BATMAN '66

VOL. 2

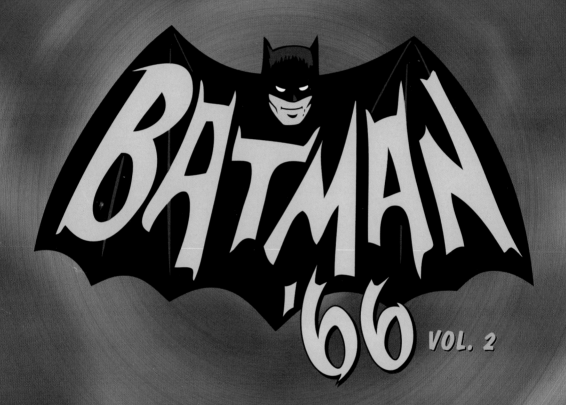

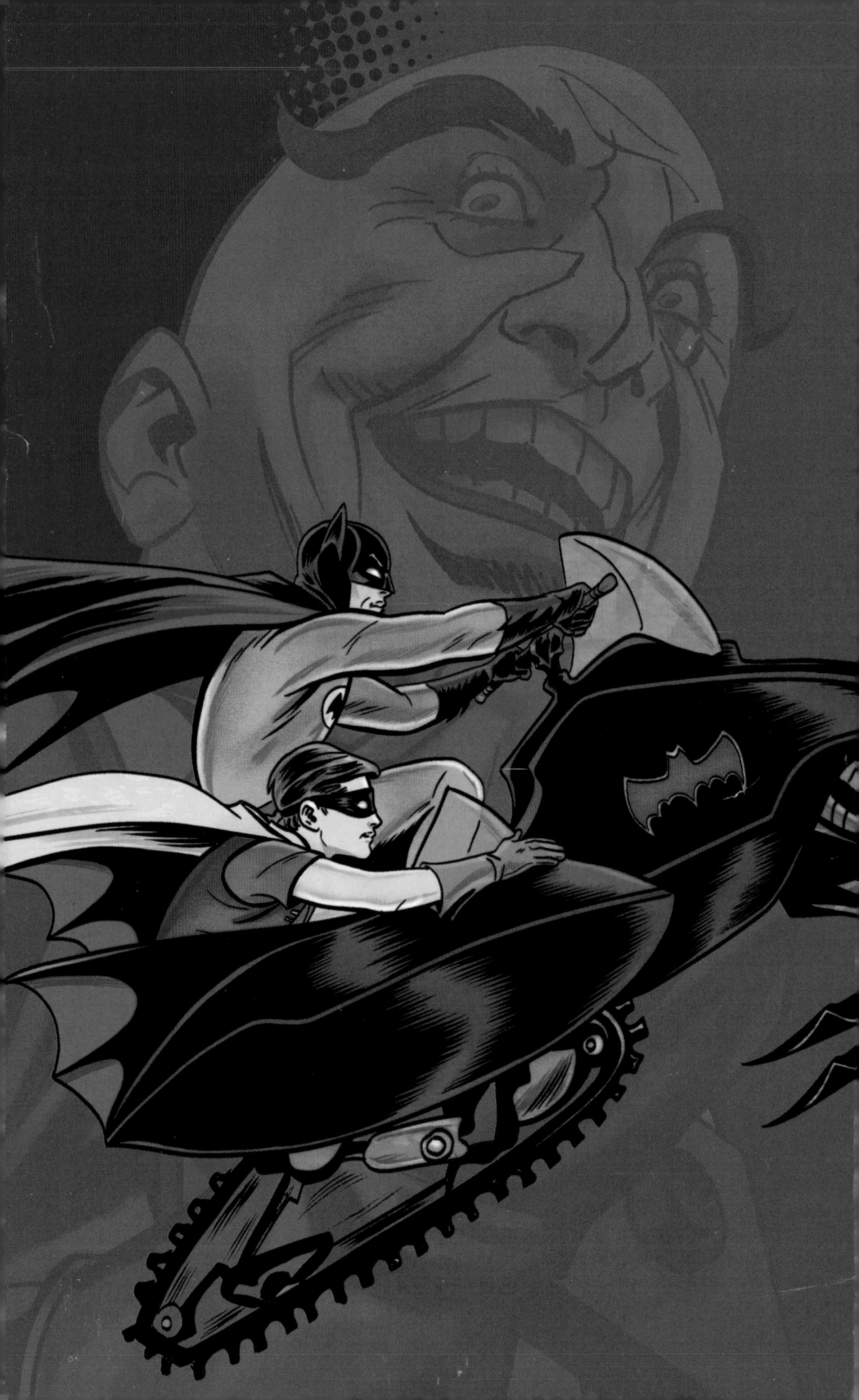

BATMAN '66 VOL. 2

Written by
JEFF PARKER
TOM PEYER

Art by
TY TEMPLETON
TED NAIFEH
CHRISTOPHER JONES
DEREC DONOVAN
RUBÉN PROCOPIO
CRAIG ROUSSEAU
CHRIS SPROUSE
KARL STORY
DAVID WILLIAMS
KELSEY SHANNON
JOËLLE JONES

Colors by
TONY AVIÑA   LEE LOUGHRIDGE
KELSEY SHANNON   NICK FILARDI

Letters by
WES ABBOTT

Cover Art & Original Series Covers by
MICHAEL & LAURA ALLRED

BATMAN created by **BOB KANE**

JIM CHADWICK
Editor – Original Series

ANIZ ANSARI
Assistant Editor – Original Series

SCOTT NYBAKKEN
Editor

ROBBIN BROSTERMAN
Design Director – Books

CURTIS KING JR.
Publication Design

HANK KANALZ
Senior VP – Vertigo & Integrated Publishing

DIANE NELSON
President

DAN DIDIO and **JIM LEE**
Co-Publishers

GEOFF JOHNS
Chief Creative Officer

AMIT DESAI
Senior VP – Marketing & Franchise Management

AMY GENKINS
Senior VP – Business & Legal Affairs

NAIRI GARDINER
Senior VP – Finance

JEFF BOISON
VP – Publishing Planning

MARK CHIARELLO
VP – Art Direction & Design

JOHN CUNNINGHAM
VP – Marketing

TERRI CUNNINGHAM
VP – Editorial Administration

LARRY GANEM
VP – Talent Relations & Services

ALISON GILL
Senior VP – Manufacturing & Operations

JAY KOGAN
VP – Business & Legal Affairs, Publishing

JACK MAHAN
VP – Business Affairs, Talent

NICK NAPOLITANO
VP – Manufacturing Administration

SUE POHJA
VP – Book Sales

FRED RUIZ
VP – Manufacturing Operations

COURTNEY SIMMONS
Senior VP – Publicity

BOB WAYNE
Senior VP – Sales

BATMAN '66 VOL. 2
Published by DC Comics.
Compilation Copyright © 2015 DC Comics. All Rights Reserved.

Originally published in single magazine form as BATMAN '66 6-10 and online as BATMAN '66 Chapters 16-30. Copyright © 2013, 2014 DC Comics. All Rights Reserved. All characters, their distinctive likenesses and related elements featured in this publication are trademarks of DC Comics. The stories, characters and incidents featured in this publication are entirely fictional. DC Comics does not read or accept unsolicited submissions of ideas, stories or artwork.

DC Comics, 1700 Broadway, New York, NY 10019
A Warner Bros. Entertainment Company.
Printed by RR Donnelley, Salem, VA, USA. 3/20/15. First Printing.
ISBN: 978-1-4012-5461-2

Library of Congress Cataloging-in-Publication Data

Parker, Jeff, 1966- author.
  Batman '66. Volume 2 / Jeff Parker, writer ; Ty Templeton, artist.
    pages cm
  ISBN 978-1-4012-5461-2 (pbk.)
  1. Graphic novels. I. Templeton, Ty, illustrator. II. Title.

PN6728.B36P373 2014
741.5'973—dc23

2014014912

TABLE OF CONTENTS

BATMAN '66 VOL. 2

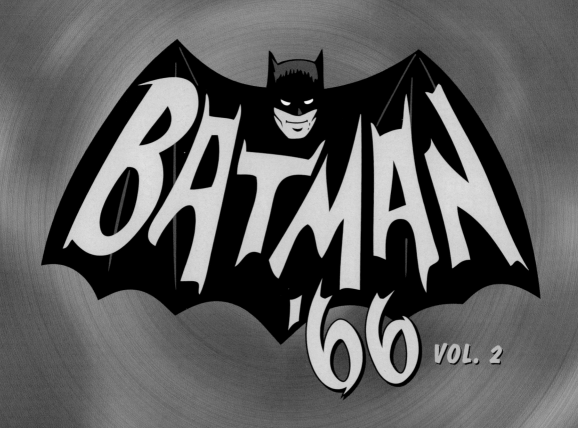

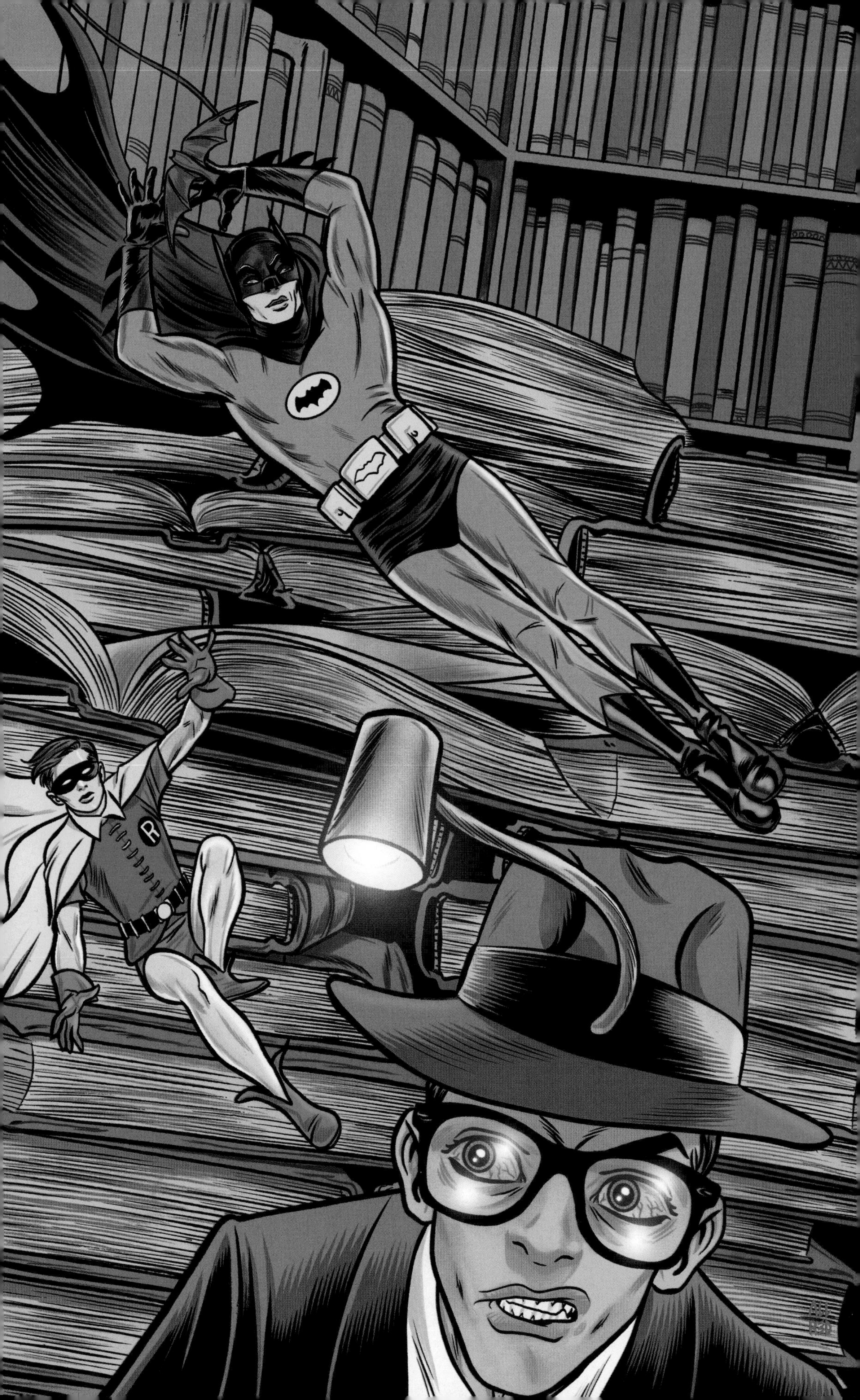

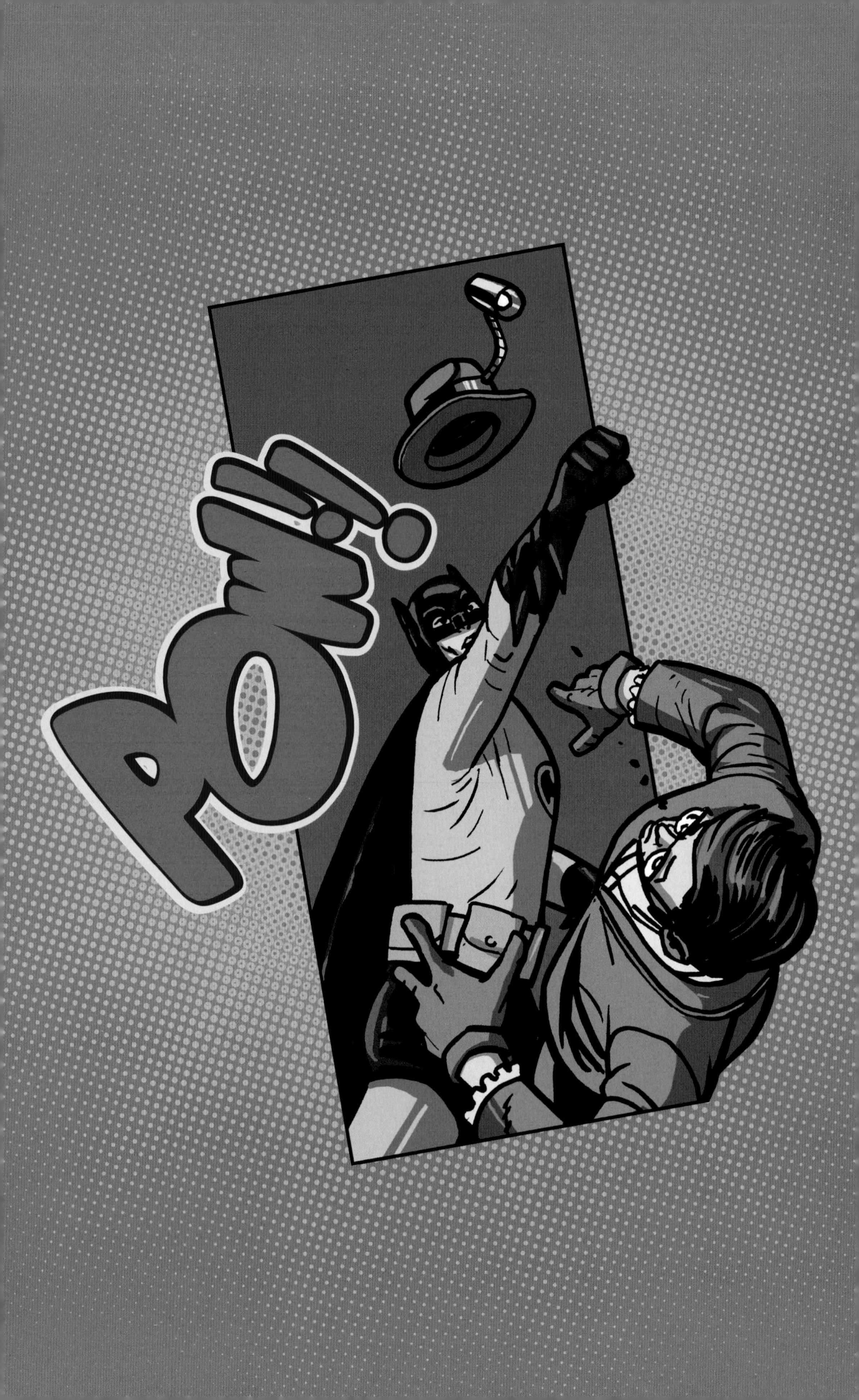
POW!!

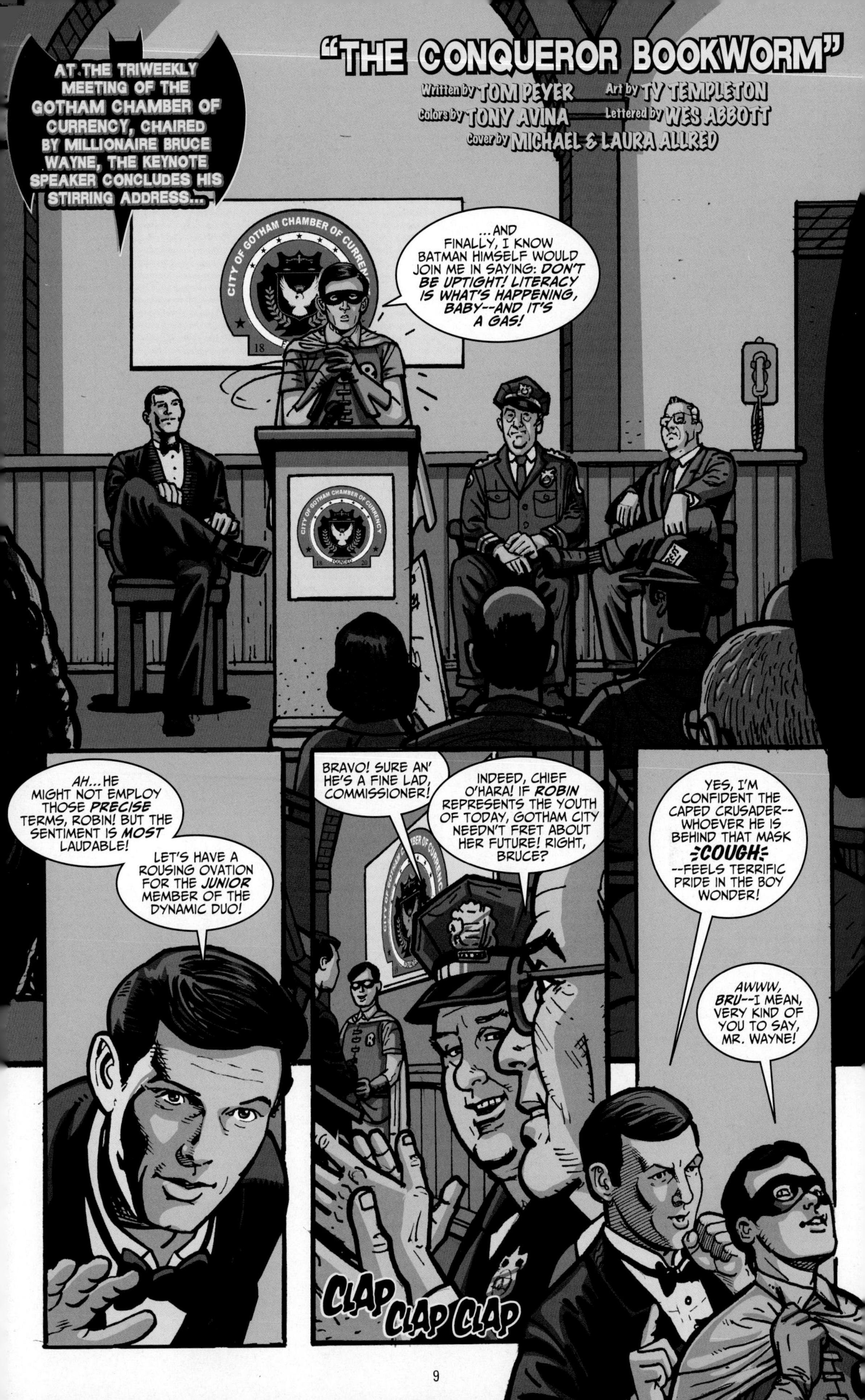

"THE CONQUEROR BOOKWORM"
Written by TOM PEYER Art by TY TEMPLETON
Colors by TONY AVINA Lettered by WES ABBOTT
Cover by MICHAEL & LAURA ALLRED
AT THE TRIWEEKLY MEETING OF THE GOTHAM CHAMBER OF CURRENCY, CHAIRED BY MILLIONAIRE BRUCE WAYNE, THE KEYNOTE SPEAKER CONCLUDES HIS STIRRING ADDRESS...
CITY OF GOTHAM CHAMBER OF CURRENCY
...AND FINALLY, I KNOW BATMAN HIMSELF WOULD JOIN ME IN SAYING: DON'T BE UPTIGHT! LITERACY IS WHAT'S HAPPENING, BABY--AND IT'S A GAS!
AH...HE MIGHT NOT EMPLOY THOSE PRECISE TERMS, ROBIN! BUT THE SENTIMENT IS MOST LAUDABLE!
LET'S HAVE A ROUSING OVATION FOR THE JUNIOR MEMBER OF THE DYNAMIC DUO!
BRAVO! SURE AN' HE'S A FINE LAD, COMMISSIONER!
INDEED, CHIEF O'HARA! IF ROBIN REPRESENTS THE YOUTH OF TODAY, GOTHAM CITY NEEDN'T FRET ABOUT HER FUTURE! RIGHT, BRUCE?
CLAP CLAP CLAP
YES, I'M CONFIDENT THE CAPED CRUSADER--WHOEVER HE IS BEHIND THAT MASK
COUGH
--FEELS TERRIFIC PRIDE IN THE BOY WONDER!
AWWW, BRU--I MEAN, VERY KIND OF YOU TO SAY, MR. WAYNE!

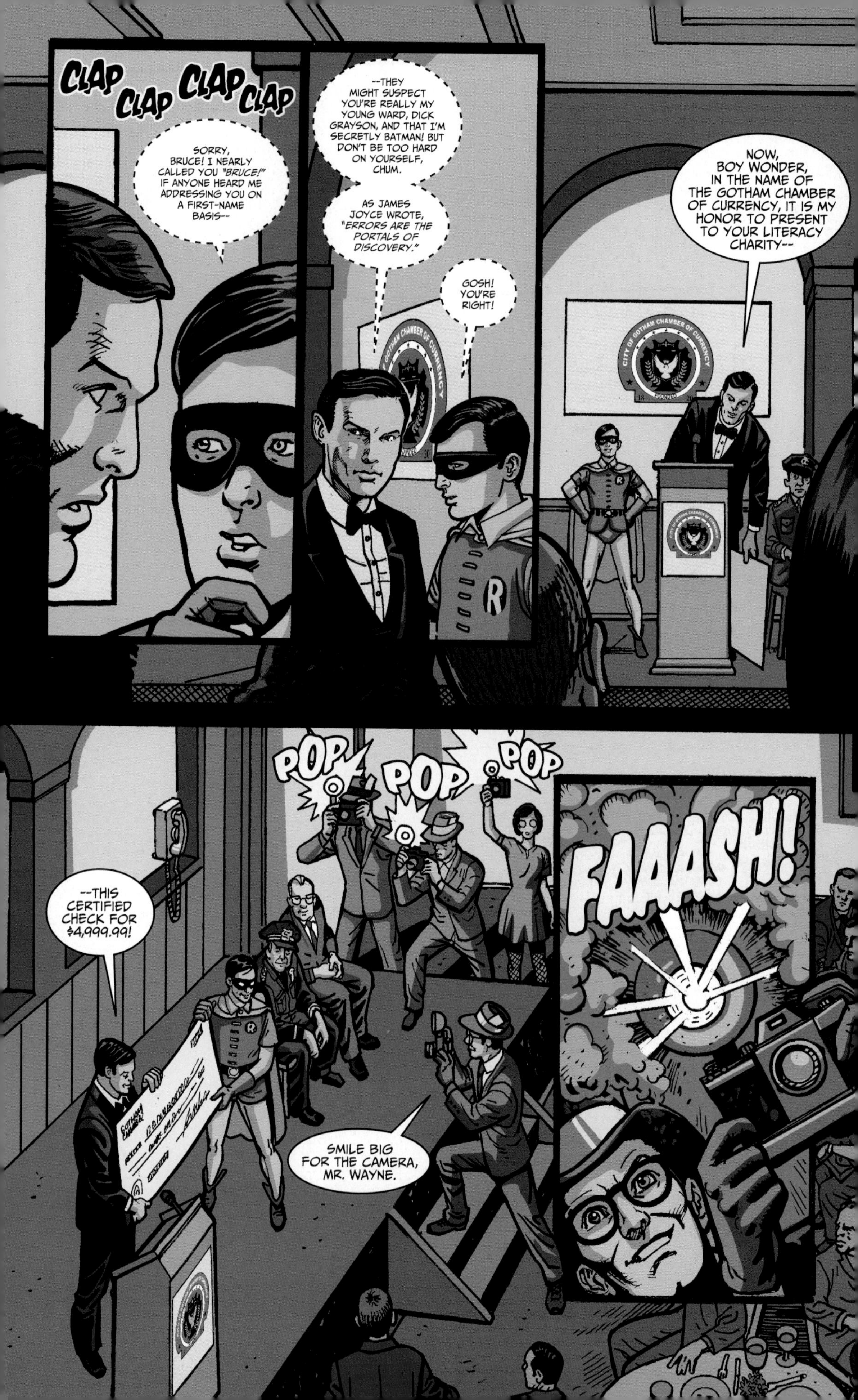
CLAP CLAP CLAP CLAP
SORRY, BRUCE! I NEARLY CALLED YOU "BRUCE!" IF ANYONE HEARD ME ADDRESSING YOU ON A FIRST-NAME BASIS--
--THEY MIGHT SUSPECT YOU'RE REALLY MY YOUNG WARD, DICK GRAYSON, AND THAT I'M SECRETLY BATMAN! BUT DON'T BE TOO HARD ON YOURSELF, CHUM.
AS JAMES JOYCE WROTE, "ERRORS ARE THE PORTALS OF DISCOVERY."
GOSH! YOU'RE RIGHT!
NOW, BOY WONDER, IN THE NAME OF THE GOTHAM CHAMBER OF CURRENCY, IT IS MY HONOR TO PRESENT TO YOUR LITERACY CHARITY--
CITY OF GOTHAM CHAMBER OF CURRENCY
POP POP POP
--THIS CERTIFIED CHECK FOR $4,999.99!
SMILE BIG FOR THE CAMERA, MR. WAYNE.
FAAASH!

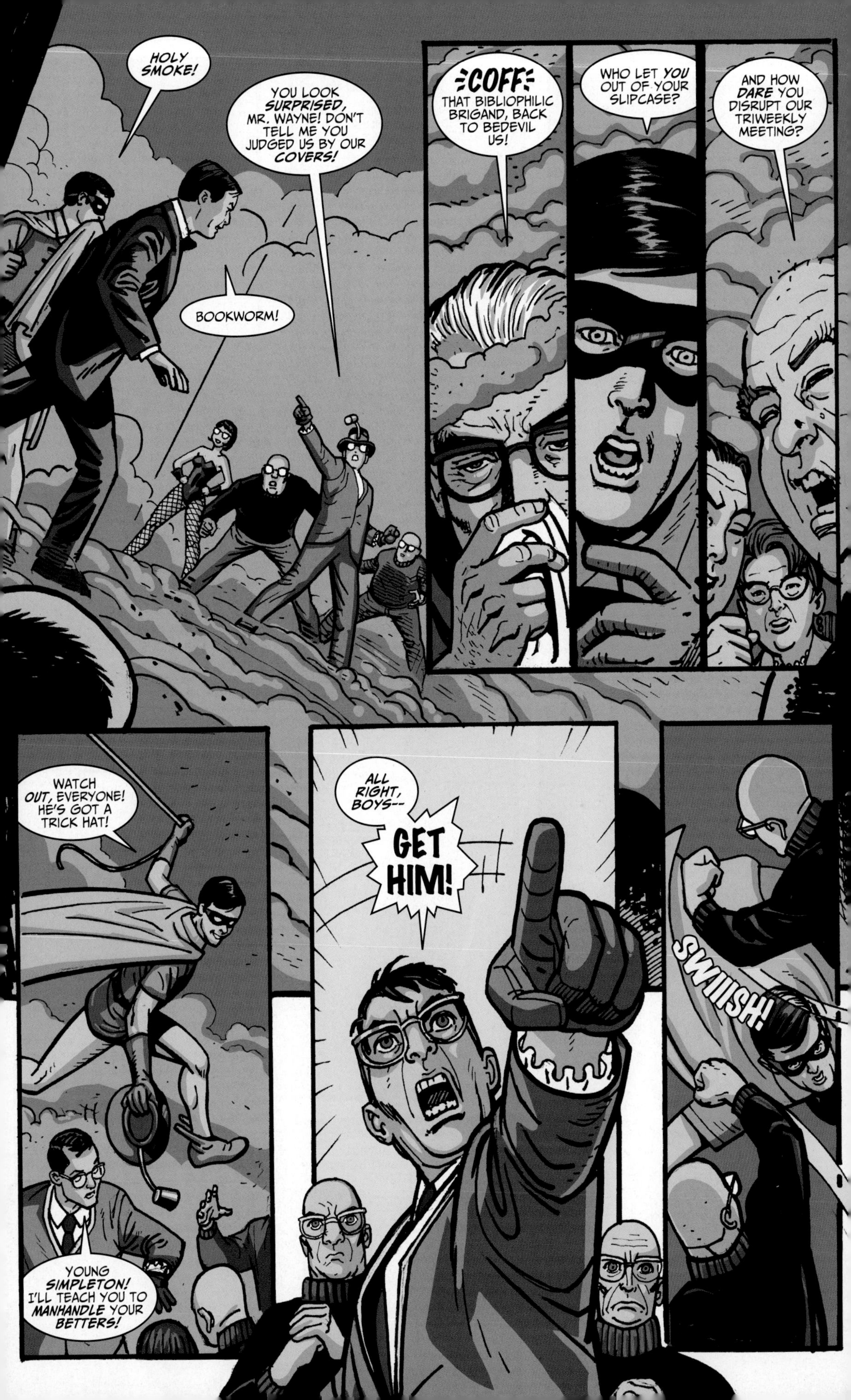
HOLY SMOKE!
YOU LOOK SURPRISED, MR. WAYNE! DON'T TELL ME YOU JUDGED US BY OUR COVERS!
BOOKWORM!
COFF
THAT BIBLIOPHILIC BRIGAND, BACK TO BEDEVIL US!
WHO LET YOU OUT OF YOUR SLIPCASE?
AND HOW DARE YOU DISRUPT OUR TRIWEEKLY MEETING?
WATCH OUT, EVERYONE! HE'S GOT A TRICK HAT!
YOUNG SIMPLETON! I'LL TEACH YOU TO MANHANDLE YOUR BETTERS!
ALL RIGHT, BOYS--
GET HIM!
SWIIISH!

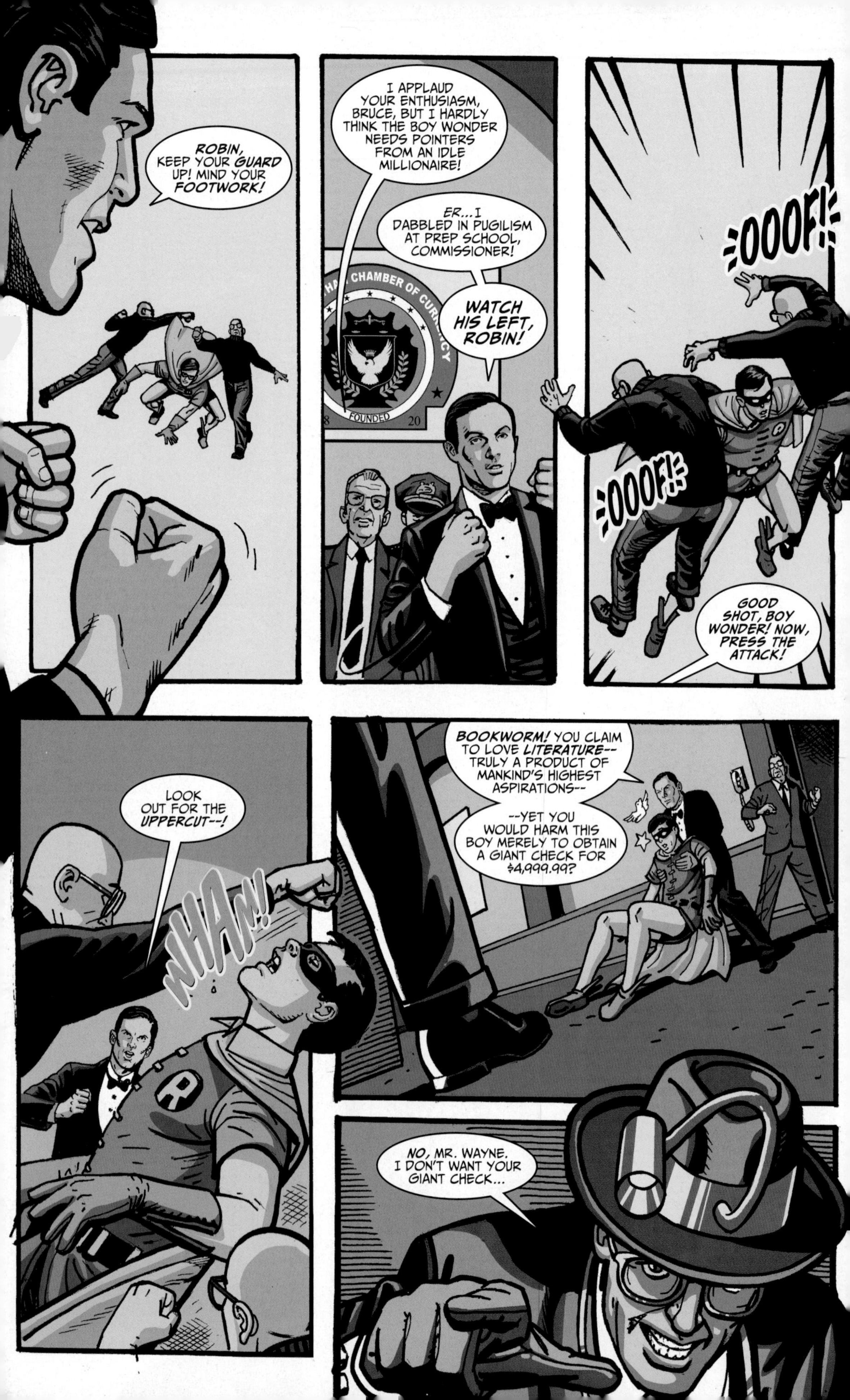
ROBIN, KEEP YOUR GUARD UP! MIND YOUR FOOTWORK!
I APPLAUD YOUR ENTHUSIASM, BRUCE, BUT I HARDLY THINK THE BOY WONDER NEEDS POINTERS FROM AN IDLE MILLIONAIRE!
ER...I DABBLED IN PUGILISM AT PREP SCHOOL, COMMISSIONER!
WATCH HIS LEFT, ROBIN!
CHAMBER OF CUR
FOUNDED
OOOF!
OOOF!
GOOD SHOT, BOY WONDER! NOW, PRESS THE ATTACK!
LOOK OUT FOR THE UPPERCUT--!
WHAM!
BOOKWORM! YOU CLAIM TO LOVE LITERATURE-- TRULY A PRODUCT OF MANKIND'S HIGHEST ASPIRATIONS--
--YET YOU WOULD HARM THIS BOY MERELY TO OBTAIN A GIANT CHECK FOR $4,999.99?
NO, MR. WAYNE. I DON'T WANT YOUR GIANT CHECK...

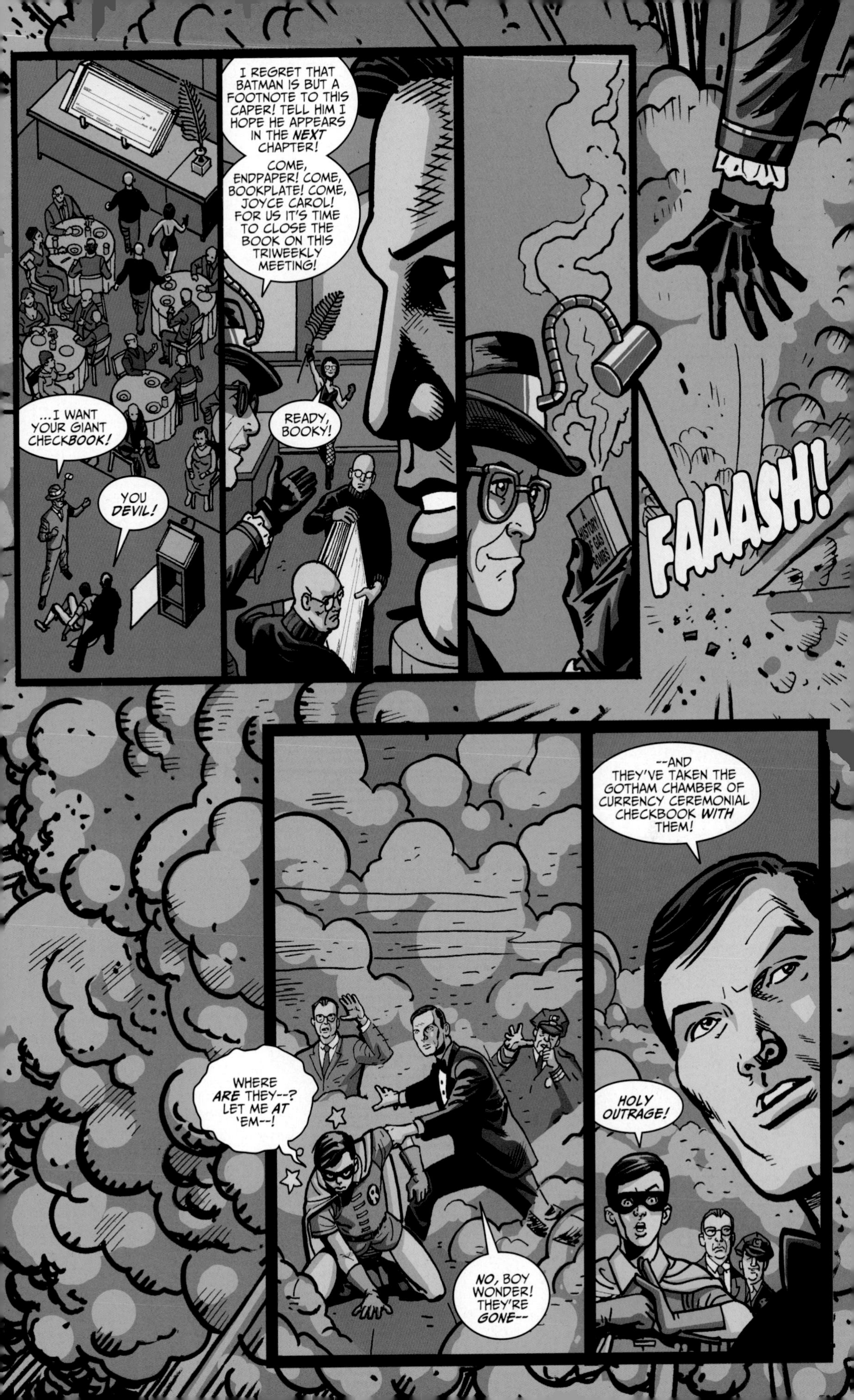
...I WANT YOUR GIANT CHECKBOOK!
YOU DEVIL!
I REGRET THAT BATMAN IS BUT A FOOTNOTE TO THIS CAPER! TELL HIM I HOPE HE APPEARS IN THE NEXT CHAPTER!
COME, ENDPAPER! COME, BOOKPLATE! COME, JOYCE CAROL! FOR US IT'S TIME TO CLOSE THE BOOK ON THIS TRIWEEKLY MEETING!
READY, BOOKY!
FAAASH!
WHERE ARE THEY--? LET ME AT 'EM--!
NO, BOY WONDER! THEY'RE GONE--
--AND THEY'VE TAKEN THE GOTHAM CHAMBER OF CURRENCY CEREMONIAL CHECKBOOK WITH THEM!
HOLY OUTRAGE!

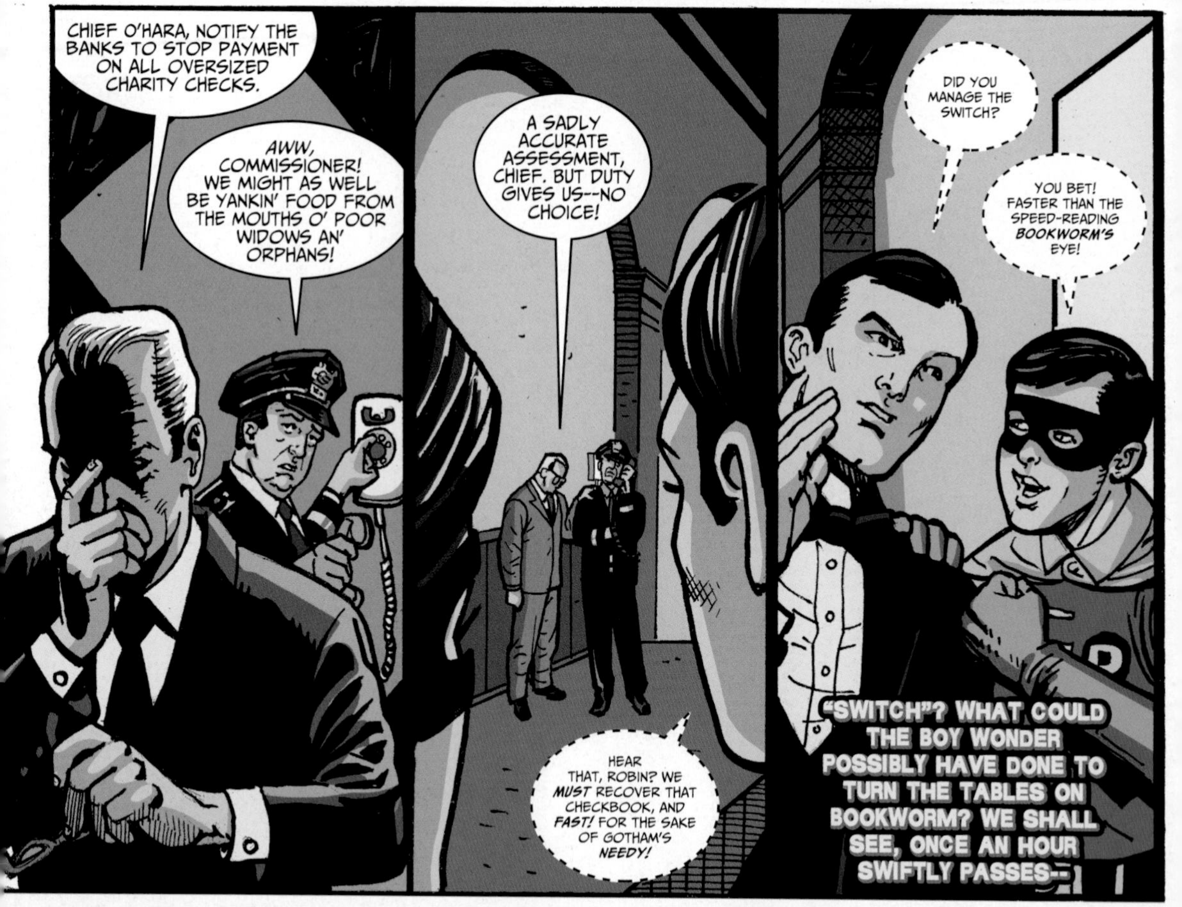
CHIEF O'HARA, NOTIFY THE BANKS TO STOP PAYMENT ON ALL OVERSIZED CHARITY CHECKS.
AWW, COMMISSIONER! WE MIGHT AS WELL BE YANKIN' FOOD FROM THE MOUTHS O' POOR WIDOWS AN' ORPHANS!
A SADLY ACCURATE ASSESSMENT, CHIEF. BUT DUTY GIVES US--NO CHOICE!
HEAR THAT, ROBIN? WE MUST RECOVER THAT CHECKBOOK, AND FAST! FOR THE SAKE OF GOTHAM'S NEEDY!
DID YOU MANAGE THE SWITCH?
YOU BET! FASTER THAN THE SPEED-READING BOOKWORM'S EYE!
"SWITCH"? WHAT COULD THE BOY WONDER POSSIBLY HAVE DONE TO TURN THE TABLES ON BOOKWORM? WE SHALL SEE, ONCE AN HOUR SWIFTLY PASSES--

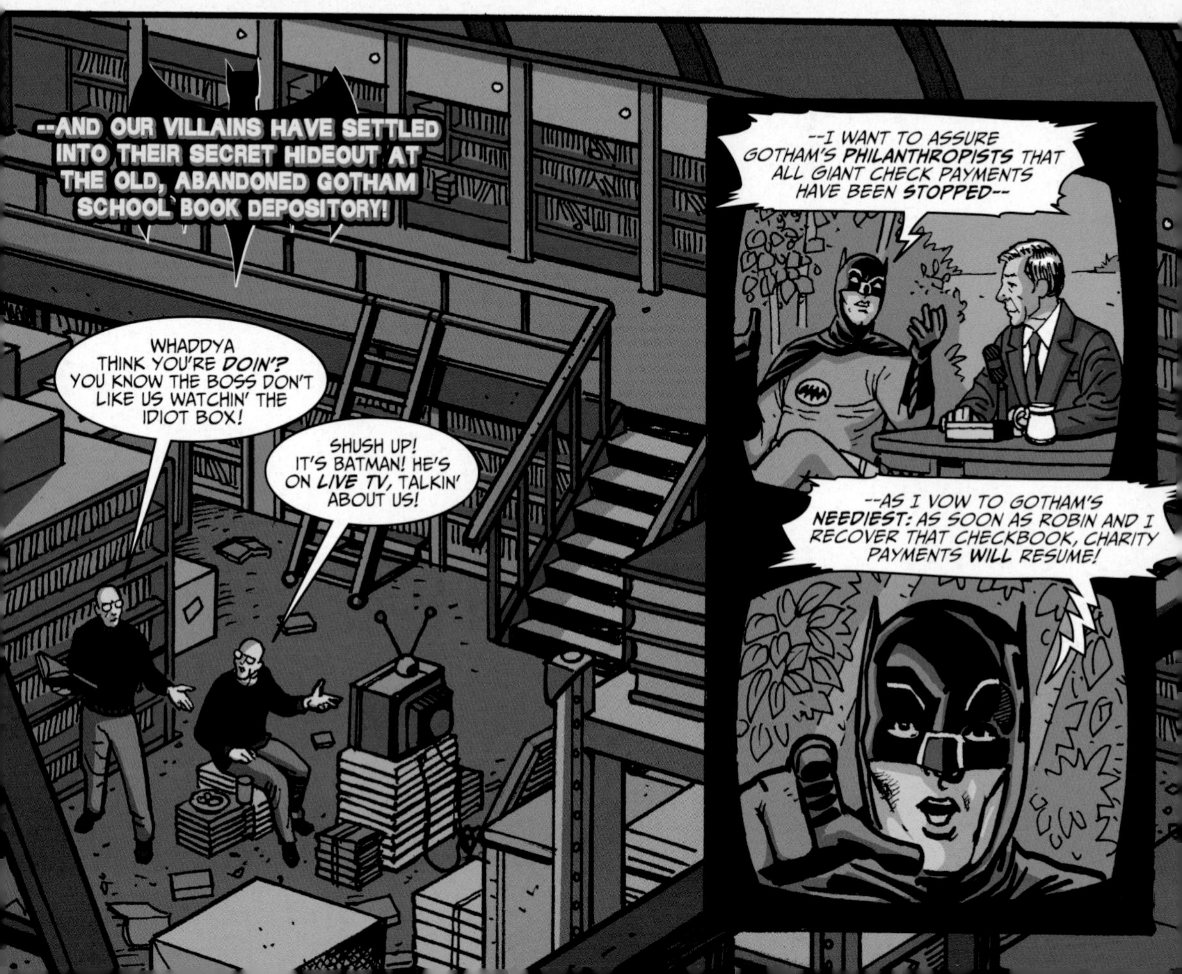
--AND OUR VILLAINS HAVE SETTLED INTO THEIR SECRET HIDEOUT AT THE OLD, ABANDONED GOTHAM SCHOOL BOOK DEPOSITORY!
WHADDYA THINK YOU'RE DOIN'? YOU KNOW THE BOSS DON'T LIKE US WATCHIN' THE IDIOT BOX!
SHUSH UP! IT'S BATMAN! HE'S ON LIVE TV, TALKIN' ABOUT US!
--I WANT TO ASSURE GOTHAM'S PHILANTHROPISTS THAT ALL GIANT CHECK PAYMENTS HAVE BEEN STOPPED--
--AS I VOW TO GOTHAM'S NEEDIEST: AS SOON AS ROBIN AND I RECOVER THAT CHECKBOOK, CHARITY PAYMENTS WILL RESUME!

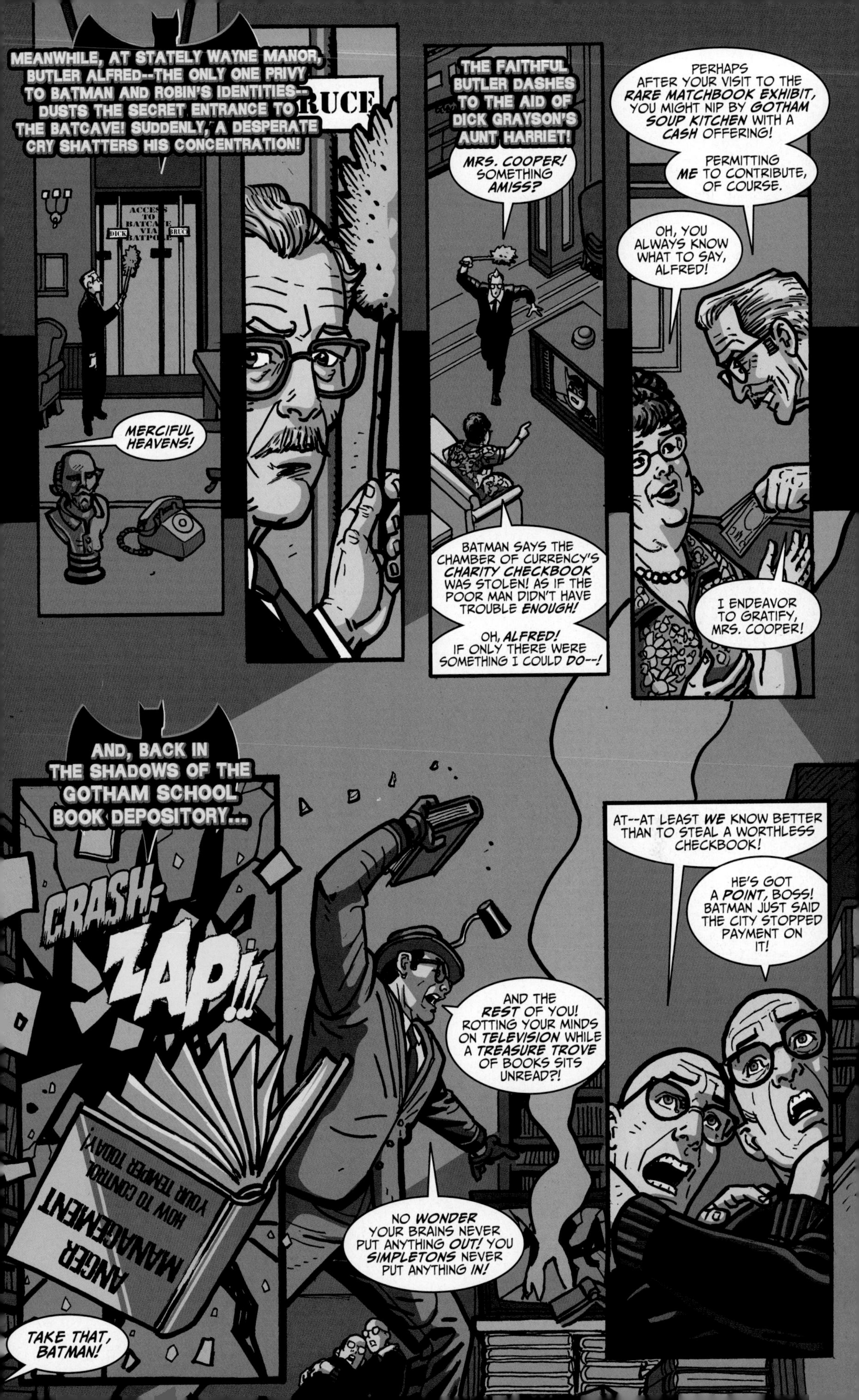

MEANWHILE, AT STATELY WAYNE MANOR, BUTLER ALFRED--THE ONLY ONE PRIVY TO BATMAN AND ROBIN'S IDENTITIES--DUSTS THE SECRET ENTRANCE TO THE BATCAVE! SUDDENLY, A DESPERATE CRY SHATTERS HIS CONCENTRATION!
BRUCE
ACCESS TO BATCAVE VIA BATPOLE
DICK
BRUCE
MERCIFUL HEAVENS!
THE FAITHFUL BUTLER DASHES TO THE AID OF DICK GRAYSON'S AUNT HARRIET!
MRS. COOPER! SOMETHING AMISS?
BATMAN SAYS THE CHAMBER OF CURRENCY'S CHARITY CHECKBOOK WAS STOLEN! AS IF THE POOR MAN DIDN'T HAVE TROUBLE ENOUGH!
OH, ALFRED! IF ONLY THERE WERE SOMETHING I COULD DO--!
PERHAPS AFTER YOUR VISIT TO THE RARE MATCHBOOK EXHIBIT, YOU MIGHT NIP BY GOTHAM SOUP KITCHEN WITH A CASH OFFERING!
PERMITTING ME TO CONTRIBUTE, OF COURSE.
OH, YOU ALWAYS KNOW WHAT TO SAY, ALFRED!
I ENDEAVOR TO GRATIFY, MRS. COOPER!
AND, BACK IN THE SHADOWS OF THE GOTHAM SCHOOL BOOK DEPOSITORY...
CRASH!
ZAP!!!
ANGER MANAGEMENT HOW TO CONTROL YOUR TEMPER TODAY!
TAKE THAT, BATMAN!
AND THE REST OF YOU! ROTTING YOUR MINDS ON TELEVISION WHILE A TREASURE TROVE OF BOOKS SITS UNREAD?!
NO WONDER YOUR BRAINS NEVER PUT ANYTHING OUT! YOU SIMPLETONS NEVER PUT ANYTHING IN!
AT--AT LEAST WE KNOW BETTER THAN TO STEAL A WORTHLESS CHECKBOOK!
HE'S GOT A POINT, BOSS! BATMAN JUST SAID THE CITY STOPPED PAYMENT ON IT!

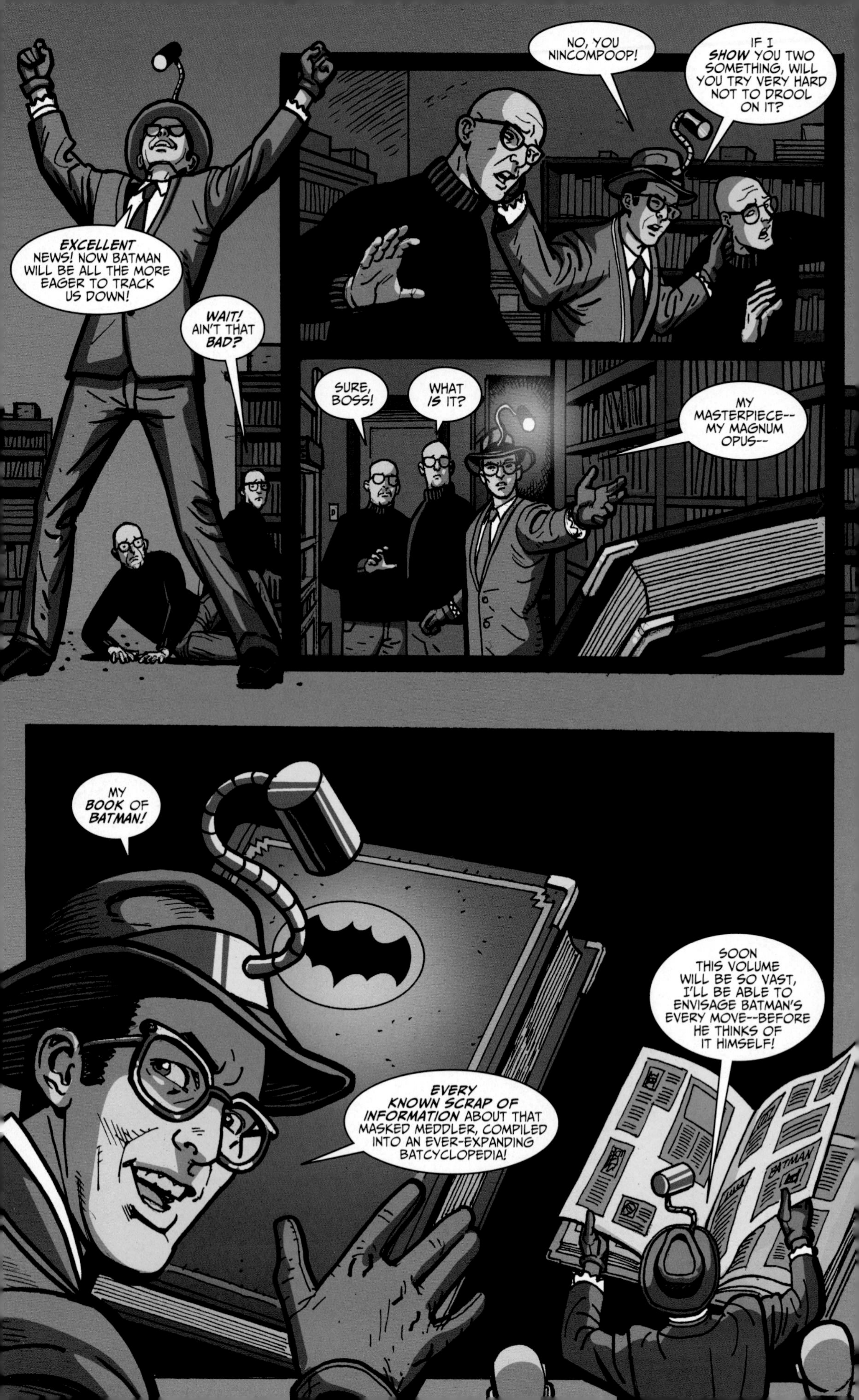
EXCELLENT NEWS! NOW BATMAN WILL BE ALL THE MORE EAGER TO TRACK US DOWN!
WAIT! AIN'T THAT BAD?
NO, YOU NINCOMPOOP!
IF I SHOW YOU TWO SOMETHING, WILL YOU TRY VERY HARD NOT TO DROOL ON IT?
SURE, BOSS!
WHAT IS IT?
MY MASTERPIECE-- MY MAGNUM OPUS--
MY BOOK OF BATMAN!
EVERY KNOWN SCRAP OF INFORMATION ABOUT THAT MASKED MEDDLER, COMPILED INTO AN EVER-EXPANDING BATCYCLOPEDIA!
SOON THIS VOLUME WILL BE SO VAST, I'LL BE ABLE TO ENVISAGE BATMAN'S EVERY MOVE--BEFORE HE THINKS OF IT HIMSELF!
BATMAN

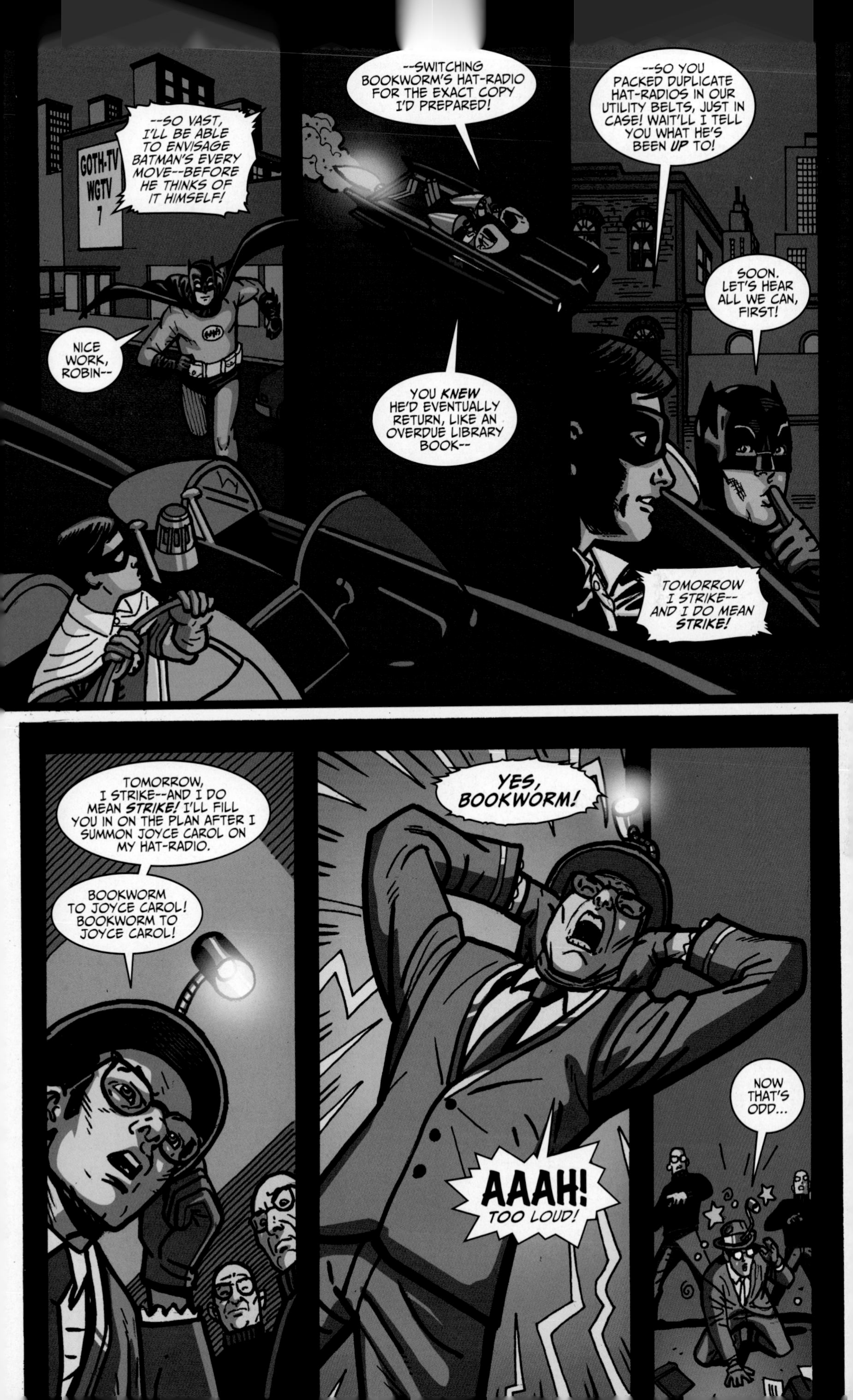

--SO VAST, I'LL BE ABLE TO ENVISAGE BATMAN'S EVERY MOVE--BEFORE HE THINKS OF IT HIMSELF!
GOTH-TV WGTV 7
NICE WORK, ROBIN--
--SWITCHING BOOKWORM'S HAT-RADIO FOR THE EXACT COPY I'D PREPARED!
YOU KNEW HE'D EVENTUALLY RETURN, LIKE AN OVERDUE LIBRARY BOOK--
--SO YOU PACKED DUPLICATE HAT-RADIOS IN OUR UTILITY BELTS, JUST IN CASE! WAIT'LL I TELL YOU WHAT HE'S BEEN UP TO!
SOON. LET'S HEAR ALL WE CAN, FIRST!
TOMORROW I STRIKE--AND I DO MEAN STRIKE!
TOMORROW, I STRIKE--AND I DO MEAN STRIKE! I'LL FILL YOU IN ON THE PLAN AFTER I SUMMON JOYCE CAROL ON MY HAT-RADIO.
BOOKWORM TO JOYCE CAROL! BOOKWORM TO JOYCE CAROL!
YES, BOOKWORM!
AAAH! TOO LOUD!
NOW THAT'S ODD...

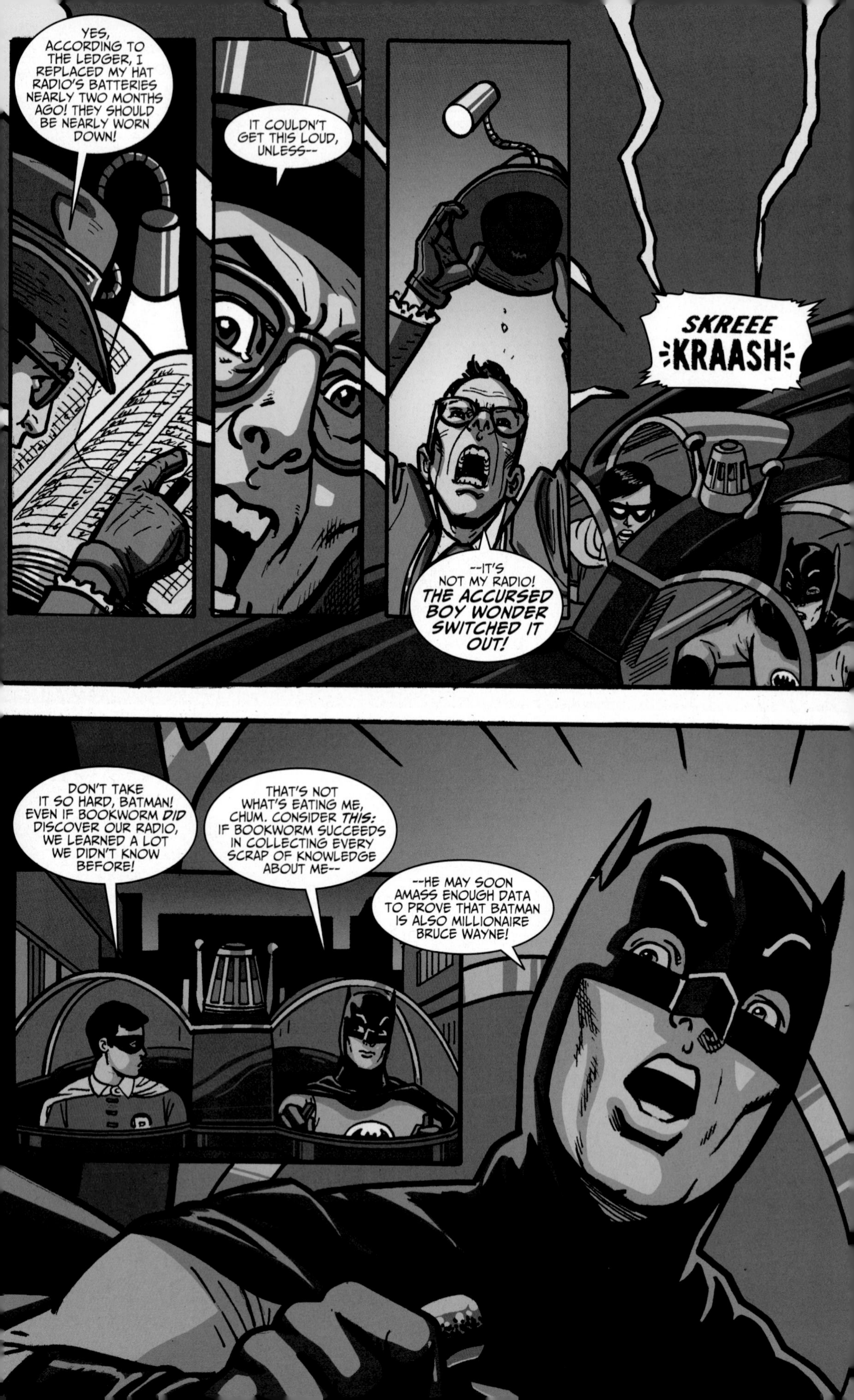
YES, ACCORDING TO THE LEDGER, I REPLACED MY HAT RADIO'S BATTERIES NEARLY TWO MONTHS AGO! THEY SHOULD BE NEARLY WORN DOWN!
IT COULDN'T GET THIS LOUD, UNLESS--
SKREEE KRAASH
--IT'S NOT MY RADIO! THE ACCURSED BOY WONDER SWITCHED IT OUT!
DON'T TAKE IT SO HARD, BATMAN! EVEN IF BOOKWORM DID DISCOVER OUR RADIO, WE LEARNED A LOT WE DIDN'T KNOW BEFORE!
THAT'S NOT WHAT'S EATING ME, CHUM. CONSIDER THIS: IF BOOKWORM SUCCEEDS IN COLLECTING EVERY SCRAP OF KNOWLEDGE ABOUT ME--
--HE MAY SOON AMASS ENOUGH DATA TO PROVE THAT BATMAN IS ALSO MILLIONAIRE BRUCE WAYNE!

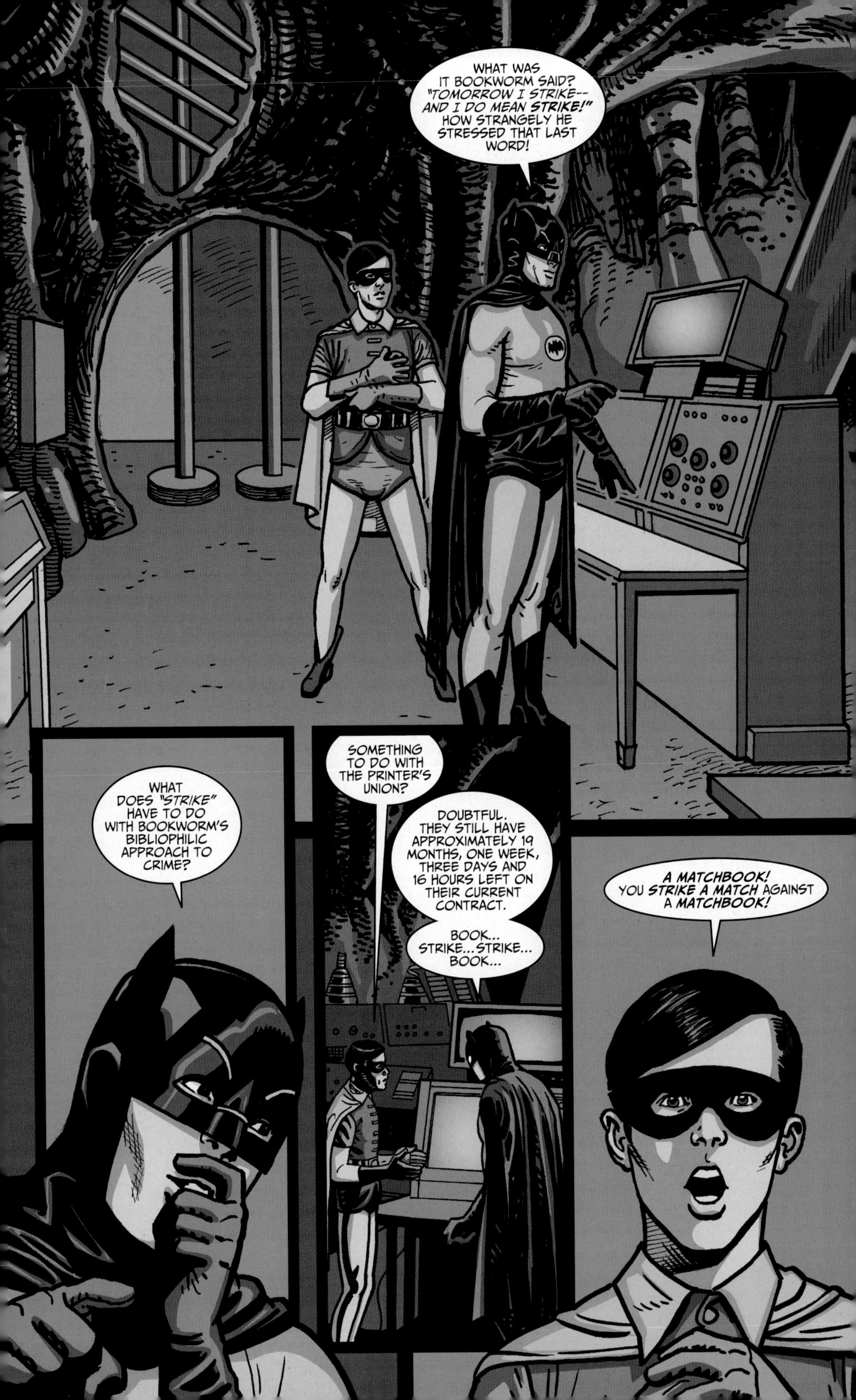
WHAT WAS IT BOOKWORM SAID? "TOMORROW I STRIKE-- AND I DO MEAN STRIKE!" HOW STRANGELY HE STRESSED THAT LAST WORD!
WHAT DOES "STRIKE" HAVE TO DO WITH BOOKWORM'S BIBLIOPHILIC APPROACH TO CRIME?
SOMETHING TO DO WITH THE PRINTER'S UNION?
DOUBTFUL. THEY STILL HAVE APPROXIMATELY 19 MONTHS, ONE WEEK, THREE DAYS AND 16 HOURS LEFT ON THEIR CURRENT CONTRACT.
BOOK... STRIKE... STRIKE... BOOK...
A MATCHBOOK! YOU STRIKE A MATCH AGAINST A MATCHBOOK!

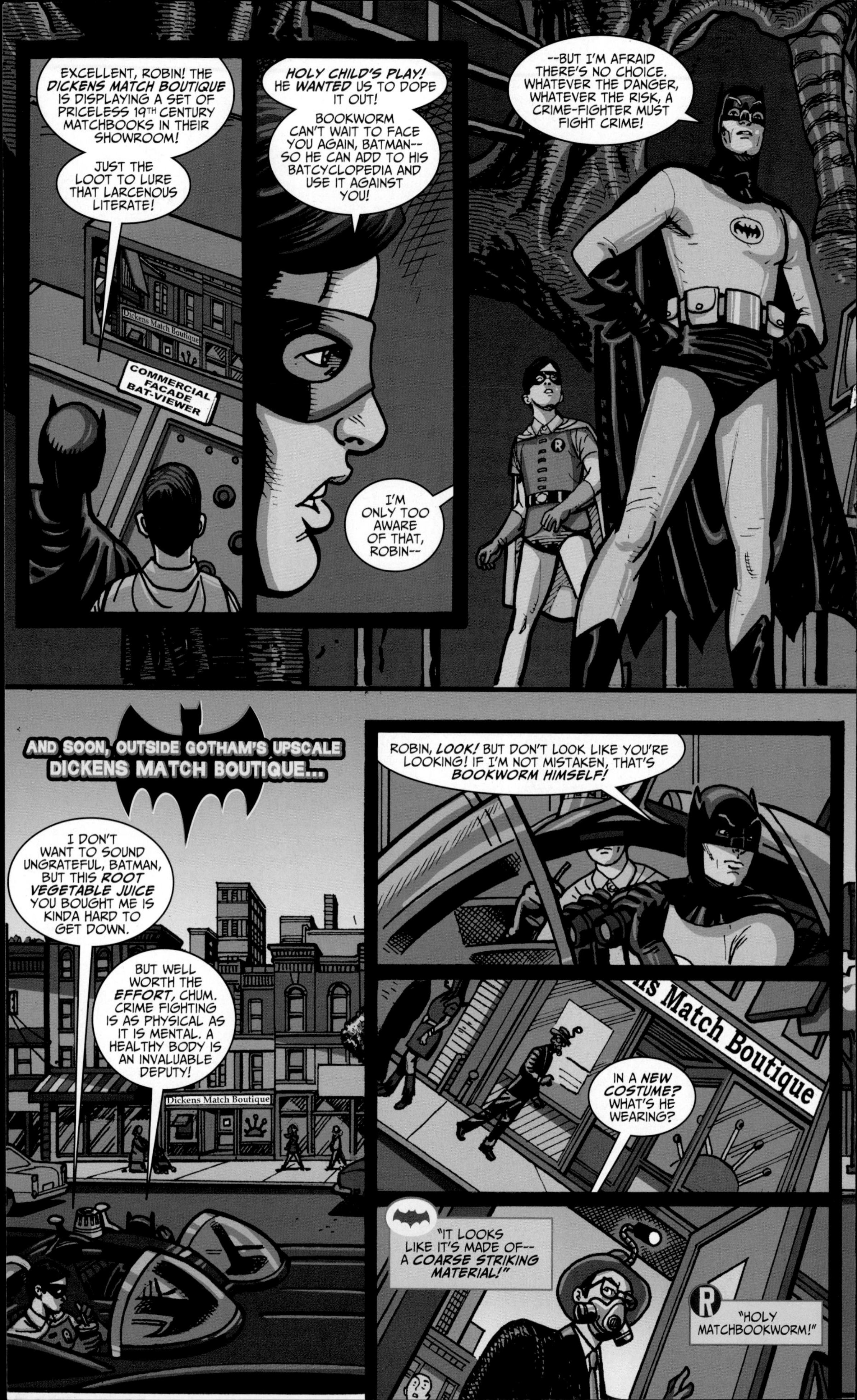
EXCELLENT, ROBIN! THE DICKENS MATCH BOUTIQUE IS DISPLAYING A SET OF PRICELESS 19TH CENTURY MATCHBOOKS IN THEIR SHOWROOM!
JUST THE LOOT TO LURE THAT LARCENOUS LITERATE!
Dickens Match Boutique
COMMERCIAL FACADE BAT-VIEWER
HOLY CHILD'S PLAY! HE WANTED US TO DOPE IT OUT!
BOOKWORM CAN'T WAIT TO FACE YOU AGAIN, BATMAN-- SO HE CAN ADD TO HIS BATCYCLOPEDIA AND USE IT AGAINST YOU!
I'M ONLY TOO AWARE OF THAT, ROBIN--
--BUT I'M AFRAID THERE'S NO CHOICE. WHATEVER THE DANGER, WHATEVER THE RISK, A CRIME-FIGHTER MUST FIGHT CRIME!
AND SOON, OUTSIDE GOTHAM'S UPSCALE DICKENS MATCH BOUTIQUE...
I DON'T WANT TO SOUND UNGRATEFUL, BATMAN, BUT THIS ROOT VEGETABLE JUICE YOU BOUGHT ME IS KINDA HARD TO GET DOWN.
BUT WELL WORTH THE EFFORT, CHUM. CRIME FIGHTING IS AS PHYSICAL AS IT IS MENTAL. A HEALTHY BODY IS AN INVALUABLE DEPUTY!
Dickens Match Boutique
ROBIN, LOOK! BUT DON'T LOOK LIKE YOU'RE LOOKING! IF I'M NOT MISTAKEN, THAT'S BOOKWORM HIMSELF!
s Match Boutique
IN A NEW COSTUME? WHAT'S HE WEARING?
"IT LOOKS LIKE IT'S MADE OF-- A COARSE STRIKING MATERIAL!"
"HOLY MATCHBOOKWORM!"

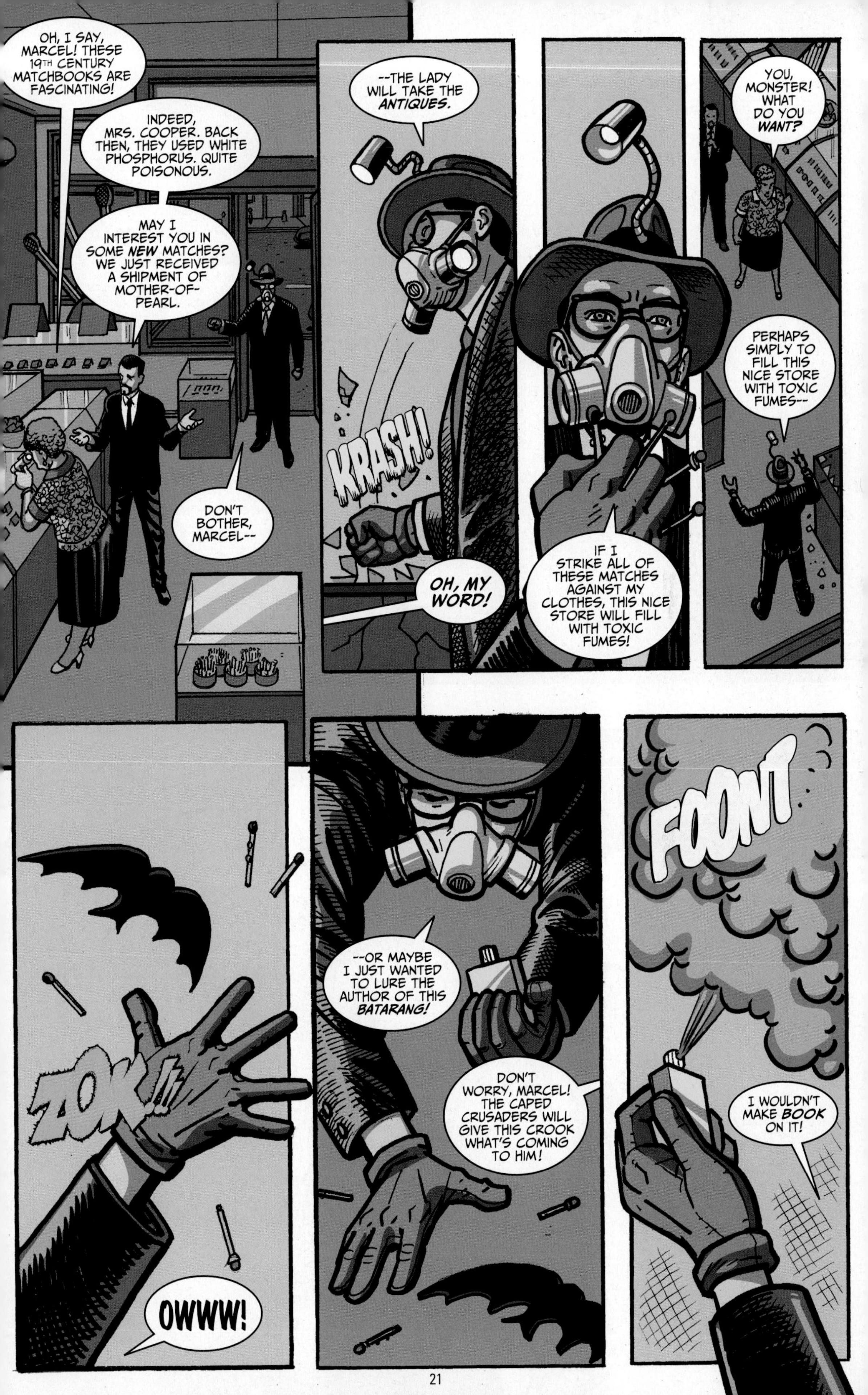
OH, I SAY, MARCEL! THESE 19TH CENTURY MATCHBOOKS ARE FASCINATING!
INDEED, MRS. COOPER. BACK THEN, THEY USED WHITE PHOSPHORUS. QUITE POISONOUS.
MAY I INTEREST YOU IN SOME NEW MATCHES? WE JUST RECEIVED A SHIPMENT OF MOTHER-OF-PEARL.
DON'T BOTHER, MARCEL--
--THE LADY WILL TAKE THE ANTIQUES.
KRASH!
OH, MY WORD!
IF I STRIKE ALL OF THESE MATCHES AGAINST MY CLOTHES, THIS NICE STORE WILL FILL WITH TOXIC FUMES!
YOU, MONSTER! WHAT DO YOU WANT?
PERHAPS SIMPLY TO FILL THIS NICE STORE WITH TOXIC FUMES--
ZOK!
OWWW!
--OR MAYBE I JUST WANTED TO LURE THE AUTHOR OF THIS BATARANG!
DON'T WORRY, MARCEL! THE CAPED CRUSADERS WILL GIVE THIS CROOK WHAT'S COMING TO HIM!
FOONT
I WOULDN'T MAKE BOOK ON IT!

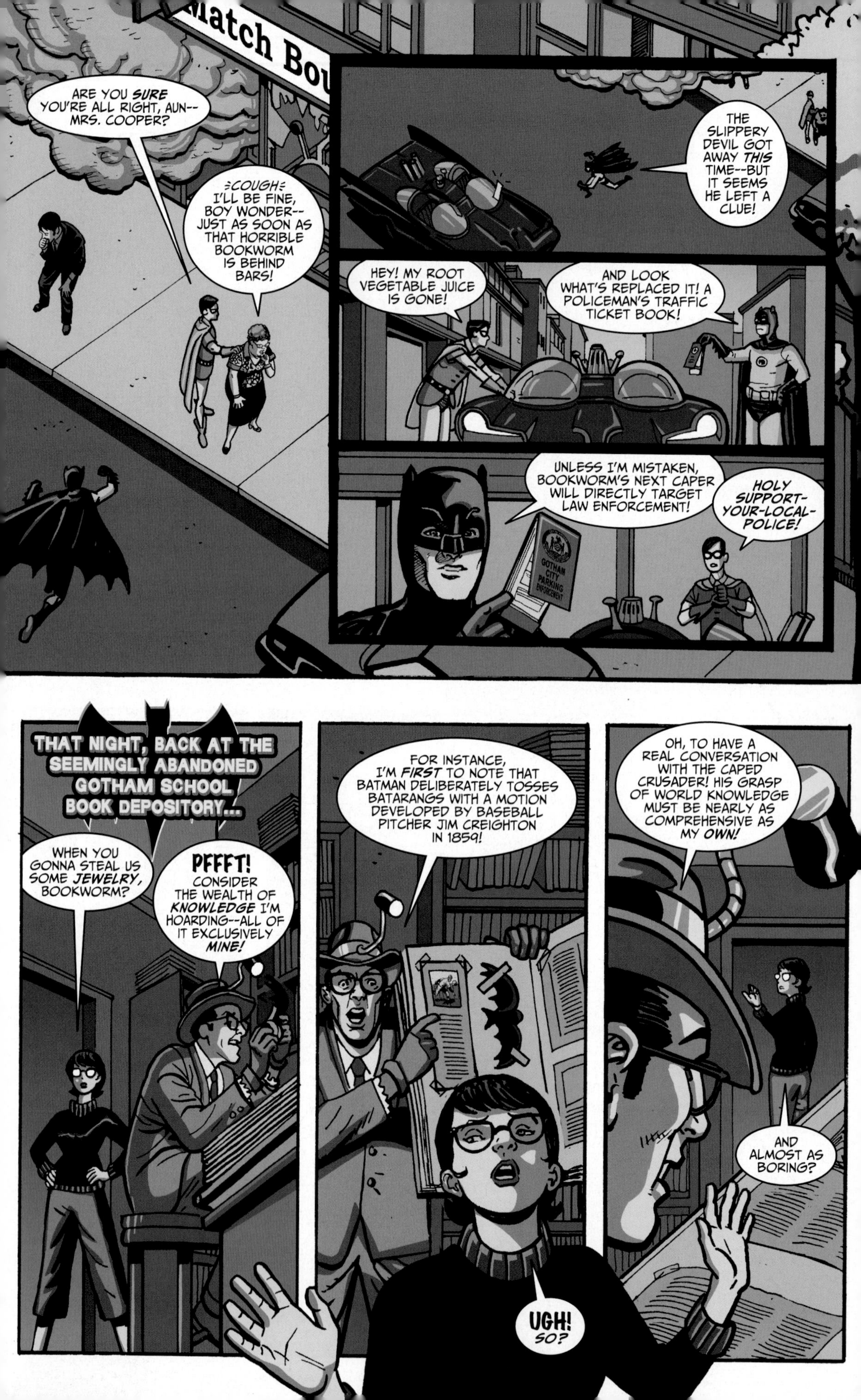
Match Bou
ARE YOU SURE YOU'RE ALL RIGHT, AUN-- MRS. COOPER?
COUGH I'LL BE FINE, BOY WONDER-- JUST AS SOON AS THAT HORRIBLE BOOKWORM IS BEHIND BARS!
THE SLIPPERY DEVIL GOT AWAY THIS TIME--BUT IT SEEMS HE LEFT A CLUE!
HEY! MY ROOT VEGETABLE JUICE IS GONE!
AND LOOK WHAT'S REPLACED IT! A POLICEMAN'S TRAFFIC TICKET BOOK!
UNLESS I'M MISTAKEN, BOOKWORM'S NEXT CAPER WILL DIRECTLY TARGET LAW ENFORCEMENT!
GOTHAM CITY PARKING ENFORCEMENT
HOLY SUPPORT-YOUR-LOCAL-POLICE!
THAT NIGHT, BACK AT THE SEEMINGLY ABANDONED GOTHAM SCHOOL BOOK DEPOSITORY...
WHEN YOU GONNA STEAL US SOME JEWELRY, BOOKWORM?
PFFFT! CONSIDER THE WEALTH OF KNOWLEDGE I'M HOARDING--ALL OF IT EXCLUSIVELY MINE!
FOR INSTANCE, I'M FIRST TO NOTE THAT BATMAN DELIBERATELY TOSSES BATARANGS WITH A MOTION DEVELOPED BY BASEBALL PITCHER JIM CREIGHTON IN 1859!
UGH! SO?
OH, TO HAVE A REAL CONVERSATION WITH THE CAPED CRUSADER! HIS GRASP OF WORLD KNOWLEDGE MUST BE NEARLY AS COMPREHENSIVE AS MY OWN!
AND ALMOST AS BORING?

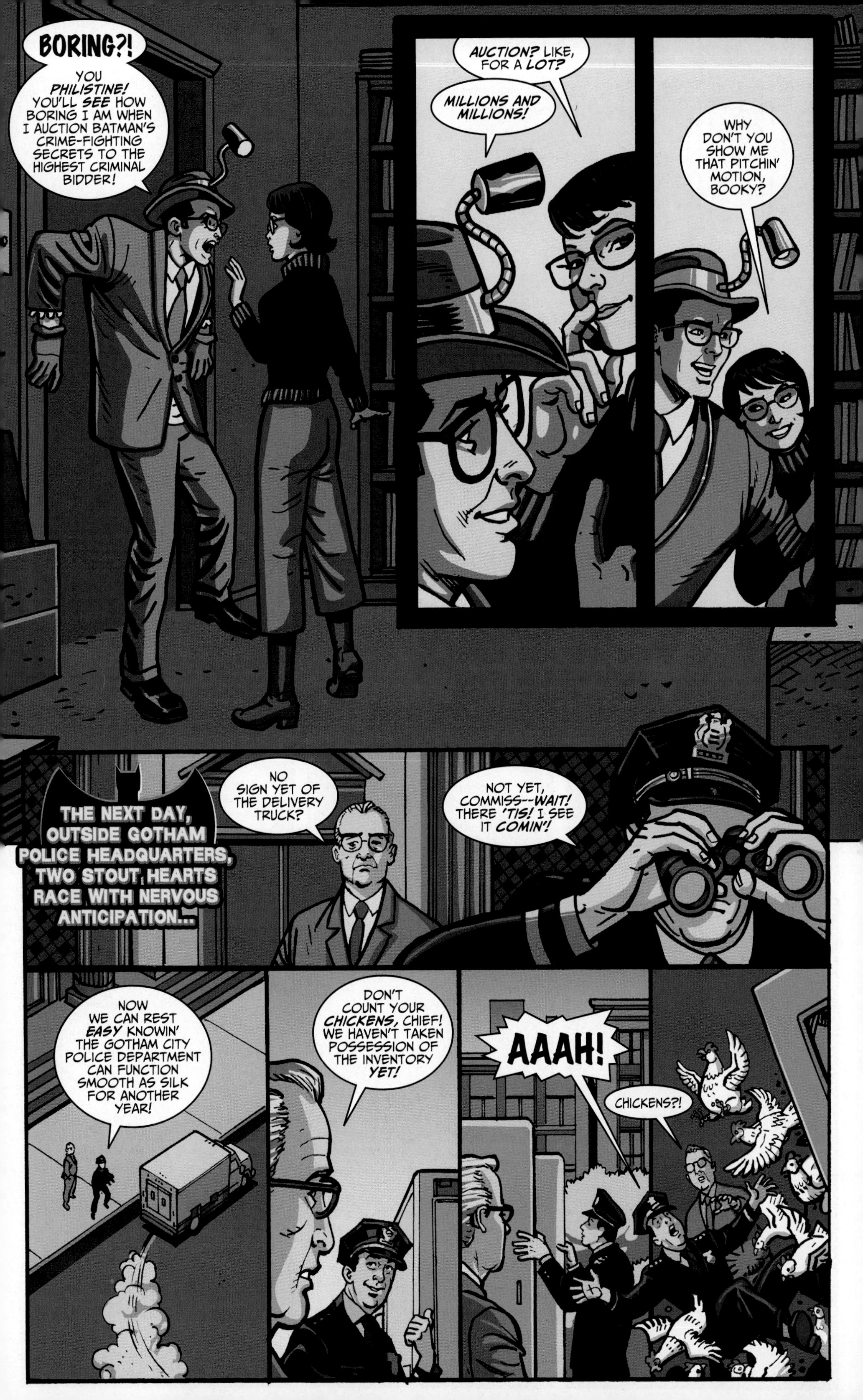
BORING?!
YOU PHILISTINE! YOU'LL SEE HOW BORING I AM WHEN I AUCTION BATMAN'S CRIME-FIGHTING SECRETS TO THE HIGHEST CRIMINAL BIDDER!
AUCTION? LIKE, FOR A LOT?
MILLIONS AND MILLIONS!
WHY DON'T YOU SHOW ME THAT PITCHIN' MOTION, BOOKY?
THE NEXT DAY, OUTSIDE GOTHAM POLICE HEADQUARTERS, TWO STOUT HEARTS RACE WITH NERVOUS ANTICIPATION...
NO SIGN YET OF THE DELIVERY TRUCK?
NOT YET, COMMISS--WAIT! THERE 'TIS! I SEE IT COMIN'!
NOW WE CAN REST EASY KNOWIN' THE GOTHAM CITY POLICE DEPARTMENT CAN FUNCTION SMOOTH AS SILK FOR ANOTHER YEAR!
DON'T COUNT YOUR CHICKENS, CHIEF! WE HAVEN'T TAKEN POSSESSION OF THE INVENTORY YET!
AAAH!
CHICKENS?!

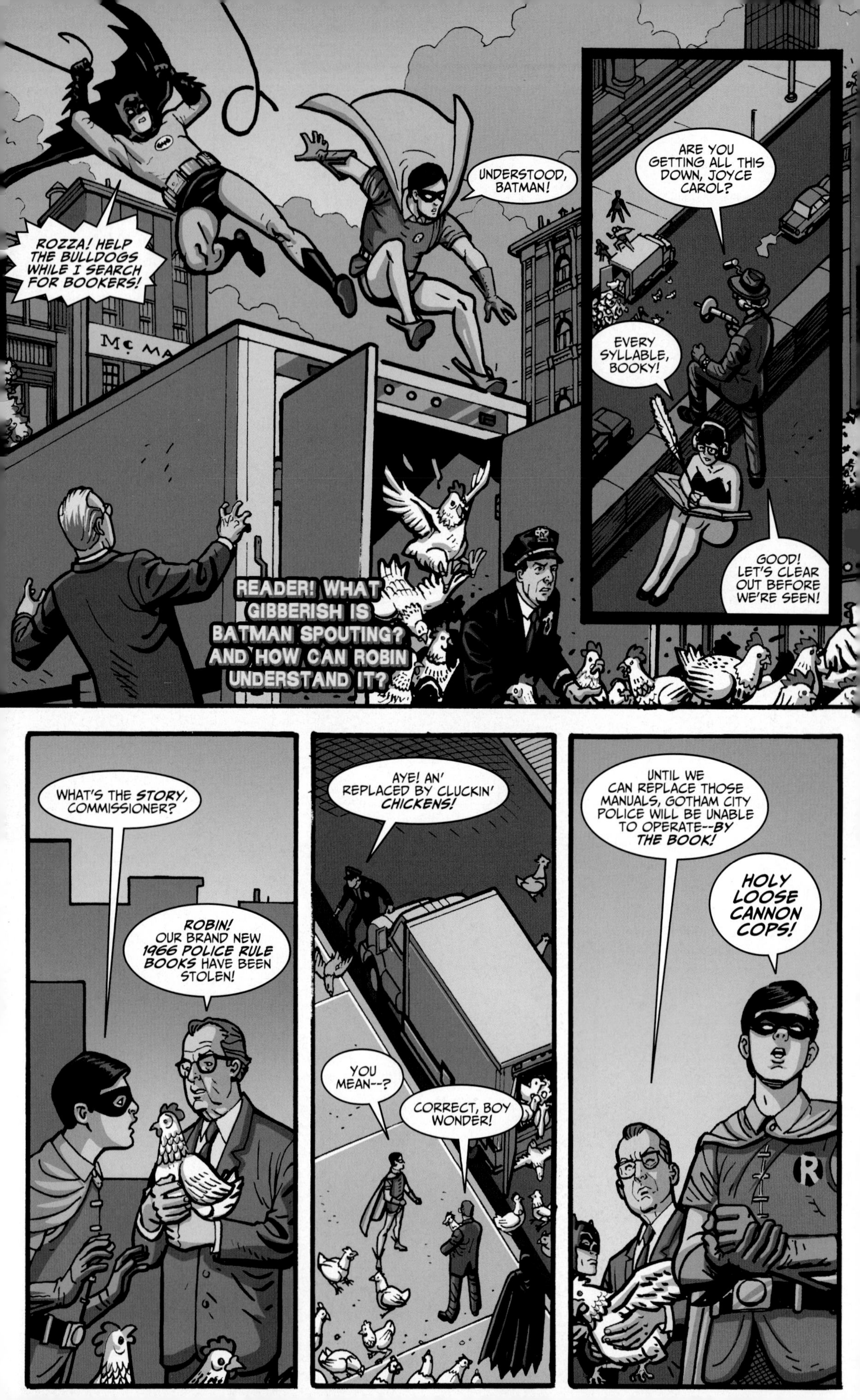
ROZZA! HELP THE BULLDOGS WHILE I SEARCH FOR BOOKERS!
UNDERSTOOD, BATMAN!
ARE YOU GETTING ALL THIS DOWN, JOYCE CAROL?
EVERY SYLLABLE, BOOKY!
GOOD! LET'S CLEAR OUT BEFORE WE'RE SEEN!
Mc MA
READER! WHAT GIBBERISH IS BATMAN SPOUTING? AND HOW CAN ROBIN UNDERSTAND IT?
WHAT'S THE STORY, COMMISSIONER?
ROBIN! OUR BRAND NEW 1966 POLICE RULE BOOKS HAVE BEEN STOLEN!
AYE! AN' REPLACED BY CLUCKIN' CHICKENS!
YOU MEAN--?
CORRECT, BOY WONDER!
UNTIL WE CAN REPLACE THOSE MANUALS, GOTHAM CITY POLICE WILL BE UNABLE TO OPERATE--BY THE BOOK!
HOLY LOOSE CANNON COPS!

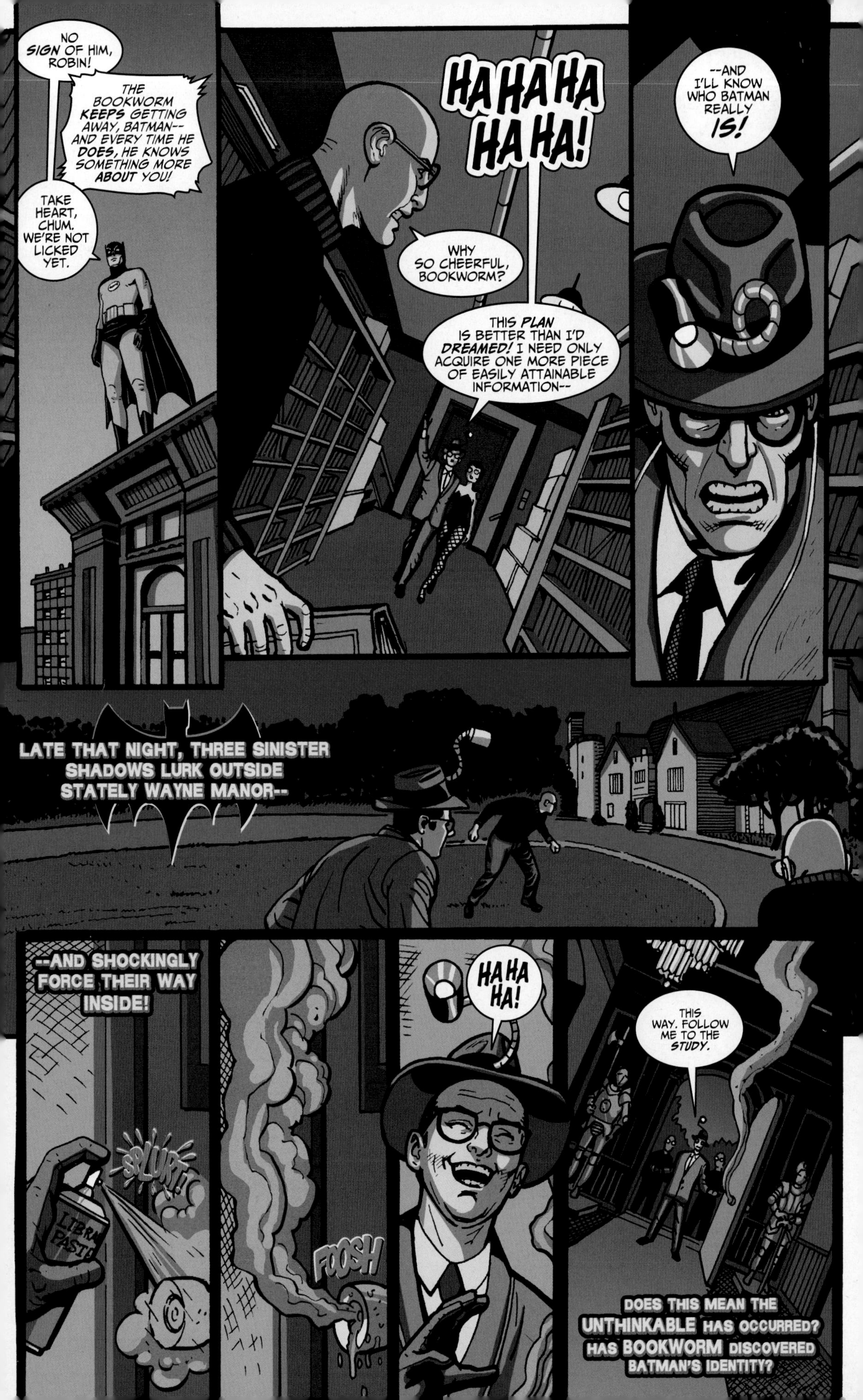
NO SIGN OF HIM, ROBIN!
THE BOOKWORM KEEPS GETTING AWAY, BATMAN-- AND EVERY TIME HE DOES, HE KNOWS SOMETHING MORE ABOUT YOU!
TAKE HEART, CHUM. WE'RE NOT LICKED YET.
WHY SO CHEERFUL, BOOKWORM?
HAHAHA HAHA!
THIS PLAN IS BETTER THAN I'D DREAMED! I NEED ONLY ACQUIRE ONE MORE PIECE OF EASILY ATTAINABLE INFORMATION--
--AND I'LL KNOW WHO BATMAN REALLY IS!
LATE THAT NIGHT, THREE SINISTER SHADOWS LURK OUTSIDE STATELY WAYNE MANOR--
--AND SHOCKINGLY FORCE THEIR WAY INSIDE!
SPLURT!
FOOSH
HAHA HA!
THIS WAY. FOLLOW ME TO THE STUDY.
DOES THIS MEAN THE UNTHINKABLE HAS OCCURRED? HAS BOOKWORM DISCOVERED BATMAN'S IDENTITY?

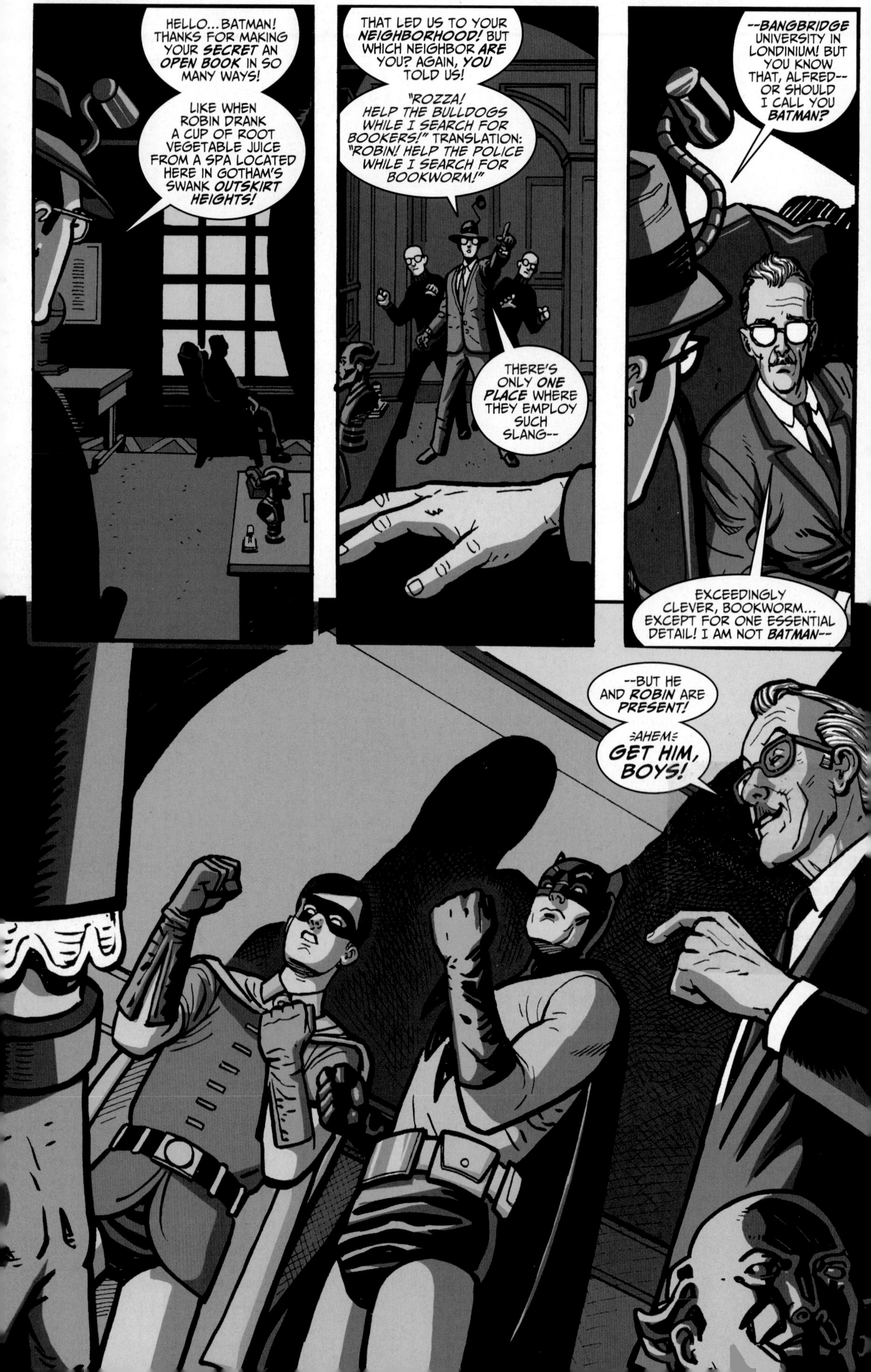
HELLO...BATMAN! THANKS FOR MAKING YOUR SECRET AN OPEN BOOK IN SO MANY WAYS!
LIKE WHEN ROBIN DRANK A CUP OF ROOT VEGETABLE JUICE FROM A SPA LOCATED HERE IN GOTHAM'S SWANK OUTSKIRT HEIGHTS!
THAT LED US TO YOUR NEIGHBORHOOD! BUT WHICH NEIGHBOR ARE YOU? AGAIN, YOU TOLD US!
"ROZZA! HELP THE BULLDOGS WHILE I SEARCH FOR BOOKERS!" TRANSLATION: "ROBIN! HELP THE POLICE WHILE I SEARCH FOR BOOKWORM!"
THERE'S ONLY ONE PLACE WHERE THEY EMPLOY SUCH SLANG--
--BANGBRIDGE UNIVERSITY IN LONDINIUM! BUT YOU KNOW THAT, ALFRED--OR SHOULD I CALL YOU BATMAN?
EXCEEDINGLY CLEVER, BOOKWORM... EXCEPT FOR ONE ESSENTIAL DETAIL! I AM NOT BATMAN--
--BUT HE AND ROBIN ARE PRESENT!
AHEM
GET HIM, BOYS!

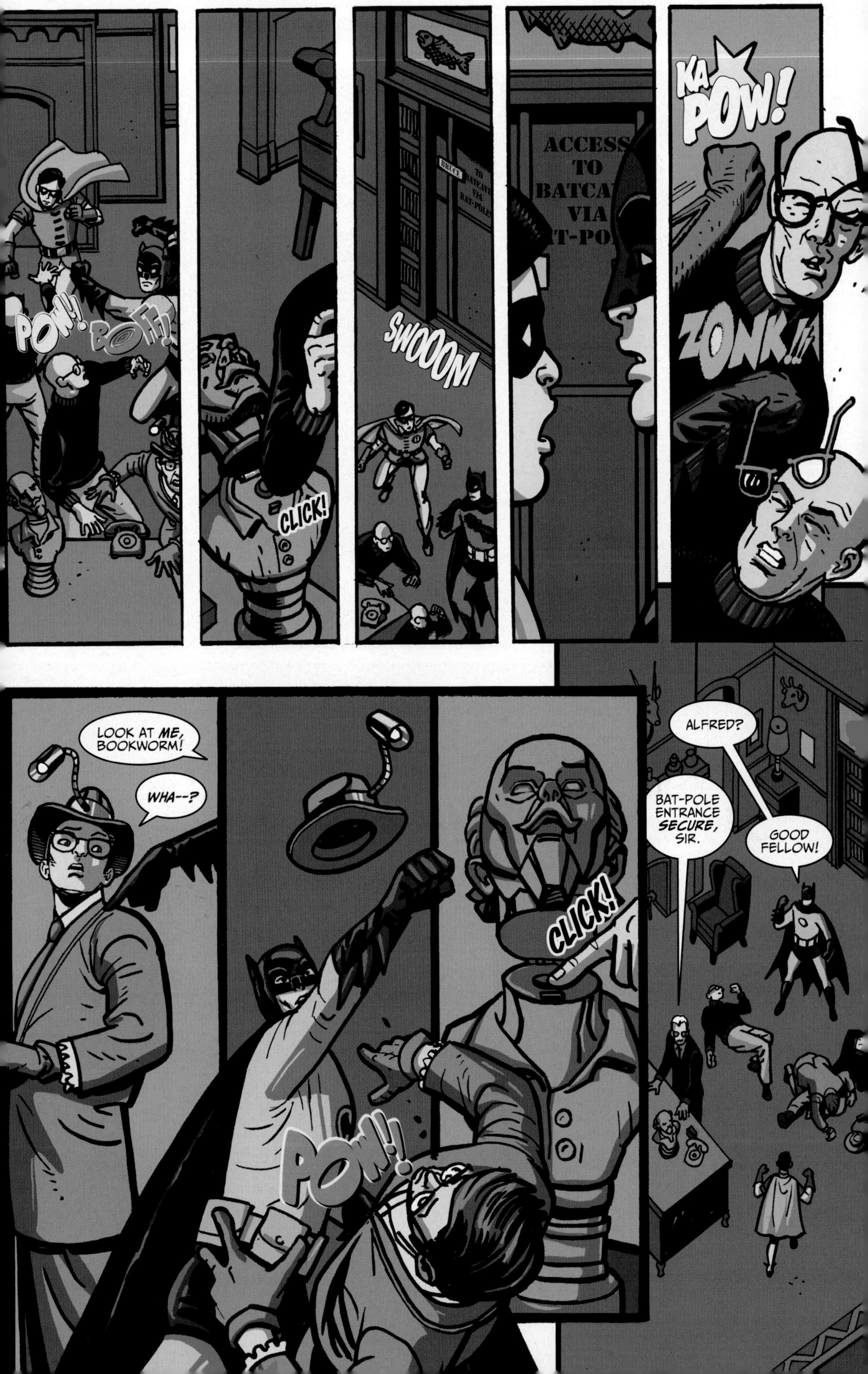
POW!! BOFF!!
CLICK!
SWOOOM
ACCESS TO BATCAVE VIA BAT-POLE
KA POW!
ZONK!!
LOOK AT ME, BOOKWORM!
WHA--?
CLICK!
POW!!
ALFRED?
BAT-POLE ENTRANCE SECURE, SIR.
GOOD FELLOW!

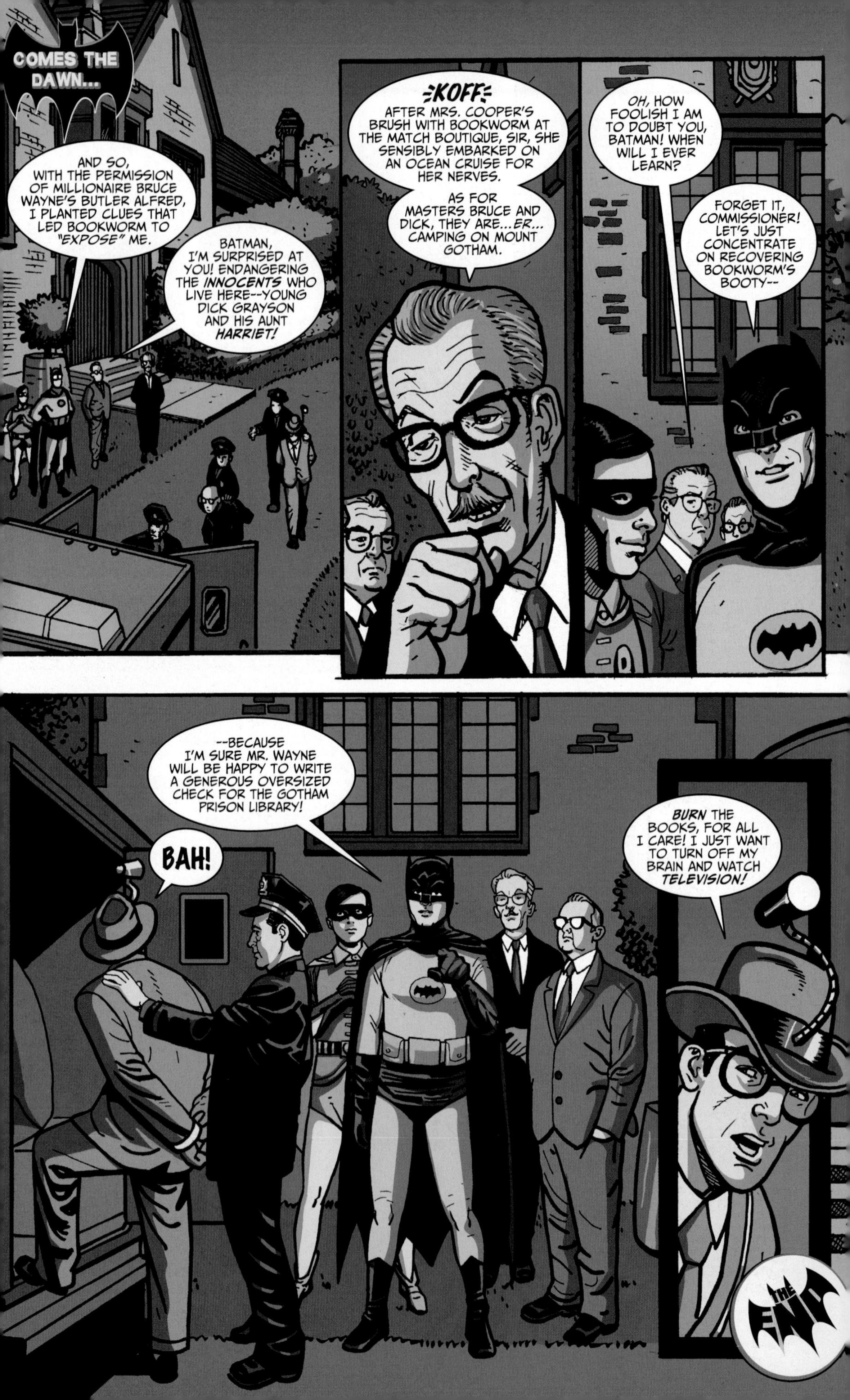
COMES THE DAWN...
AND SO, WITH THE PERMISSION OF MILLIONAIRE BRUCE WAYNE'S BUTLER ALFRED, I PLANTED CLUES THAT LED BOOKWORM TO "EXPOSE" ME.
BATMAN, I'M SURPRISED AT YOU! ENDANGERING THE INNOCENTS WHO LIVE HERE--YOUNG DICK GRAYSON AND HIS AUNT HARRIET!
KOFF
AFTER MRS. COOPER'S BRUSH WITH BOOKWORM AT THE MATCH BOUTIQUE, SIR, SHE SENSIBLY EMBARKED ON AN OCEAN CRUISE FOR HER NERVES.
AS FOR MASTERS BRUCE AND DICK, THEY ARE...ER... CAMPING ON MOUNT GOTHAM.
OH, HOW FOOLISH I AM TO DOUBT YOU, BATMAN! WHEN WILL I EVER LEARN?
FORGET IT, COMMISSIONER! LET'S JUST CONCENTRATE ON RECOVERING BOOKWORM'S BOOTY--
--BECAUSE I'M SURE MR. WAYNE WILL BE HAPPY TO WRITE A GENEROUS OVERSIZED CHECK FOR THE GOTHAM PRISON LIBRARY!
BAH!
BURN THE BOOKS, FOR ALL I CARE! I JUST WANT TO TURN OFF MY BRAIN AND WATCH TELEVISION!
THE END

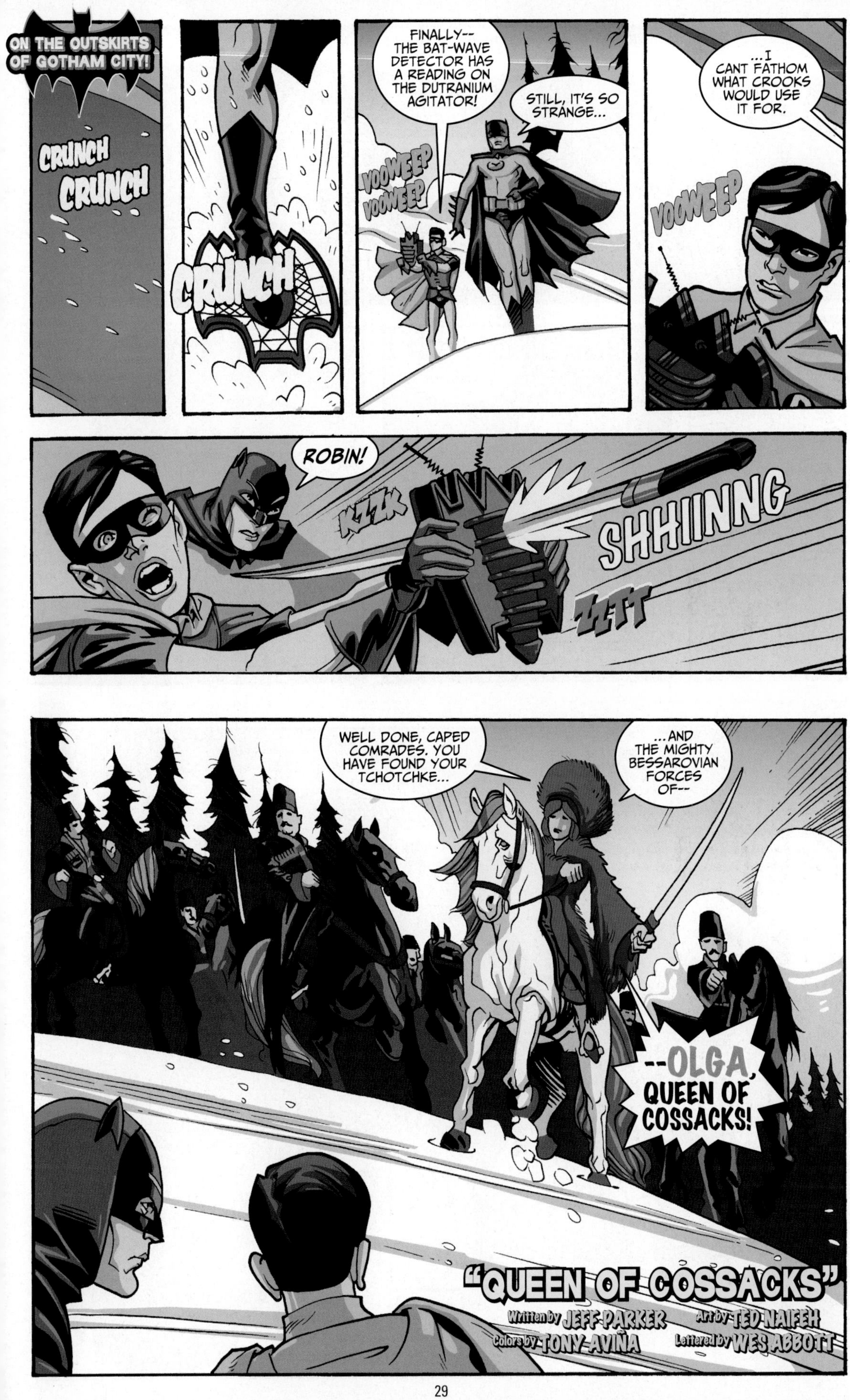
ON THE OUTSKIRTS OF GOTHAM CITY!
CRUNCH
CRUNCH
CRUNCH
FINALLY-- THE BAT-WAVE DETECTOR HAS A READING ON THE DUTRANIUM AGITATOR!
STILL, IT'S SO STRANGE...
VOOWEEP
VOOWEEP
...I CANT FATHOM WHAT CROOKS WOULD USE IT FOR.
VOOWEEP
ROBIN!
KZZK
SHHIINNG
ZZTT
WELL DONE, CAPED COMRADES. YOU HAVE FOUND YOUR TCHOTCHKE...
...AND THE MIGHTY BESSAROVIAN FORCES OF--
--OLGA, QUEEN OF COSSACKS!
"QUEEN OF COSSACKS"
Written by JEFF PARKER
Art by TED NAIFEH
Colors by TONY AVIÑA
Lettered by WES ABBOTT

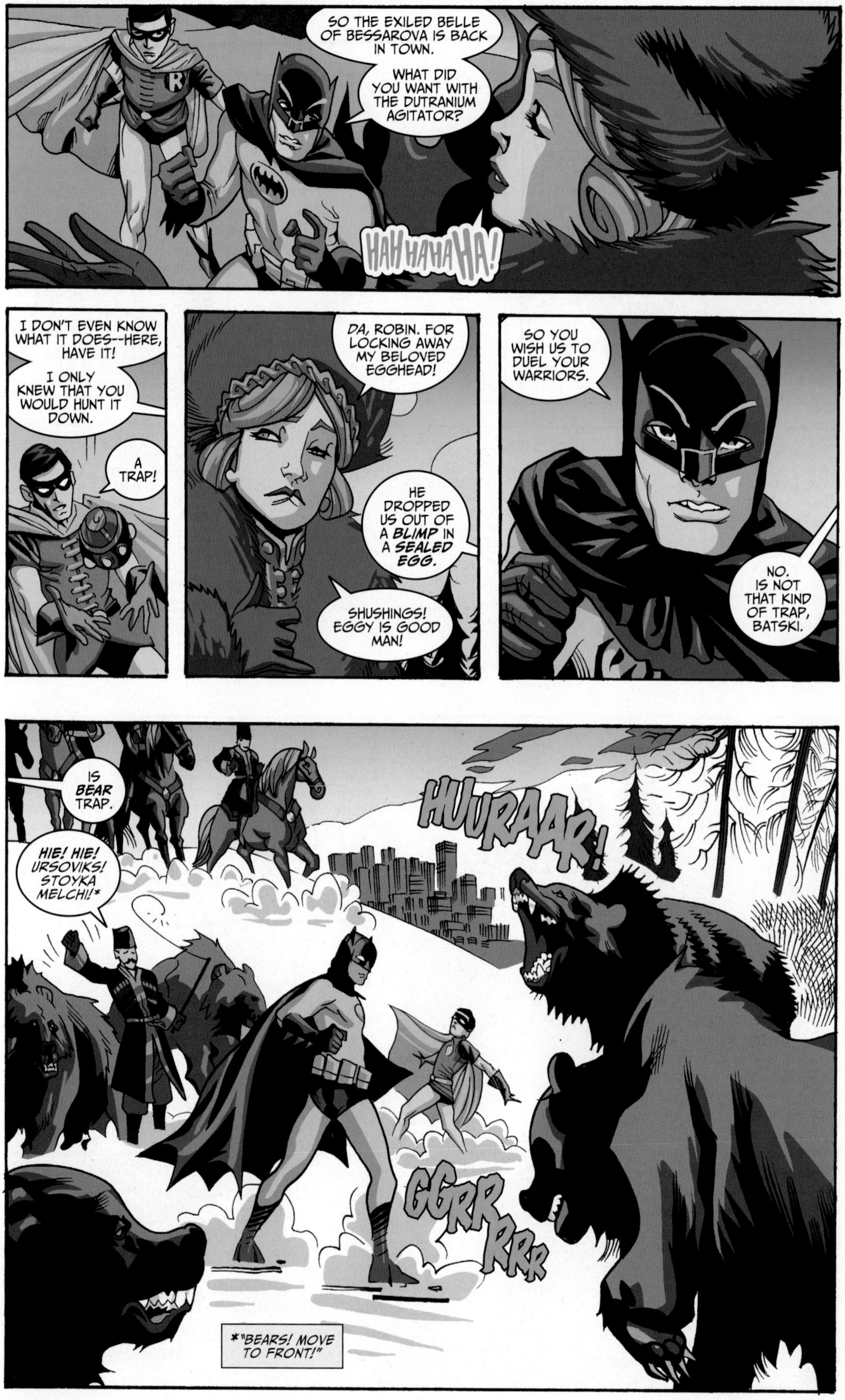
SO THE EXILED BELLE OF BESSAROVA IS BACK IN TOWN.
WHAT DID YOU WANT WITH THE DUTRANIUM AGITATOR?
HAHHAHAHA!
I DON'T EVEN KNOW WHAT IT DOES--HERE, HAVE IT!
I ONLY KNEW THAT YOU WOULD HUNT IT DOWN.
A TRAP!
DA, ROBIN. FOR LOCKING AWAY MY BELOVED EGGHEAD!
HE DROPPED US OUT OF A BLIMP IN A SEALED EGG.
SHUSHINGS! EGGY IS GOOD MAN!
SO YOU WISH US TO DUEL YOUR WARRIORS.
NO. IS NOT THAT KIND OF TRAP, BATSKI.
IS BEAR TRAP.
HUURAAAR!
HIE! HIE! URSOVIKS! STOYKA MELCHI!*
GGRRRRR
*"BEARS! MOVE TO FRONT!"

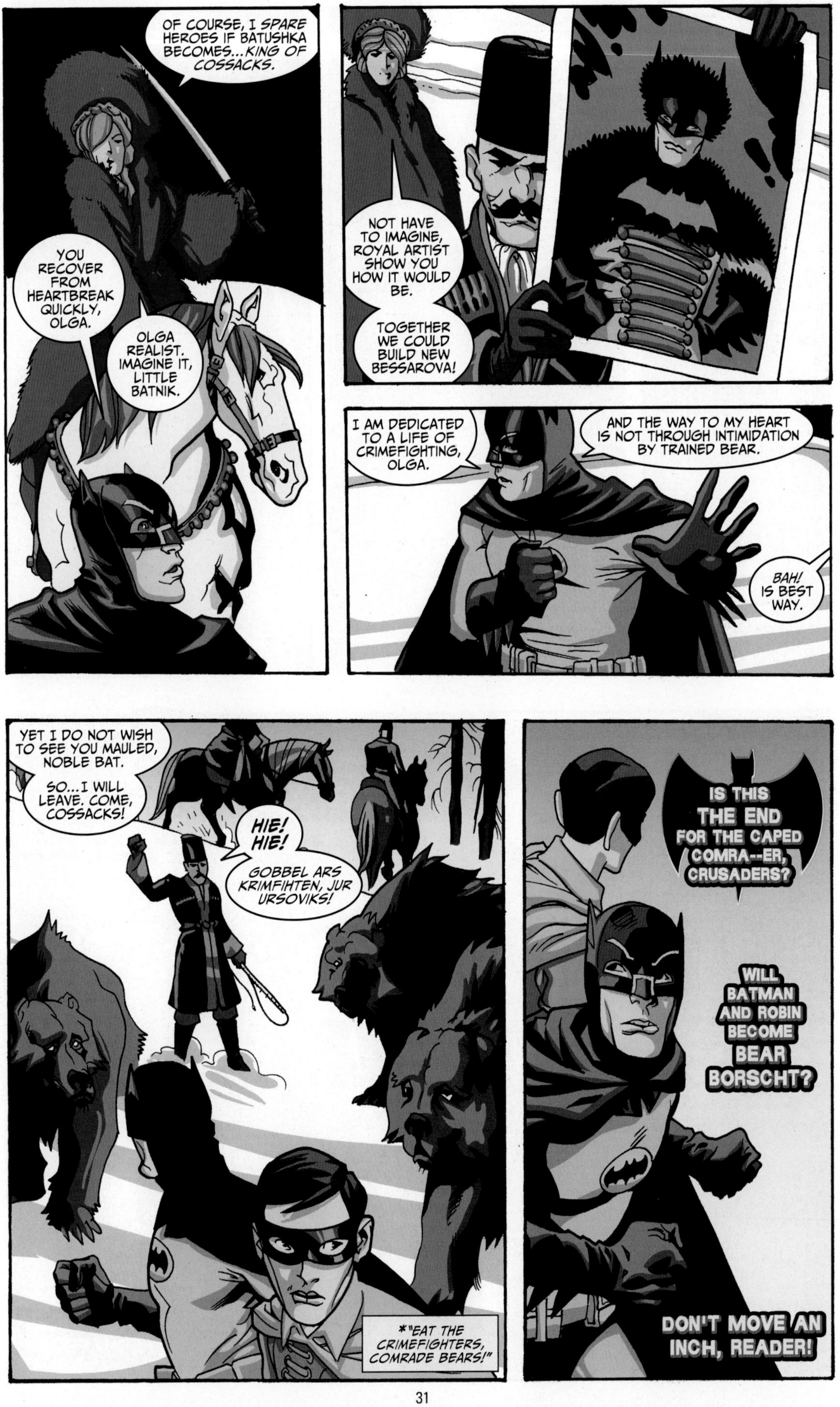
OF COURSE, I SPARE HEROES IF BATUSHKA BECOMES...KING OF COSSACKS.
YOU RECOVER FROM HEARTBREAK QUICKLY, OLGA.
OLGA REALIST. IMAGINE IT, LITTLE BATNIK.
NOT HAVE TO IMAGINE, ROYAL ARTIST SHOW YOU HOW IT WOULD BE.
TOGETHER WE COULD BUILD NEW BESSAROVA!
I AM DEDICATED TO A LIFE OF CRIMEFIGHTING, OLGA.
AND THE WAY TO MY HEART IS NOT THROUGH INTIMIDATION BY TRAINED BEAR.
BAH! IS BEST WAY.
YET I DO NOT WISH TO SEE YOU MAULED, NOBLE BAT.
SO...I WILL LEAVE. COME, COSSACKS!
HIE! HIE!
GOBBEL ARS KRIMFIHTEN, JUR URSOVIKS!
*"EAT THE CRIMEFIGHTERS, COMRADE BEARS!"
IS THIS THE END FOR THE CAPED COMRA--ER, CRUSADERS?
WILL BATMAN AND ROBIN BECOME BEAR BORSCHT?
DON'T MOVE AN INCH, READER!

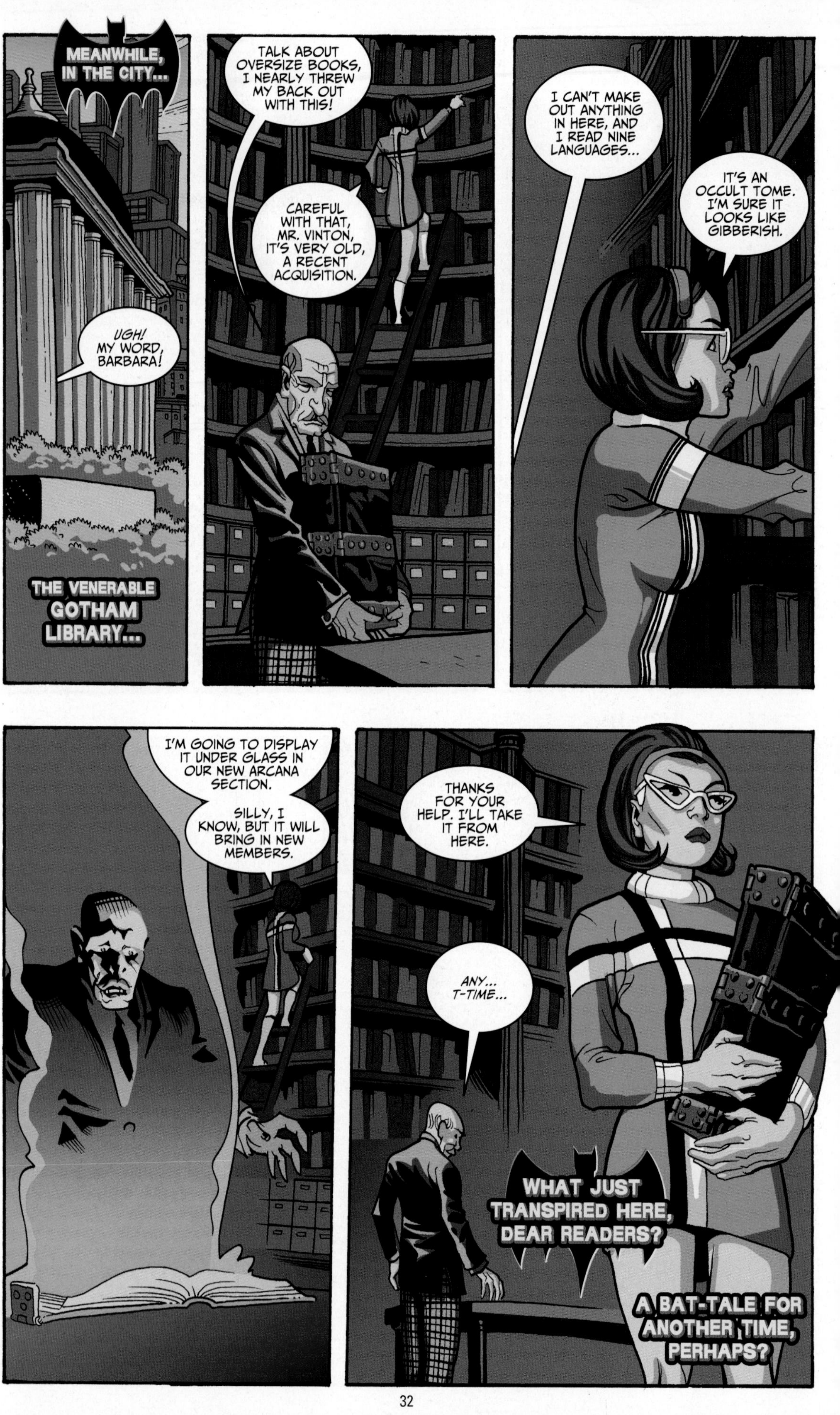
MEANWHILE, IN THE CITY...
UGH! MY WORD, BARBARA!
THE VENERABLE GOTHAM LIBRARY...
TALK ABOUT OVERSIZE BOOKS, I NEARLY THREW MY BACK OUT WITH THIS!
CAREFUL WITH THAT, MR. VINTON, IT'S VERY OLD, A RECENT ACQUISITION.
I CAN'T MAKE OUT ANYTHING IN HERE, AND I READ NINE LANGUAGES...
IT'S AN OCCULT TOME. I'M SURE IT LOOKS LIKE GIBBERISH.
I'M GOING TO DISPLAY IT UNDER GLASS IN OUR NEW ARCANA SECTION.
SILLY, I KNOW, BUT IT WILL BRING IN NEW MEMBERS.
THANKS FOR YOUR HELP. I'LL TAKE IT FROM HERE.
ANY... T-TIME...
WHAT JUST TRANSPIRED HERE, DEAR READERS?
A BAT-TALE FOR ANOTHER TIME, PERHAPS?

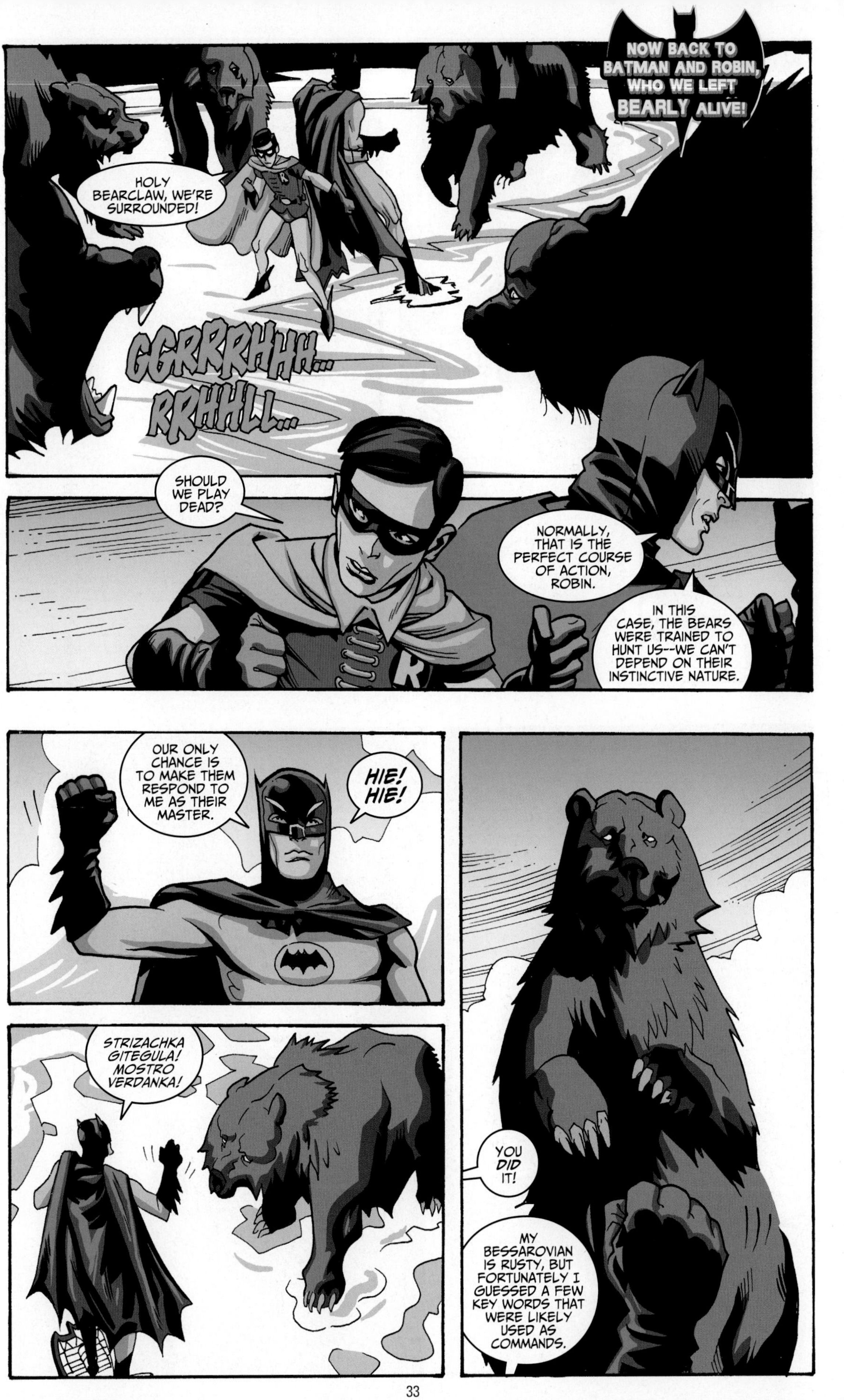
NOW BACK TO BATMAN AND ROBIN, WHO WE LEFT BEARLY ALIVE!
HOLY BEARCLAW, WE'RE SURROUNDED!
GGRRRHHH... RRHHLL...
SHOULD WE PLAY DEAD?
NORMALLY, THAT IS THE PERFECT COURSE OF ACTION, ROBIN.
IN THIS CASE, THE BEARS WERE TRAINED TO HUNT US--WE CAN'T DEPEND ON THEIR INSTINCTIVE NATURE.
OUR ONLY CHANCE IS TO MAKE THEM RESPOND TO ME AS THEIR MASTER.
HIE! HIE!
STRIZACHKA GITEGULA! MOSTRO VERDANKA!
YOU DID IT!
MY BESSAROVIAN IS RUSTY, BUT FORTUNATELY I GUESSED A FEW KEY WORDS THAT WERE LIKELY USED AS COMMANDS.

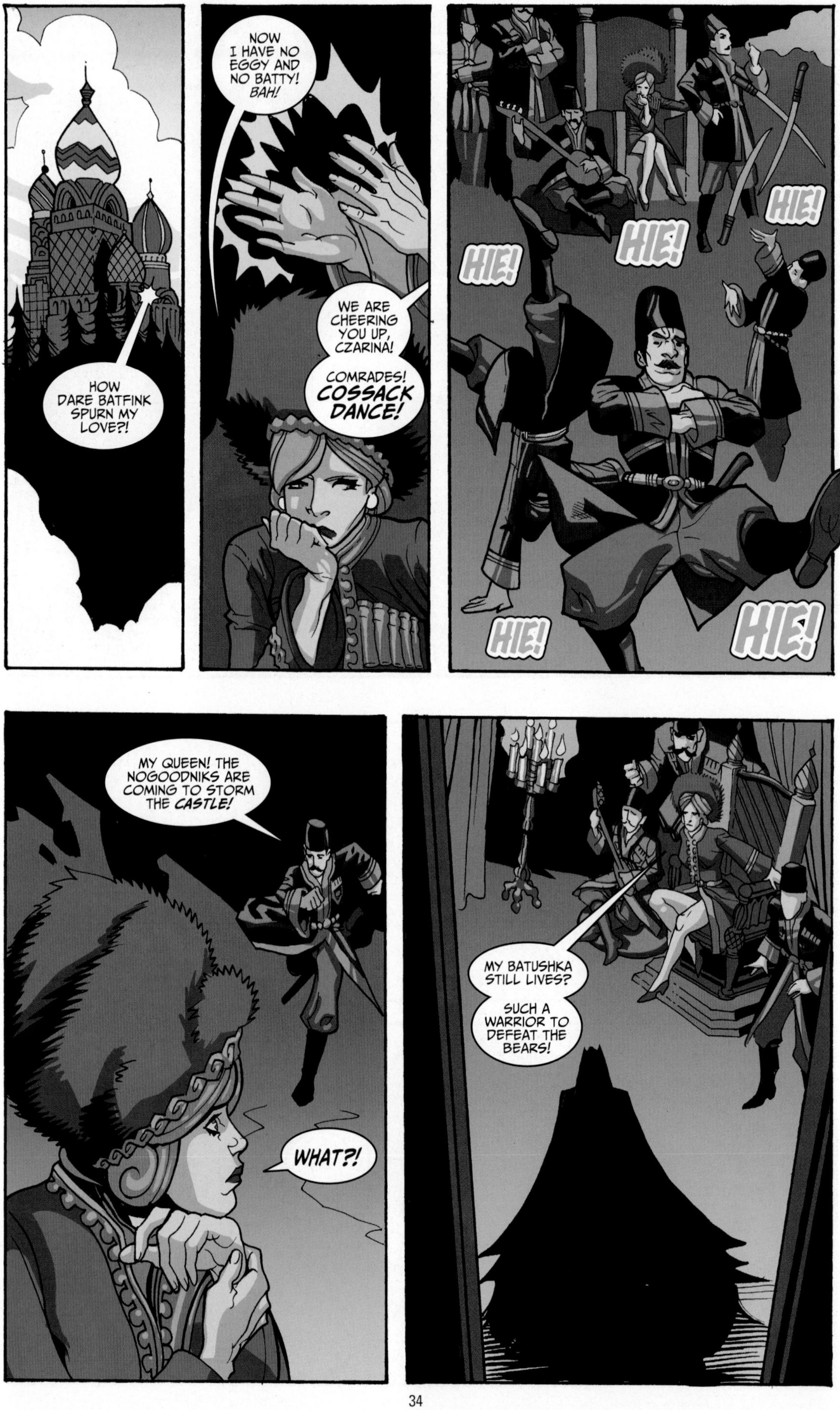
HOW DARE BATFINK SPURN MY LOVE?!
NOW I HAVE NO EGGY AND NO BATTY! BAH!
WE ARE CHEERING YOU UP, CZARINA!
COMRADES! COSSACK DANCE!
HIE!
HIE!
HIE!
HIE!
HIE!
MY QUEEN! THE NOGOODNIKS ARE COMING TO STORM THE CASTLE!
WHAT?!
MY BATUSHKA STILL LIVES?
SUCH A WARRIOR TO DEFEAT THE BEARS!

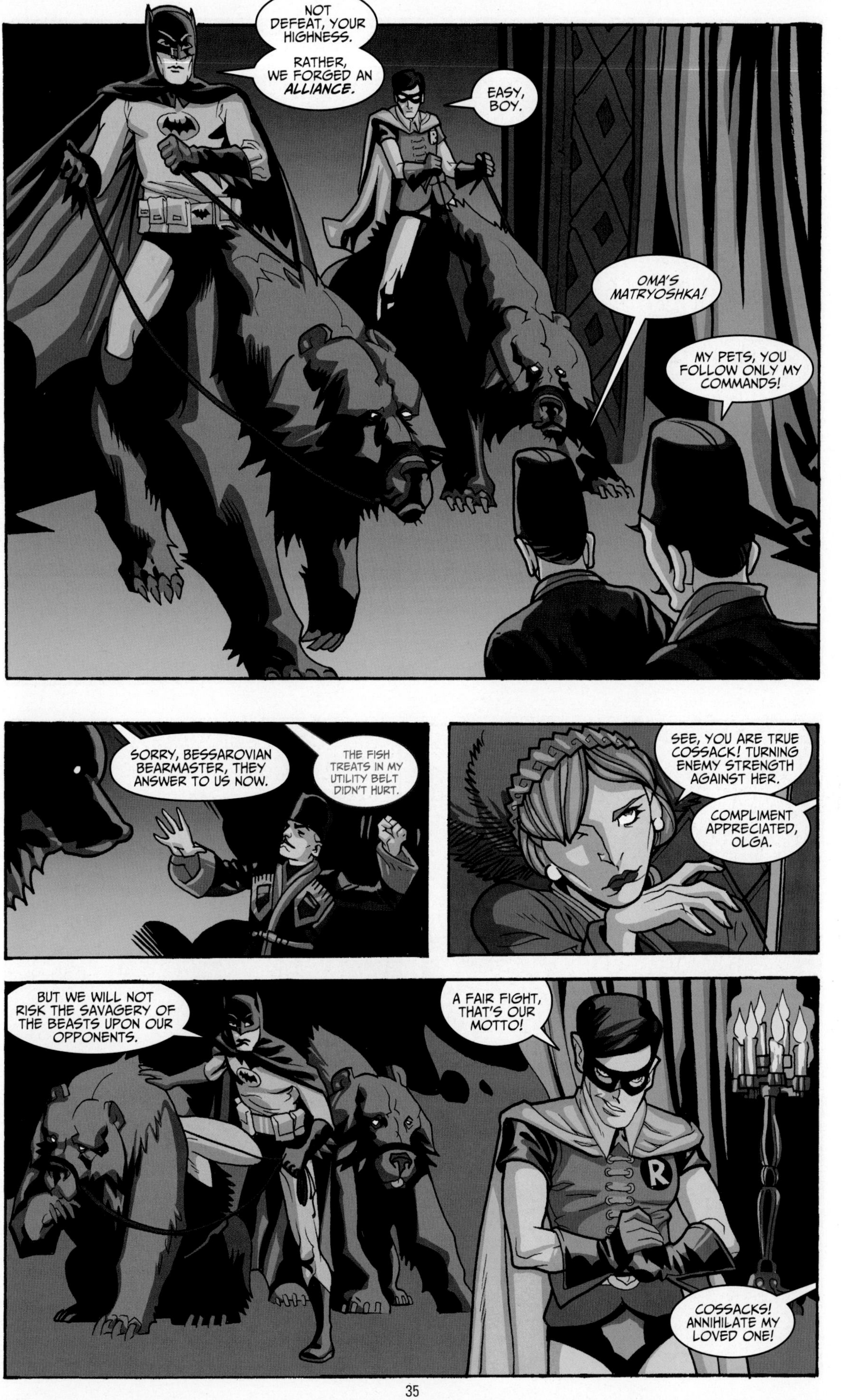
NOT DEFEAT, YOUR HIGHNESS.
RATHER, WE FORGED AN ALLIANCE.
EASY, BOY.
OMA'S MATRYOSHKA!
MY PETS, YOU FOLLOW ONLY MY COMMANDS!
SORRY, BESSAROVIAN BEARMASTER, THEY ANSWER TO US NOW.
THE FISH TREATS IN MY UTILITY BELT DIDN'T HURT.
SEE, YOU ARE TRUE COSSACK! TURNING ENEMY STRENGTH AGAINST HER.
COMPLIMENT APPRECIATED, OLGA.
BUT WE WILL NOT RISK THE SAVAGERY OF THE BEASTS UPON OUR OPPONENTS.
A FAIR FIGHT, THAT'S OUR MOTTO!
COSSACKS! ANNIHILATE MY LOVED ONE!

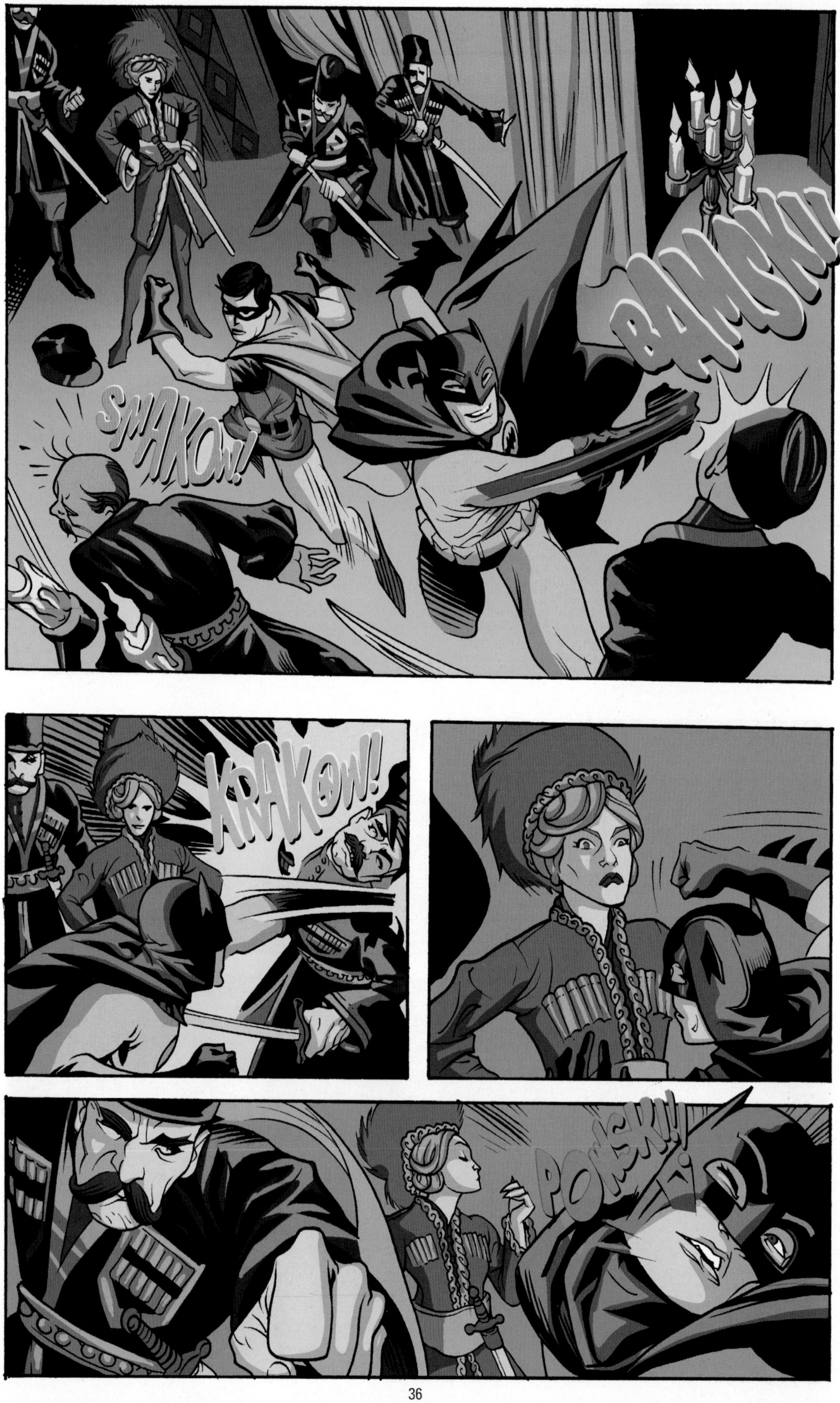
SMAKOW!
BAMSK!!
KRAKOW!!
POWSK!!!

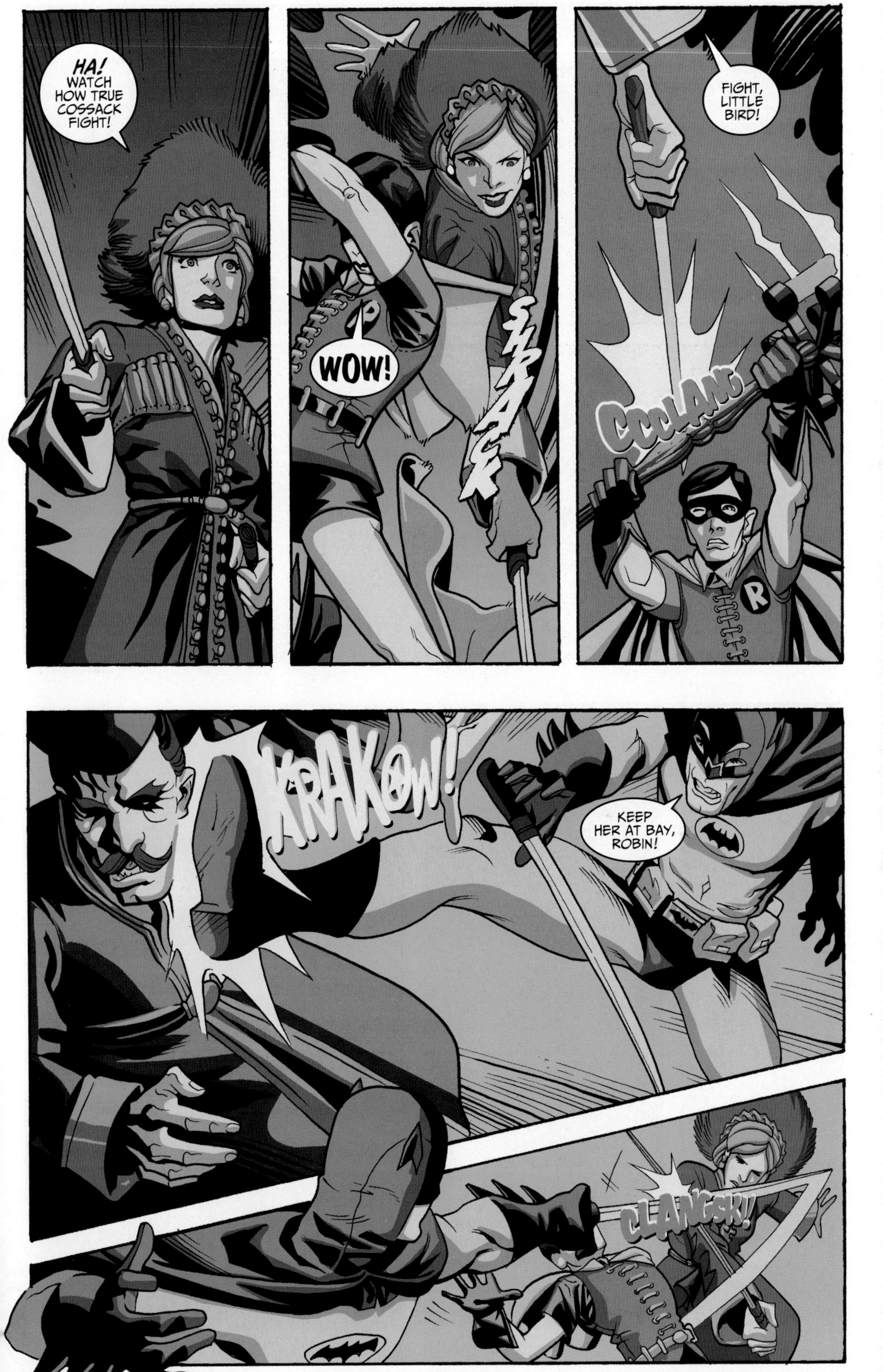
HA! WATCH HOW TRUE COSSACK FIGHT!
WOW!
SHRAACK
FIGHT, LITTLE BIRD!
CCCLANG
KRAKOW!
KEEP HER AT BAY, ROBIN!
CLANGSK!

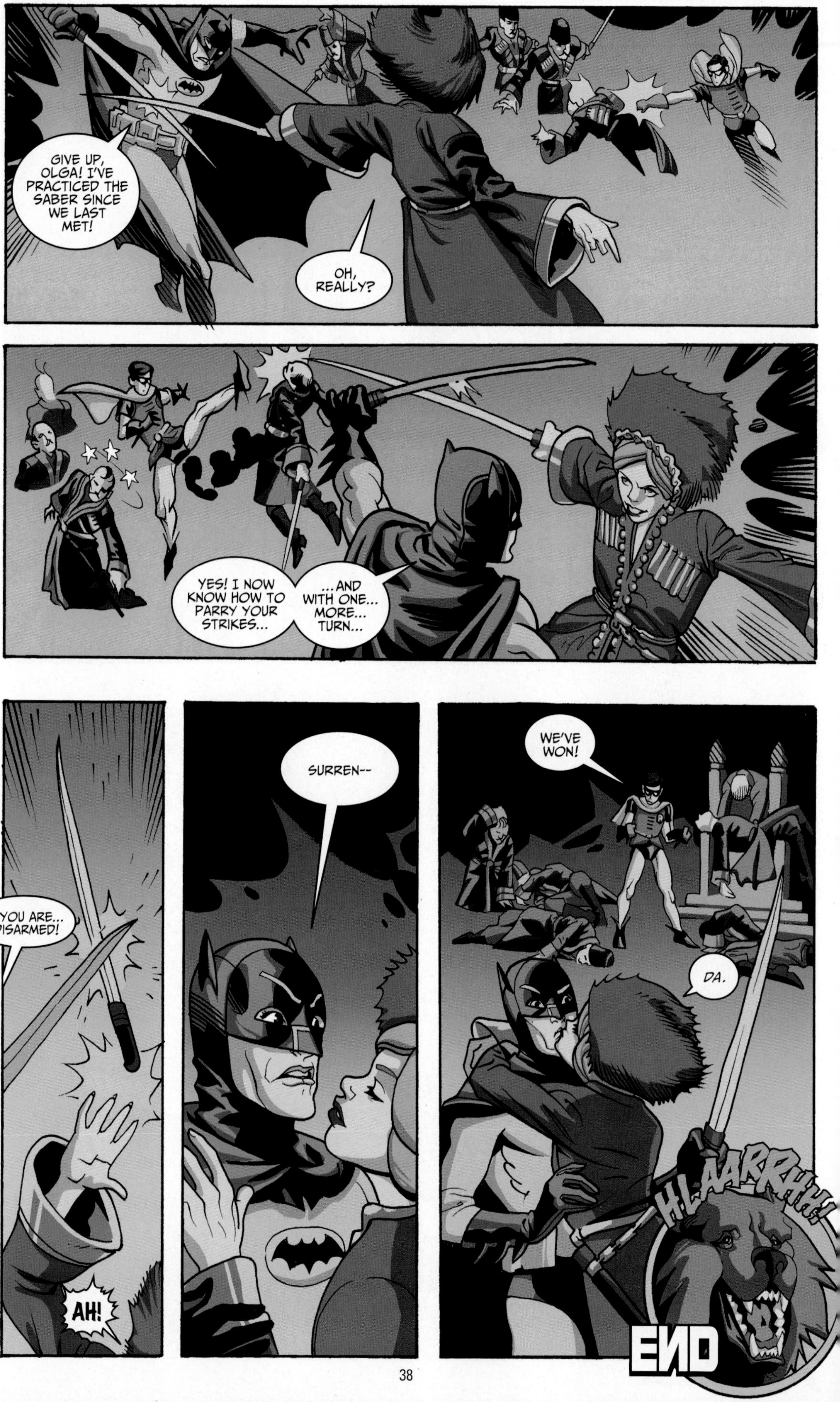
GIVE UP, OLGA! I'VE PRACTICED THE SABER SINCE WE LAST MET!
OH, REALLY?
YES! I NOW KNOW HOW TO PARRY YOUR STRIKES...
...AND WITH ONE... MORE... TURN...
...YOU ARE... DISARMED!
AH!
SURREN--
WE'VE WON!
DA.
HLAARRHH!
END

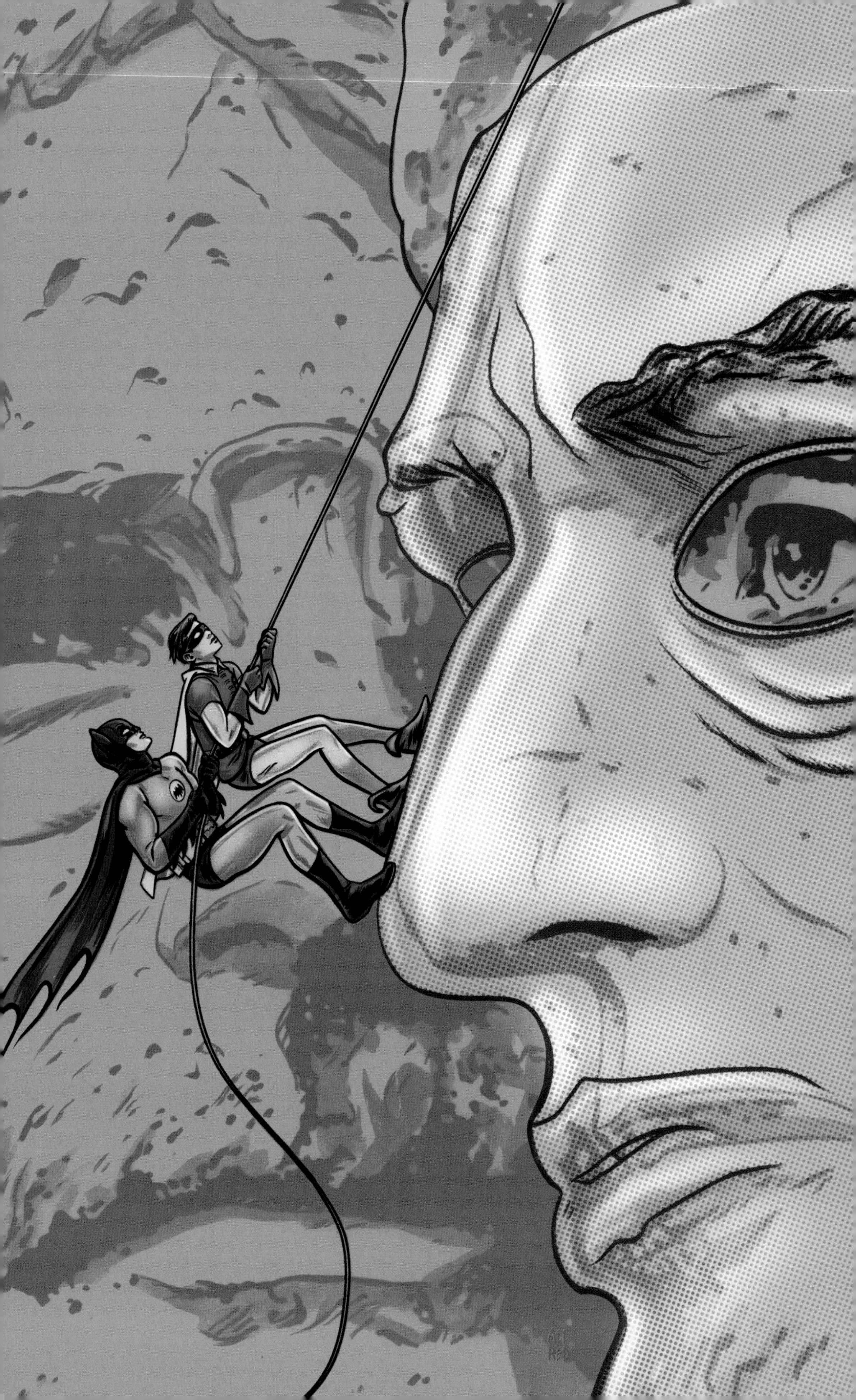

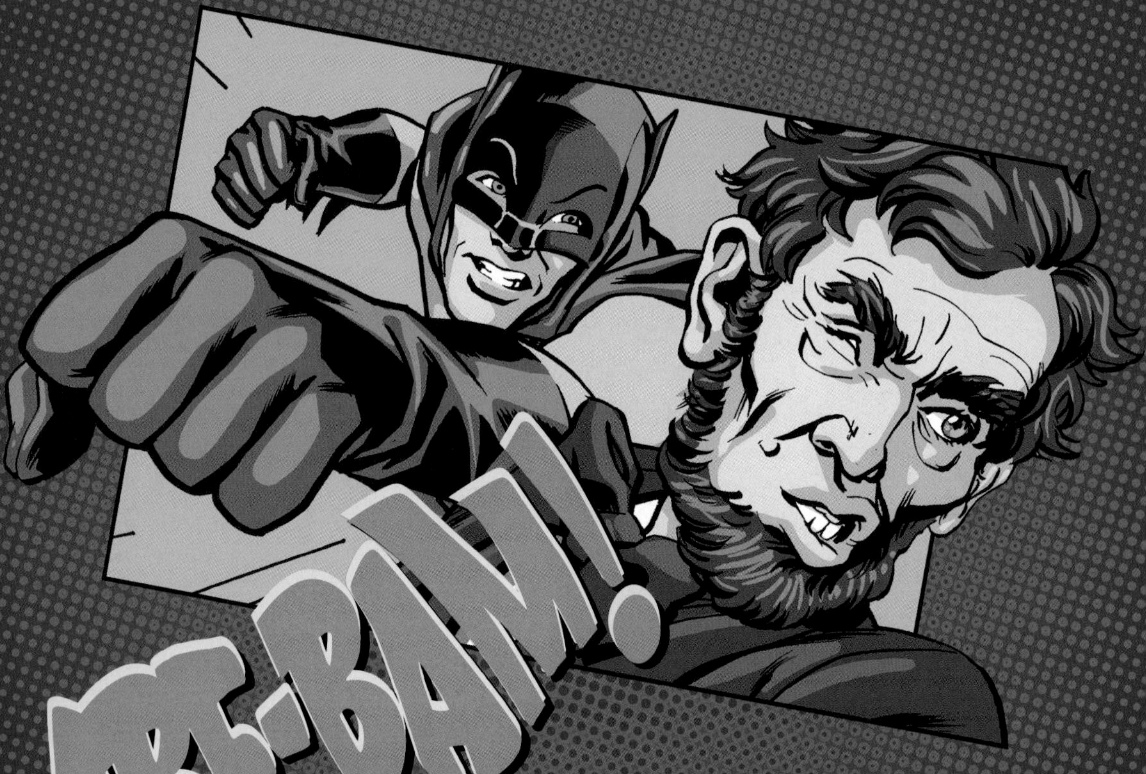
ABE-BAM!

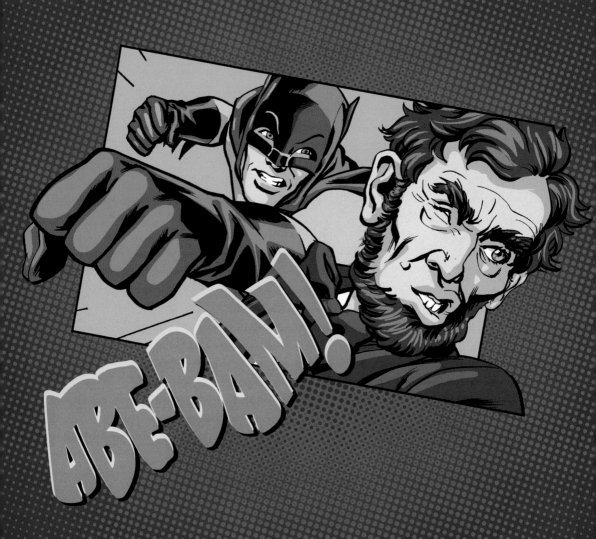

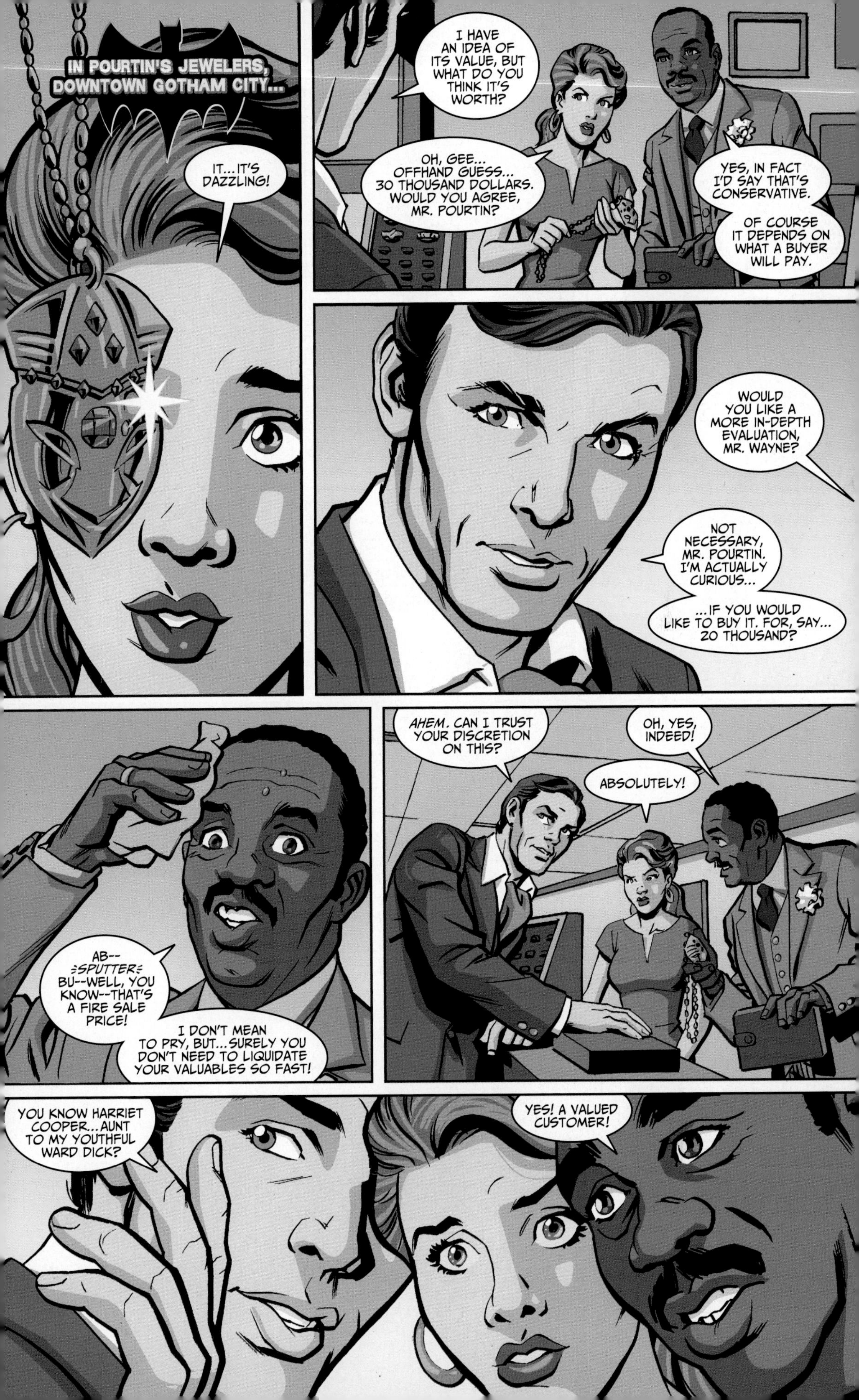

IN POURTIN'S JEWELERS, DOWNTOWN GOTHAM CITY...
IT...IT'S DAZZLING!
I HAVE AN IDEA OF ITS VALUE, BUT WHAT DO YOU THINK IT'S WORTH?
OH, GEE... OFFHAND GUESS... 30 THOUSAND DOLLARS. WOULD YOU AGREE, MR. POURTIN?
YES, IN FACT I'D SAY THAT'S CONSERVATIVE.
OF COURSE IT DEPENDS ON WHAT A BUYER WILL PAY.
WOULD YOU LIKE A MORE IN-DEPTH EVALUATION, MR. WAYNE?
NOT NECESSARY, MR. POURTIN. I'M ACTUALLY CURIOUS...
...IF YOU WOULD LIKE TO BUY IT. FOR, SAY... 20 THOUSAND?
AB-- =SPUTTER= BU--WELL, YOU KNOW--THAT'S A FIRE SALE PRICE!
I DON'T MEAN TO PRY, BUT...SURELY YOU DON'T NEED TO LIQUIDATE YOUR VALUABLES SO FAST!
AHEM. CAN I TRUST YOUR DISCRETION ON THIS?
OH, YES, INDEED!
ABSOLUTELY!
YOU KNOW HARRIET COOPER...AUNT TO MY YOUTHFUL WARD DICK?
YES! A VALUED CUSTOMER!

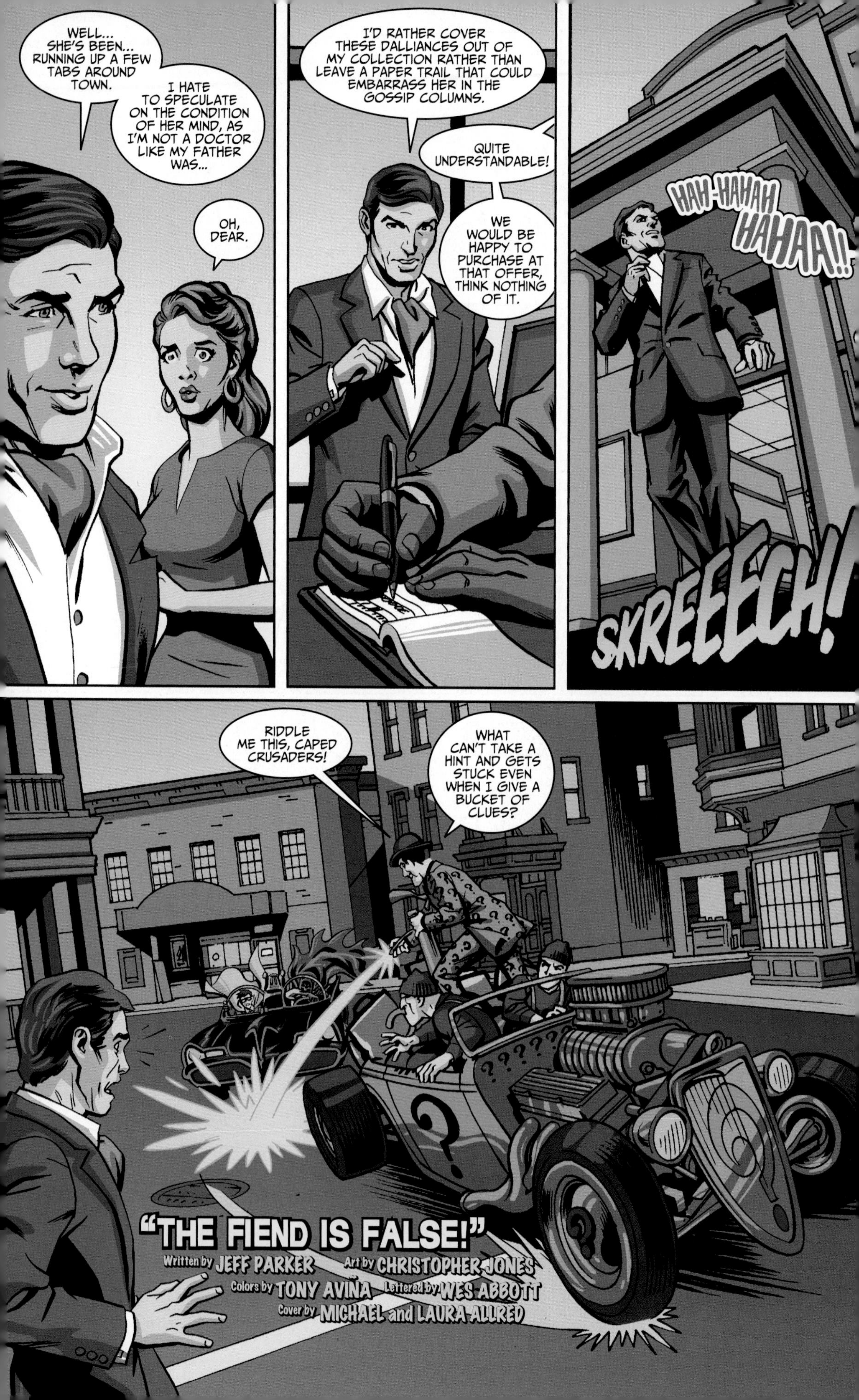
WELL... SHE'S BEEN... RUNNING UP A FEW TABS AROUND TOWN.
I HATE TO SPECULATE ON THE CONDITION OF HER MIND, AS I'M NOT A DOCTOR LIKE MY FATHER WAS...
OH, DEAR.
I'D RATHER COVER THESE DALLIANCES OUT OF MY COLLECTION RATHER THAN LEAVE A PAPER TRAIL THAT COULD EMBARRASS HER IN THE GOSSIP COLUMNS.
QUITE UNDERSTANDABLE!
WE WOULD BE HAPPY TO PURCHASE AT THAT OFFER, THINK NOTHING OF IT.
HAH-HAHAH HAHAA!!
SKREEECH!
RIDDLE ME THIS, CAPED CRUSADERS!
WHAT CAN'T TAKE A HINT AND GETS STUCK EVEN WHEN I GIVE A BUCKET OF CLUES?
"THE FIEND IS FALSE!"
Written by JEFF PARKER Art by CHRISTOPHER JONES
Colors by TONY AVIÑA Lettered by WES ABBOTT
Cover by MICHAEL and LAURA ALLRED

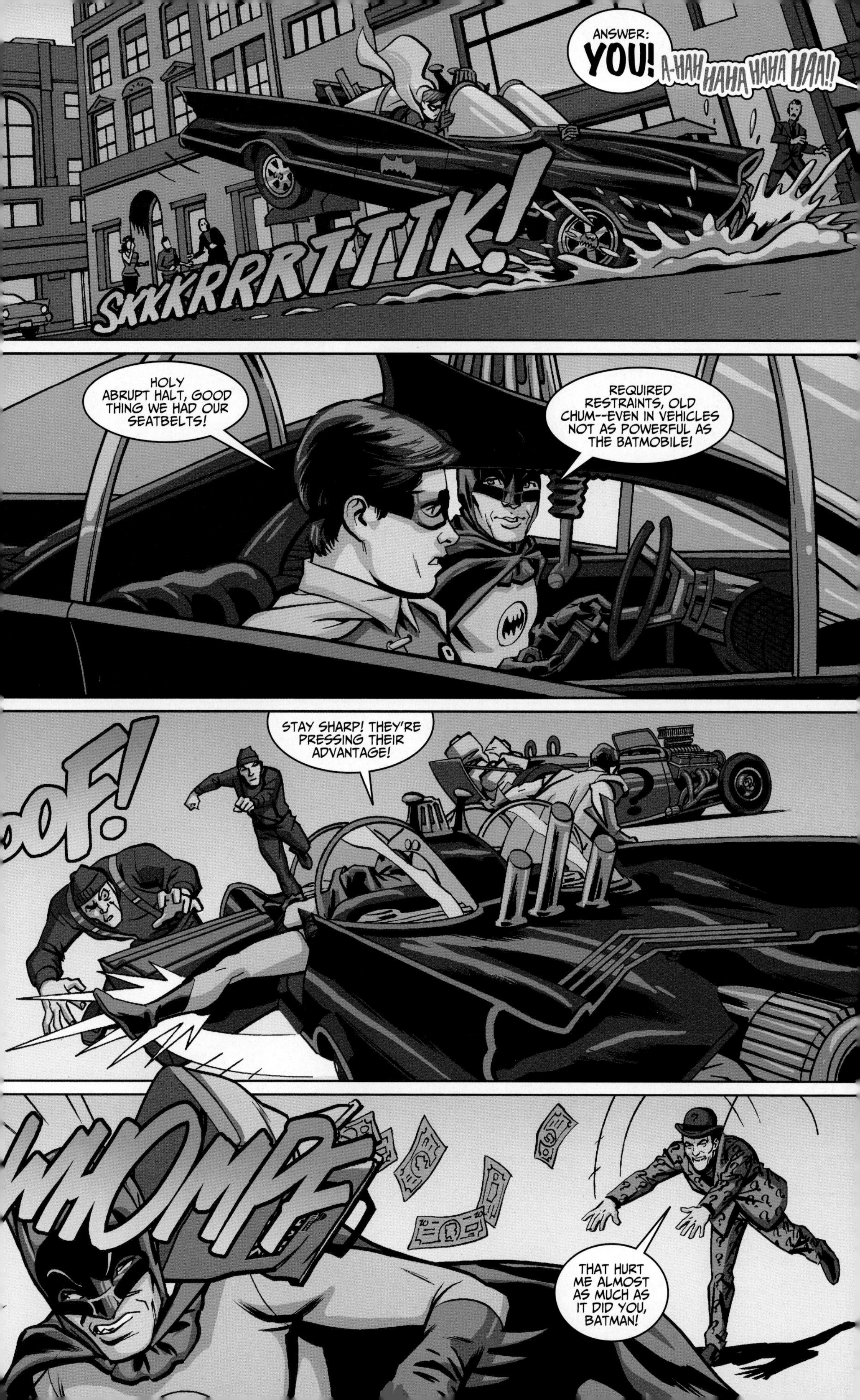
ANSWER: YOU! A-HAH HAHA HAHA HAA!!
SKKKRRRRTTTK!
HOLY ABRUPT HALT, GOOD THING WE HAD OUR SEATBELTS!
REQUIRED RESTRAINTS, OLD CHUM--EVEN IN VEHICLES NOT AS POWERFUL AS THE BATMOBILE!
STAY SHARP! THEY'RE PRESSING THEIR ADVANTAGE!
OOF!
WHOMP!
THAT HURT ME ALMOST AS MUCH AS IT DID YOU, BATMAN!

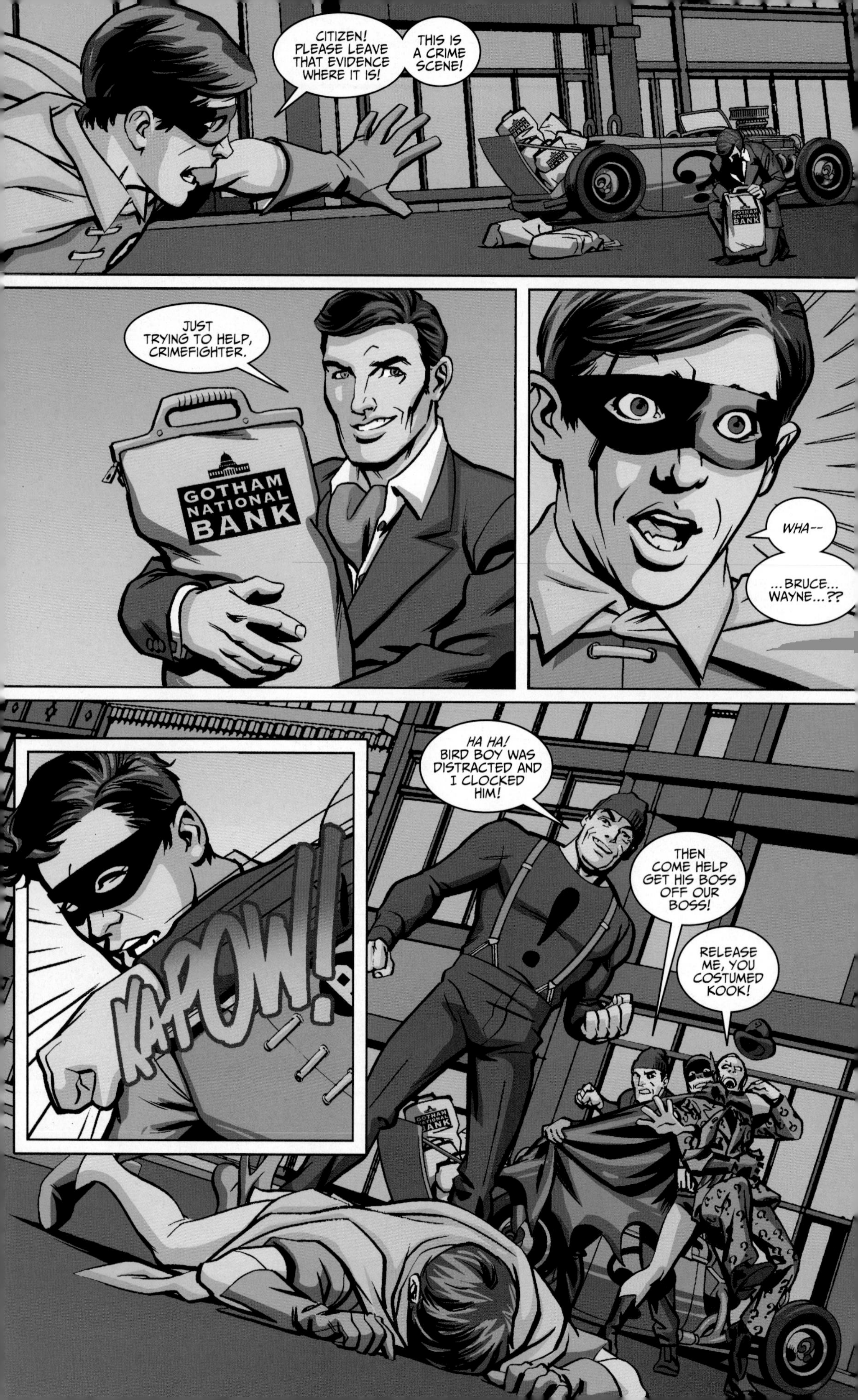
CITIZEN! PLEASE LEAVE THAT EVIDENCE WHERE IT IS!
THIS IS A CRIME SCENE!
GOTHAM NATIONAL BANK
JUST TRYING TO HELP, CRIMEFIGHTER.
GOTHAM NATIONAL BANK
WHA--
...BRUCE... WAYNE...??
KA-POW!!
HA HA! BIRD BOY WAS DISTRACTED AND I CLOCKED HIM!
THEN COME HELP GET HIS BOSS OFF OUR BOSS!
RELEASE ME, YOU COSTUMED KOOK!

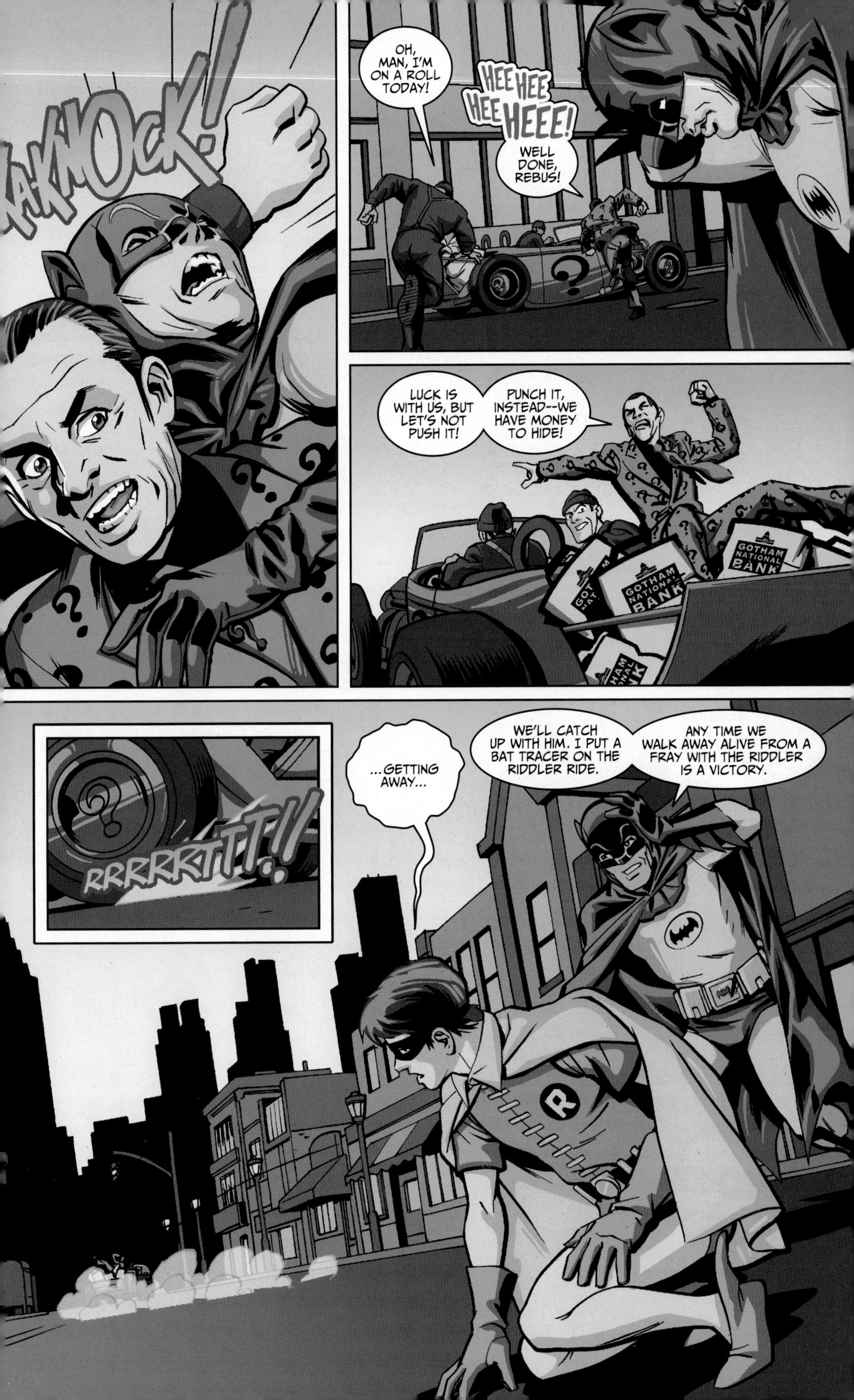
KAKNOCK!
OH, MAN, I'M ON A ROLL TODAY!
HEE HEE HEE HEEE!
WELL DONE, REBUS!
LUCK IS WITH US, BUT LET'S NOT PUSH IT!
PUNCH IT, INSTEAD--WE HAVE MONEY TO HIDE!
GOTHAM NATIONAL BANK
RRRRRTTT!!
...GETTING AWAY...
WE'LL CATCH UP WITH HIM. I PUT A BAT TRACER ON THE RIDDLER RIDE.
ANY TIME WE WALK AWAY ALIVE FROM A FRAY WITH THE RIDDLER IS A VICTORY.

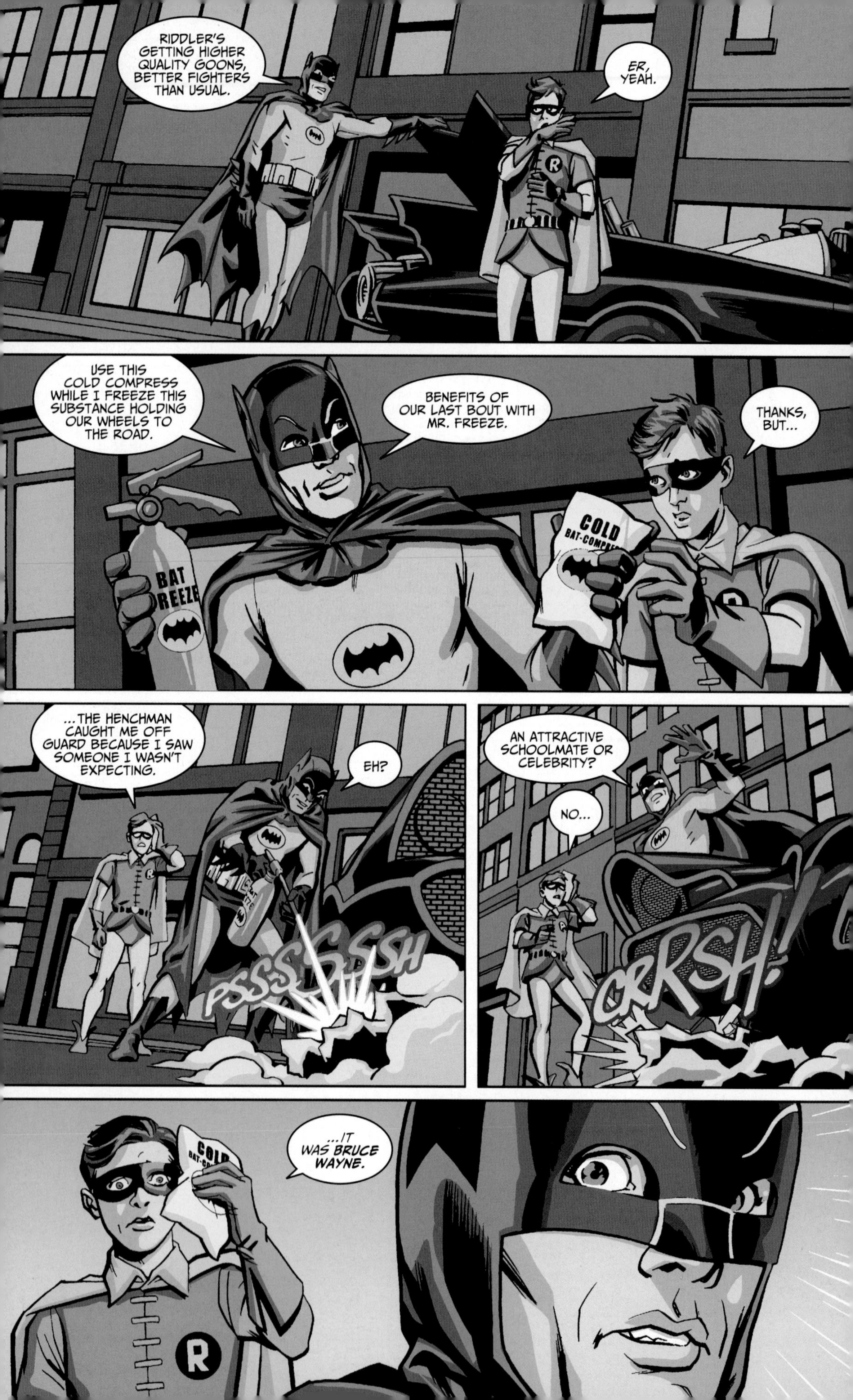
RIDDLER'S GETTING HIGHER QUALITY GOONS, BETTER FIGHTERS THAN USUAL.
ER, YEAH.
USE THIS COLD COMPRESS WHILE I FREEZE THIS SUBSTANCE HOLDING OUR WHEELS TO THE ROAD.
BENEFITS OF OUR LAST BOUT WITH MR. FREEZE.
THANKS, BUT...
BAT FREEZE
COLD BAT-COMPRESS
...THE HENCHMAN CAUGHT ME OFF GUARD BECAUSE I SAW SOMEONE I WASN'T EXPECTING.
EH?
PSSSSSSSH
AN ATTRACTIVE SCHOOLMATE OR CELEBRITY?
NO...
CRRSH!
...IT WAS BRUCE WAYNE.

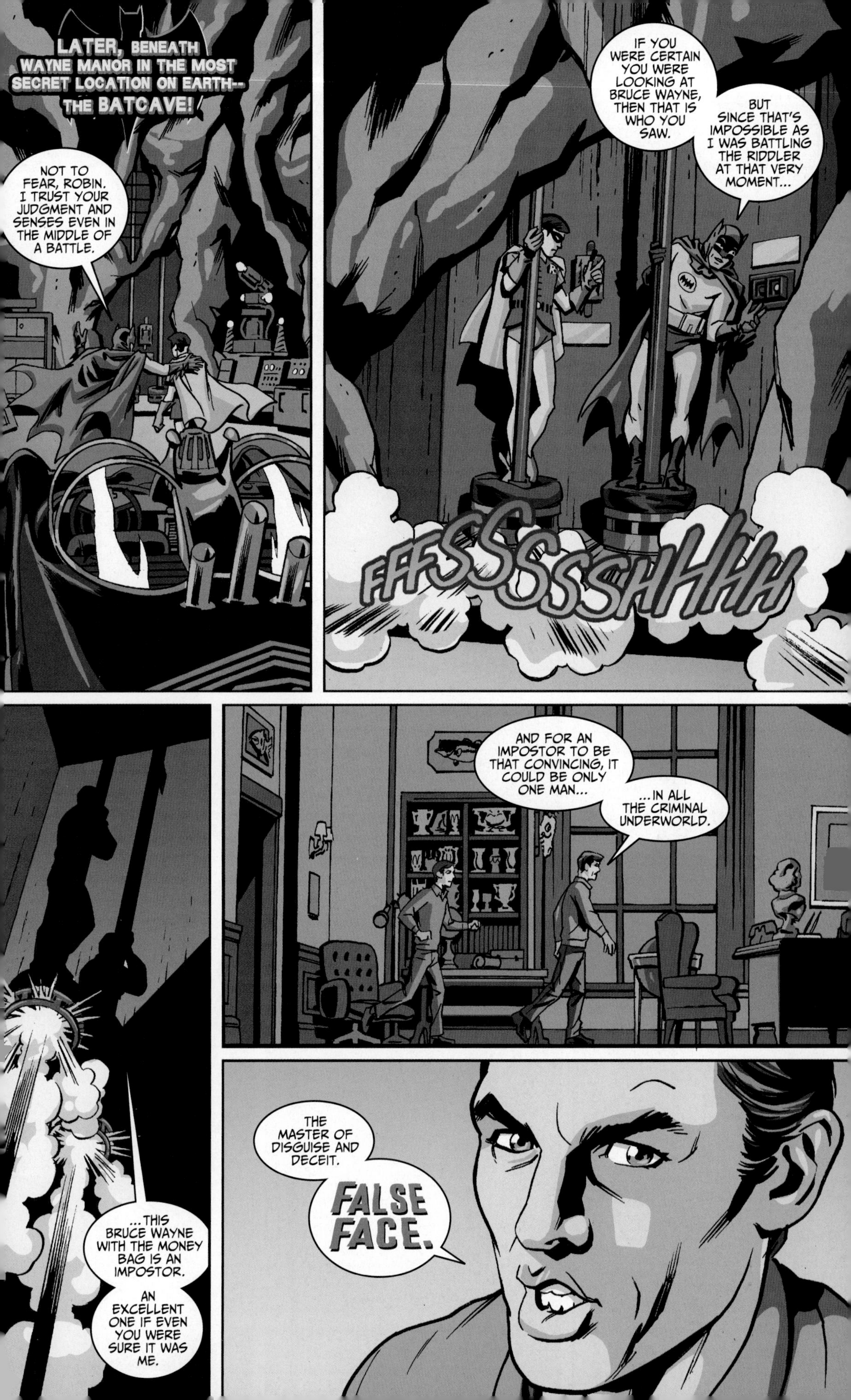
LATER, BENEATH WAYNE MANOR IN THE MOST SECRET LOCATION ON EARTH-- THE BATCAVE!
NOT TO FEAR, ROBIN. I TRUST YOUR JUDGMENT AND SENSES EVEN IN THE MIDDLE OF A BATTLE.
IF YOU WERE CERTAIN YOU WERE LOOKING AT BRUCE WAYNE, THEN THAT IS WHO YOU SAW.
BUT SINCE THAT'S IMPOSSIBLE AS I WAS BATTLING THE RIDDLER AT THAT VERY MOMENT...
FFFSSSSSSHHHH
...THIS BRUCE WAYNE WITH THE MONEY BAG IS AN IMPOSTOR.
AN EXCELLENT ONE IF EVEN YOU WERE SURE IT WAS ME.
AND FOR AN IMPOSTOR TO BE THAT CONVINCING, IT COULD BE ONLY ONE MAN...
...IN ALL THE CRIMINAL UNDERWORLD.
THE MASTER OF DISGUISE AND DECEIT.
FALSE FACE.

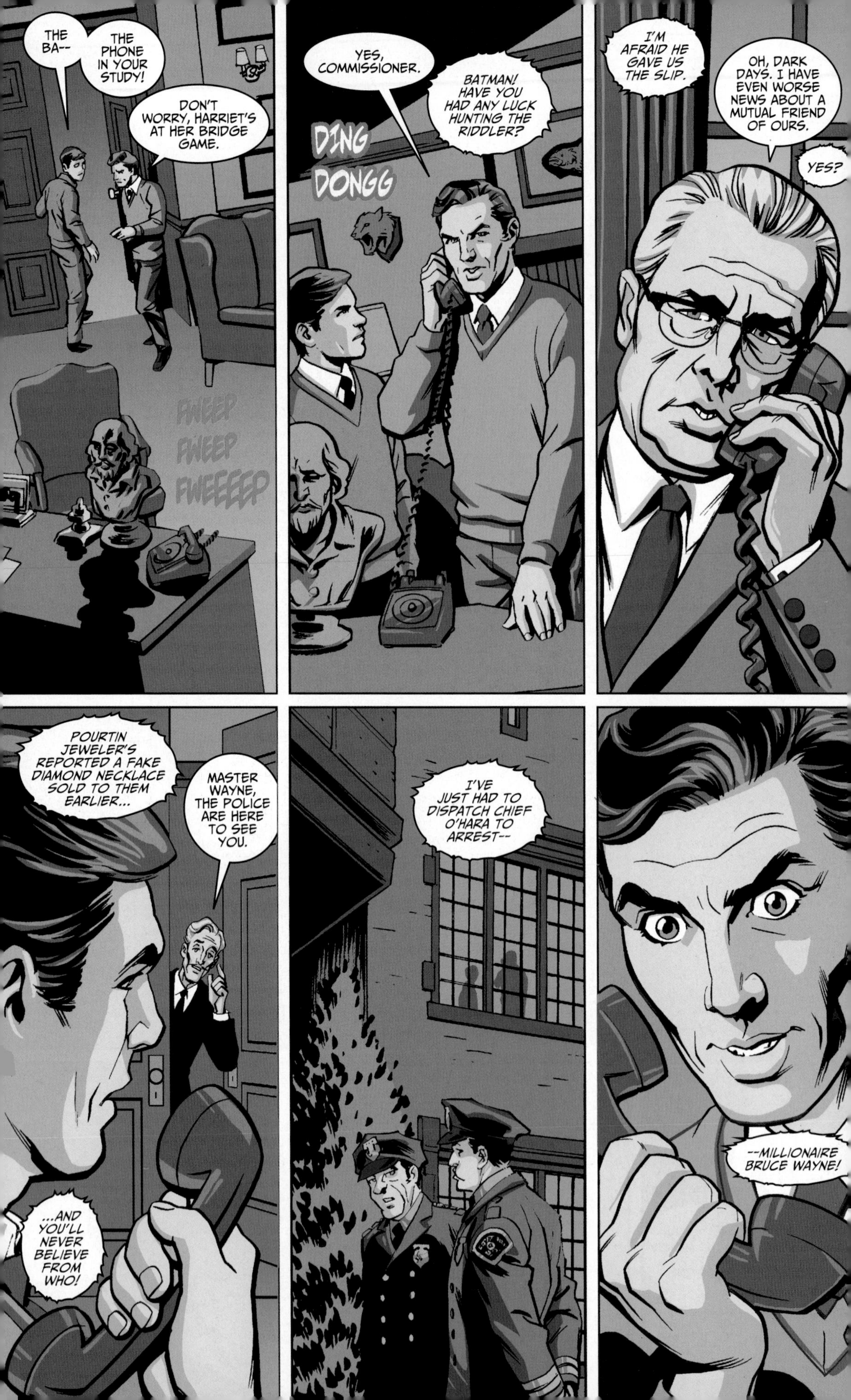
THE BA--
THE PHONE IN YOUR STUDY!
DON'T WORRY, HARRIET'S AT HER BRIDGE GAME.
FWEEP FWEEP FWEEEEP
DING DONGG
YES, COMMISSIONER.
BATMAN! HAVE YOU HAD ANY LUCK HUNTING THE RIDDLER?
I'M AFRAID HE GAVE US THE SLIP.
OH, DARK DAYS. I HAVE EVEN WORSE NEWS ABOUT A MUTUAL FRIEND OF OURS.
YES?
POURTIN JEWELER'S REPORTED A FAKE DIAMOND NECKLACE SOLD TO THEM EARLIER...
MASTER WAYNE, THE POLICE ARE HERE TO SEE YOU.
...AND YOU'LL NEVER BELIEVE FROM WHO!
I'VE JUST HAD TO DISPATCH CHIEF O'HARA TO ARREST--
--MILLIONAIRE BRUCE WAYNE!

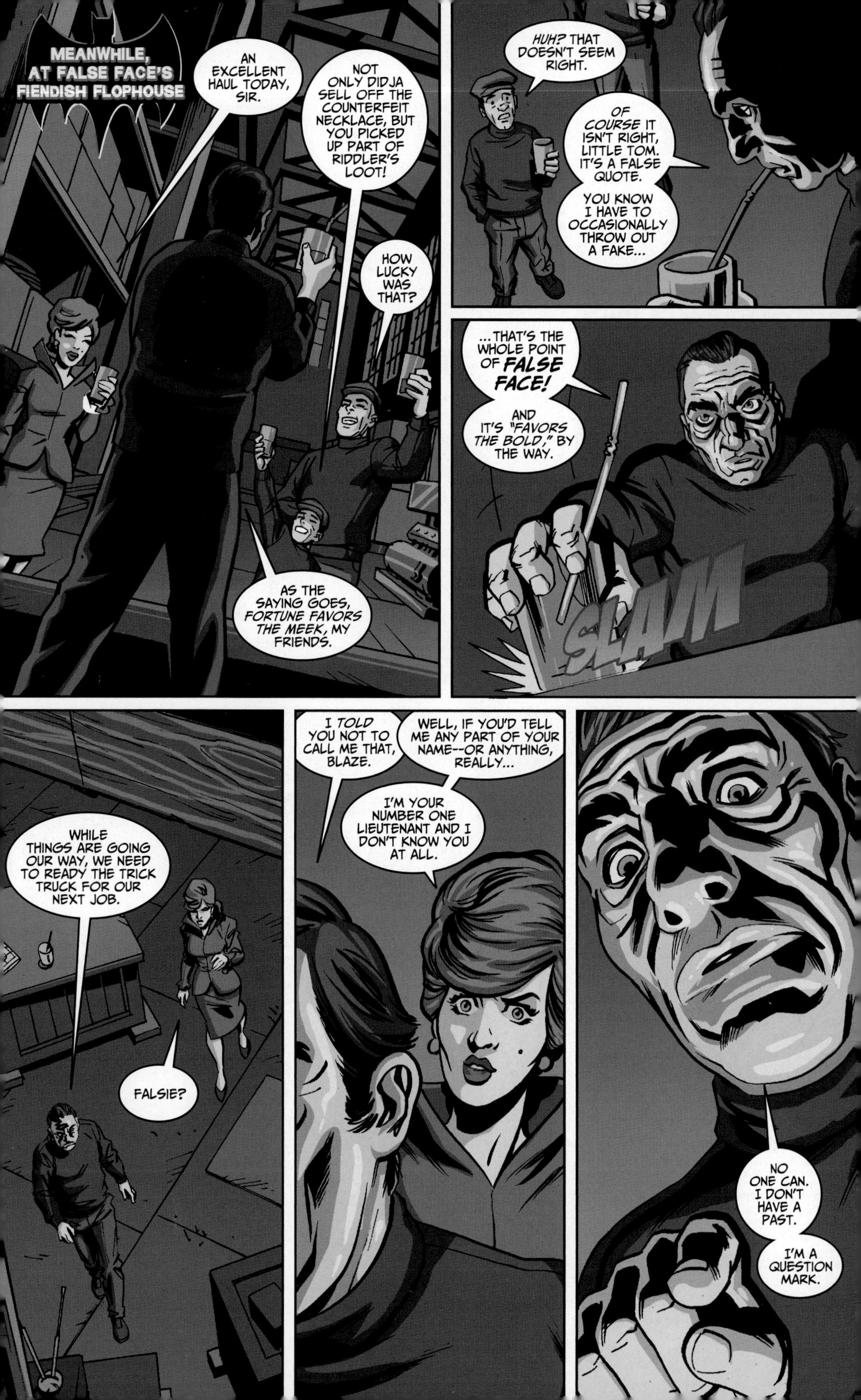
MEANWHILE, AT FALSE FACE'S FIENDISH FLOPHOUSE
AN EXCELLENT HAUL TODAY, SIR.
NOT ONLY DIDJA SELL OFF THE COUNTERFEIT NECKLACE, BUT YOU PICKED UP PART OF RIDDLER'S LOOT!
HOW LUCKY WAS THAT?
AS THE SAYING GOES, *FORTUNE FAVORS THE MEEK,* MY FRIENDS.
HUH? THAT DOESN'T SEEM RIGHT.
OF COURSE IT ISN'T RIGHT, LITTLE TOM. IT'S A FALSE QUOTE.
YOU KNOW I HAVE TO OCCASIONALLY THROW OUT A FAKE...
...THAT'S THE WHOLE POINT OF **FALSE FACE!**
AND IT'S *"FAVORS THE BOLD,"* BY THE WAY.
SLAM
WHILE THINGS ARE GOING OUR WAY, WE NEED TO READY THE TRICK TRUCK FOR OUR NEXT JOB.
FALSIE?
I *TOLD* YOU NOT TO CALL ME THAT, BLAZE.
WELL, IF YOU'D TELL ME ANY PART OF YOUR NAME--OR ANYTHING, REALLY...
I'M YOUR NUMBER ONE LIEUTENANT AND I DON'T KNOW YOU AT ALL.
NO ONE CAN. I DON'T HAVE A PAST.
I'M A QUESTION MARK.

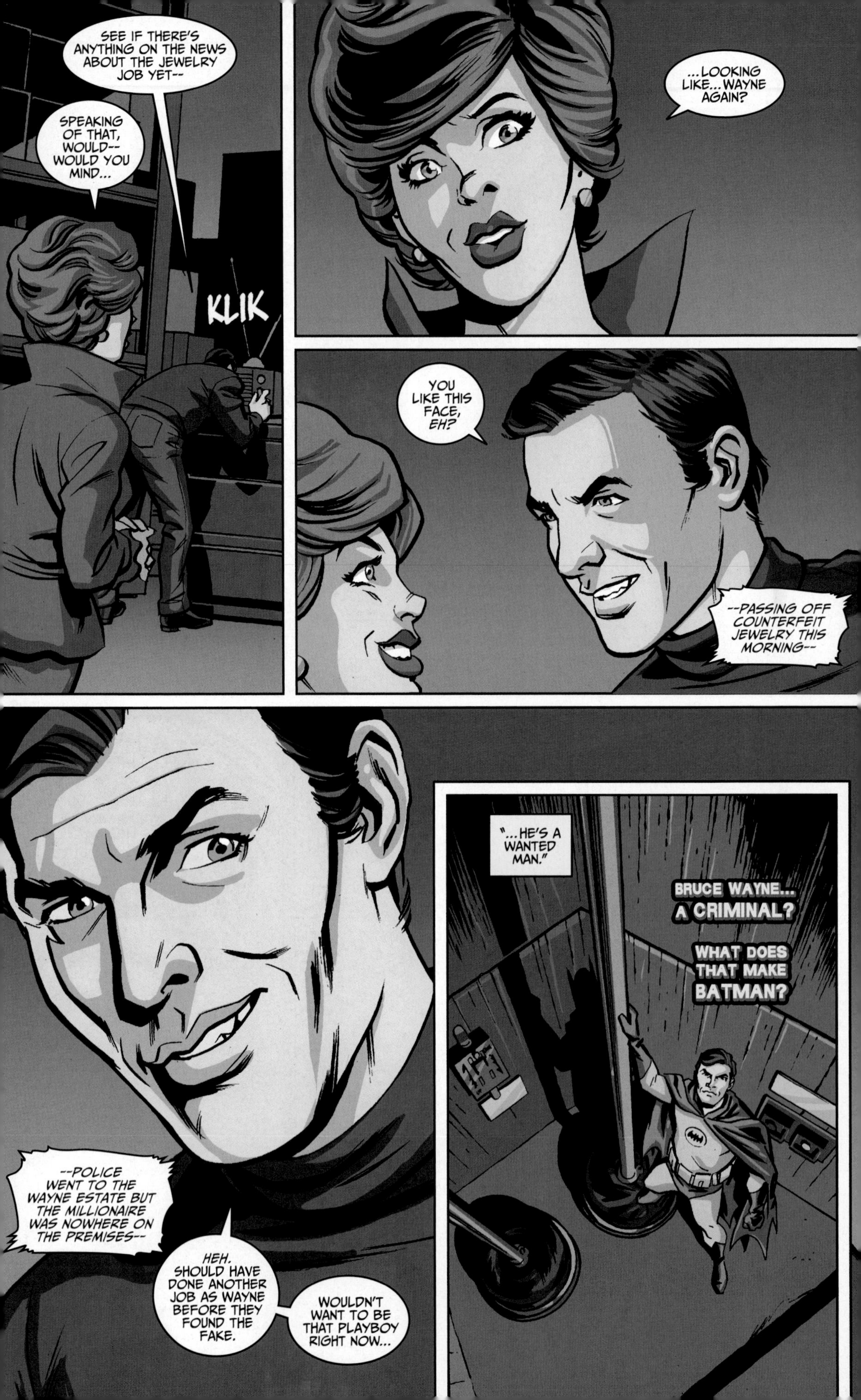
SEE IF THERE'S ANYTHING ON THE NEWS ABOUT THE JEWELRY JOB YET--
SPEAKING OF THAT, WOULD-- WOULD YOU MIND...
KLIK
...LOOKING LIKE...WAYNE AGAIN?
YOU LIKE THIS FACE, EH?
--PASSING OFF COUNTERFEIT JEWELRY THIS MORNING--
--POLICE WENT TO THE WAYNE ESTATE BUT THE MILLIONAIRE WAS NOWHERE ON THE PREMISES--
HEH. SHOULD HAVE DONE ANOTHER JOB AS WAYNE BEFORE THEY FOUND THE FAKE.
WOULDN'T WANT TO BE THAT PLAYBOY RIGHT NOW...
"...HE'S A WANTED MAN."
BRUCE WAYNE... A CRIMINAL?
WHAT DOES THAT MAKE BATMAN?

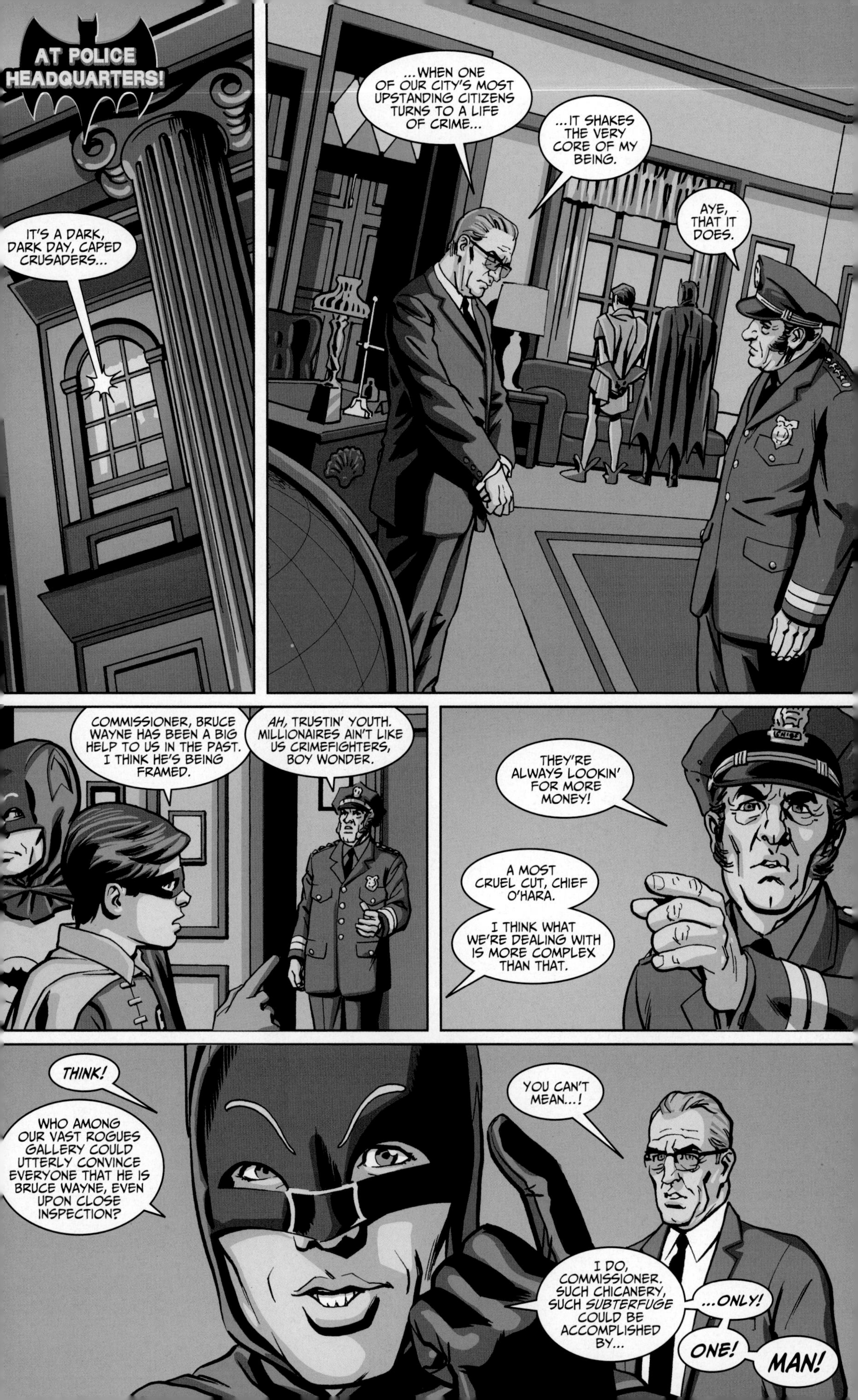
AT POLICE HEADQUARTERS!
IT'S A DARK, DARK DAY, CAPED CRUSADERS...
...WHEN ONE OF OUR CITY'S MOST UPSTANDING CITIZENS TURNS TO A LIFE OF CRIME...
...IT SHAKES THE VERY CORE OF MY BEING.
AYE, THAT IT DOES.
COMMISSIONER, BRUCE WAYNE HAS BEEN A BIG HELP TO US IN THE PAST. I THINK HE'S BEING FRAMED.
AH, TRUSTIN' YOUTH. MILLIONAIRES AIN'T LIKE US CRIMEFIGHTERS, BOY WONDER.
THEY'RE ALWAYS LOOKIN' FOR MORE MONEY!
A MOST CRUEL CUT, CHIEF O'HARA.
I THINK WHAT WE'RE DEALING WITH IS MORE COMPLEX THAN THAT.
THINK!
WHO AMONG OUR VAST ROGUES GALLERY COULD UTTERLY CONVINCE EVERYONE THAT HE IS BRUCE WAYNE, EVEN UPON CLOSE INSPECTION?
YOU CAN'T MEAN...!
I DO, COMMISSIONER. SUCH CHICANERY, SUCH SUBTERFUGE COULD BE ACCOMPLISHED BY...
...ONLY!
ONE!
MAN!

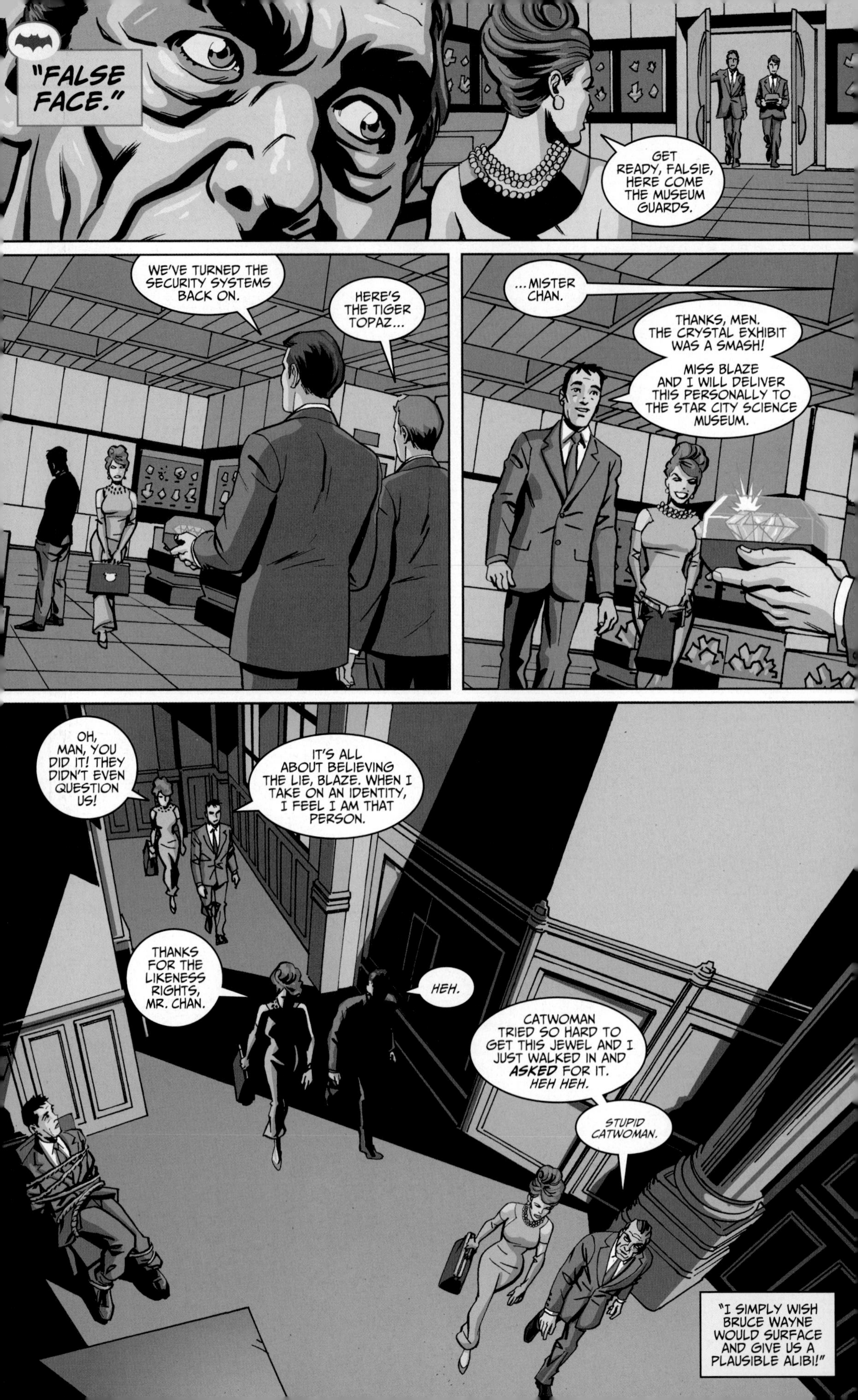
"FALSE FACE."
GET READY, FALSIE, HERE COME THE MUSEUM GUARDS.
WE'VE TURNED THE SECURITY SYSTEMS BACK ON.
HERE'S THE TIGER TOPAZ...
...MISTER CHAN.
THANKS, MEN. THE CRYSTAL EXHIBIT WAS A SMASH!
MISS BLAZE AND I WILL DELIVER THIS PERSONALLY TO THE STAR CITY SCIENCE MUSEUM.
OH, MAN, YOU DID IT! THEY DIDN'T EVEN QUESTION US!
IT'S ALL ABOUT BELIEVING THE LIE, BLAZE. WHEN I TAKE ON AN IDENTITY, I FEEL I AM THAT PERSON.
THANKS FOR THE LIKENESS RIGHTS, MR. CHAN.
HEH.
CATWOMAN TRIED SO HARD TO GET THIS JEWEL AND I JUST WALKED IN AND ASKED FOR IT. HEH HEH.
STUPID CATWOMAN.
"I SIMPLY WISH BRUCE WAYNE WOULD SURFACE AND GIVE US A PLAUSIBLE ALIBI!"

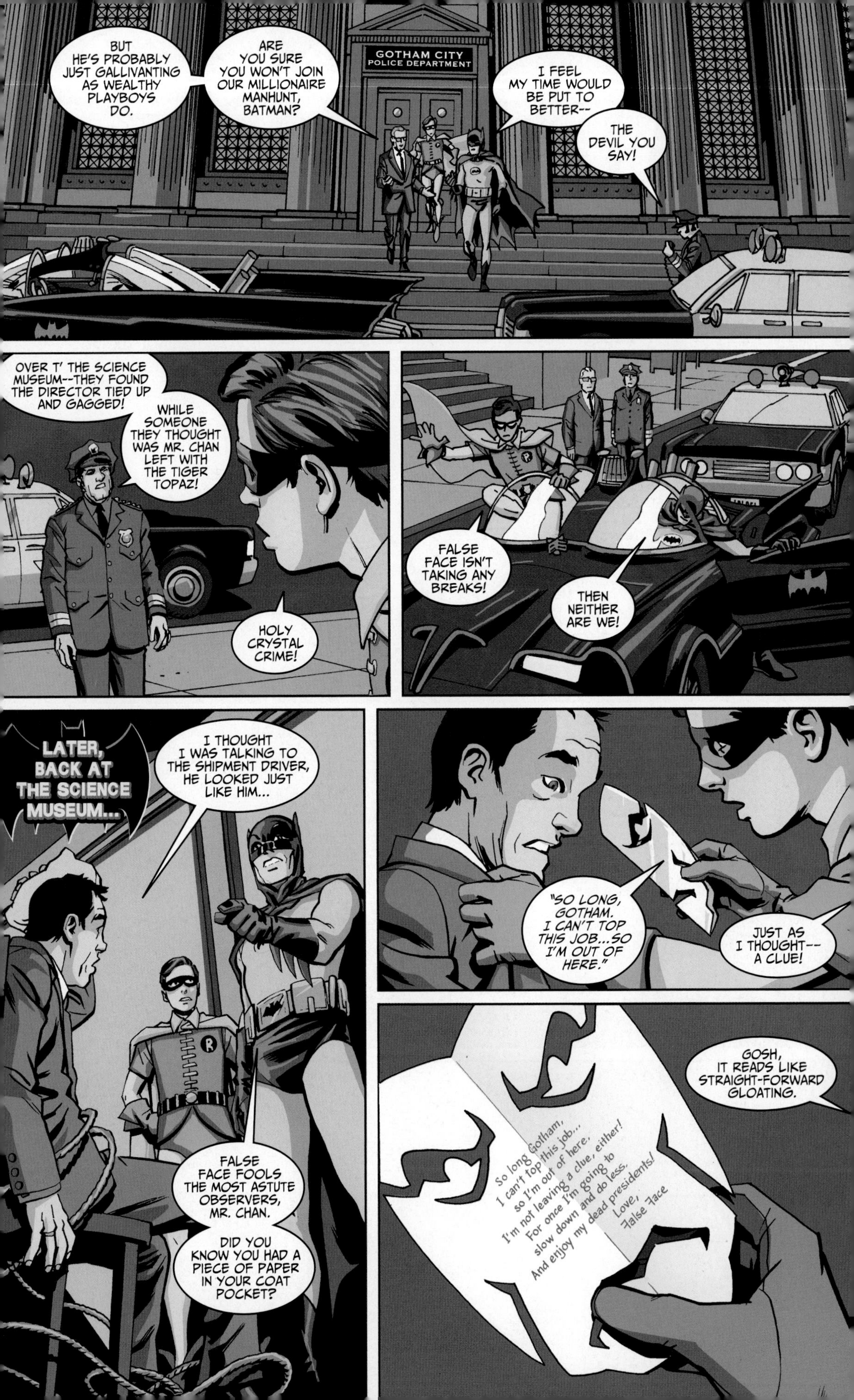
GOTHAM CITY POLICE DEPARTMENT
BUT HE'S PROBABLY JUST GALLIVANTING AS WEALTHY PLAYBOYS DO.
ARE YOU SURE YOU WON'T JOIN OUR MILLIONAIRE MANHUNT, BATMAN?
I FEEL MY TIME WOULD BE PUT TO BETTER--
THE DEVIL YOU SAY!
OVER T' THE SCIENCE MUSEUM--THEY FOUND THE DIRECTOR TIED UP AND GAGGED!
WHILE SOMEONE THEY THOUGHT WAS MR. CHAN LEFT WITH THE TIGER TOPAZ!
HOLY CRYSTAL CRIME!
FALSE FACE ISN'T TAKING ANY BREAKS!
THEN NEITHER ARE WE!
LATER, BACK AT THE SCIENCE MUSEUM...
I THOUGHT I WAS TALKING TO THE SHIPMENT DRIVER, HE LOOKED JUST LIKE HIM...
FALSE FACE FOOLS THE MOST ASTUTE OBSERVERS, MR. CHAN.
DID YOU KNOW YOU HAD A PIECE OF PAPER IN YOUR COAT POCKET?
"SO LONG, GOTHAM. I CAN'T TOP THIS JOB...SO I'M OUT OF HERE."
JUST AS I THOUGHT-- A CLUE!
GOSH, IT READS LIKE STRAIGHT-FORWARD GLOATING.
So long Gotham,
I can't top this job...
so I'm out of here.
I'm not leaving a clue, either!
For once I'm going to
slow down and do less.
And enjoy my dead presidents!
Love,
False Face

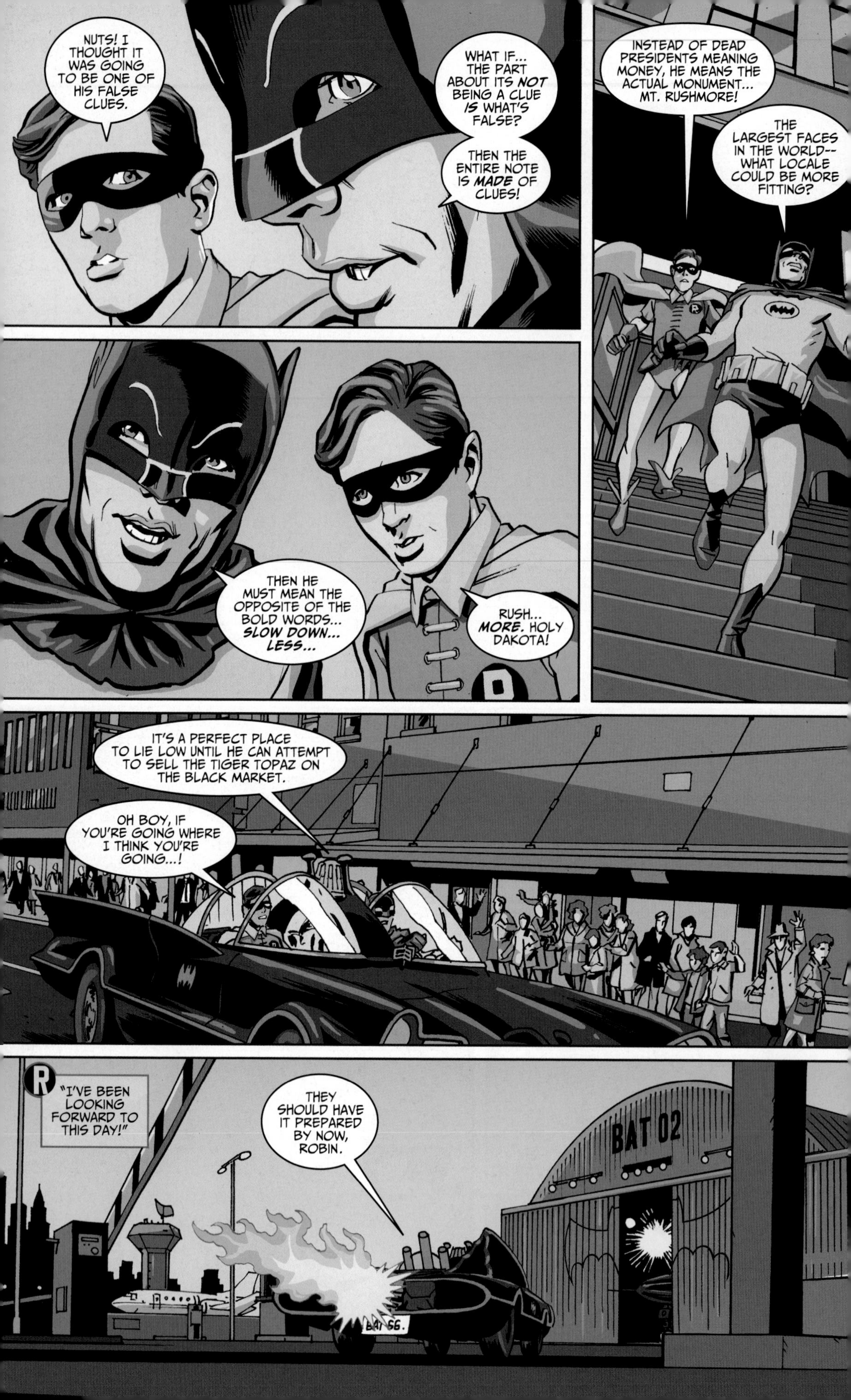
NUTS! I THOUGHT IT WAS GOING TO BE ONE OF HIS FALSE CLUES.
WHAT IF... THE PART ABOUT ITS NOT BEING A CLUE IS WHAT'S FALSE?
THEN THE ENTIRE NOTE IS MADE OF CLUES!
THEN HE MUST MEAN THE OPPOSITE OF THE BOLD WORDS... SLOW DOWN... LESS...
RUSH... MORE. HOLY DAKOTA!
INSTEAD OF DEAD PRESIDENTS MEANING MONEY, HE MEANS THE ACTUAL MONUMENT... MT. RUSHMORE!
THE LARGEST FACES IN THE WORLD-- WHAT LOCALE COULD BE MORE FITTING?
IT'S A PERFECT PLACE TO LIE LOW UNTIL HE CAN ATTEMPT TO SELL THE TIGER TOPAZ ON THE BLACK MARKET.
OH BOY, IF YOU'RE GOING WHERE I THINK YOU'RE GOING...!
"I'VE BEEN LOOKING FORWARD TO THIS DAY!"
THEY SHOULD HAVE IT PREPARED BY NOW, ROBIN.
BAT 02
BAT 66.

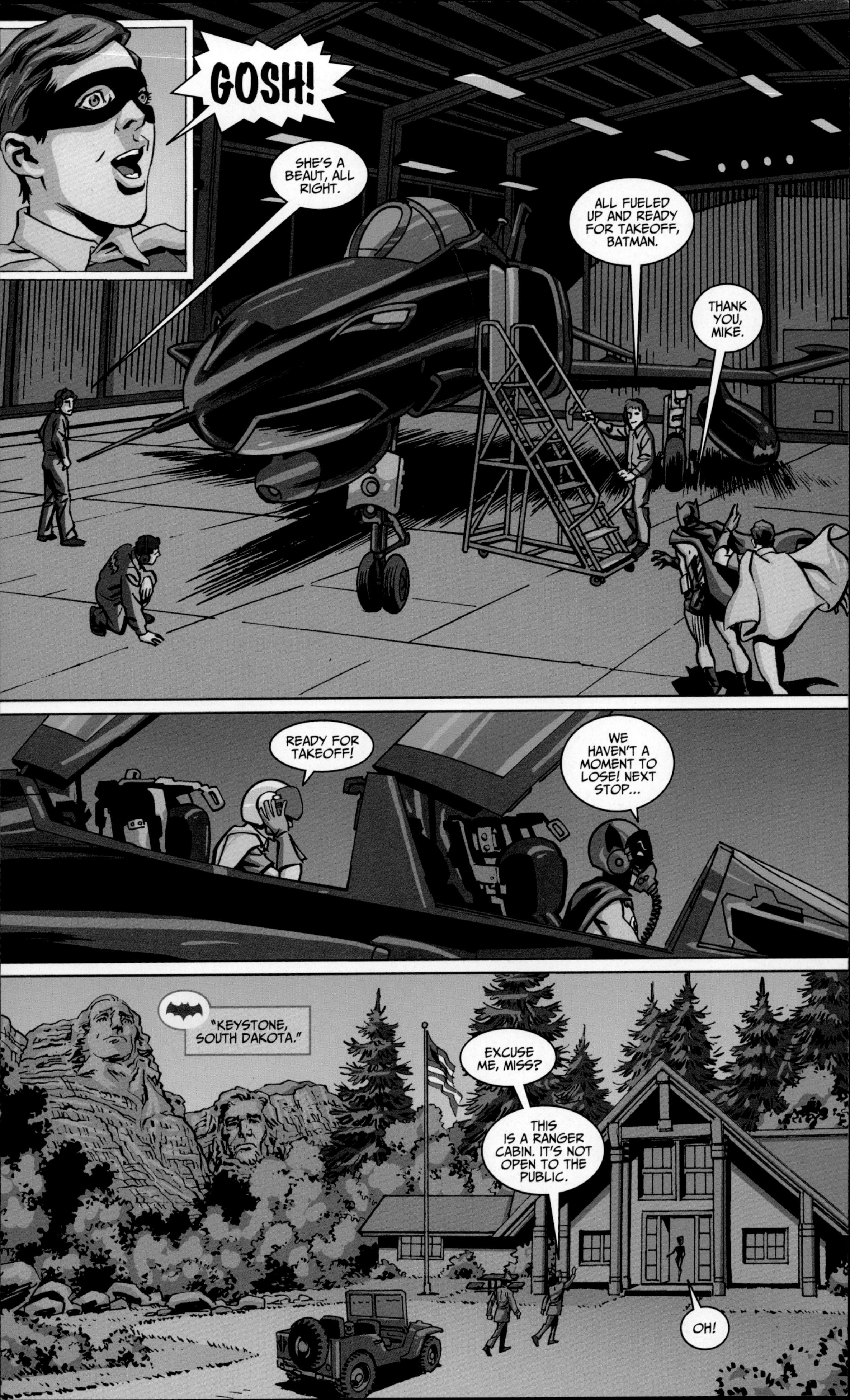
GOSH!
SHE'S A BEAUT, ALL RIGHT.
ALL FUELED UP AND READY FOR TAKEOFF, BATMAN.
THANK YOU, MIKE.
READY FOR TAKEOFF!
WE HAVEN'T A MOMENT TO LOSE! NEXT STOP...
"KEYSTONE, SOUTH DAKOTA."
EXCUSE ME, MISS?
THIS IS A RANGER CABIN. IT'S NOT OPEN TO THE PUBLIC.
OH!

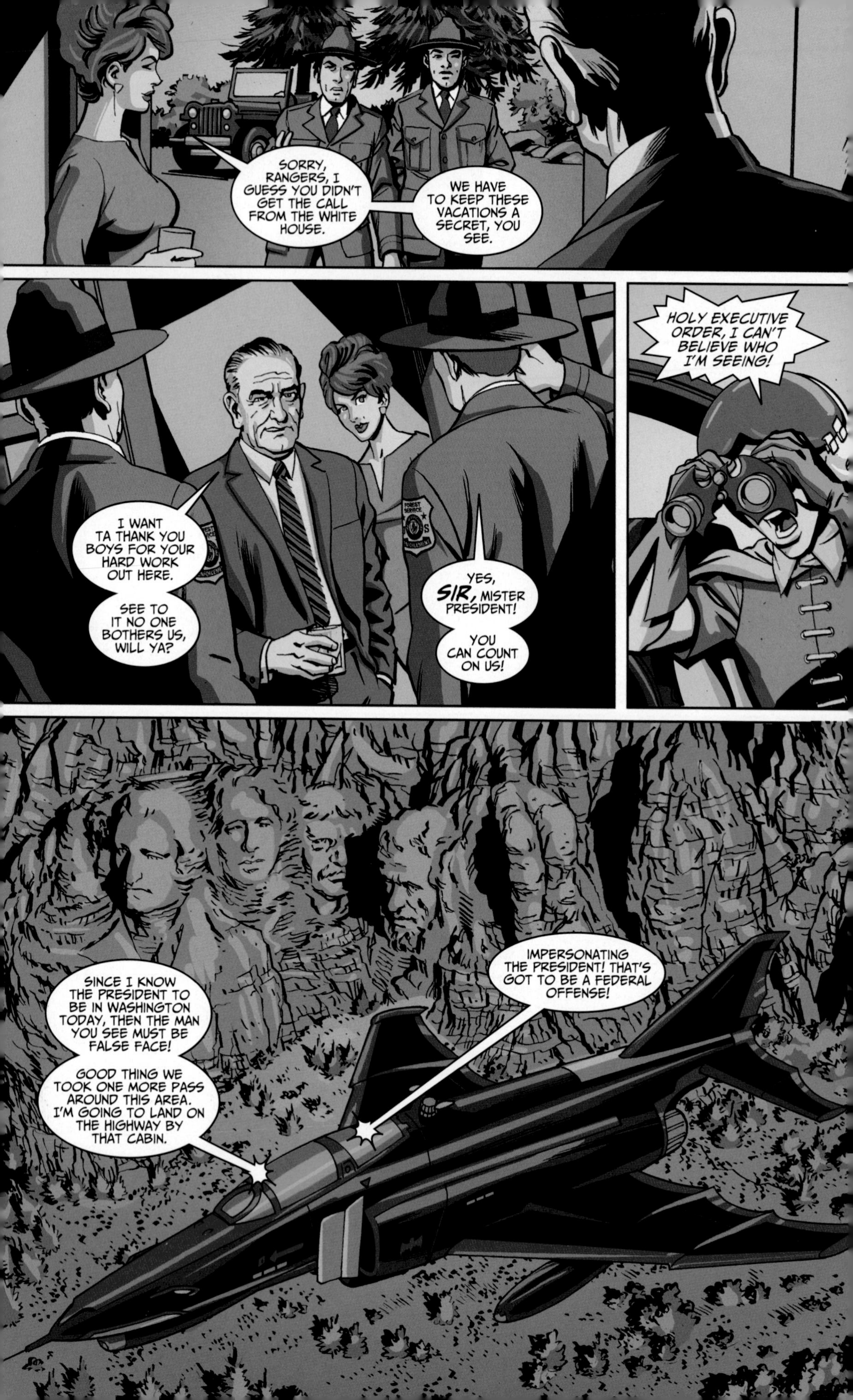
SORRY, RANGERS, I GUESS YOU DIDN'T GET THE CALL FROM THE WHITE HOUSE.
WE HAVE TO KEEP THESE VACATIONS A SECRET, YOU SEE.
I WANT TA THANK YOU BOYS FOR YOUR HARD WORK OUT HERE.
SEE TO IT NO ONE BOTHERS US, WILL YA?
YES, SIR, MISTER PRESIDENT!
YOU CAN COUNT ON US!
HOLY EXECUTIVE ORDER, I CAN'T BELIEVE WHO I'M SEEING!
SINCE I KNOW THE PRESIDENT TO BE IN WASHINGTON TODAY, THEN THE MAN YOU SEE MUST BE FALSE FACE!
GOOD THING WE TOOK ONE MORE PASS AROUND THIS AREA. I'M GOING TO LAND ON THE HIGHWAY BY THAT CABIN.
IMPERSONATING THE PRESIDENT! THAT'S GOT TO BE A FEDERAL OFFENSE!

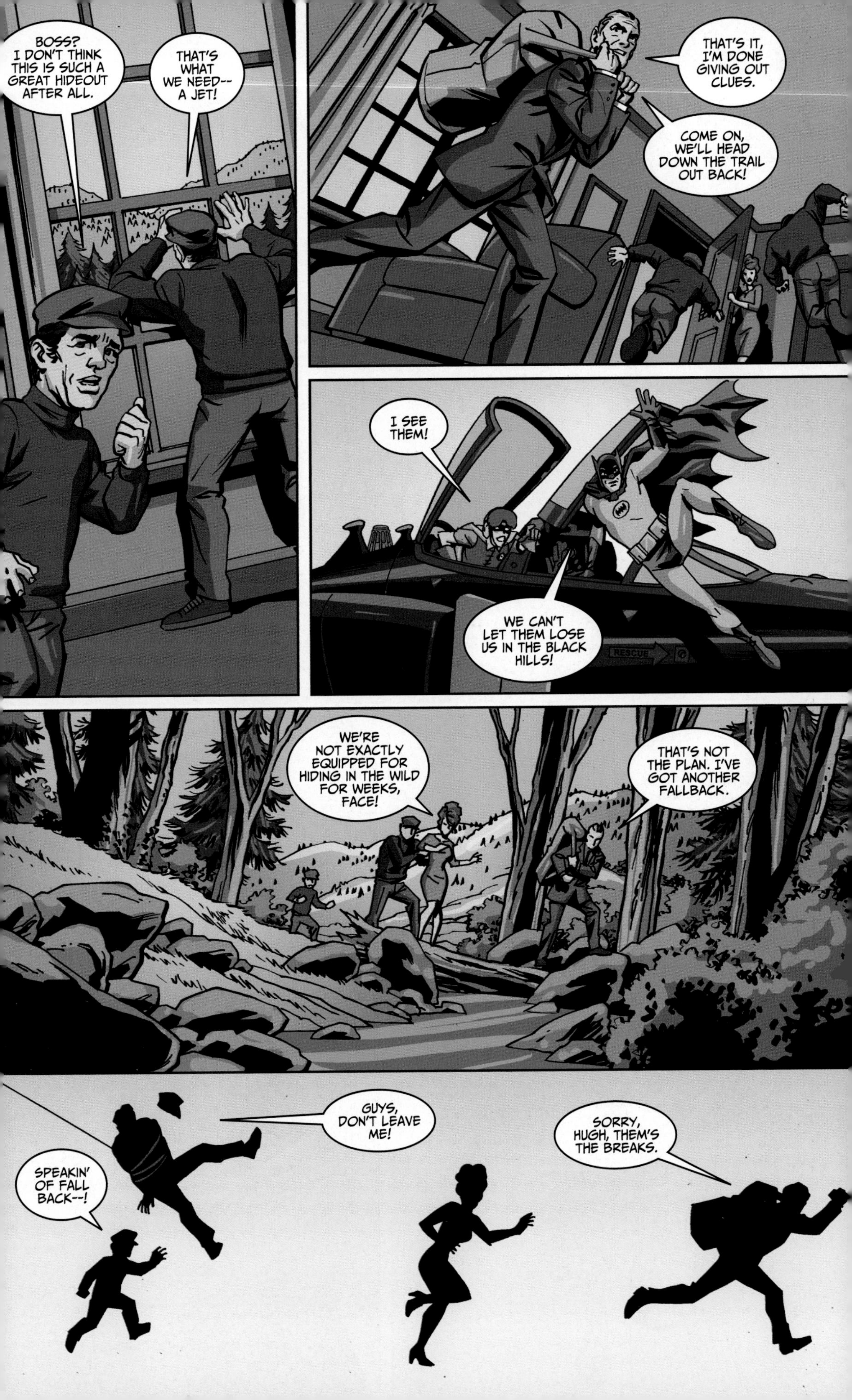
BOSS? I DON'T THINK THIS IS SUCH A GREAT HIDEOUT AFTER ALL.
THAT'S WHAT WE NEED-- A JET!
THAT'S IT, I'M DONE GIVING OUT CLUES.
COME ON, WE'LL HEAD DOWN THE TRAIL OUT BACK!
I SEE THEM!
WE CAN'T LET THEM LOSE US IN THE BLACK HILLS!
RESCUE
WE'RE NOT EXACTLY EQUIPPED FOR HIDING IN THE WILD FOR WEEKS, FACE!
THAT'S NOT THE PLAN. I'VE GOT ANOTHER FALLBACK.
GUYS, DON'T LEAVE ME!
SPEAKIN' OF FALL BACK--!
SORRY, HUGH, THEM'S THE BREAKS.

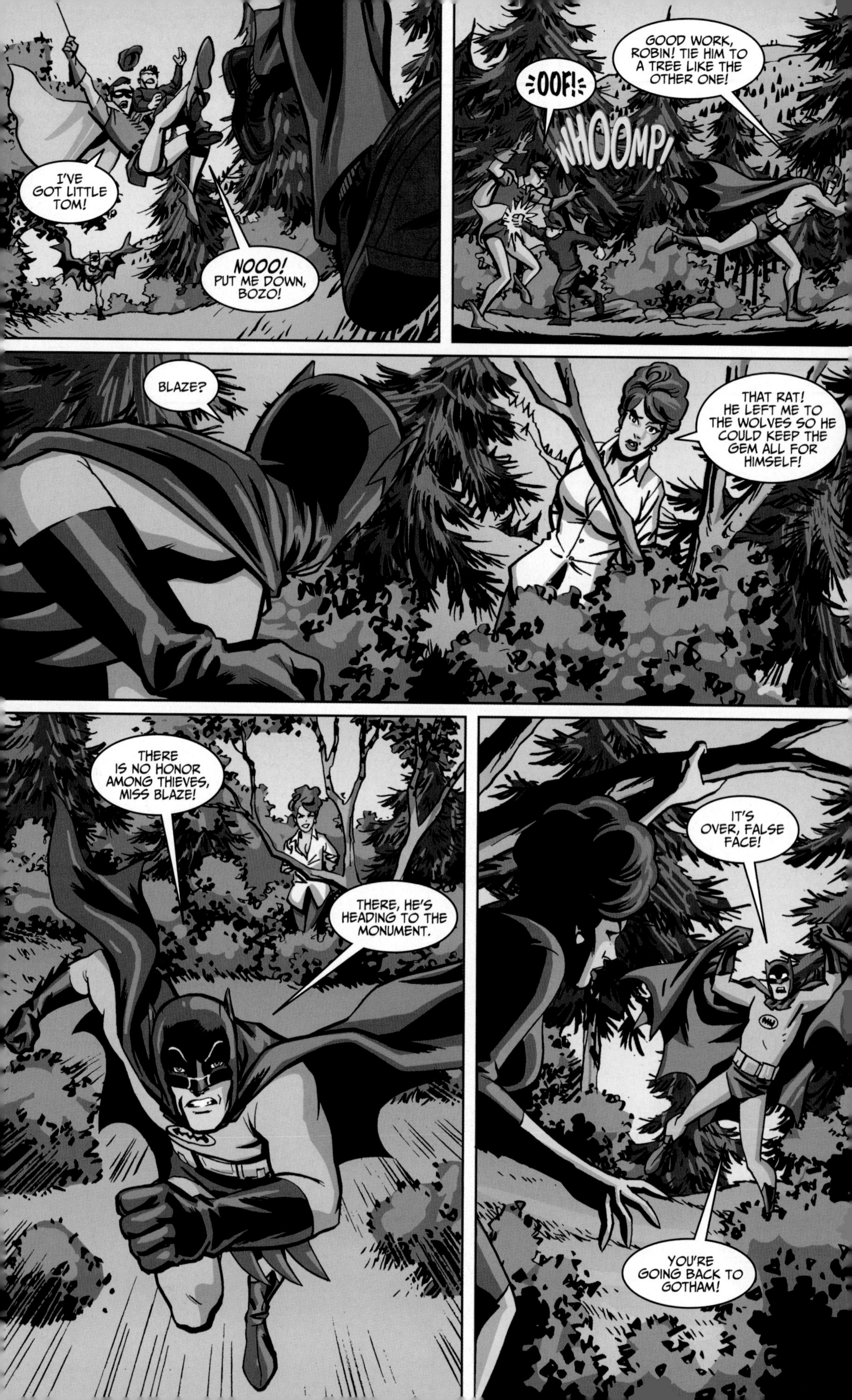
I'VE GOT LITTLE TOM!
NOOO! PUT ME DOWN, BOZO!
OOF!
WHOOMP!
GOOD WORK, ROBIN! TIE HIM TO A TREE LIKE THE OTHER ONE!
BLAZE?
THAT RAT! HE LEFT ME TO THE WOLVES SO HE COULD KEEP THE GEM ALL FOR HIMSELF!
THERE IS NO HONOR AMONG THIEVES, MISS BLAZE!
THERE, HE'S HEADING TO THE MONUMENT.
IT'S OVER, FALSE FACE!
YOU'RE GOING BACK TO GOTHAM!

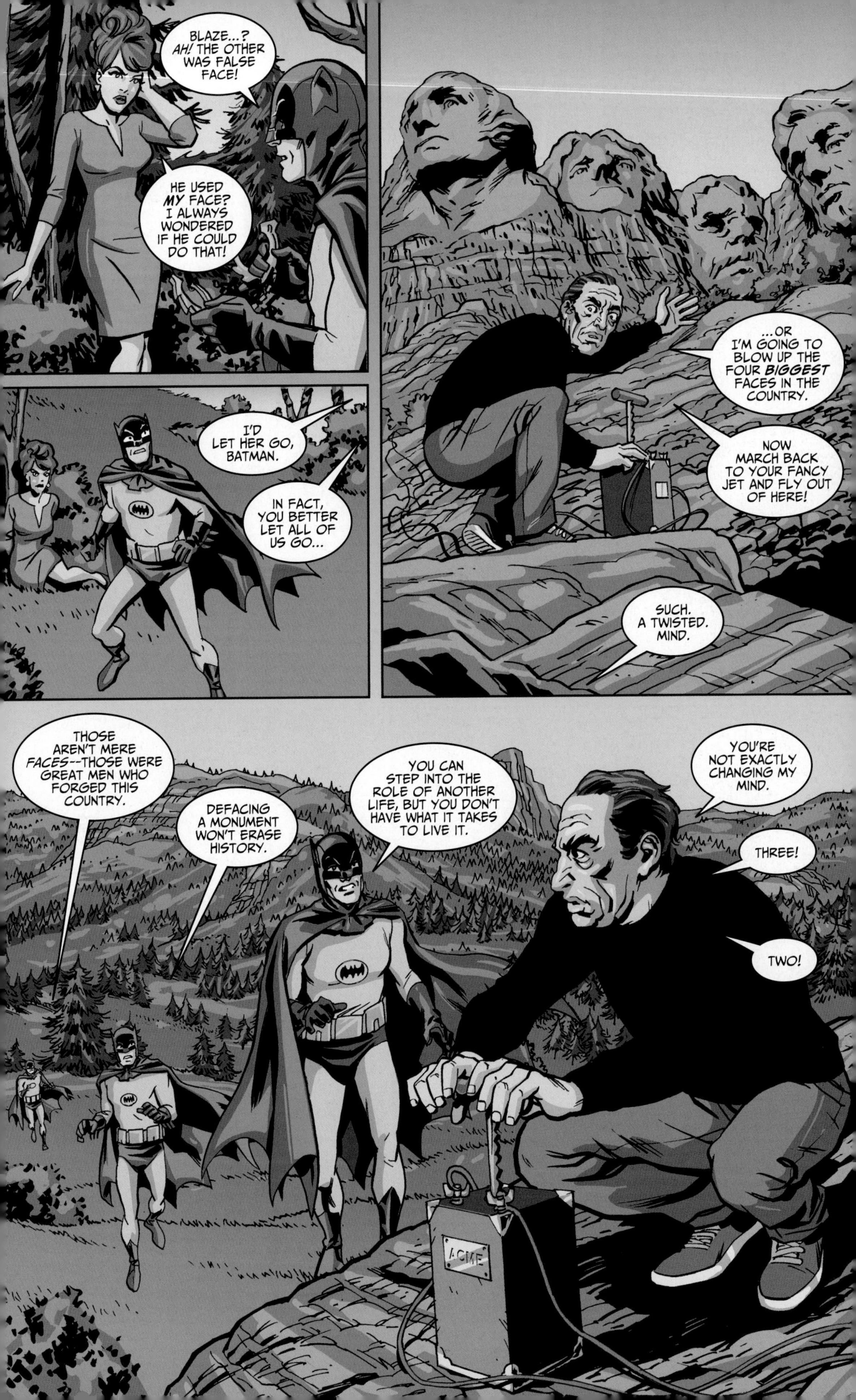
BLAZE...? AH! THE OTHER WAS FALSE FACE!
HE USED MY FACE? I ALWAYS WONDERED IF HE COULD DO THAT!
I'D LET HER GO, BATMAN.
IN FACT, YOU BETTER LET ALL OF US GO...
...OR I'M GOING TO BLOW UP THE FOUR BIGGEST FACES IN THE COUNTRY.
NOW MARCH BACK TO YOUR FANCY JET AND FLY OUT OF HERE!
SUCH. A TWISTED. MIND.
THOSE AREN'T MERE FACES--THOSE WERE GREAT MEN WHO FORGED THIS COUNTRY.
DEFACING A MONUMENT WON'T ERASE HISTORY.
YOU CAN STEP INTO THE ROLE OF ANOTHER LIFE, BUT YOU DON'T HAVE WHAT IT TAKES TO LIVE IT.
YOU'RE NOT EXACTLY CHANGING MY MIND.
THREE!
TWO!
ACME

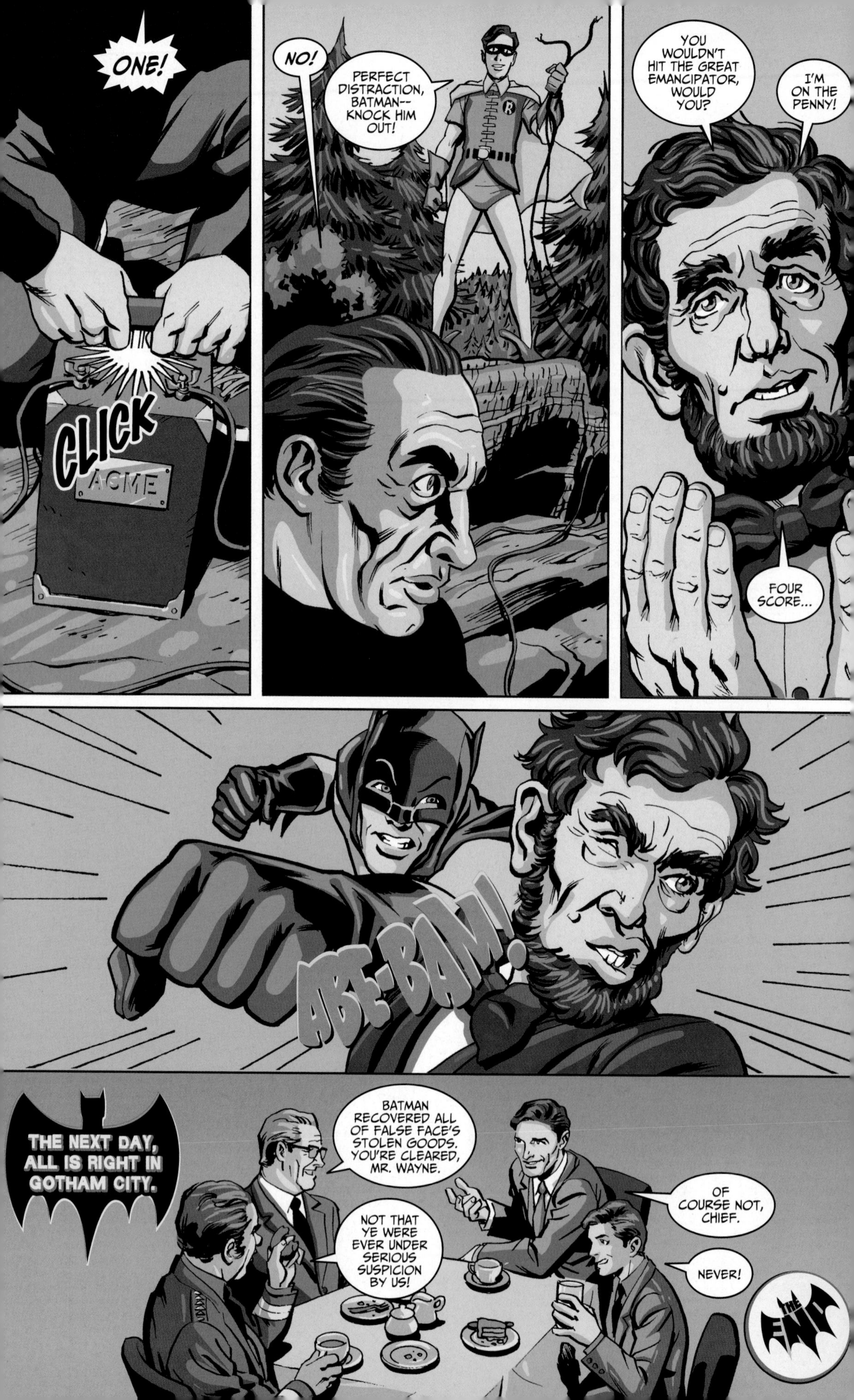
ONE!
CLICK
ACME
NO!
PERFECT DISTRACTION, BATMAN-- KNOCK HIM OUT!
YOU WOULDN'T HIT THE GREAT EMANCIPATOR, WOULD YOU?
I'M ON THE PENNY!
FOUR SCORE...
ABE-BAM!
THE NEXT DAY, ALL IS RIGHT IN GOTHAM CITY.
BATMAN RECOVERED ALL OF FALSE FACE'S STOLEN GOODS. YOU'RE CLEARED, MR. WAYNE.
NOT THAT YE WERE EVER UNDER SERIOUS SUSPICION BY US!
OF COURSE NOT, CHIEF.
NEVER!
THE END

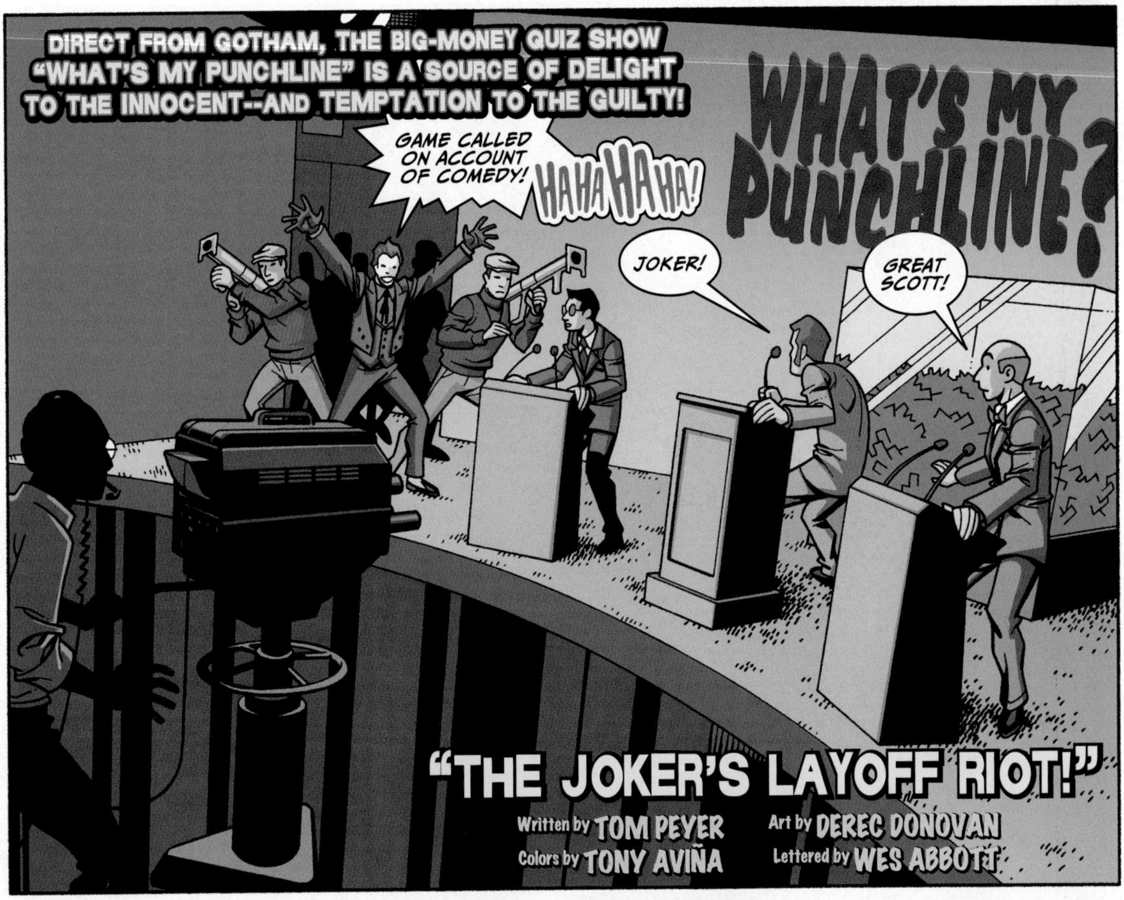
DIRECT FROM GOTHAM, THE BIG-MONEY QUIZ SHOW "WHAT'S MY PUNCHLINE" IS A SOURCE OF DELIGHT TO THE INNOCENT--AND TEMPTATION TO THE GUILTY!
WHAT'S MY PUNCHLINE?
GAME CALLED ON ACCOUNT OF COMEDY!
HAHAHAHAHA!
JOKER!
GREAT SCOTT!
"THE JOKER'S LAYOFF RIOT!"
Written by TOM PEYER
Art by DEREC DONOVAN
Colors by TONY AVIÑA
Lettered by WES ABBOTT

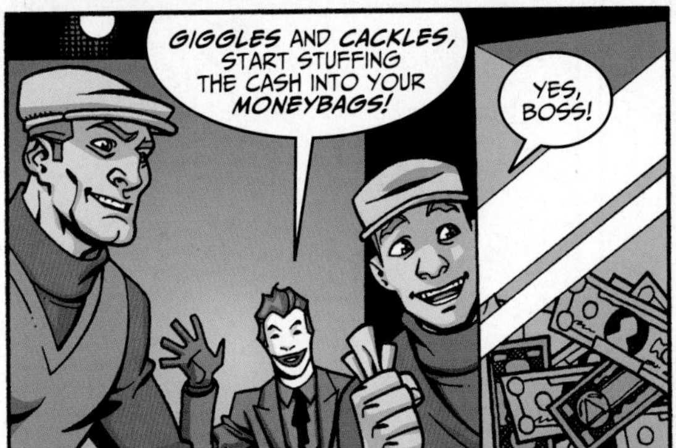
GIGGLES AND CACKLES, START STUFFING THE CASH INTO YOUR MONEYBAGS!
YES, BOSS!

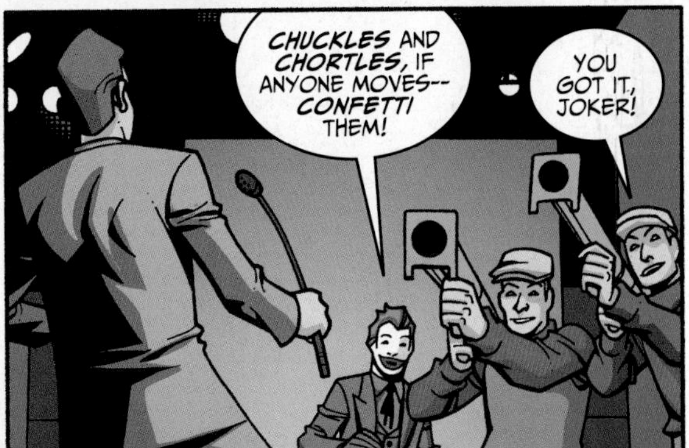
CHUCKLES AND CHORTLES, IF ANYONE MOVES-- CONFETTI THEM!
YOU GOT IT, JOKER!

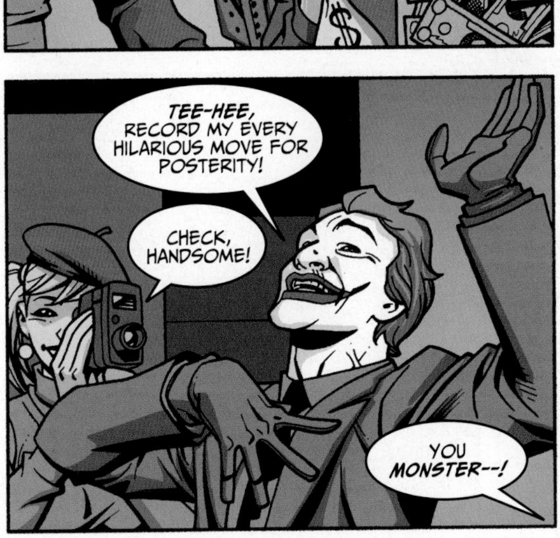
TEE-HEE, RECORD MY EVERY HILARIOUS MOVE FOR POSTERITY!
CHECK, HANDSOME!
YOU MONSTER--!

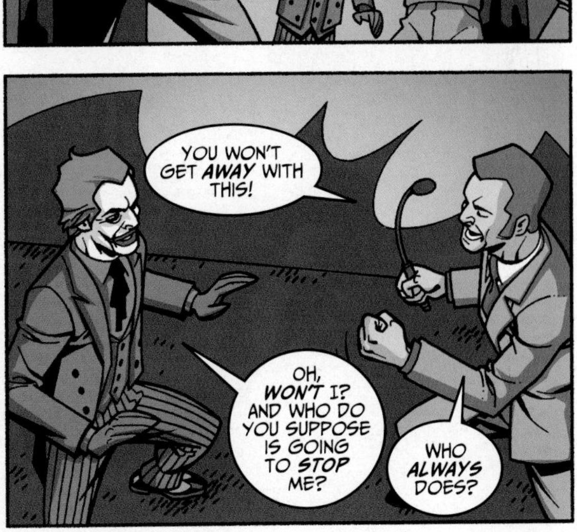
YOU WON'T GET AWAY WITH THIS!
OH, WON'T I? AND WHO DO YOU SUPPOSE IS GOING TO STOP ME?
WHO ALWAYS DOES?

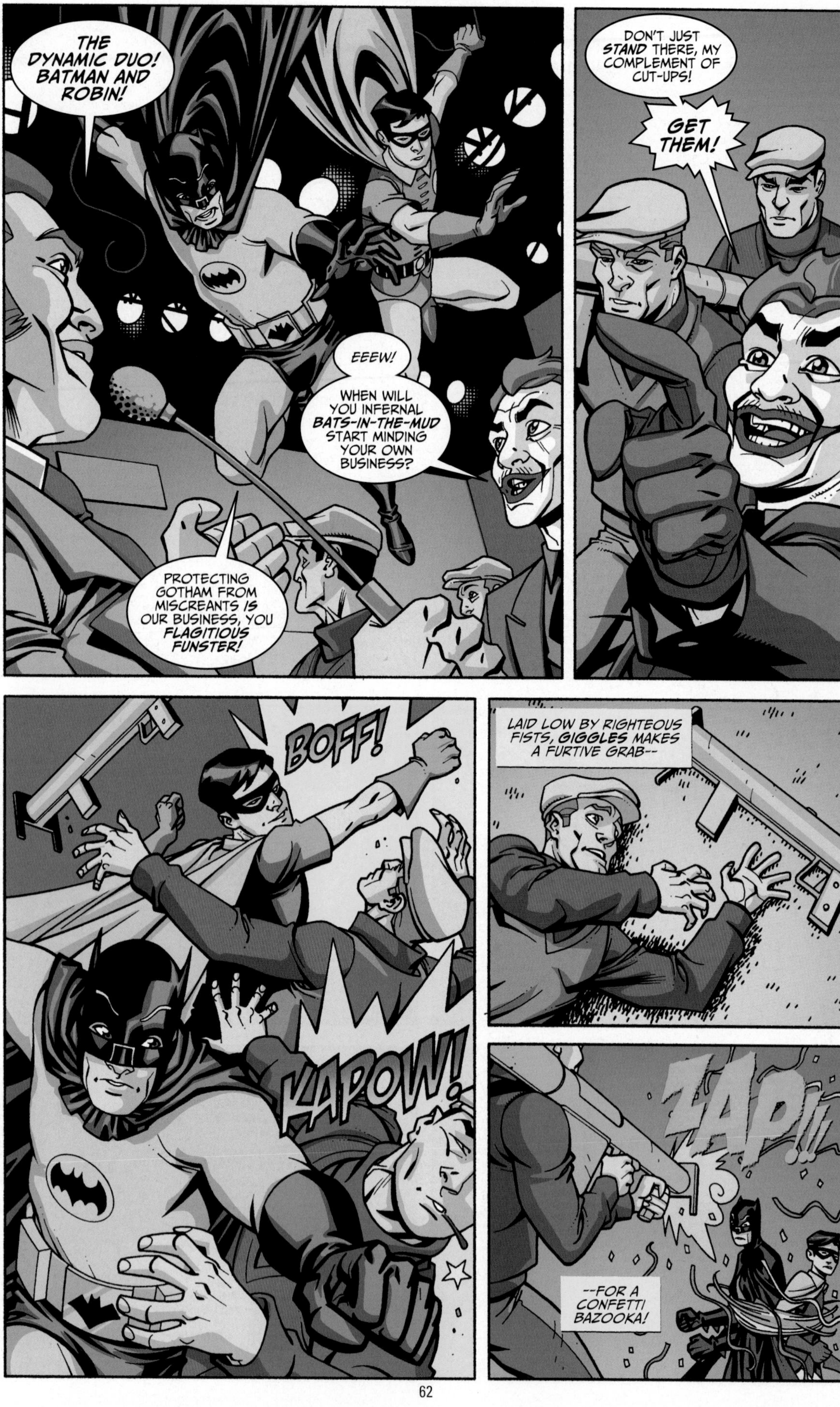

THE DYNAMIC DUO! BATMAN AND ROBIN!
EEEW!
WHEN WILL YOU INFERNAL BATS-IN-THE-MUD START MINDING YOUR OWN BUSINESS?
PROTECTING GOTHAM FROM MISCREANTS IS OUR BUSINESS, YOU FLAGITIOUS FUNSTER!
DON'T JUST STAND THERE, MY COMPLEMENT OF CUT-UPS!
GET THEM!
BOFF!
KAPOW!
LAID LOW BY RIGHTEOUS FISTS, GIGGLES MAKES A FURTIVE GRAB--
ZAP!!!
--FOR A CONFETTI BAZOOKA!

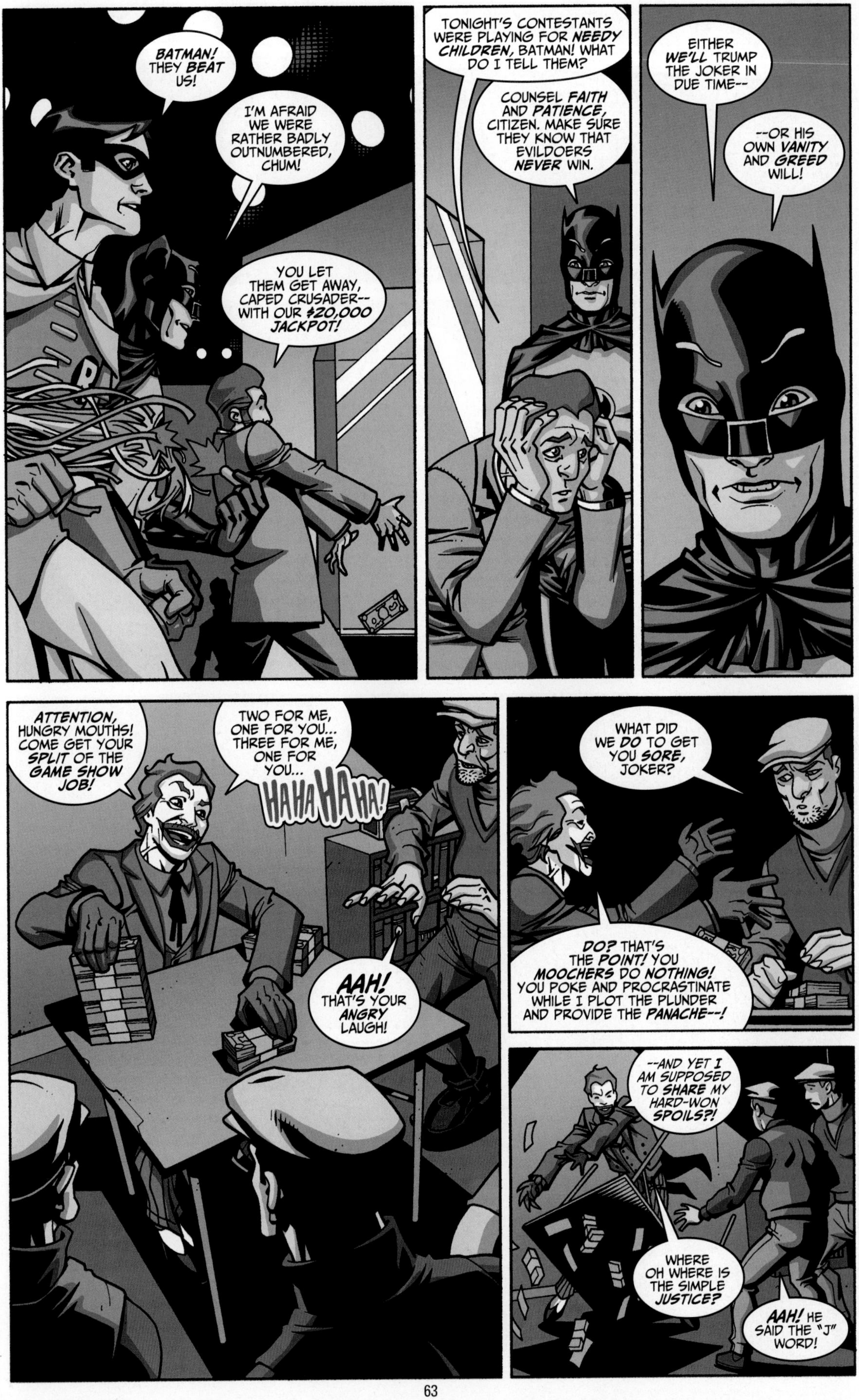
BATMAN! THEY BEAT US!
I'M AFRAID WE WERE RATHER BADLY OUTNUMBERED, CHUM!
YOU LET THEM GET AWAY, CAPED CRUSADER-- WITH OUR $20,000 JACKPOT!
TONIGHT'S CONTESTANTS WERE PLAYING FOR NEEDY CHILDREN, BATMAN! WHAT DO I TELL THEM?
COUNSEL FAITH AND PATIENCE, CITIZEN. MAKE SURE THEY KNOW THAT EVILDOERS NEVER WIN.
EITHER WE'LL TRUMP THE JOKER IN DUE TIME--
--OR HIS OWN VANITY AND GREED WILL!
ATTENTION, HUNGRY MOUTHS! COME GET YOUR SPLIT OF THE GAME SHOW JOB!
TWO FOR ME, ONE FOR YOU... THREE FOR ME, ONE FOR YOU...
HAHAHAHA!
AAH! THAT'S YOUR ANGRY LAUGH!
WHAT DID WE DO TO GET YOU SORE, JOKER?
DO? THAT'S THE POINT! YOU MOOCHERS DO NOTHING! YOU POKE AND PROCRASTINATE WHILE I PLOT THE PLUNDER AND PROVIDE THE PANACHE--!
--AND YET I AM SUPPOSED TO SHARE MY HARD-WON SPOILS?!
WHERE OH WHERE IS THE SIMPLE JUSTICE?
AAH! HE SAID THE "J" WORD!

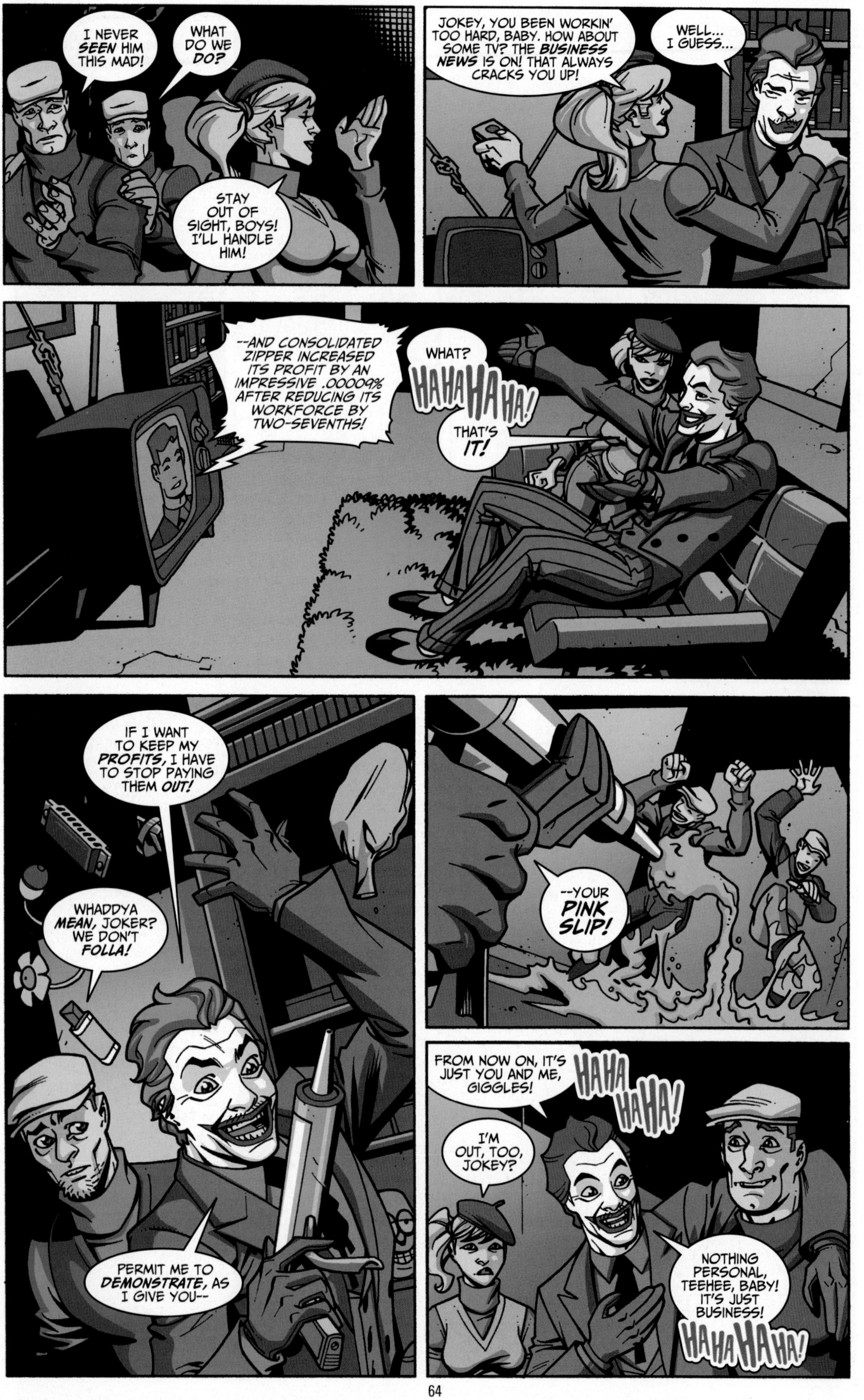
I NEVER SEEN HIM THIS MAD!
WHAT DO WE DO?
STAY OUT OF SIGHT, BOYS! I'LL HANDLE HIM!
JOKEY, YOU BEEN WORKIN' TOO HARD, BABY. HOW ABOUT SOME TV? THE BUSINESS NEWS IS ON! THAT ALWAYS CRACKS YOU UP!
WELL... I GUESS...
--AND CONSOLIDATED ZIPPER INCREASED ITS PROFIT BY AN IMPRESSIVE .00009% AFTER REDUCING ITS WORKFORCE BY TWO-SEVENTHS!
WHAT?
HAHAHAHA!
THAT'S IT!
IF I WANT TO KEEP MY PROFITS, I HAVE TO STOP PAYING THEM OUT!
WHADDYA MEAN, JOKER? WE DON'T FOLLA!
PERMIT ME TO DEMONSTRATE, AS I GIVE YOU--
--YOUR PINK SLIP!
FROM NOW ON, IT'S JUST YOU AND ME, GIGGLES!
HAHA HAHA!
I'M OUT, TOO, JOKEY?
NOTHING PERSONAL, TEEHEE, BABY! IT'S JUST BUSINESS!
HAHAHAHA!

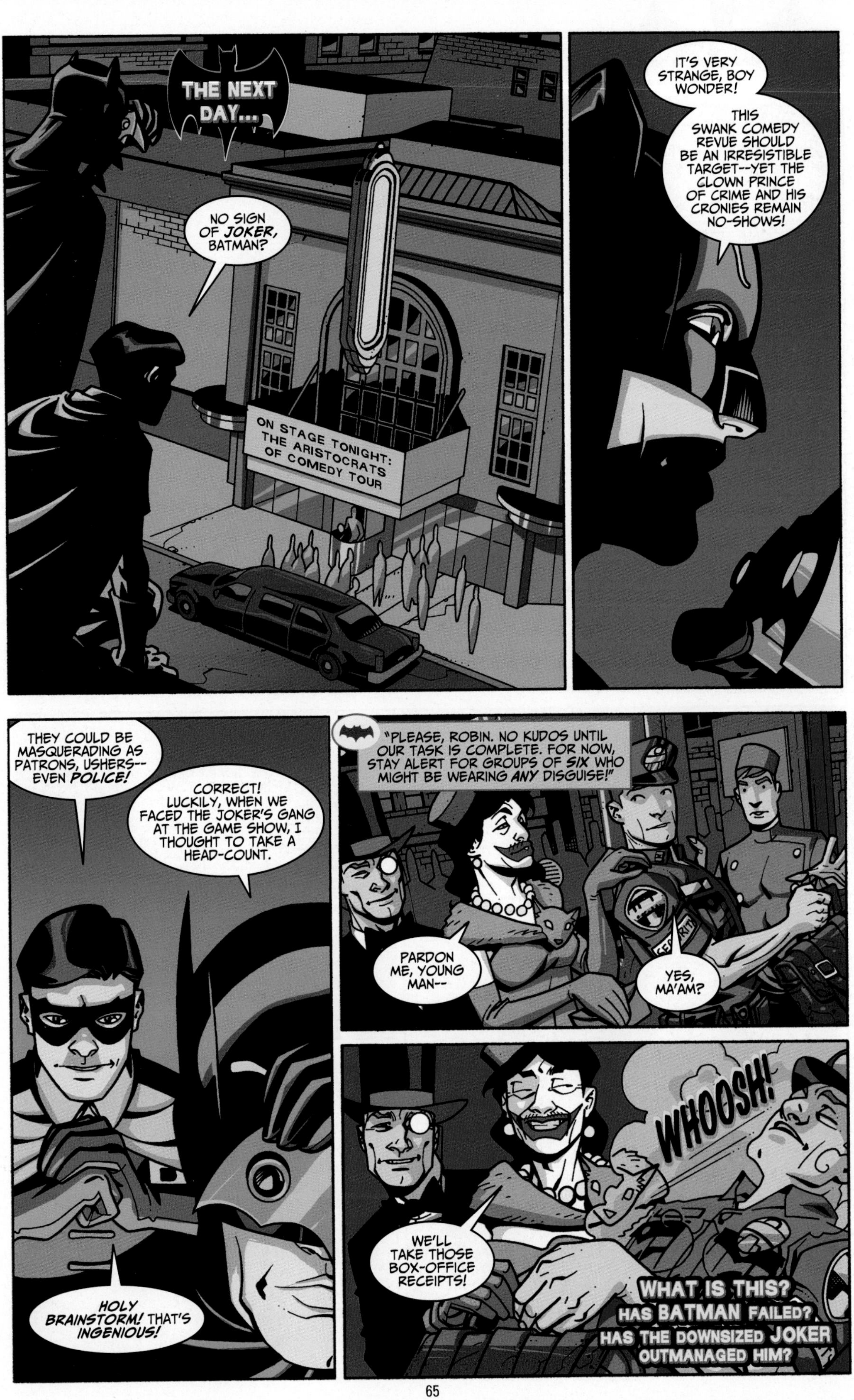
THE NEXT DAY...
NO SIGN OF JOKER, BATMAN?
ON STAGE TONIGHT: THE ARISTOCRATS OF COMEDY TOUR
IT'S VERY STRANGE, BOY WONDER!
THIS SWANK COMEDY REVUE SHOULD BE AN IRRESISTIBLE TARGET--YET THE CLOWN PRINCE OF CRIME AND HIS CRONIES REMAIN NO-SHOWS!
THEY COULD BE MASQUERADING AS PATRONS, USHERS--EVEN POLICE!
CORRECT! LUCKILY, WHEN WE FACED THE JOKER'S GANG AT THE GAME SHOW, I THOUGHT TO TAKE A HEAD-COUNT.
HOLY BRAINSTORM! THAT'S INGENIOUS!
"PLEASE, ROBIN. NO KUDOS UNTIL OUR TASK IS COMPLETE. FOR NOW, STAY ALERT FOR GROUPS OF SIX WHO MIGHT BE WEARING ANY DISGUISE!"
PARDON ME, YOUNG MAN--
YES, MA'AM?
WHOOSH!
WE'LL TAKE THOSE BOX-OFFICE RECEIPTS!
WHAT IS THIS? HAS BATMAN FAILED? HAS THE DOWNSIZED JOKER OUTMANAGED HIM?

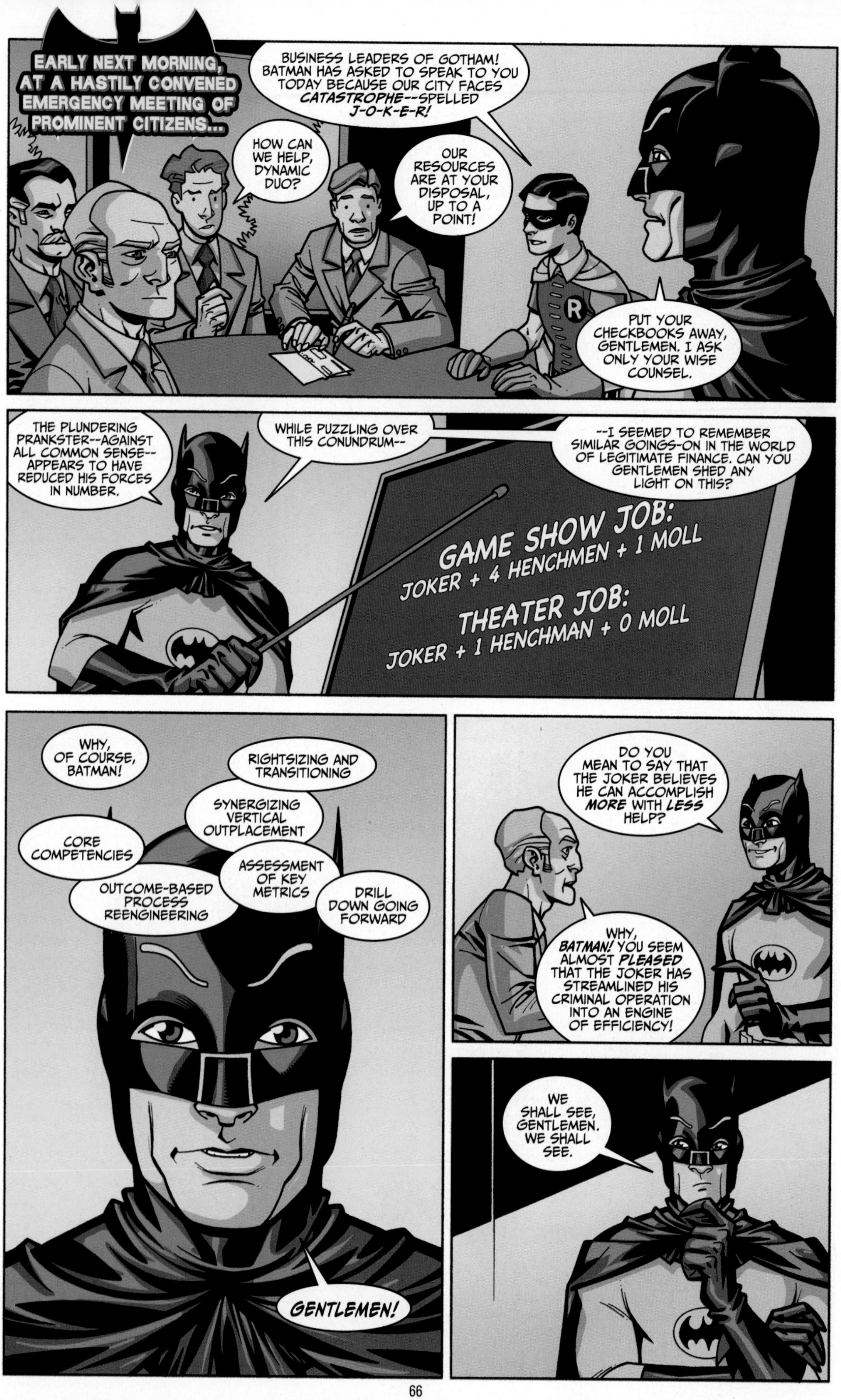

EARLY NEXT MORNING, AT A HASTILY CONVENED EMERGENCY MEETING OF PROMINENT CITIZENS...
BUSINESS LEADERS OF GOTHAM! BATMAN HAS ASKED TO SPEAK TO YOU TODAY BECAUSE OUR CITY FACES CATASTROPHE--SPELLED J-O-K-E-R!
HOW CAN WE HELP, DYNAMIC DUO?
OUR RESOURCES ARE AT YOUR DISPOSAL, UP TO A POINT!
PUT YOUR CHECKBOOKS AWAY, GENTLEMEN. I ASK ONLY YOUR WISE COUNSEL.
THE PLUNDERING PRANKSTER--AGAINST ALL COMMON SENSE--APPEARS TO HAVE REDUCED HIS FORCES IN NUMBER.
WHILE PUZZLING OVER THIS CONUNDRUM--
--I SEEMED TO REMEMBER SIMILAR GOINGS-ON IN THE WORLD OF LEGITIMATE FINANCE. CAN YOU GENTLEMEN SHED ANY LIGHT ON THIS?
GAME SHOW JOB:
JOKER + 4 HENCHMEN + 1 MOLL
THEATER JOB:
JOKER + 1 HENCHMAN + 0 MOLL
WHY, OF COURSE, BATMAN!
RIGHTSIZING AND TRANSITIONING
SYNERGIZING VERTICAL OUTPLACEMENT
CORE COMPETENCIES
ASSESSMENT OF KEY METRICS
OUTCOME-BASED PROCESS REENGINEERING
DRILL DOWN GOING FORWARD
GENTLEMEN!
DO YOU MEAN TO SAY THAT THE JOKER BELIEVES HE CAN ACCOMPLISH MORE WITH LESS HELP?
WHY, BATMAN! YOU SEEM ALMOST PLEASED THAT THE JOKER HAS STREAMLINED HIS CRIMINAL OPERATION INTO AN ENGINE OF EFFICIENCY!
WE SHALL SEE, GENTLEMEN. WE SHALL SEE.

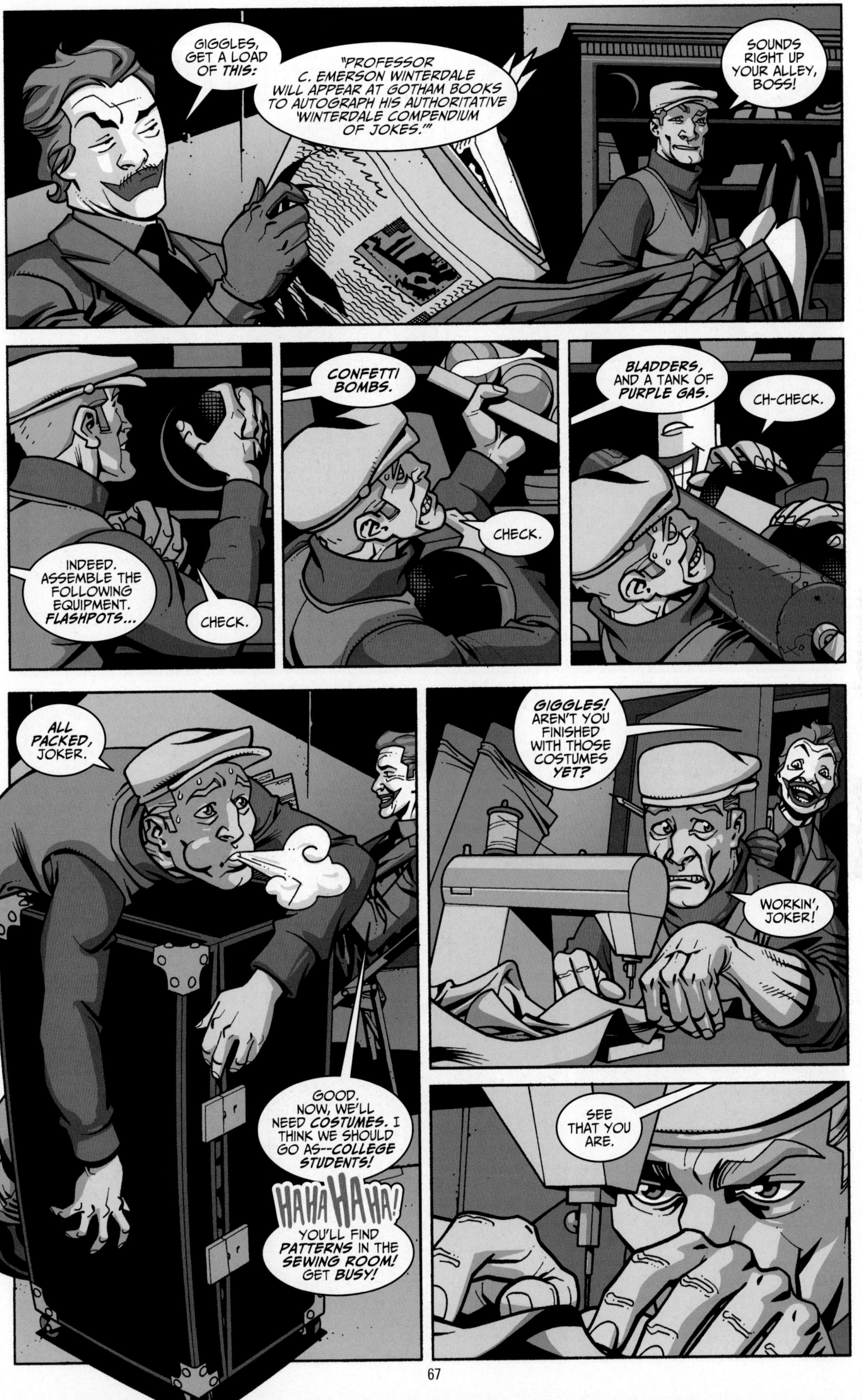
GIGGLES, GET A LOAD OF THIS:
"PROFESSOR C. EMERSON WINTERDALE WILL APPEAR AT GOTHAM BOOKS TO AUTOGRAPH HIS AUTHORITATIVE 'WINTERDALE COMPENDIUM OF JOKES.'"
SOUNDS RIGHT UP YOUR ALLEY, BOSS!
INDEED. ASSEMBLE THE FOLLOWING EQUIPMENT. FLASHPOTS...
CHECK.
CONFETTI BOMBS.
CHECK.
BLADDERS, AND A TANK OF PURPLE GAS.
CH-CHECK.
ALL PACKED, JOKER.
GOOD. NOW, WE'LL NEED COSTUMES. I THINK WE SHOULD GO AS--COLLEGE STUDENTS!
HAHAHAHA!
YOU'LL FIND PATTERNS IN THE SEWING ROOM! GET BUSY!
GIGGLES! AREN'T YOU FINISHED WITH THOSE COSTUMES YET?
WORKIN', JOKER!
SEE THAT YOU ARE.

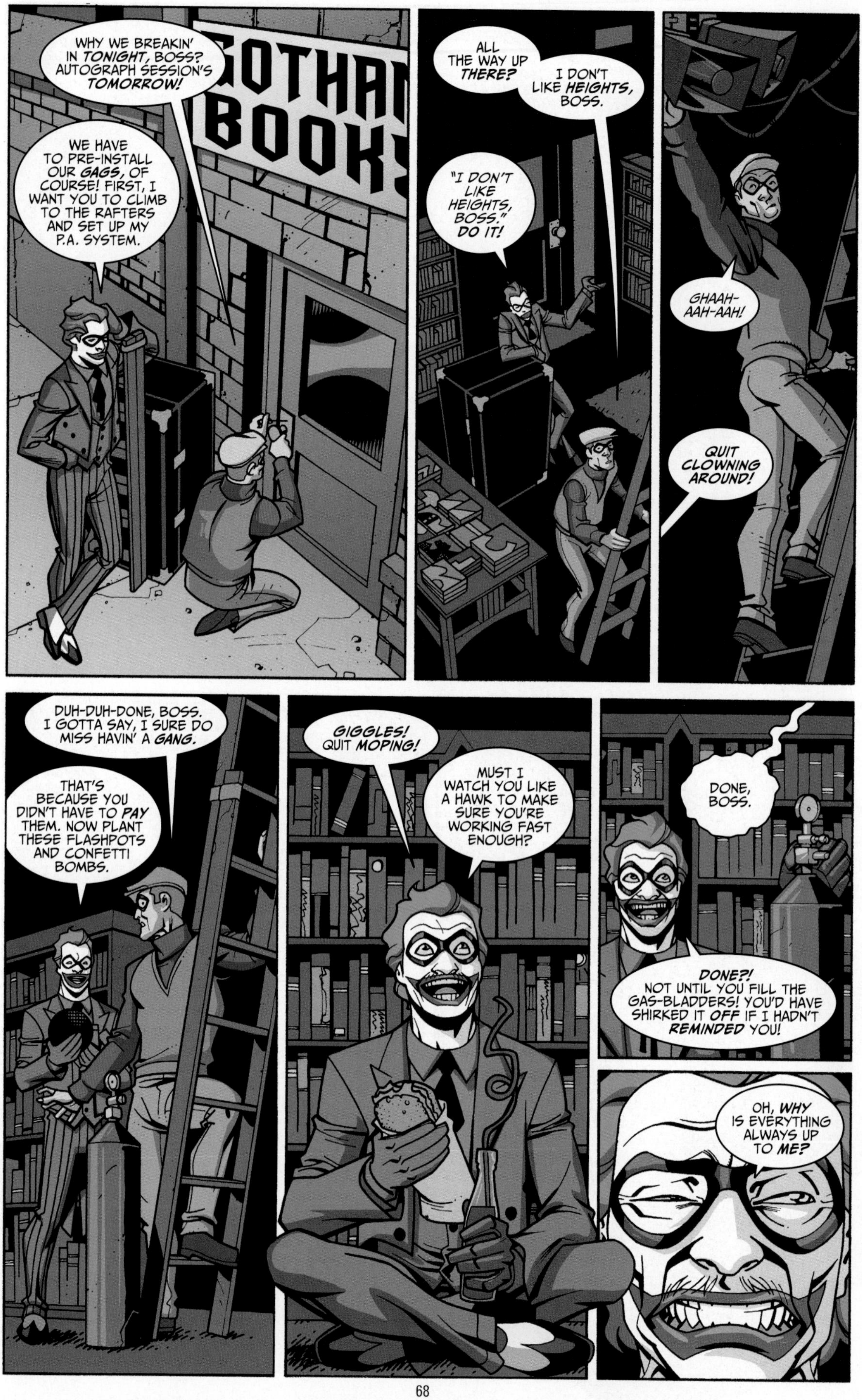
GOTHAM BOOKS
WHY WE BREAKIN' IN TONIGHT, BOSS? AUTOGRAPH SESSION'S TOMORROW!
WE HAVE TO PRE-INSTALL OUR GAGS, OF COURSE! FIRST, I WANT YOU TO CLIMB TO THE RAFTERS AND SET UP MY P.A. SYSTEM.
ALL THE WAY UP THERE?
I DON'T LIKE HEIGHTS, BOSS.
"I DON'T LIKE HEIGHTS, BOSS." DO IT!
GHAAH-AAH-AAH!
QUIT CLOWNING AROUND!
DUH-DUH-DONE, BOSS. I GOTTA SAY, I SURE DO MISS HAVIN' A GANG.
THAT'S BECAUSE YOU DIDN'T HAVE TO PAY THEM. NOW PLANT THESE FLASHPOTS AND CONFETTI BOMBS.
GIGGLES! QUIT MOPING!
MUST I WATCH YOU LIKE A HAWK TO MAKE SURE YOU'RE WORKING FAST ENOUGH?
DONE, BOSS.
DONE?! NOT UNTIL YOU FILL THE GAS-BLADDERS! YOU'D HAVE SHIRKED IT OFF IF I HADN'T REMINDED YOU!
OH, WHY IS EVERYTHING ALWAYS UP TO ME?

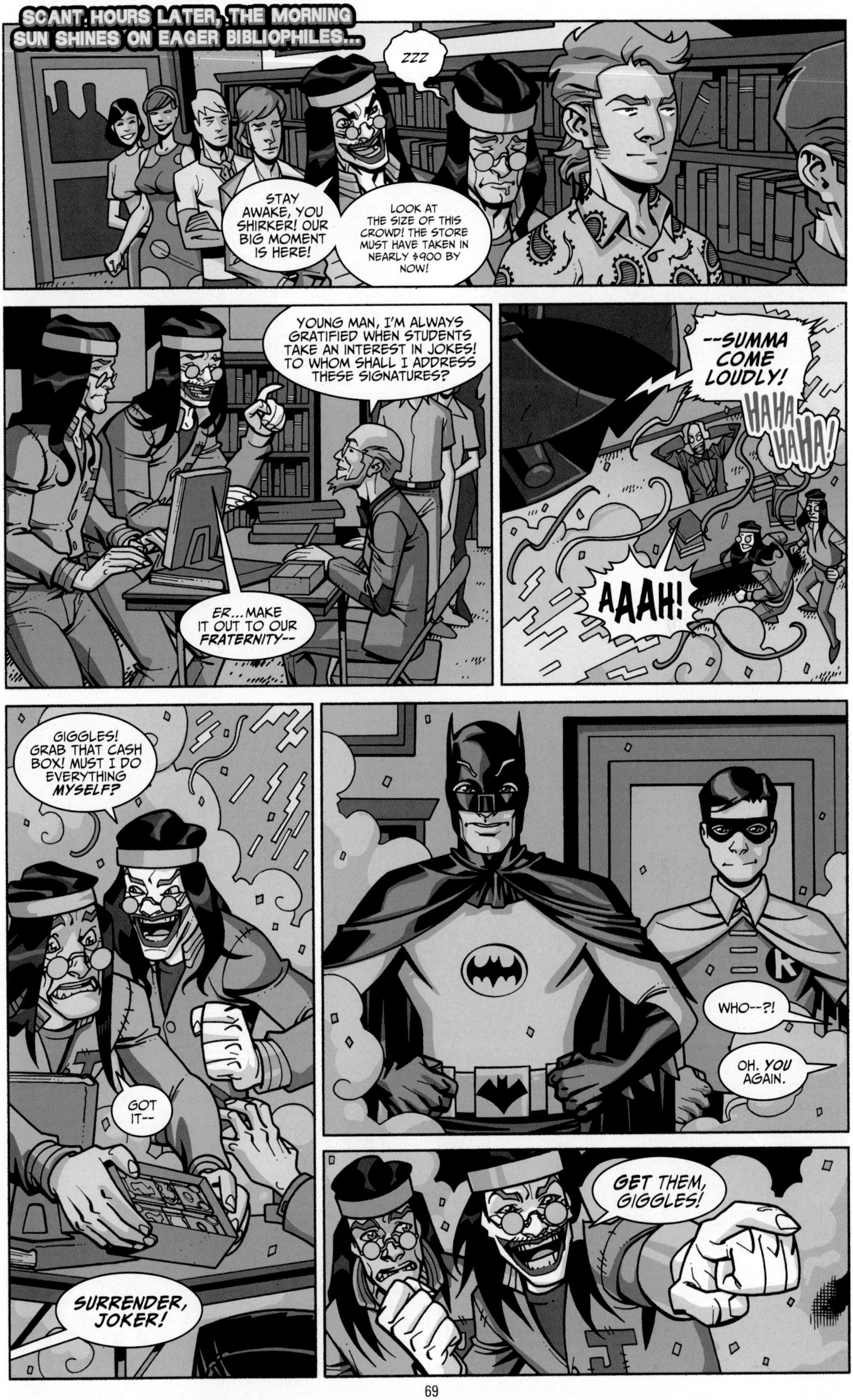
SCANT HOURS LATER, THE MORNING SUN SHINES ON EAGER BIBLIOPHILES...
ZZZ
STAY AWAKE, YOU SHIRKER! OUR BIG MOMENT IS HERE!
LOOK AT THE SIZE OF THIS CROWD! THE STORE MUST HAVE TAKEN IN NEARLY $900 BY NOW!
YOUNG MAN, I'M ALWAYS GRATIFIED WHEN STUDENTS TAKE AN INTEREST IN JOKES! TO WHOM SHALL I ADDRESS THESE SIGNATURES?
ER... MAKE IT OUT TO OUR FRATERNITY--
--SUMMA COME LOUDLY!
HAHA HAHA!
AAAH!
GIGGLES! GRAB THAT CASH BOX! MUST I DO EVERYTHING MYSELF?
GOT IT--
SURRENDER, JOKER!
WHO--?!
OH. YOU AGAIN.
GET THEM, GIGGLES!

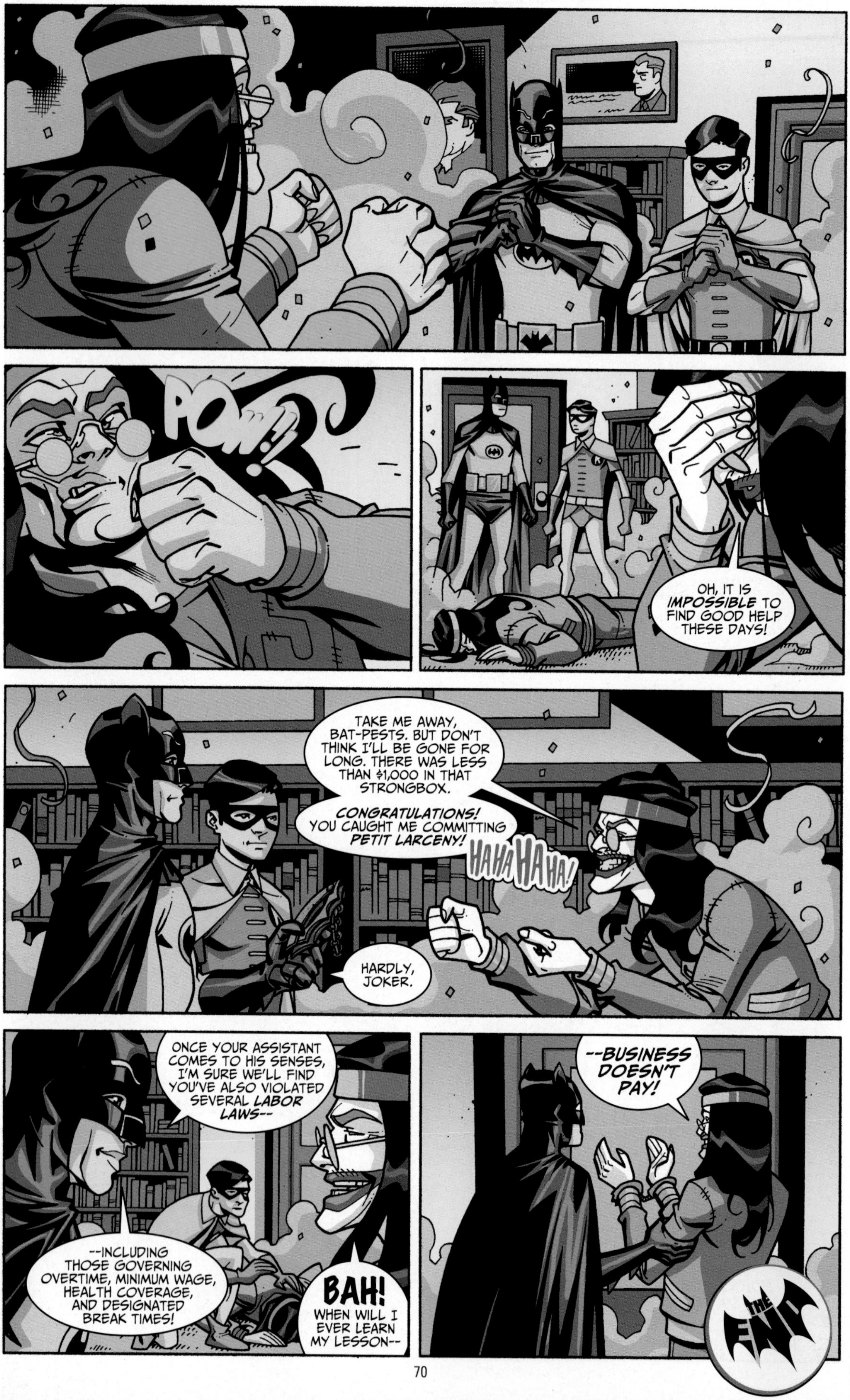
POW!
OH, IT IS IMPOSSIBLE TO FIND GOOD HELP THESE DAYS!
TAKE ME AWAY, BAT-PESTS. BUT DON'T THINK I'LL BE GONE FOR LONG. THERE WAS LESS THAN $1,000 IN THAT STRONGBOX.
CONGRATULATIONS! YOU CAUGHT ME COMMITTING PETIT LARCENY!
HAHAHAHA!
HARDLY, JOKER.
ONCE YOUR ASSISTANT COMES TO HIS SENSES, I'M SURE WE'LL FIND YOU'VE ALSO VIOLATED SEVERAL LABOR LAWS--
--INCLUDING THOSE GOVERNING OVERTIME, MINIMUM WAGE, HEALTH COVERAGE, AND DESIGNATED BREAK TIMES!
BAH! WHEN WILL I EVER LEARN MY LESSON--
--BUSINESS DOESN'T PAY!
THE END

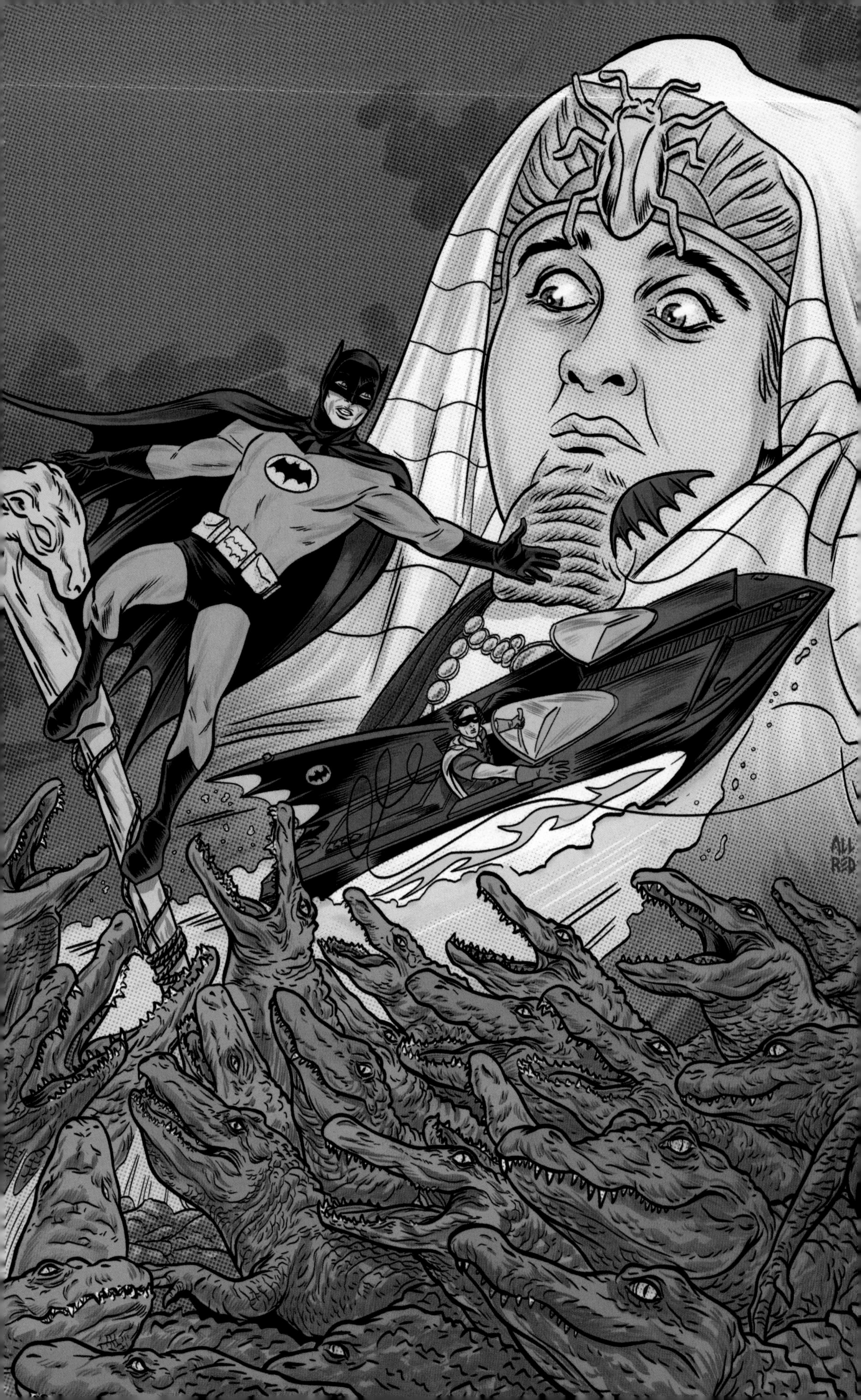
ALL
RED

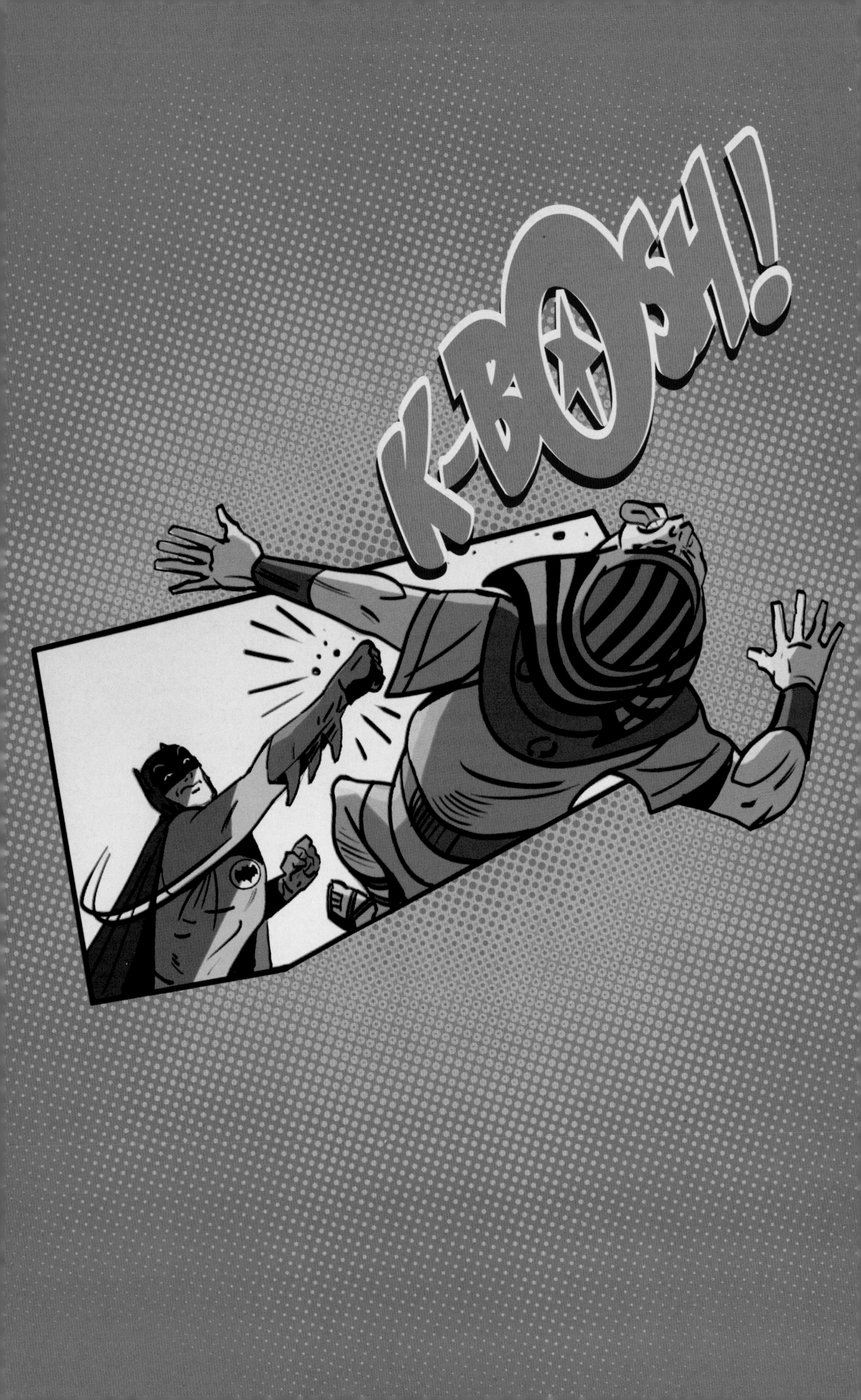
K-BOOSH!!

AT THE GOTHAM RIVER, A STRANGE SIGHT SUMMONS THE CITIZENRY!

IT MUST BE SOME KIND OF A STUNT.

MAYBE THEY'RE FILMING A MOVIE?

I DON'T SEE ANY CAMERAS...

THAT IS DEFINITELY A ROYAL BARGE.

ONE SIDE, PLEASE!

BATMAN!

AND ROBIN, THE BOY WONDER!

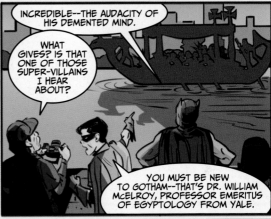

INCREDIBLE--THE AUDACITY OF HIS DEMENTED MIND.

WHAT GIVES? IS THAT ONE OF THOSE SUPER-VILLAINS I HEAR ABOUT?

YOU MUST BE NEW TO GOTHAM--THAT'S DR. WILLIAM McELROY, PROFESSOR EMERITUS OF EGYPTOLOGY FROM YALE.

R "HE WAS HIT IN THE HEAD DURING STUDENT RIOTING AND AWOKE BELIEVING HIMSELF TO BE THE REINCARNATION OF..."

"...KING TUT."

"KING TUT BARGES IN"

Written by JEFF PARKER   Art by RUBEN PROCOPIO
Colors by LEE LOUGHRIDGE   Lettered by WES ABBOTT
Cover by MICHAEL and LAURA ALLRED

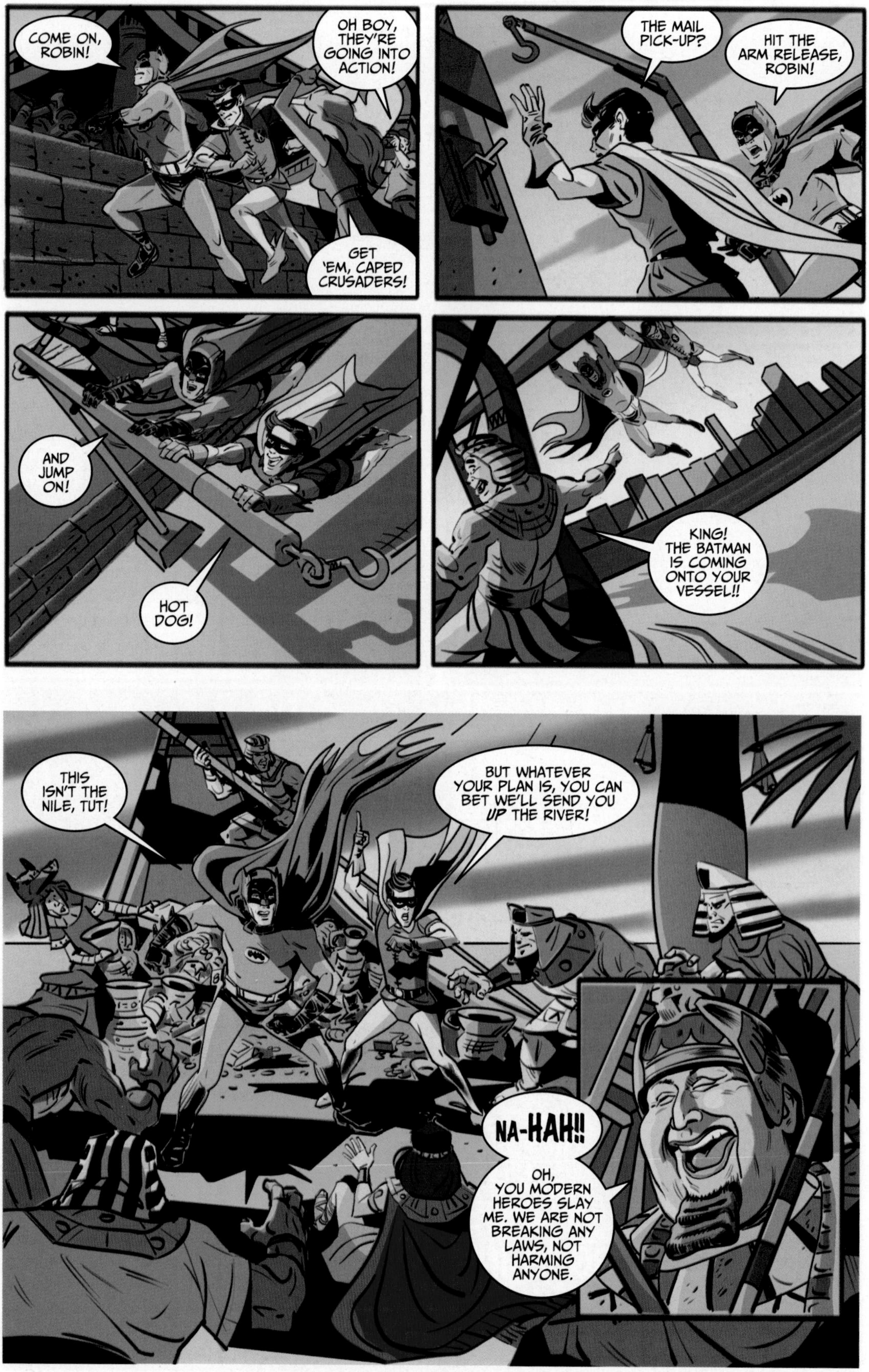
COME ON, ROBIN!
OH BOY, THEY'RE GOING INTO ACTION!
GET 'EM, CAPED CRUSADERS!
THE MAIL PICK-UP?
HIT THE ARM RELEASE, ROBIN!
AND JUMP ON!
HOT DOG!
KING! THE BATMAN IS COMING ONTO YOUR VESSEL!!
THIS ISN'T THE NILE, TUT!
BUT WHATEVER YOUR PLAN IS, YOU CAN BET WE'LL SEND YOU *UP* THE RIVER!
NA-HAH!!
OH, YOU MODERN HEROES SLAY ME. WE ARE NOT BREAKING ANY LAWS, NOT HARMING ANYONE.

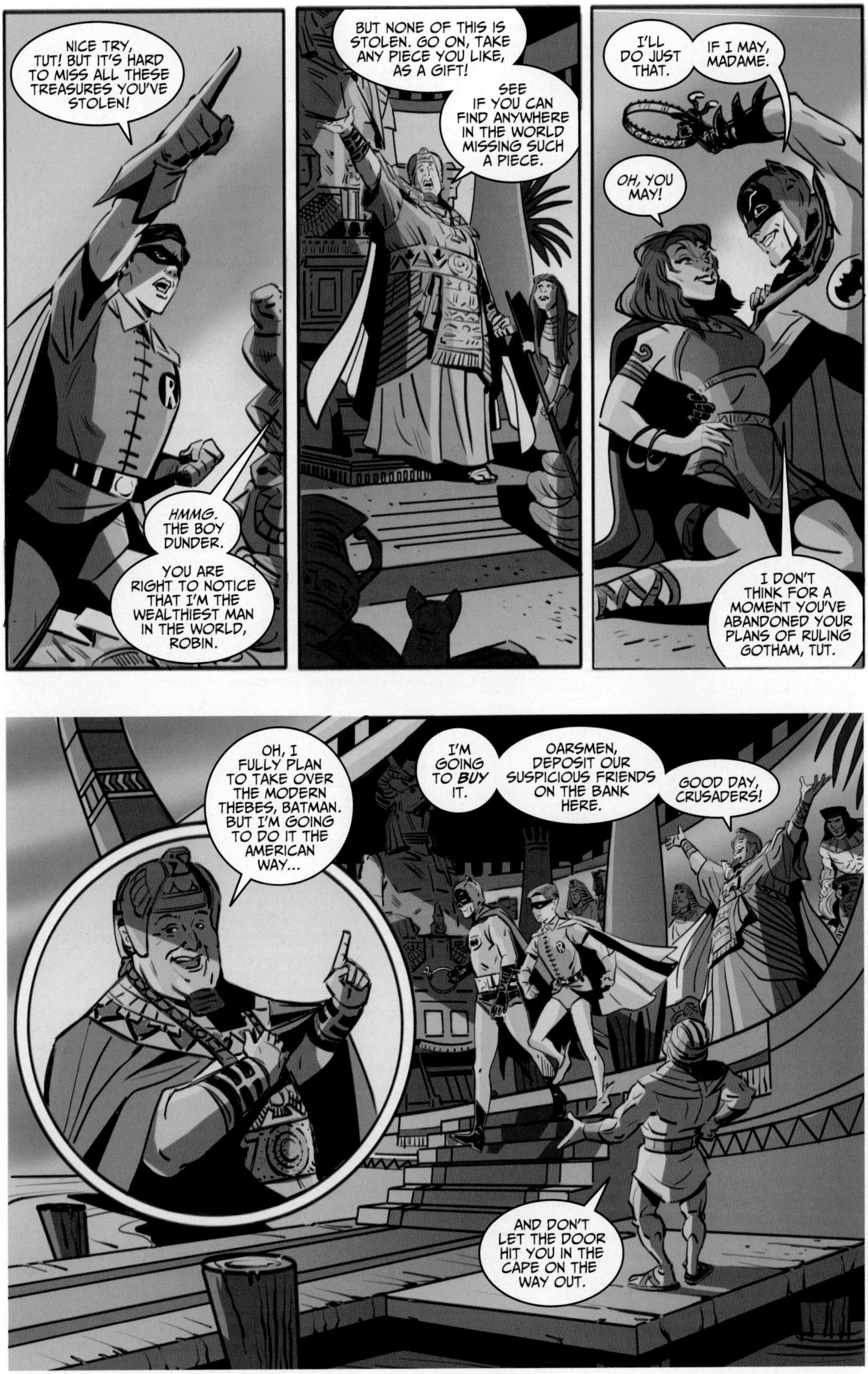
NICE TRY, TUT! BUT IT'S HARD TO MISS ALL THESE TREASURES YOU'VE STOLEN!
HMMG. THE BOY DUNDER.
YOU ARE RIGHT TO NOTICE THAT I'M THE WEALTHIEST MAN IN THE WORLD, ROBIN.
BUT NONE OF THIS IS STOLEN. GO ON, TAKE ANY PIECE YOU LIKE, AS A GIFT!
SEE IF YOU CAN FIND ANYWHERE IN THE WORLD MISSING SUCH A PIECE.
I'LL DO JUST THAT.
IF I MAY, MADAME.
OH, YOU MAY!
I DON'T THINK FOR A MOMENT YOU'VE ABANDONED YOUR PLANS OF RULING GOTHAM, TUT.
OH, I FULLY PLAN TO TAKE OVER THE MODERN THEBES, BATMAN. BUT I'M GOING TO DO IT THE AMERICAN WAY...
I'M GOING TO BUY IT.
OARSMEN, DEPOSIT OUR SUSPICIOUS FRIENDS ON THE BANK HERE.
GOOD DAY, CRUSADERS!
AND DON'T LET THE DOOR HIT YOU IN THE CAPE ON THE WAY OUT.

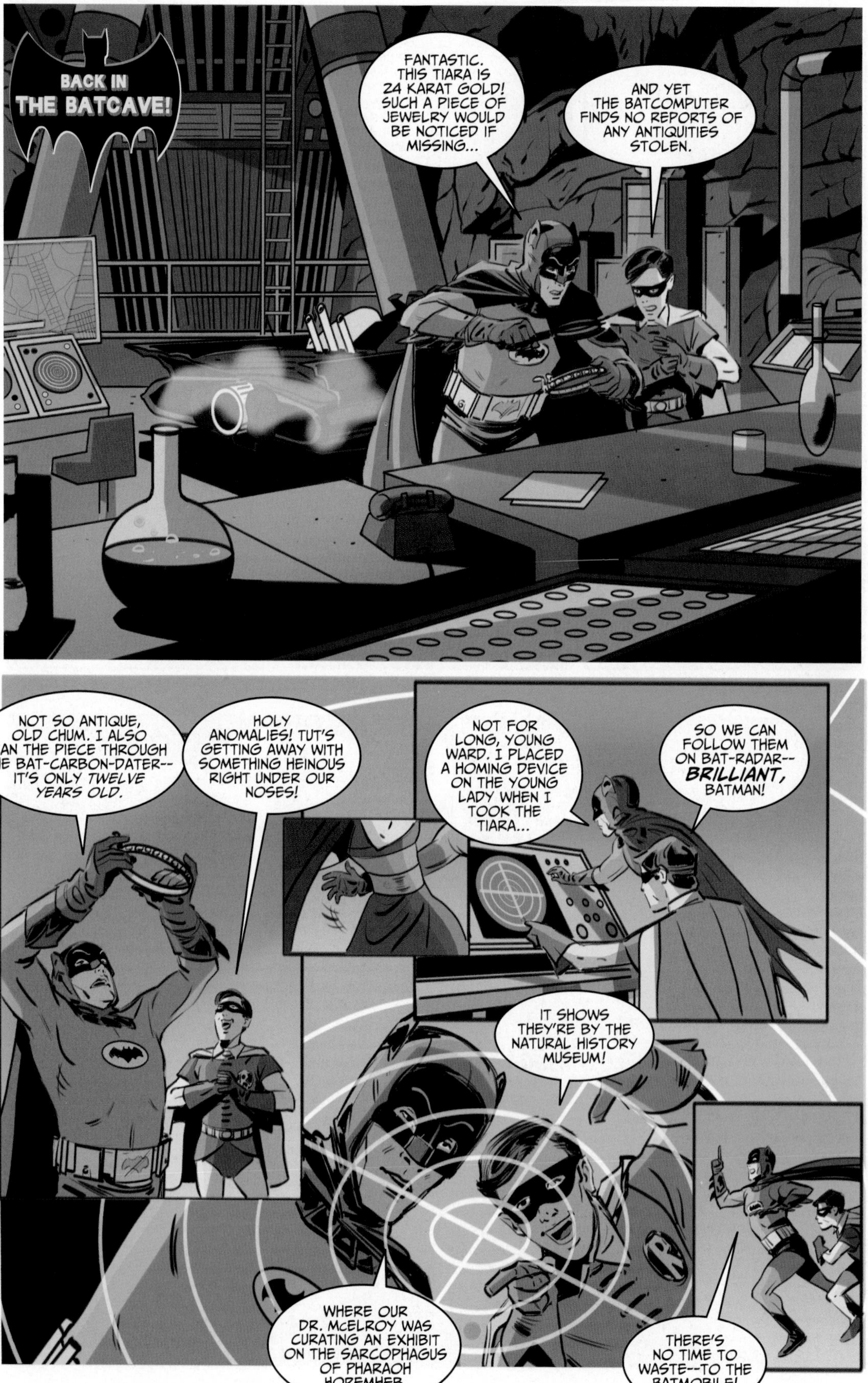
BACK IN THE BATCAVE!
FANTASTIC. THIS TIARA IS 24 KARAT GOLD! SUCH A PIECE OF JEWELRY WOULD BE NOTICED IF MISSING...
AND YET THE BATCOMPUTER FINDS NO REPORTS OF ANY ANTIQUITIES STOLEN.
NOT SO ANTIQUE, OLD CHUM. I ALSO RAN THE PIECE THROUGH THE BAT-CARBON-DATER-- IT'S ONLY *TWELVE YEARS OLD.*
HOLY ANOMALIES! TUT'S GETTING AWAY WITH SOMETHING HEINOUS RIGHT UNDER OUR NOSES!
NOT FOR LONG, YOUNG WARD. I PLACED A HOMING DEVICE ON THE YOUNG LADY WHEN I TOOK THE TIARA...
SO WE CAN FOLLOW THEM ON BAT-RADAR-- ***BRILLIANT,*** BATMAN!
IT SHOWS THEY'RE BY THE NATURAL HISTORY MUSEUM!
WHERE OUR DR. McELROY WAS CURATING AN EXHIBIT ON THE SARCOPHAGUS OF PHARAOH HOREMHEB.
THERE'S NO TIME TO WASTE--TO THE BATMOBILE!

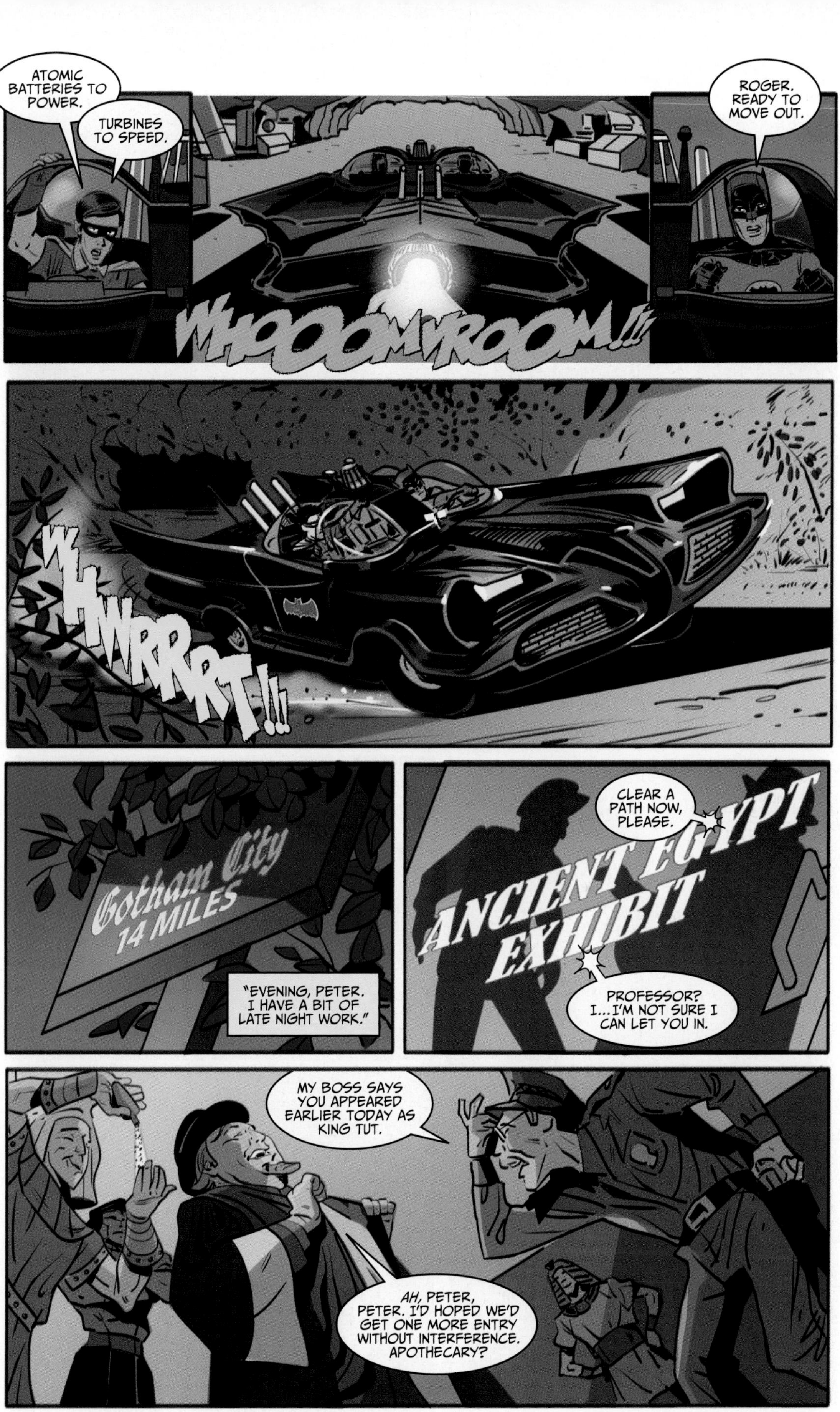
ATOMIC BATTERIES TO POWER.
TURBINES TO SPEED.
ROGER. READY TO MOVE OUT.
WHOOOOMVROOM!!
WHWRRRRT!!!
Gotham City 14 MILES
"EVENING, PETER. I HAVE A BIT OF LATE NIGHT WORK."
ANCIENT EGYPT EXHIBIT
CLEAR A PATH NOW, PLEASE.
PROFESSOR? I...I'M NOT SURE I CAN LET YOU IN.
MY BOSS SAYS YOU APPEARED EARLIER TODAY AS KING TUT.
AH, PETER, PETER. I'D HOPED WE'D GET ONE MORE ENTRY WITHOUT INTERFERENCE. APOTHECARY?

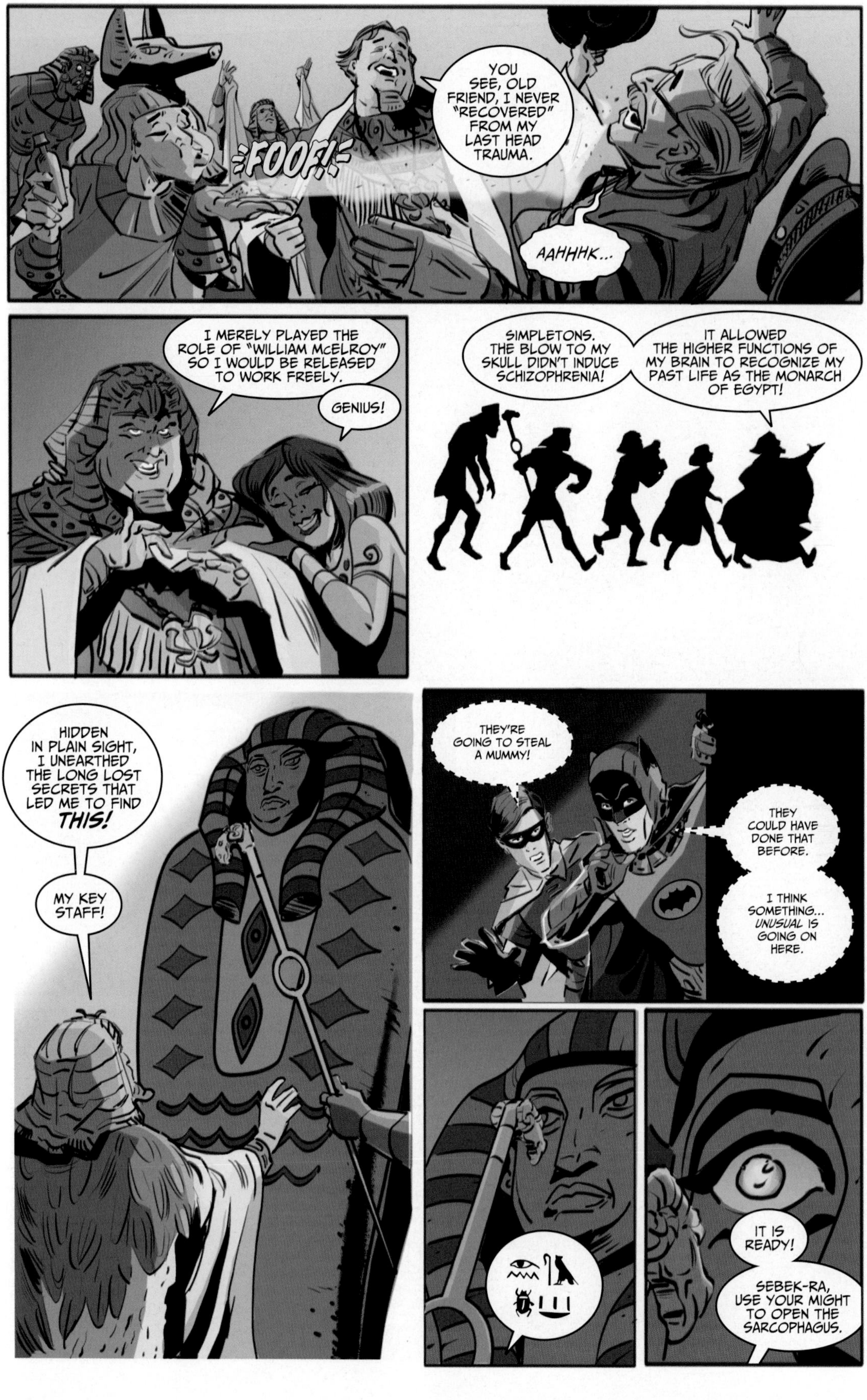

YOU SEE, OLD FRIEND, I NEVER "RECOVERED" FROM MY LAST HEAD TRAUMA.
FOOF!
AAHHHK...
I MERELY PLAYED THE ROLE OF "WILLIAM McELROY" SO I WOULD BE RELEASED TO WORK FREELY.
GENIUS!
SIMPLETONS. THE BLOW TO MY SKULL DIDN'T INDUCE SCHIZOPHRENIA!
IT ALLOWED THE HIGHER FUNCTIONS OF MY BRAIN TO RECOGNIZE MY PAST LIFE AS THE MONARCH OF EGYPT!
HIDDEN IN PLAIN SIGHT, I UNEARTHED THE LONG LOST SECRETS THAT LED ME TO FIND *THIS!*
MY KEY STAFF!
THEY'RE GOING TO STEAL A MUMMY!
THEY COULD HAVE DONE THAT BEFORE.
I THINK SOMETHING... *UNUSUAL* IS GOING ON HERE.
IT IS READY!
SEBEK-RA, USE YOUR MIGHT TO OPEN THE SARCOPHAGUS.

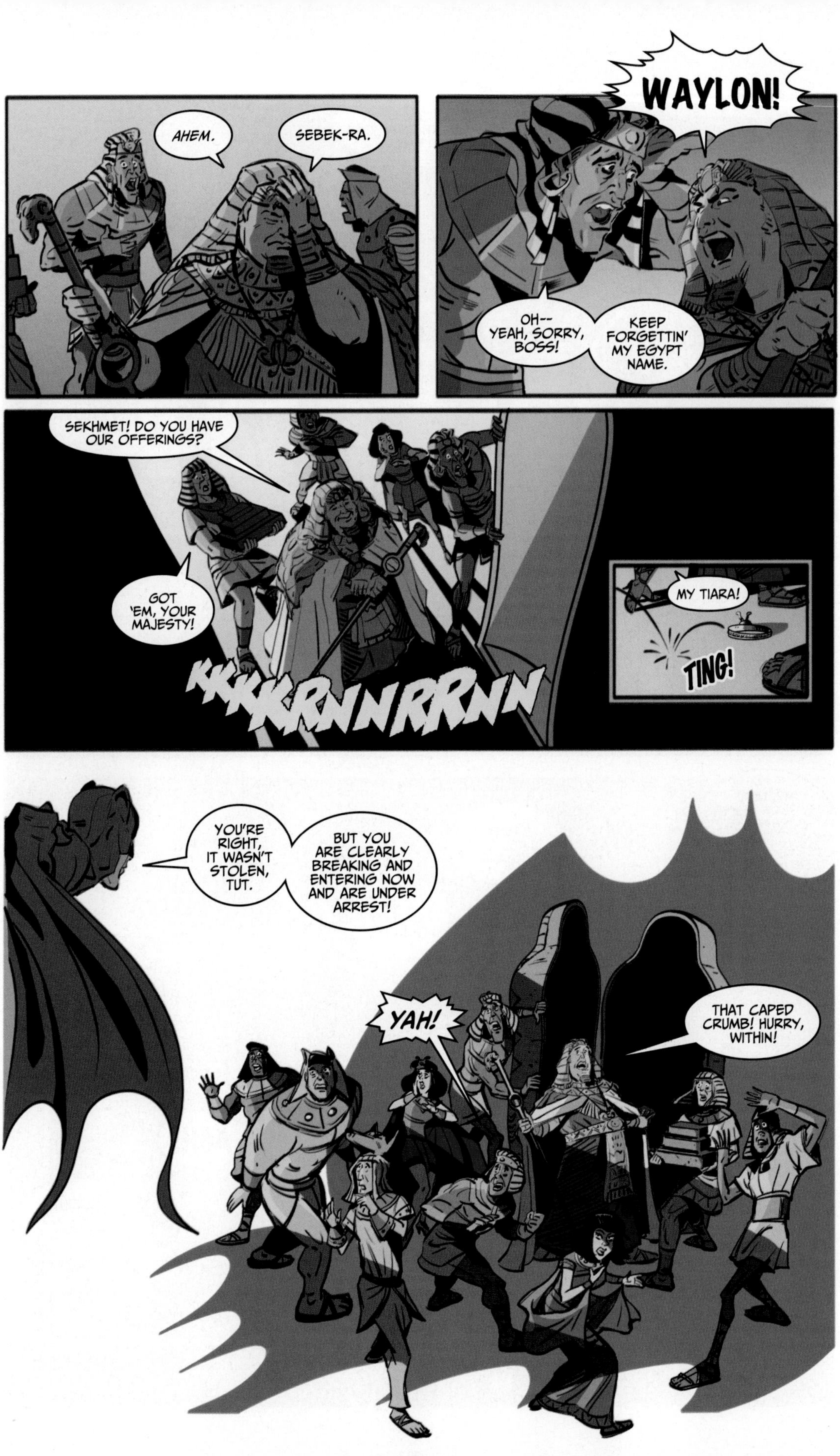
AHEM.
SEBEK-RA.
WAYLON!
OH-- YEAH, SORRY, BOSS!
KEEP FORGETTIN' MY EGYPT NAME.
SEKHMET! DO YOU HAVE OUR OFFERINGS?
GOT 'EM, YOUR MAJESTY!
KKKKRNNNRRRNN
MY TIARA!
TING!
YOU'RE RIGHT, IT WASN'T STOLEN, TUT.
BUT YOU ARE CLEARLY BREAKING AND ENTERING NOW AND ARE UNDER ARREST!
YAH!
THAT CAPED CRUMB! HURRY, WITHIN!

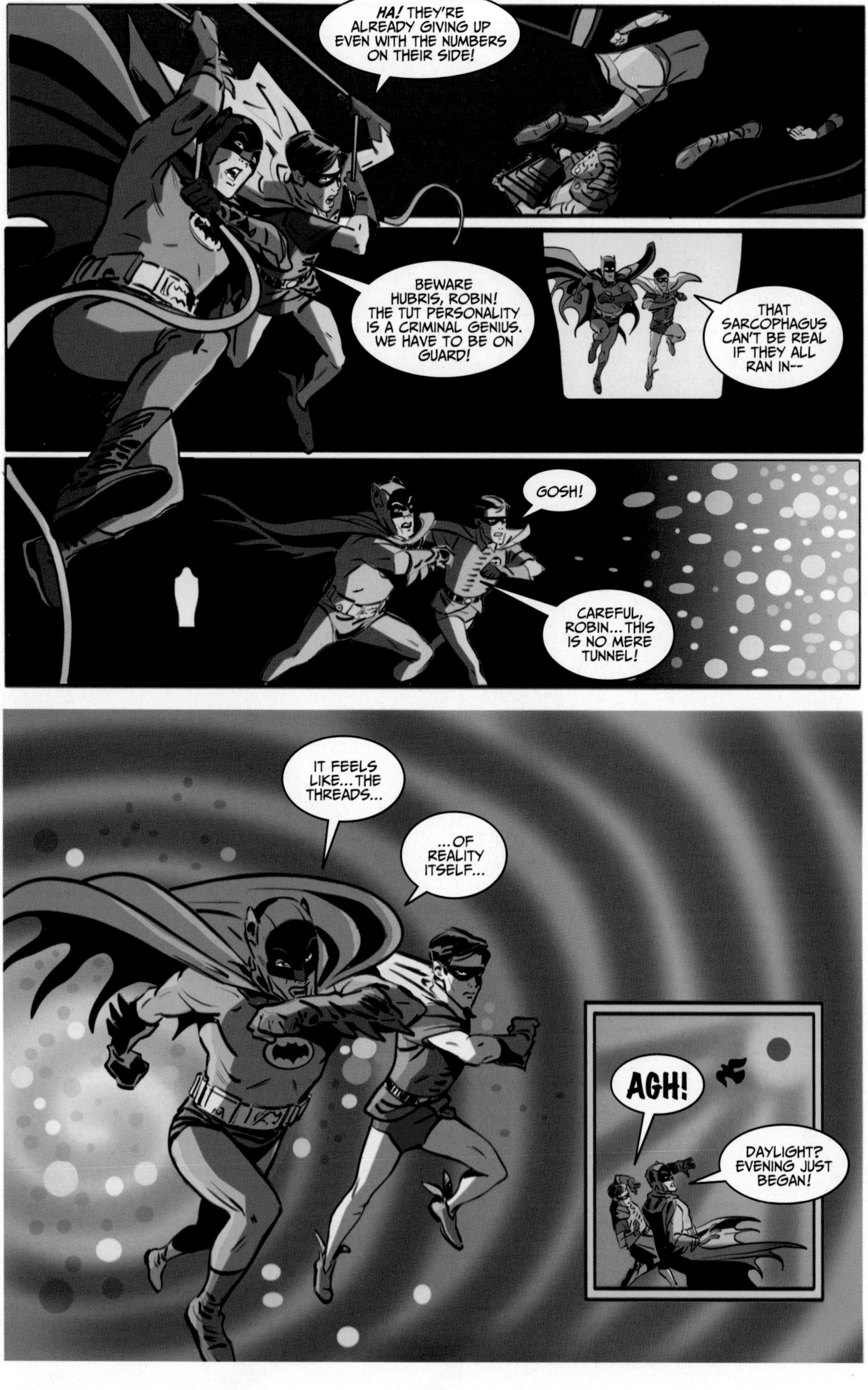
HA! THEY'RE ALREADY GIVING UP EVEN WITH THE NUMBERS ON THEIR SIDE!
BEWARE HUBRIS, ROBIN! THE TUT PERSONALITY IS A CRIMINAL GENIUS. WE HAVE TO BE ON GUARD!
THAT SARCOPHAGUS CAN'T BE REAL IF THEY ALL RAN IN--
GOSH!
CAREFUL, ROBIN... THIS IS NO MERE TUNNEL!
IT FEELS LIKE... THE THREADS...
...OF REALITY ITSELF...
AGH!
DAYLIGHT? EVENING JUST BEGAN!

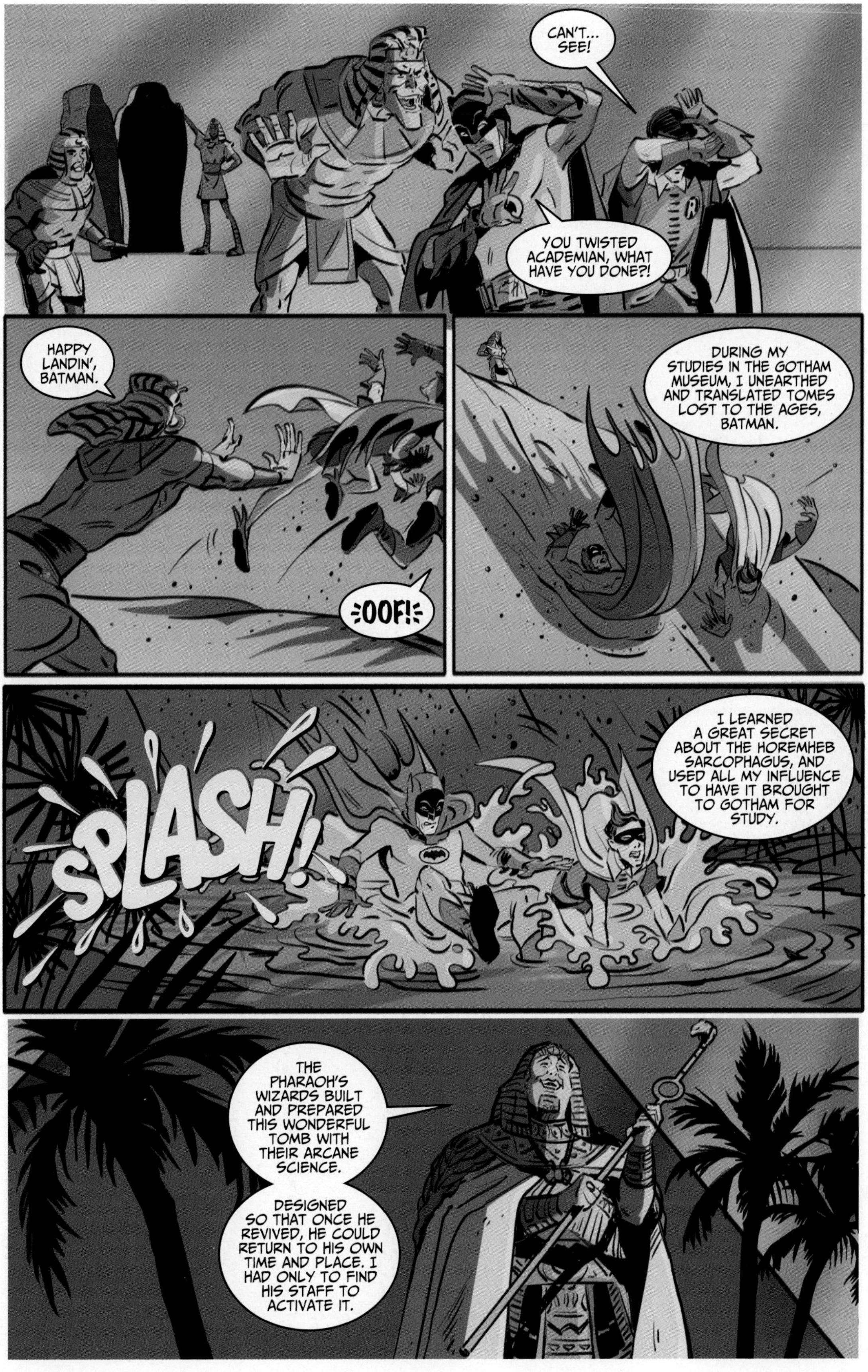
CAN'T... SEE!
YOU TWISTED ACADEMIAN, WHAT HAVE YOU DONE?!
HAPPY LANDIN', BATMAN.
OOF!
DURING MY STUDIES IN THE GOTHAM MUSEUM, I UNEARTHED AND TRANSLATED TOMES LOST TO THE AGES, BATMAN.
SPLASH!
I LEARNED A GREAT SECRET ABOUT THE HOREMHEB SARCOPHAGUS, AND USED ALL MY INFLUENCE TO HAVE IT BROUGHT TO GOTHAM FOR STUDY.
THE PHARAOH'S WIZARDS BUILT AND PREPARED THIS WONDERFUL TOMB WITH THEIR ARCANE SCIENCE.
DESIGNED SO THAT ONCE HE REVIVED, HE COULD RETURN TO HIS OWN TIME AND PLACE. I HAD ONLY TO FIND HIS STAFF TO ACTIVATE IT.

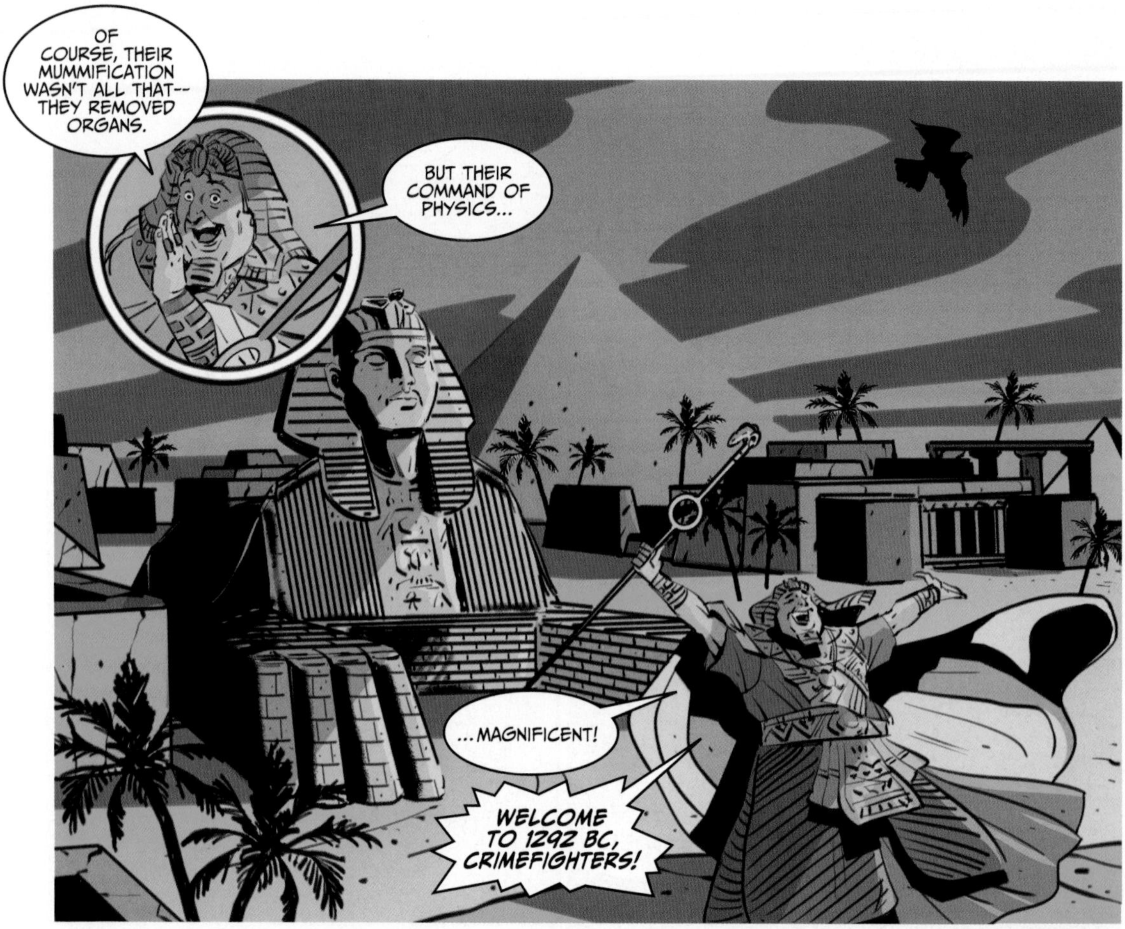
OF COURSE, THEIR MUMMIFICATION WASN'T ALL THAT-- THEY REMOVED ORGANS.
BUT THEIR COMMAND OF PHYSICS...
...MAGNIFICENT!
WELCOME TO 1292 BC, CRIMEFIGHTERS!

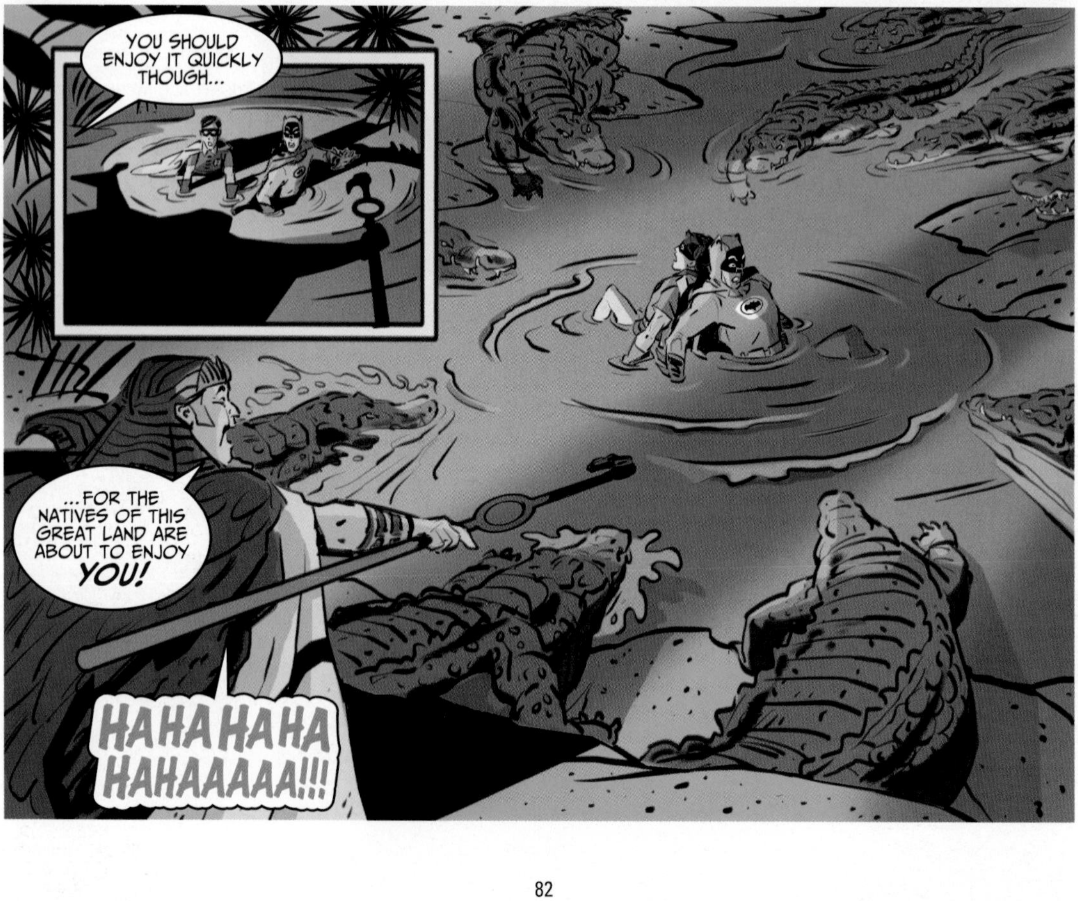
YOU SHOULD ENJOY IT QUICKLY THOUGH...
...FOR THE NATIVES OF THIS GREAT LAND ARE ABOUT TO ENJOY YOU!
HAHAHAHA HAHAAAAA!!!

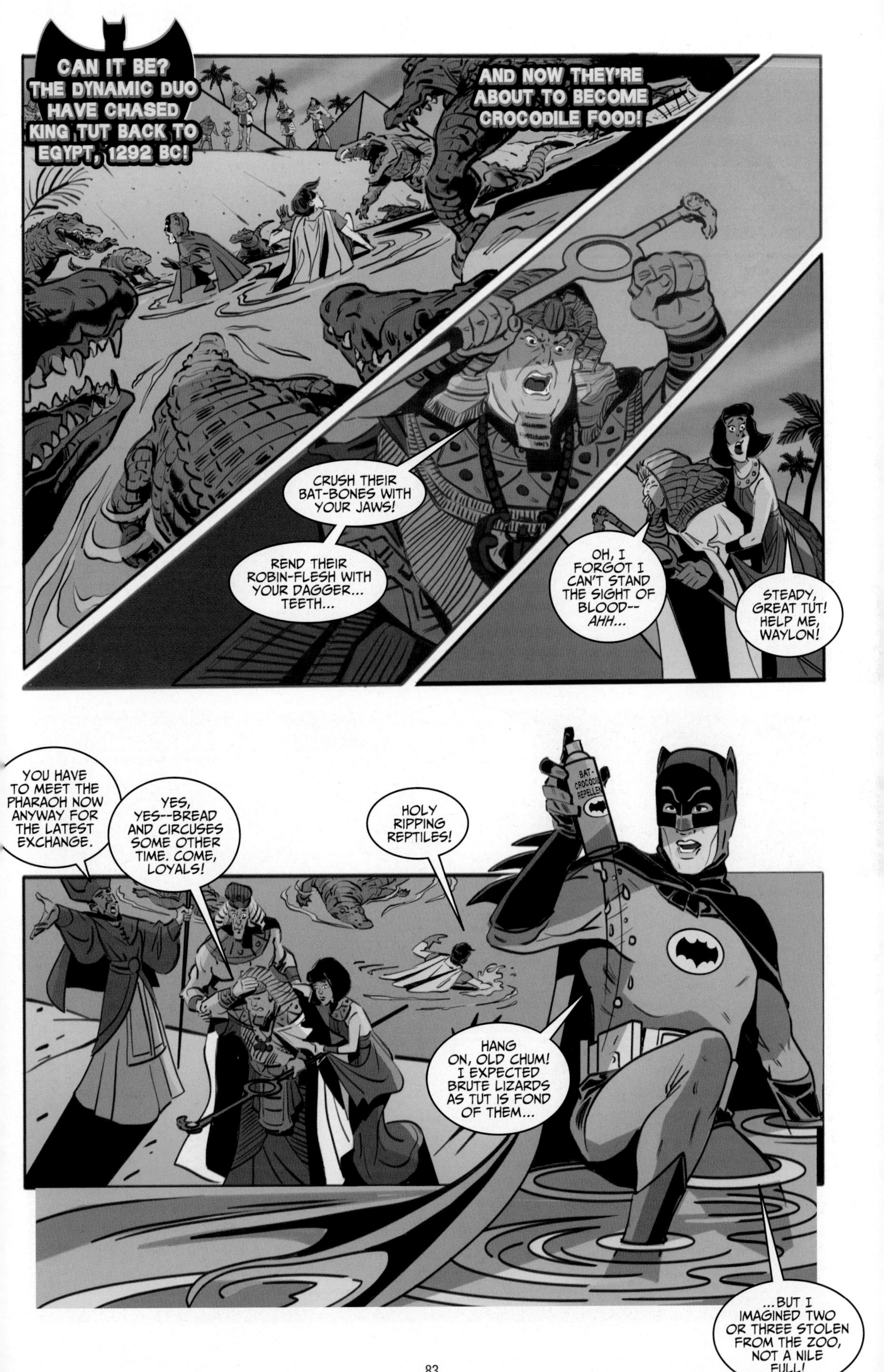
CAN IT BE? THE DYNAMIC DUO HAVE CHASED KING TUT BACK TO EGYPT, 1292 BC!
AND NOW THEY'RE ABOUT TO BECOME CROCODILE FOOD!
CRUSH THEIR BAT-BONES WITH YOUR JAWS!
REND THEIR ROBIN-FLESH WITH YOUR DAGGER... TEETH...
OH, I FORGOT I CAN'T STAND THE SIGHT OF BLOOD-- AHH...
STEADY, GREAT TUT! HELP ME, WAYLON!
YOU HAVE TO MEET THE PHARAOH NOW ANYWAY FOR THE LATEST EXCHANGE.
YES, YES--BREAD AND CIRCUSES SOME OTHER TIME. COME, LOYALS!
HOLY RIPPING REPTILES!
BAT-CROCODILE REPELLEN
HANG ON, OLD CHUM! I EXPECTED BRUTE LIZARDS AS TUT IS FOND OF THEM...
...BUT I IMAGINED TWO OR THREE STOLEN FROM THE ZOO, NOT A NILE FULL!

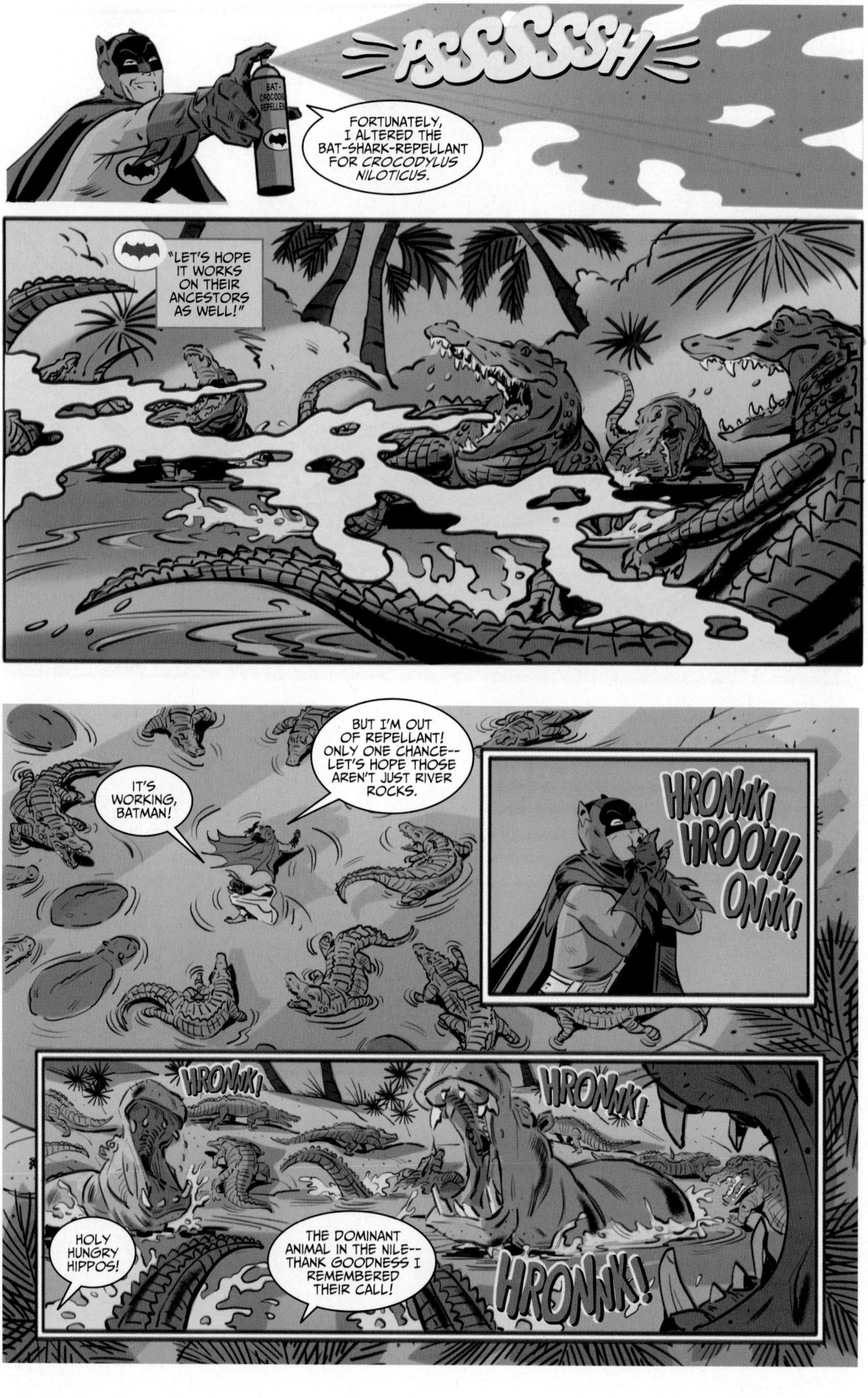

PSSSSSH
BAT-CROCODILE REPELLENT
FORTUNATELY, I ALTERED THE BAT-SHARK-REPELLANT FOR CROCODYLUS NILOTICUS.
"LET'S HOPE IT WORKS ON THEIR ANCESTORS AS WELL!"
IT'S WORKING, BATMAN!
BUT I'M OUT OF REPELLANT! ONLY ONE CHANCE--LET'S HOPE THOSE AREN'T JUST RIVER ROCKS.
HRONNK! HROOH!! ONNK!
HRONNK!
HRONNK!
HOLY HUNGRY HIPPOS!
THE DOMINANT ANIMAL IN THE NILE--THANK GOODNESS I REMEMBERED THEIR CALL!
HRONNK!

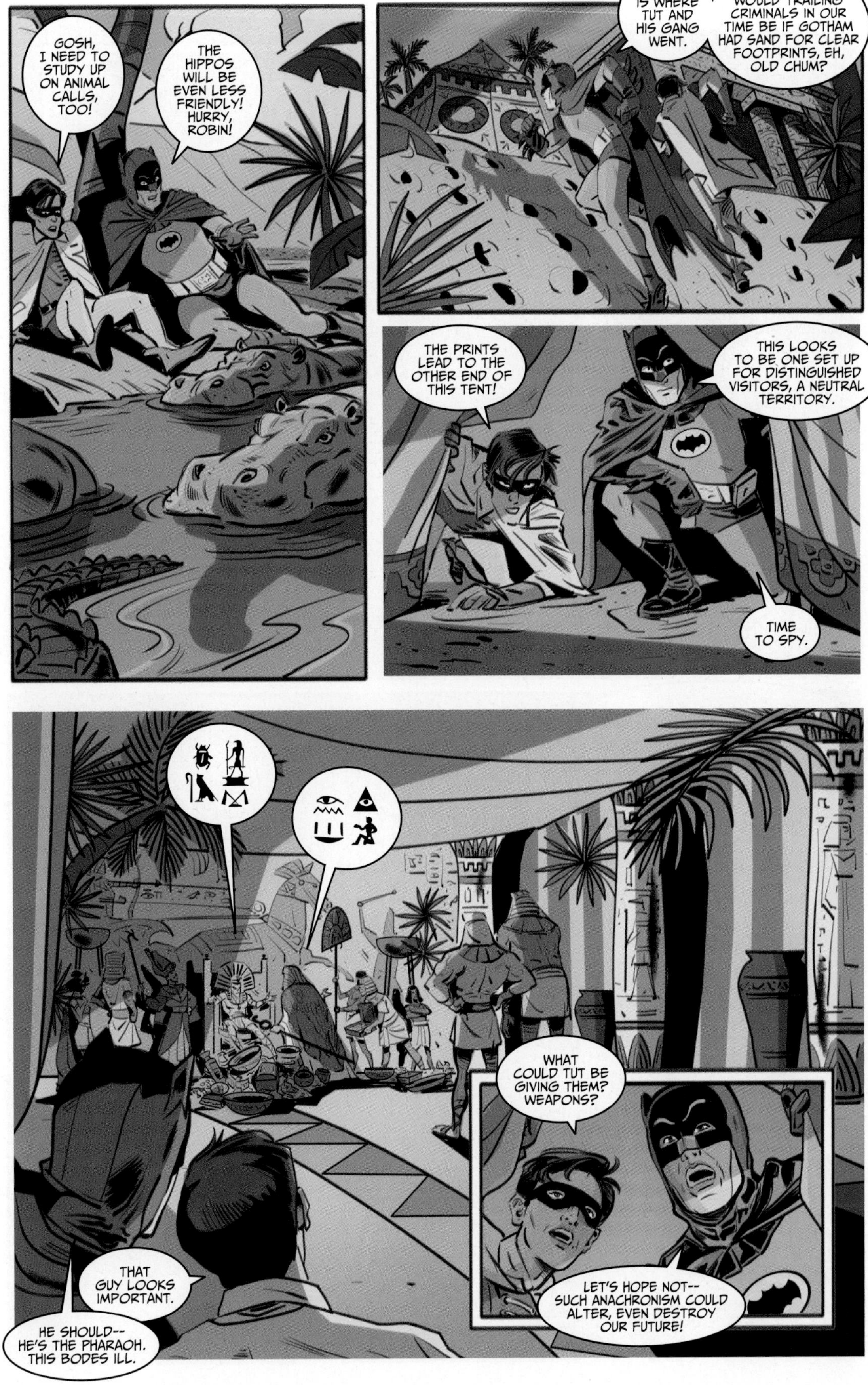
GOSH, I NEED TO STUDY UP ON ANIMAL CALLS, TOO!
THE HIPPOS WILL BE EVEN LESS FRIENDLY! HURRY, ROBIN!
THIS IS WHERE TUT AND HIS GANG WENT.
HOW EASY WOULD TRAILING CRIMINALS IN OUR TIME BE IF GOTHAM HAD SAND FOR CLEAR FOOTPRINTS, EH, OLD CHUM?
THE PRINTS LEAD TO THE OTHER END OF THIS TENT!
THIS LOOKS TO BE ONE SET UP FOR DISTINGUISHED VISITORS, A NEUTRAL TERRITORY.
TIME TO SPY.
THAT GUY LOOKS IMPORTANT.
HE SHOULD-- HE'S THE PHARAOH. THIS BODES ILL.
WHAT COULD TUT BE GIVING THEM? WEAPONS?
LET'S HOPE NOT-- SUCH ANACHRONISM COULD ALTER, EVEN DESTROY OUR FUTURE!

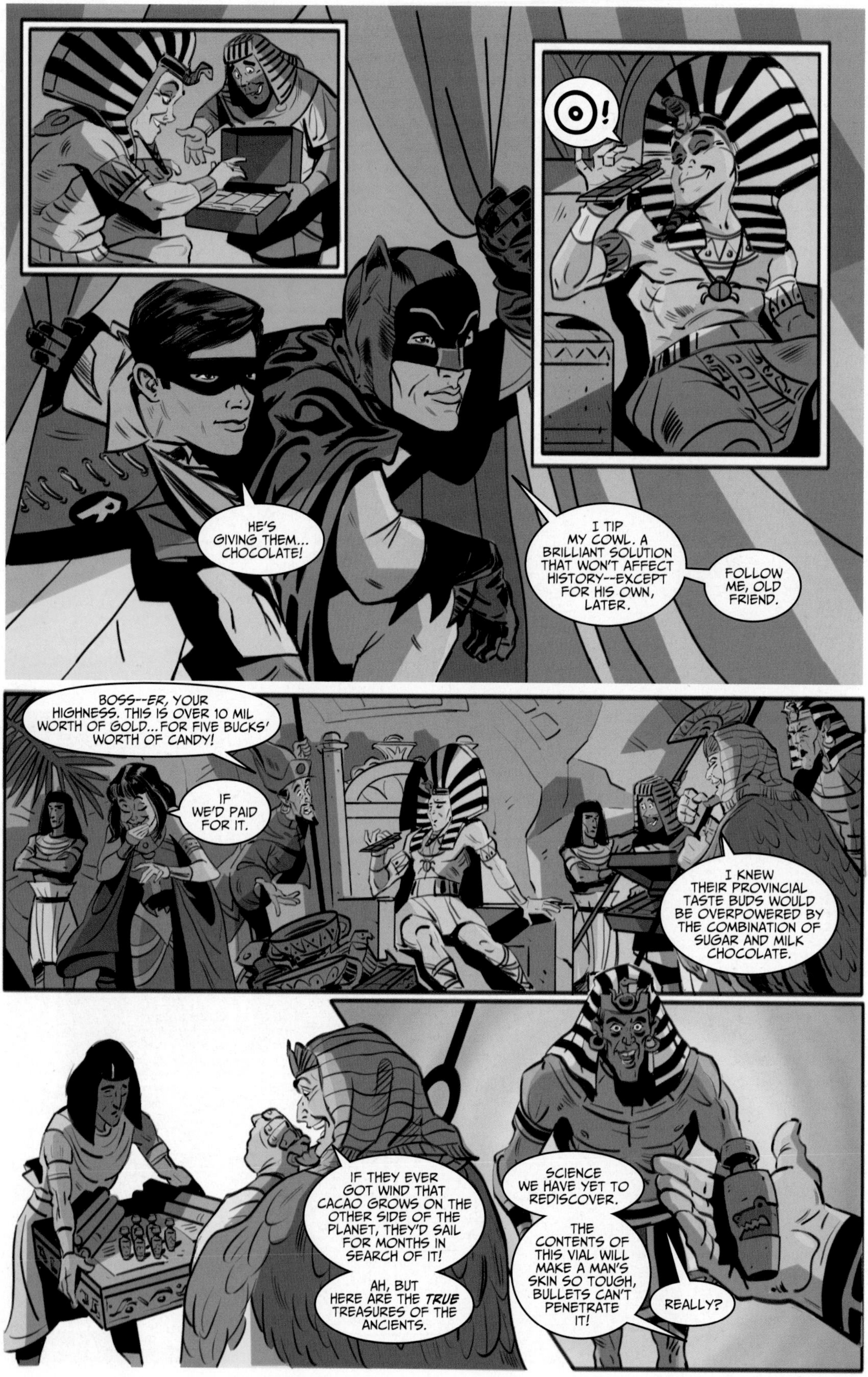
HE'S GIVING THEM... CHOCOLATE!
I TIP MY COWL. A BRILLIANT SOLUTION THAT WON'T AFFECT HISTORY--EXCEPT FOR HIS OWN, LATER.
FOLLOW ME, OLD FRIEND.
BOSS--ER, YOUR HIGHNESS. THIS IS OVER 10 MIL WORTH OF GOLD...FOR FIVE BUCKS' WORTH OF CANDY!
IF WE'D PAID FOR IT.
I KNEW THEIR PROVINCIAL TASTE BUDS WOULD BE OVERPOWERED BY THE COMBINATION OF SUGAR AND MILK CHOCOLATE.
IF THEY EVER GOT WIND THAT CACAO GROWS ON THE OTHER SIDE OF THE PLANET, THEY'D SAIL FOR MONTHS IN SEARCH OF IT!
AH, BUT HERE ARE THE *TRUE* TREASURES OF THE ANCIENTS.
SCIENCE WE HAVE YET TO REDISCOVER.
THE CONTENTS OF THIS VIAL WILL MAKE A MAN'S SKIN SO TOUGH, BULLETS CAN'T PENETRATE IT!
REALLY?

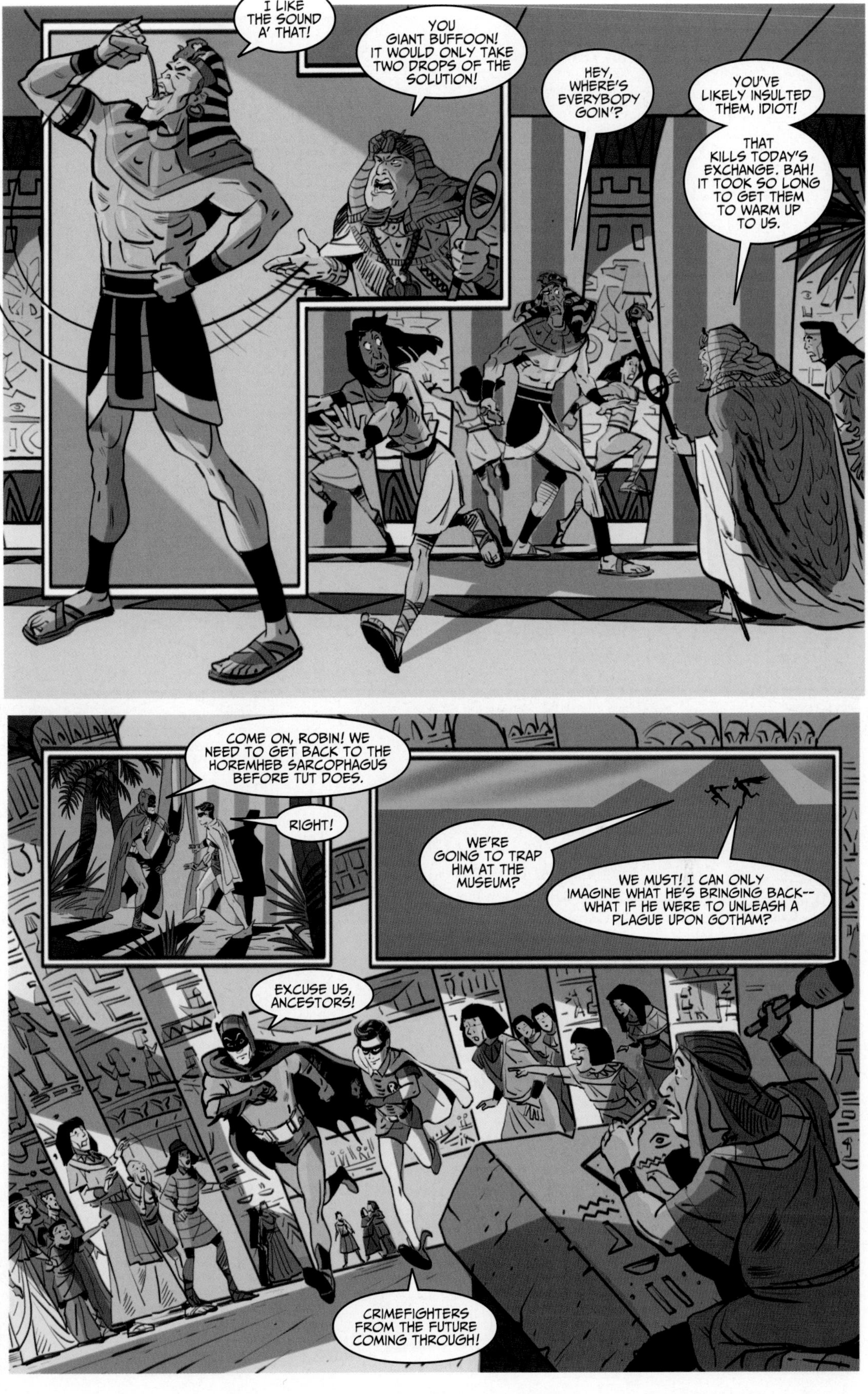
I LIKE THE SOUND A' THAT!
YOU GIANT BUFFOON! IT WOULD ONLY TAKE TWO DROPS OF THE SOLUTION!
HEY, WHERE'S EVERYBODY GOIN'?
YOU'VE LIKELY INSULTED THEM, IDIOT!
THAT KILLS TODAY'S EXCHANGE. BAH! IT TOOK SO LONG TO GET THEM TO WARM UP TO US.
COME ON, ROBIN! WE NEED TO GET BACK TO THE HOREMHEB SARCOPHAGUS BEFORE TUT DOES.
RIGHT!
WE'RE GOING TO TRAP HIM AT THE MUSEUM?
WE MUST! I CAN ONLY IMAGINE WHAT HE'S BRINGING BACK-- WHAT IF HE WERE TO UNLEASH A PLAGUE UPON GOTHAM?
EXCUSE US, ANCESTORS!
CRIMEFIGHTERS FROM THE FUTURE COMING THROUGH!

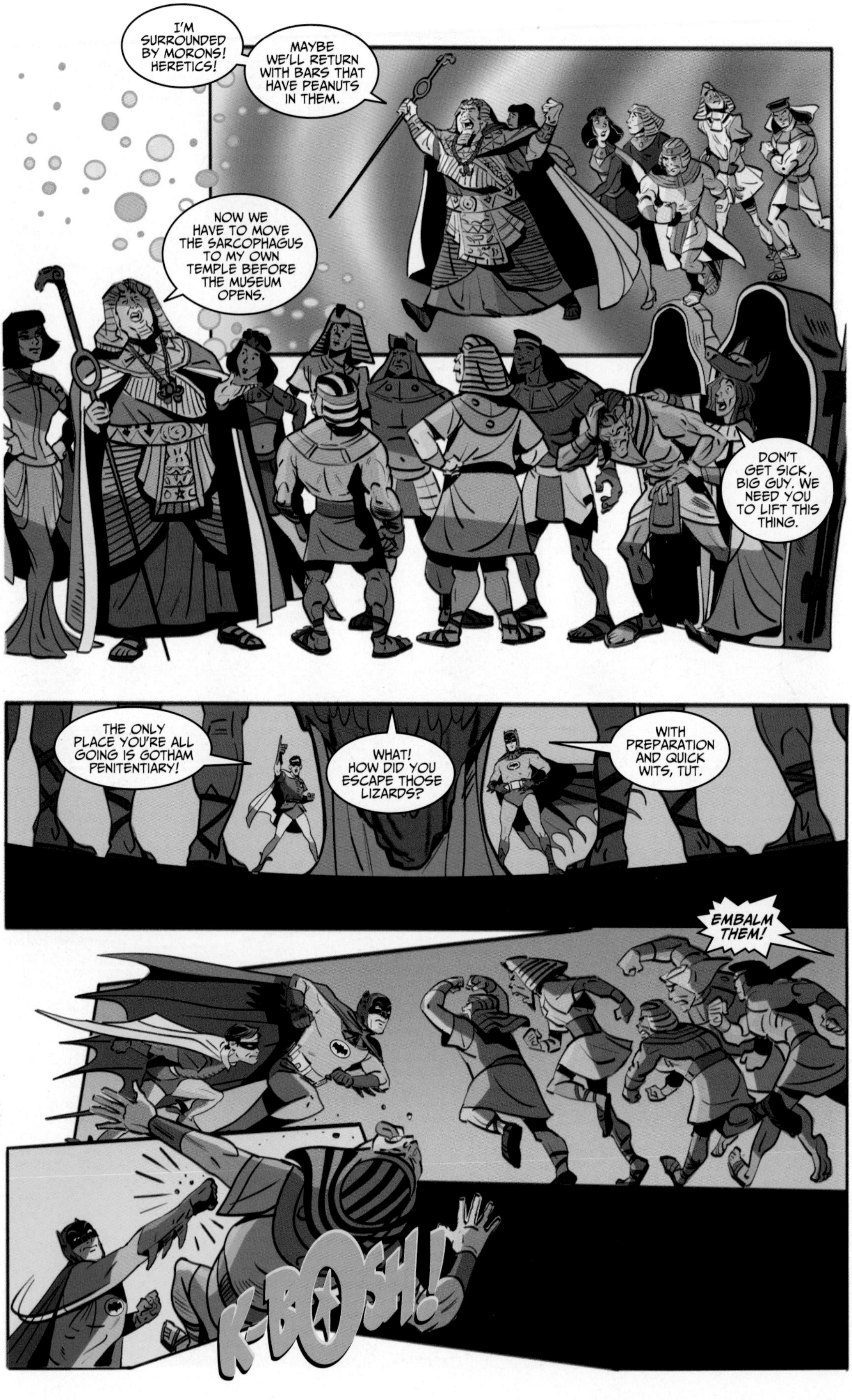
I'M SURROUNDED BY MORONS! HERETICS!
MAYBE WE'LL RETURN WITH BARS THAT HAVE PEANUTS IN THEM.
NOW WE HAVE TO MOVE THE SARCOPHAGUS TO MY OWN TEMPLE BEFORE THE MUSEUM OPENS.
DON'T GET SICK, BIG GUY. WE NEED YOU TO LIFT THIS THING.
THE ONLY PLACE YOU'RE ALL GOING IS GOTHAM PENITENTIARY!
WHAT! HOW DID YOU ESCAPE THOSE LIZARDS?
WITH PREPARATION AND QUICK WITS, TUT.
EMBALM THEM!
K-BOSH!

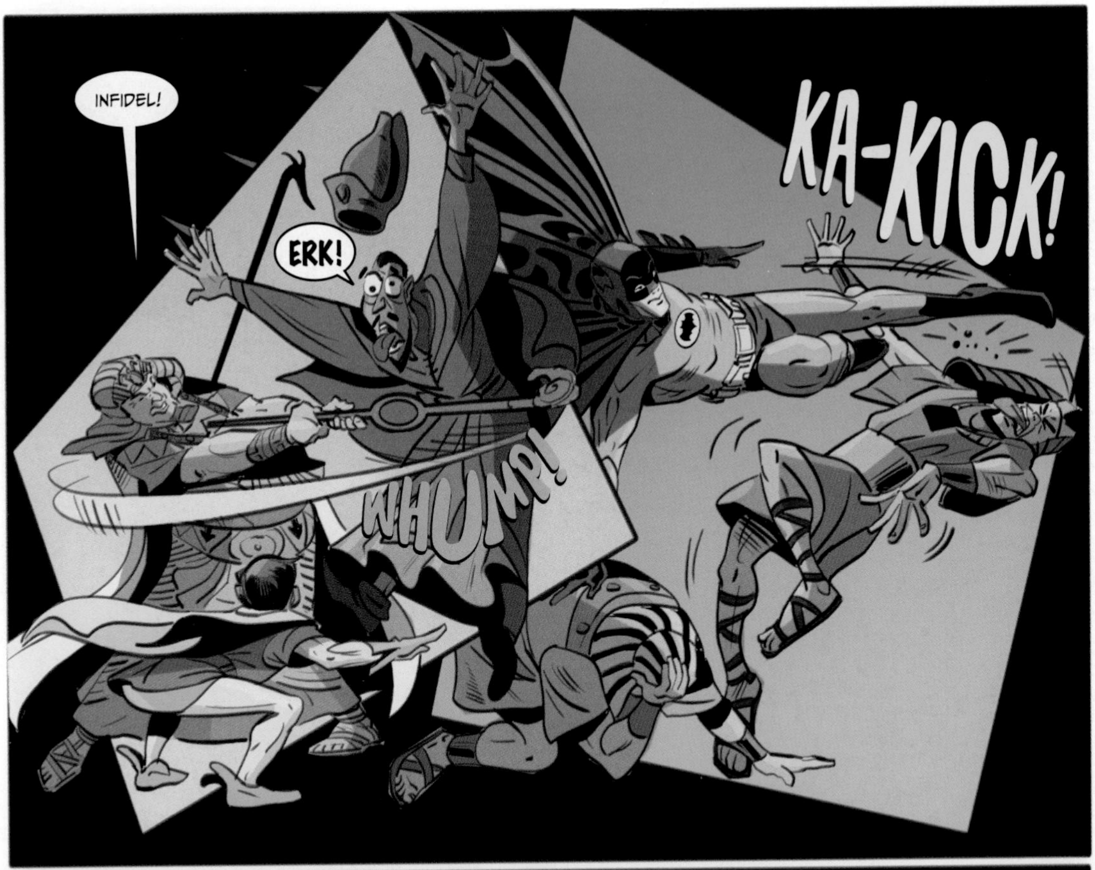
INFIDEL!
ERK!
KA-KICK!
WHUMP!

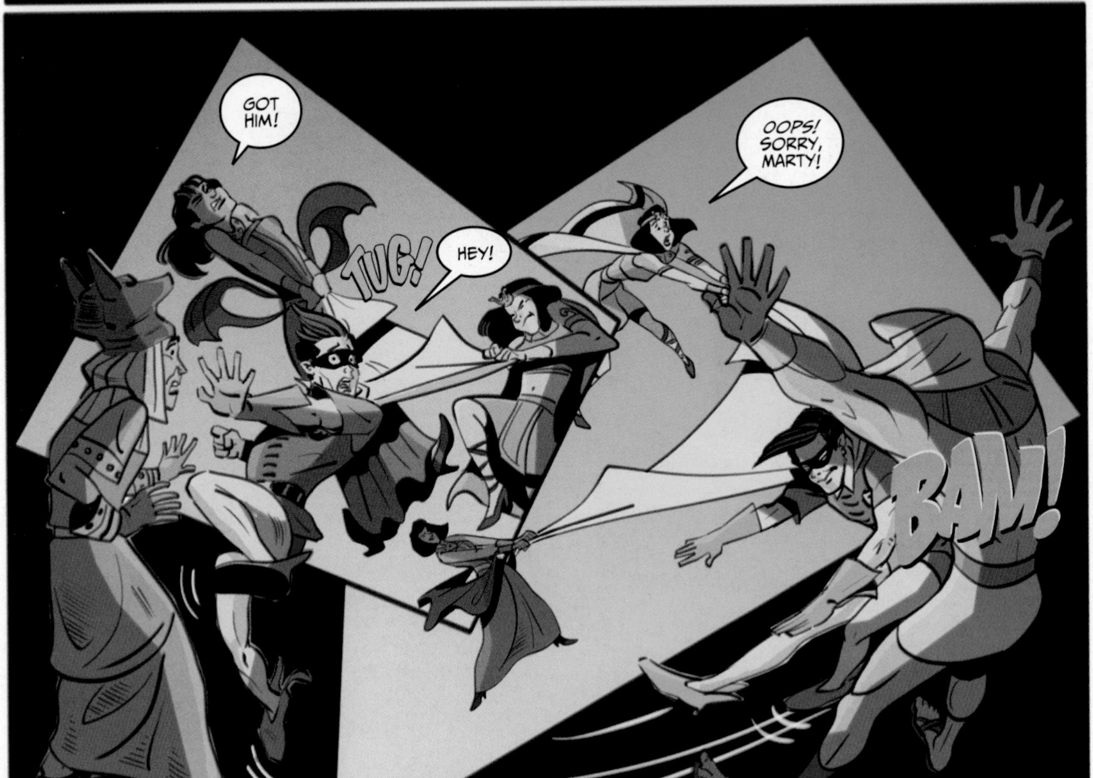
GOT HIM!
TUG!
HEY!
OOPS! SORRY, MARTY!
BAM!

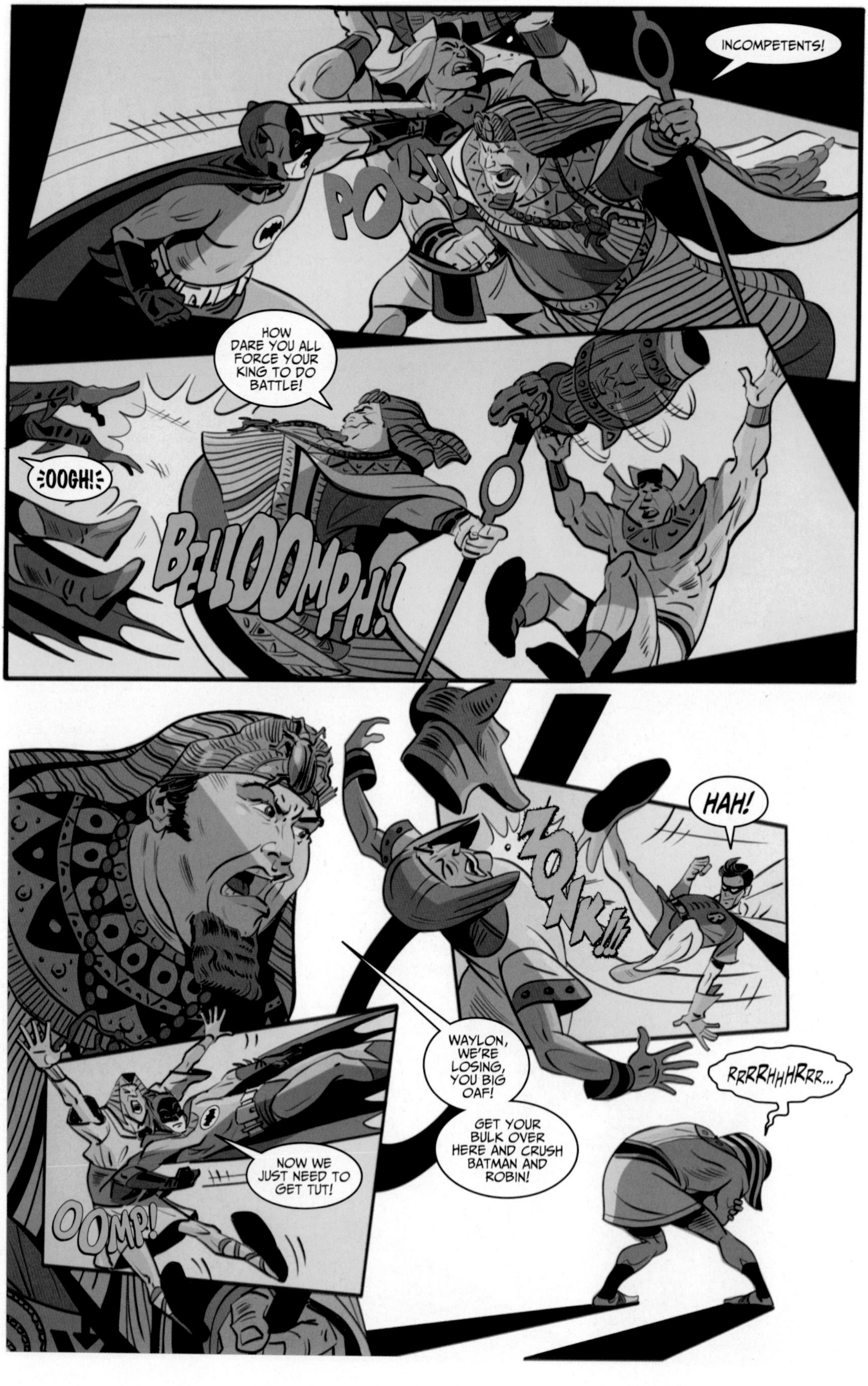
INCOMPETENTS!
POK!!
HOW DARE YOU ALL FORCE YOUR KING TO DO BATTLE!
OOGH!
BELLOOMPH!
HAH!
ZONK!!!
WAYLON, WE'RE LOSING, YOU BIG OAF!
GET YOUR BULK OVER HERE AND CRUSH BATMAN AND ROBIN!
RRRRHHHRRR...
NOW WE JUST NEED TO GET TUT!
OOMP!

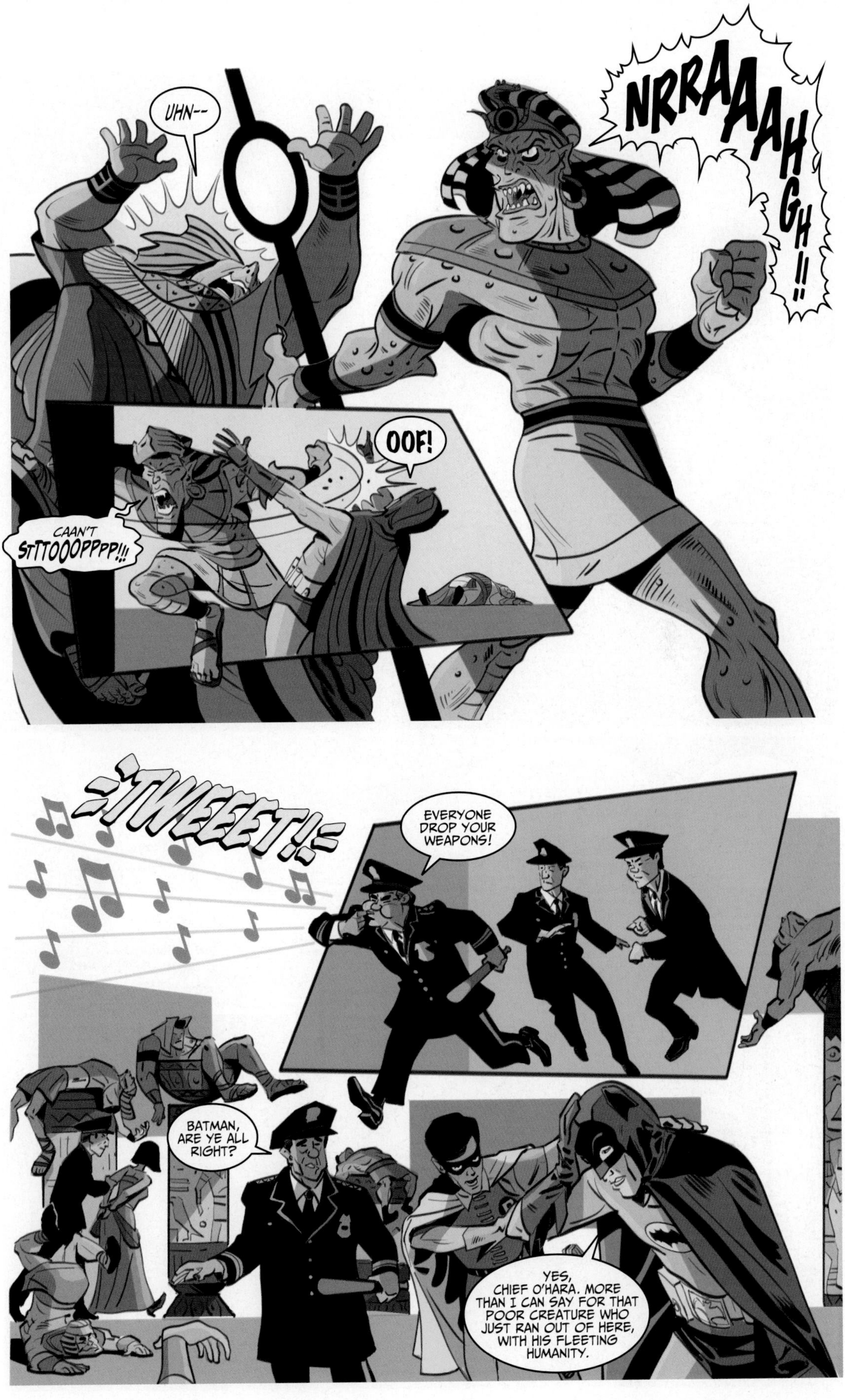
UHN--
NRRAAAAHGH!!
OOF!
CAAN'T STTTOOOPPPP!!!
TWEEET!!
EVERYONE DROP YOUR WEAPONS!
BATMAN, ARE YE ALL RIGHT?
YES, CHIEF O'HARA. MORE THAN I CAN SAY FOR THAT POOR CREATURE WHO JUST RAN OUT OF HERE, WITH HIS FLEETING HUMANITY.

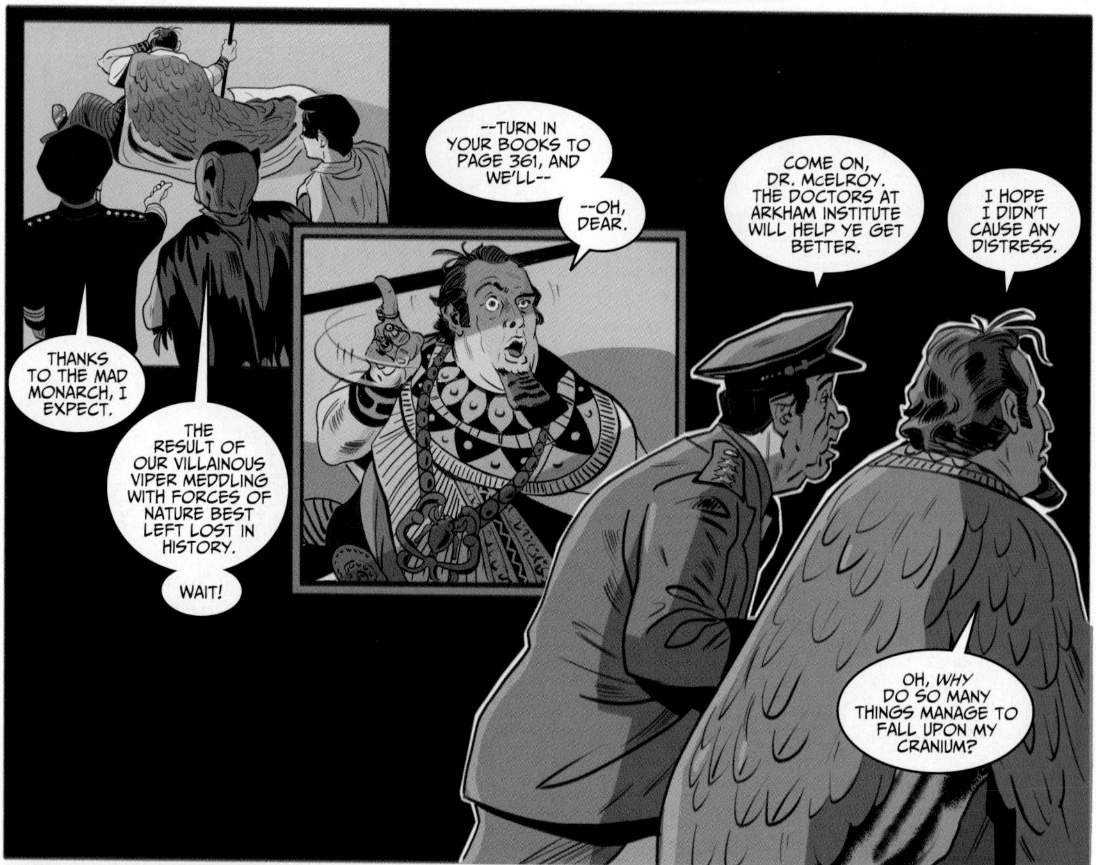
THANKS TO THE MAD MONARCH, I EXPECT.
THE RESULT OF OUR VILLAINOUS VIPER MEDDLING WITH FORCES OF NATURE BEST LEFT LOST IN HISTORY.
WAIT!
--TURN IN YOUR BOOKS TO PAGE 361, AND WE'LL--
--OH, DEAR.
COME ON, DR. McELROY. THE DOCTORS AT ARKHAM INSTITUTE WILL HELP YE GET BETTER.
I HOPE I DIDN'T CAUSE ANY DISTRESS.
OH, WHY DO SO MANY THINGS MANAGE TO FALL UPON MY CRANIUM?

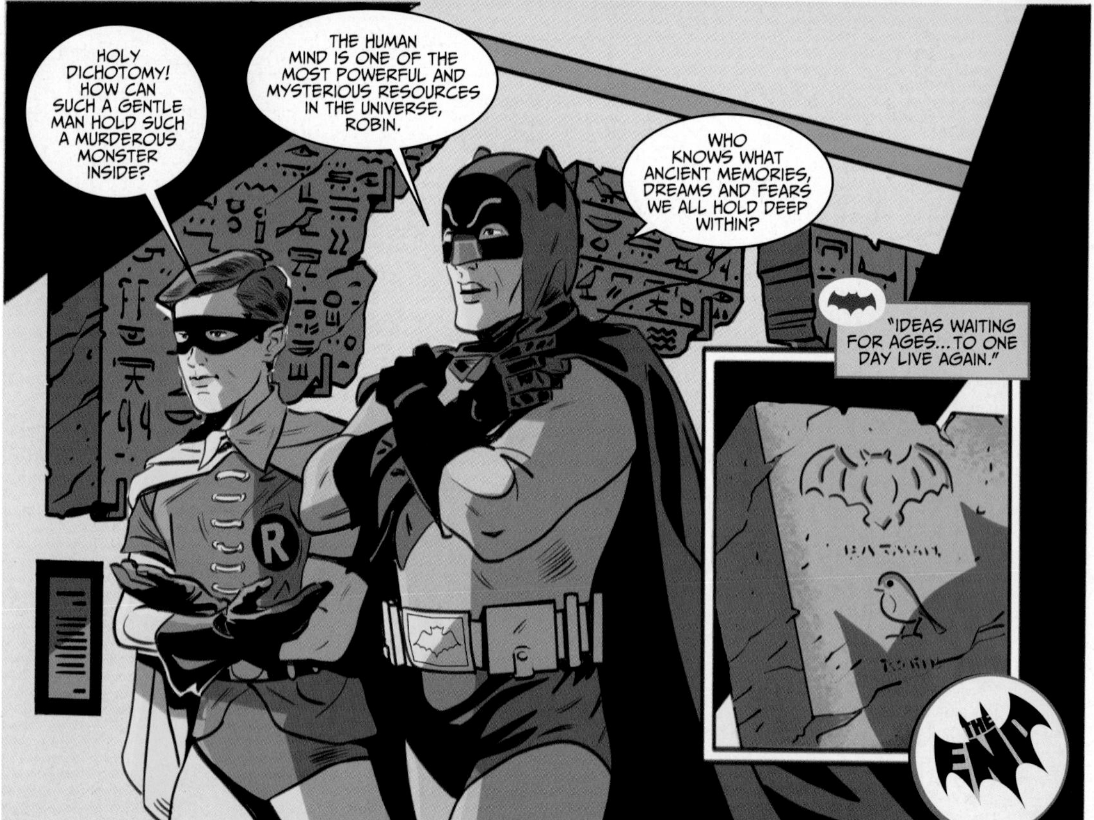
HOLY DICHOTOMY! HOW CAN SUCH A GENTLE MAN HOLD SUCH A MURDEROUS MONSTER INSIDE?
THE HUMAN MIND IS ONE OF THE MOST POWERFUL AND MYSTERIOUS RESOURCES IN THE UNIVERSE, ROBIN.
WHO KNOWS WHAT ANCIENT MEMORIES, DREAMS AND FEARS WE ALL HOLD DEEP WITHIN?
"IDEAS WAITING FOR AGES...TO ONE DAY LIVE AGAIN."
THE END

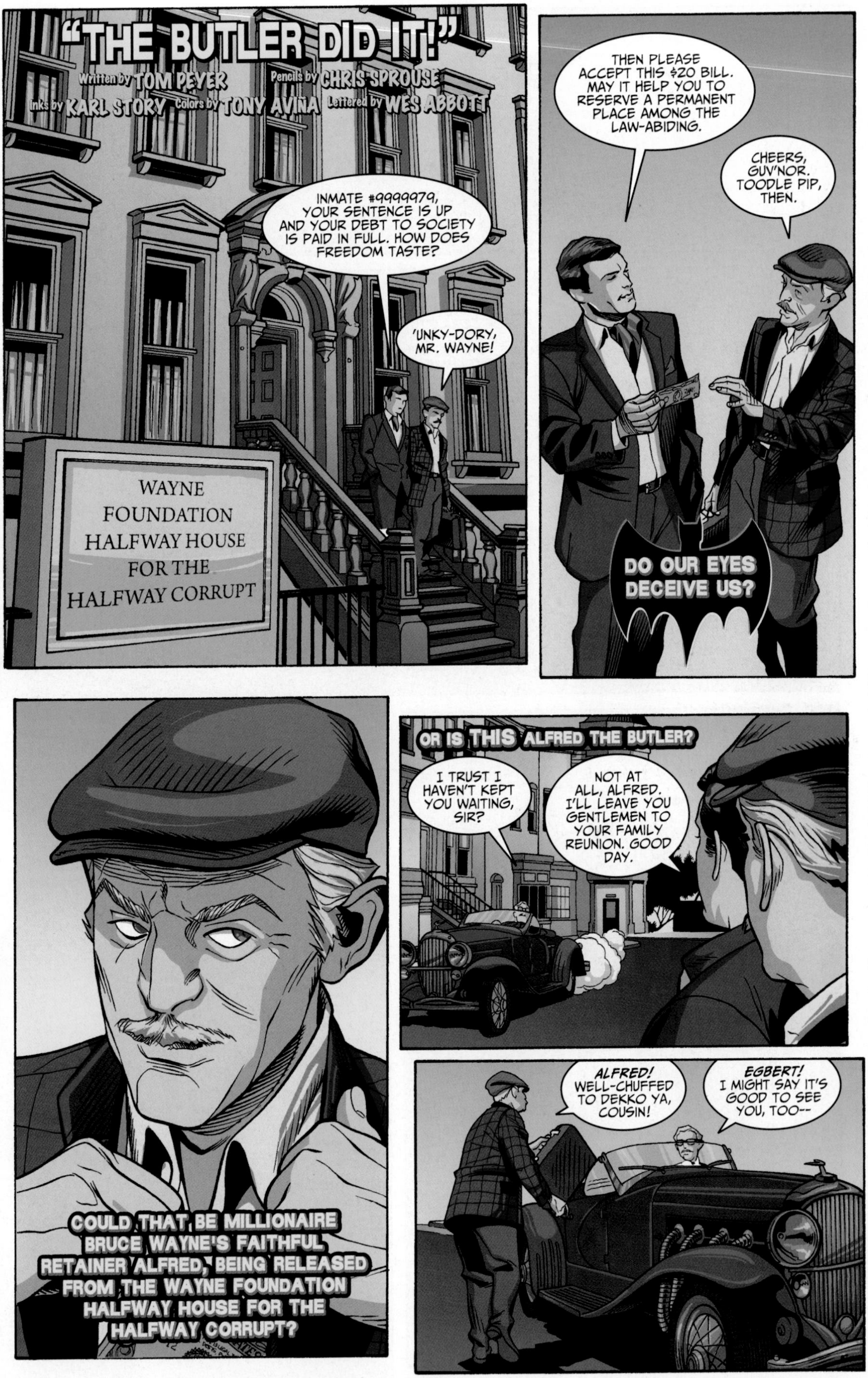

"THE BUTLER DID IT!"
Written by TOM PEYER Pencils by CHRIS SPROUSE
Inks by KARL STORY Colors by TONY AVIÑA Lettered by WES ABBOTT
INMATE #9999979, YOUR SENTENCE IS UP AND YOUR DEBT TO SOCIETY IS PAID IN FULL. HOW DOES FREEDOM TASTE?
'UNKY-DORY, MR. WAYNE!
WAYNE FOUNDATION HALFWAY HOUSE FOR THE HALFWAY CORRUPT
THEN PLEASE ACCEPT THIS $20 BILL. MAY IT HELP YOU TO RESERVE A PERMANENT PLACE AMONG THE LAW-ABIDING.
CHEERS, GUV'NOR. TOODLE PIP, THEN.
DO OUR EYES DECEIVE US?
COULD THAT BE MILLIONAIRE BRUCE WAYNE'S FAITHFUL RETAINER ALFRED, BEING RELEASED FROM THE WAYNE FOUNDATION HALFWAY HOUSE FOR THE HALFWAY CORRUPT?
OR IS THIS ALFRED THE BUTLER?
I TRUST I HAVEN'T KEPT YOU WAITING, SIR?
NOT AT ALL, ALFRED. I'LL LEAVE YOU GENTLEMEN TO YOUR FAMILY REUNION. GOOD DAY.
ALFRED! WELL-CHUFFED TO DEKKO YA, COUSIN!
EGBERT! I MIGHT SAY IT'S GOOD TO SEE YOU, TOO--

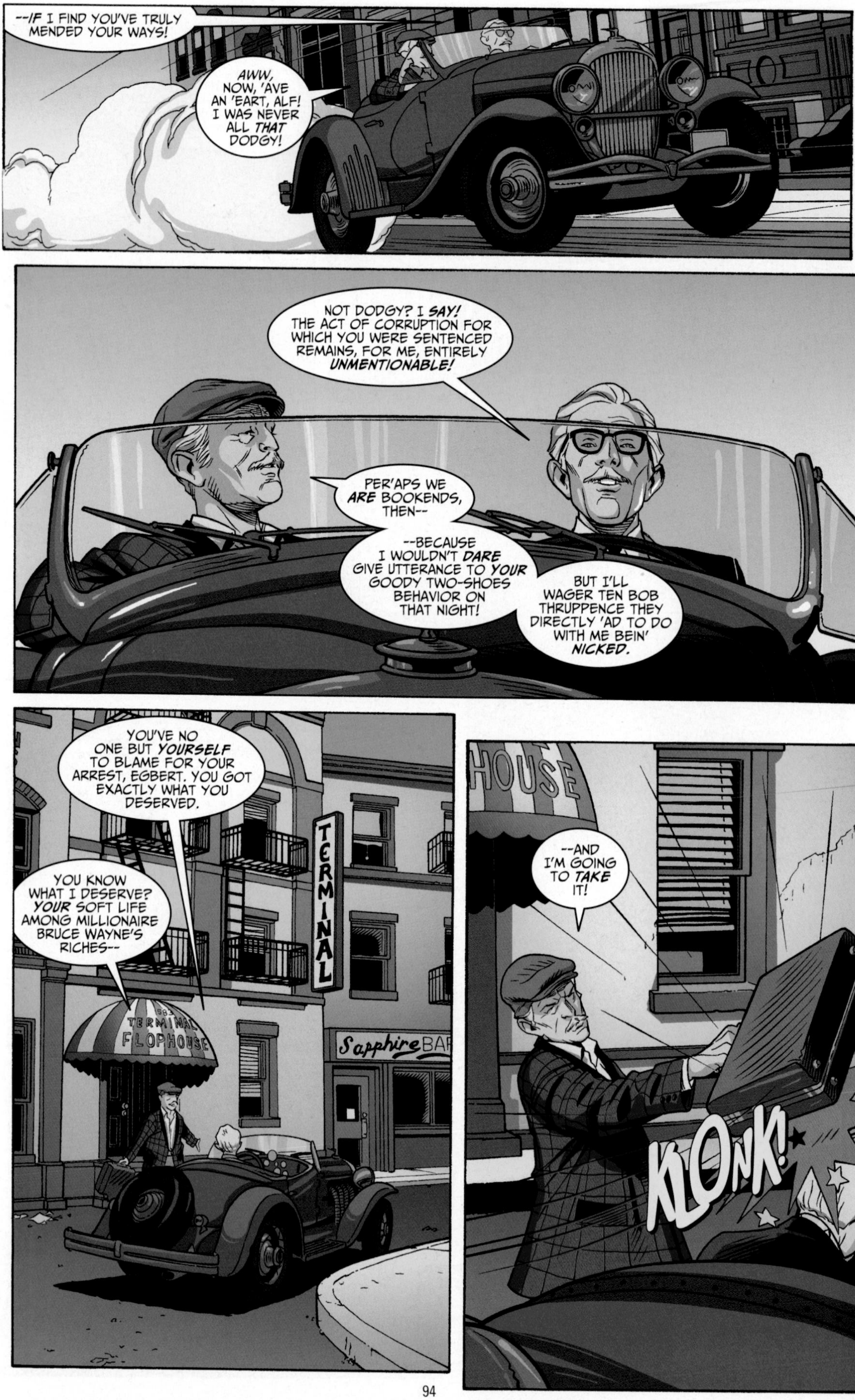
--IF I FIND YOU'VE TRULY MENDED YOUR WAYS!
AWW, NOW, 'AVE AN 'EART, ALF! I WAS NEVER ALL THAT DODGY!
NOT DODGY? I SAY! THE ACT OF CORRUPTION FOR WHICH YOU WERE SENTENCED REMAINS, FOR ME, ENTIRELY UNMENTIONABLE!
PER'APS WE ARE BOOKENDS, THEN--
--BECAUSE I WOULDN'T DARE GIVE UTTERANCE TO YOUR GOODY TWO-SHOES BEHAVIOR ON THAT NIGHT!
BUT I'LL WAGER TEN BOB THRUPPENCE THEY DIRECTLY 'AD TO DO WITH ME BEIN' NICKED.
YOU'VE NO ONE BUT YOURSELF TO BLAME FOR YOUR ARREST, EGBERT. YOU GOT EXACTLY WHAT YOU DESERVED.
YOU KNOW WHAT I DESERVE? YOUR SOFT LIFE AMONG MILLIONAIRE BRUCE WAYNE'S RICHES--
TERMINAL
583 TERMINAL FLOPHOUSE
Sapphire BAR
--AND I'M GOING TO TAKE IT!
HOUSE
KLONK!

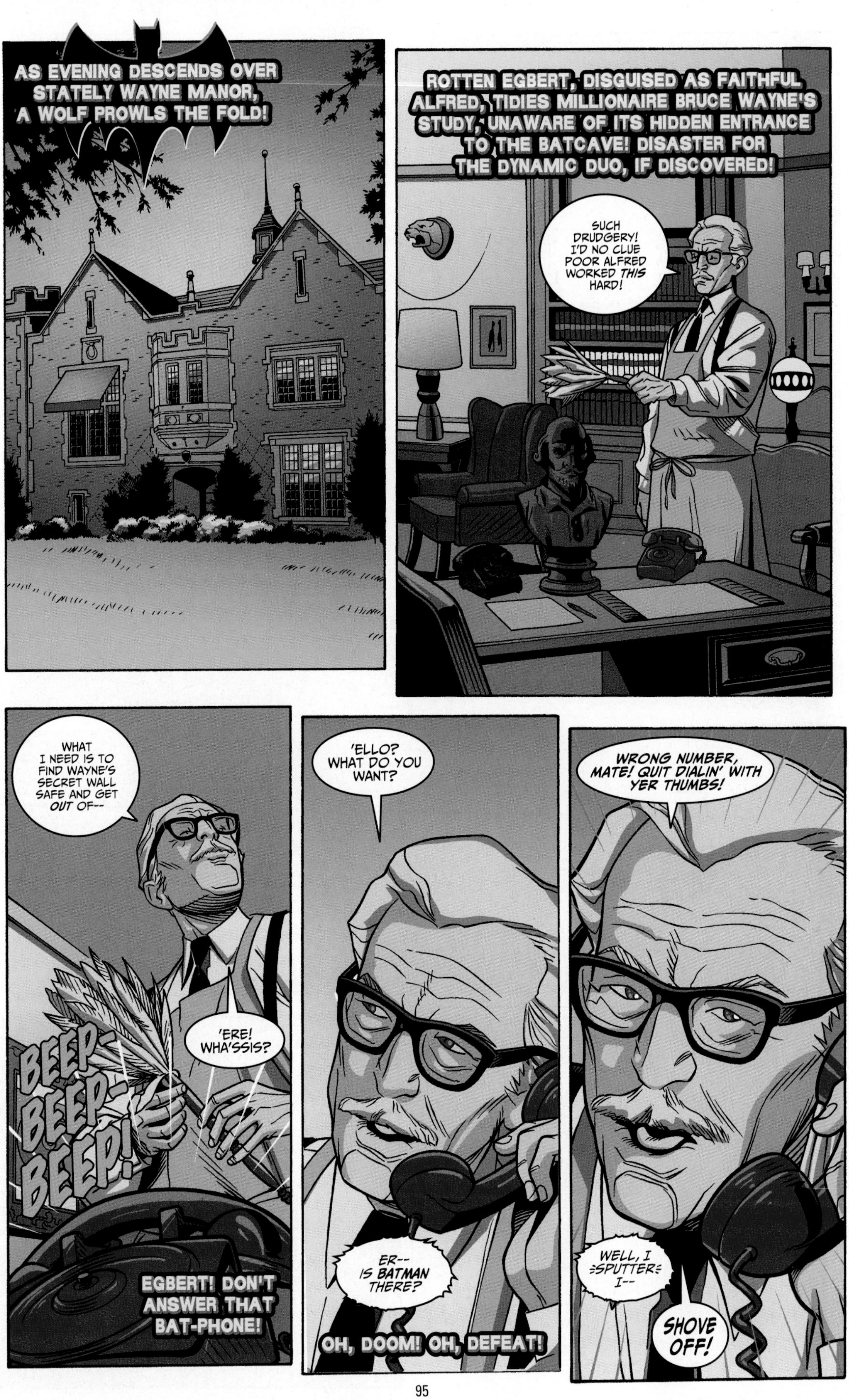
AS EVENING DESCENDS OVER STATELY WAYNE MANOR, A WOLF PROWLS THE FOLD!
ROTTEN EGBERT, DISGUISED AS FAITHFUL ALFRED, TIDIES MILLIONAIRE BRUCE WAYNE'S STUDY, UNAWARE OF ITS HIDDEN ENTRANCE TO THE BATCAVE! DISASTER FOR THE DYNAMIC DUO, IF DISCOVERED!
SUCH DRUDGERY! I'D NO CLUE POOR ALFRED WORKED *THIS* HARD!
WHAT I NEED IS TO FIND WAYNE'S SECRET WALL SAFE AND GET *OUT* OF--
BEEP-BEEP-BEEP!
'ERE! WHA'SSIS?
EGBERT! DON'T ANSWER THAT BAT-PHONE!
'ELLO? WHAT DO YOU WANT?
ER-- IS *BATMAN* THERE?
OH, DOOM! OH, DEFEAT!
WRONG NUMBER, MATE! QUIT DIALIN' WITH YER THUMBS!
WELL, I *SPUTTER* I--
SHOVE OFF!

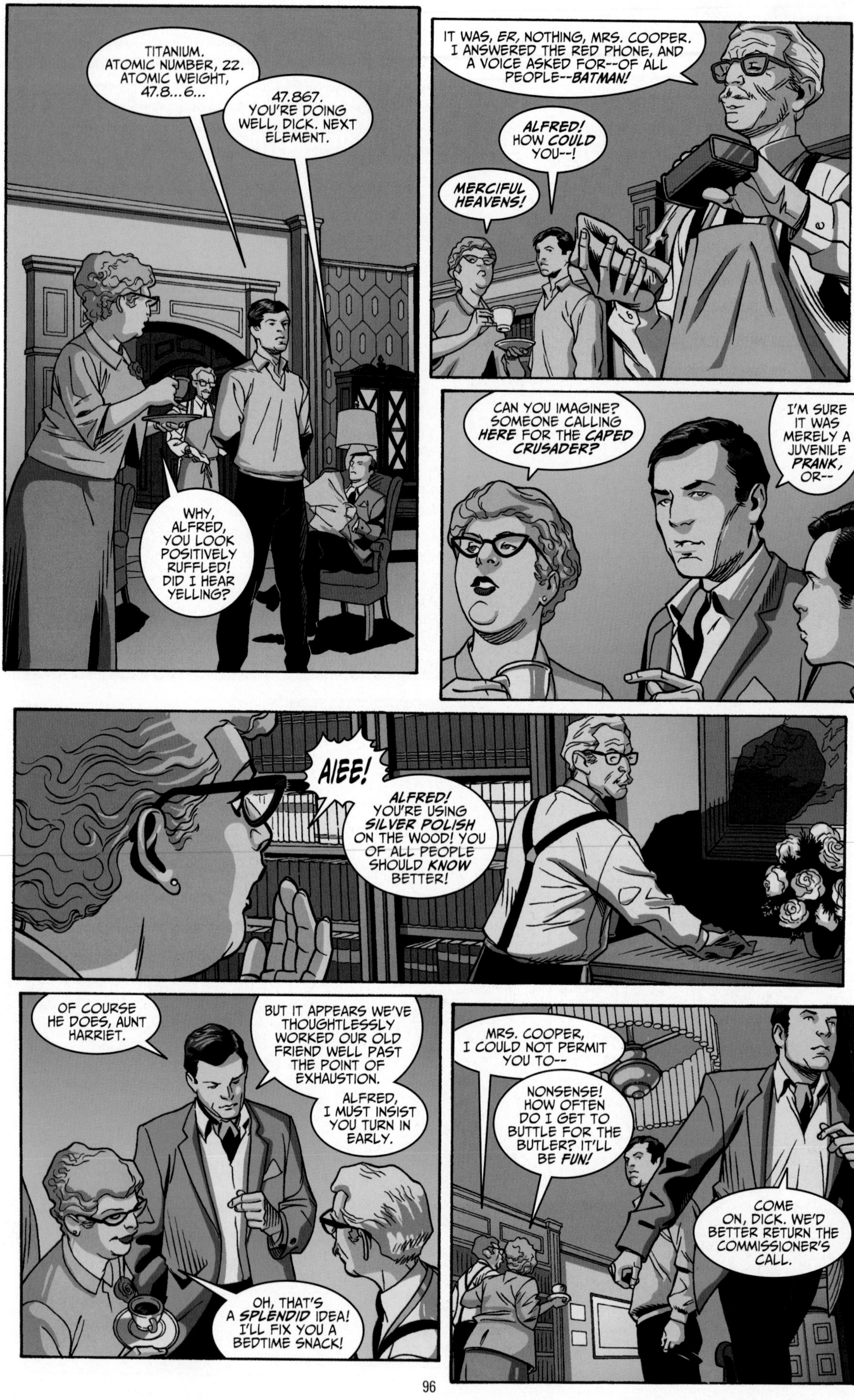
TITANIUM. ATOMIC NUMBER, 22. ATOMIC WEIGHT, 47.8...6...
47.867. YOU'RE DOING WELL, DICK. NEXT ELEMENT.
WHY, ALFRED, YOU LOOK POSITIVELY RUFFLED! DID I HEAR YELLING?
IT WAS, ER, NOTHING, MRS. COOPER. I ANSWERED THE RED PHONE, AND A VOICE ASKED FOR--OF ALL PEOPLE--BATMAN!
ALFRED! HOW COULD YOU--!
MERCIFUL HEAVENS!
CAN YOU IMAGINE? SOMEONE CALLING HERE FOR THE CAPED CRUSADER?
I'M SURE IT WAS MERELY A JUVENILE PRANK, OR--
AIEE!
ALFRED! YOU'RE USING SILVER POLISH ON THE WOOD! YOU OF ALL PEOPLE SHOULD KNOW BETTER!
OF COURSE HE DOES, AUNT HARRIET.
BUT IT APPEARS WE'VE THOUGHTLESSLY WORKED OUR OLD FRIEND WELL PAST THE POINT OF EXHAUSTION.
ALFRED, I MUST INSIST YOU TURN IN EARLY.
OH, THAT'S A SPLENDID IDEA! I'LL FIX YOU A BEDTIME SNACK!
MRS. COOPER, I COULD NOT PERMIT YOU TO--
NONSENSE! HOW OFTEN DO I GET TO BUTTLE FOR THE BUTLER? IT'LL BE FUN!
COME ON, DICK. WE'D BETTER RETURN THE COMMISSIONER'S CALL.

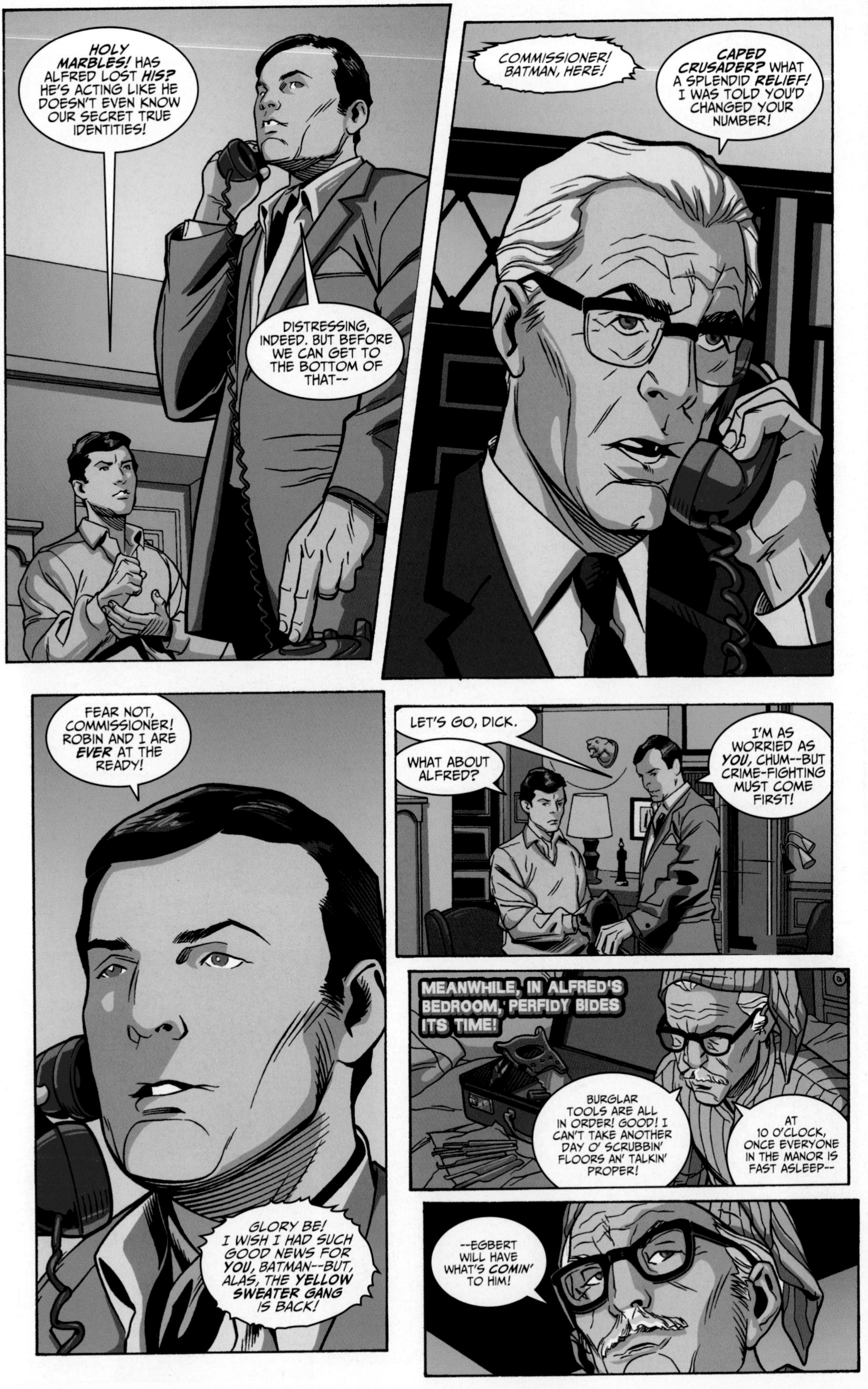
HOLY MARBLES! HAS ALFRED LOST HIS? HE'S ACTING LIKE HE DOESN'T EVEN KNOW OUR SECRET TRUE IDENTITIES!
DISTRESSING, INDEED. BUT BEFORE WE CAN GET TO THE BOTTOM OF THAT--
COMMISSIONER! BATMAN, HERE!
CAPED CRUSADER? WHAT A SPLENDID RELIEF! I WAS TOLD YOU'D CHANGED YOUR NUMBER!
FEAR NOT, COMMISSIONER! ROBIN AND I ARE EVER AT THE READY!
GLORY BE! I WISH I HAD SUCH GOOD NEWS FOR YOU, BATMAN--BUT, ALAS, THE YELLOW SWEATER GANG IS BACK!
LET'S GO, DICK.
WHAT ABOUT ALFRED?
I'M AS WORRIED AS YOU, CHUM--BUT CRIME-FIGHTING MUST COME FIRST!
MEANWHILE, IN ALFRED'S BEDROOM, PERFIDY BIDES ITS TIME!
BURGLAR TOOLS ARE ALL IN ORDER! GOOD! I CAN'T TAKE ANOTHER DAY O' SCRUBBIN' FLOORS AN' TALKIN' PROPER!
AT 10 O'CLOCK, ONCE EVERYONE IN THE MANOR IS FAST ASLEEP--
--EGBERT WILL HAVE WHAT'S COMIN' TO HIM!

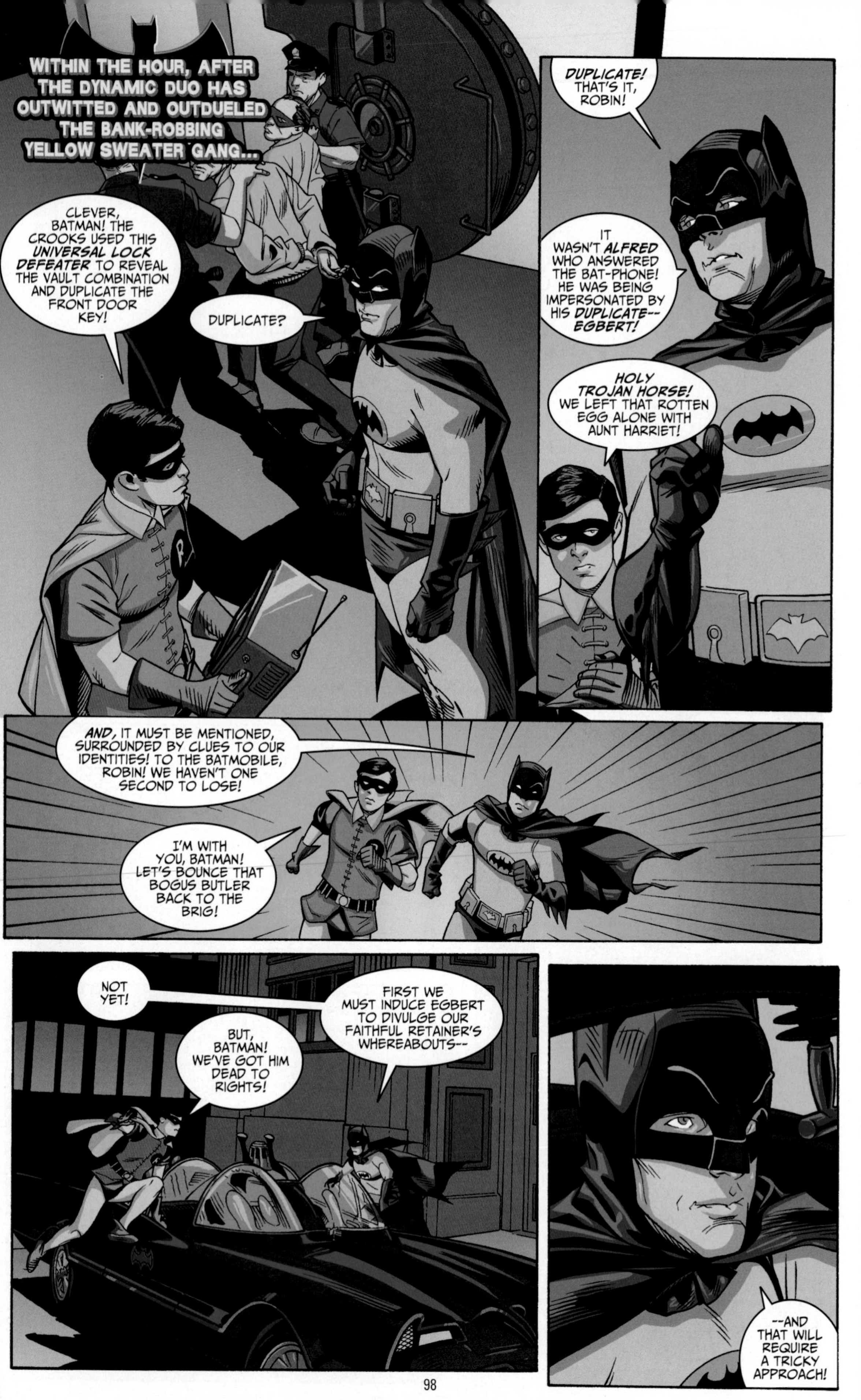
WITHIN THE HOUR, AFTER THE DYNAMIC DUO HAS OUTWITTED AND OUTDUELED THE BANK-ROBBING YELLOW SWEATER GANG...
CLEVER, BATMAN! THE CROOKS USED THIS UNIVERSAL LOCK DEFEATER TO REVEAL THE VAULT COMBINATION AND DUPLICATE THE FRONT DOOR KEY!
DUPLICATE?
DUPLICATE! THAT'S IT, ROBIN!
IT WASN'T ALFRED WHO ANSWERED THE BAT-PHONE! HE WAS BEING IMPERSONATED BY HIS DUPLICATE-- EGBERT!
HOLY TROJAN HORSE! WE LEFT THAT ROTTEN EGG ALONE WITH AUNT HARRIET!
AND, IT MUST BE MENTIONED, SURROUNDED BY CLUES TO OUR IDENTITIES! TO THE BATMOBILE, ROBIN! WE HAVEN'T ONE SECOND TO LOSE!
I'M WITH YOU, BATMAN! LET'S BOUNCE THAT BOGUS BUTLER BACK TO THE BRIG!
NOT YET!
FIRST WE MUST INDUCE EGBERT TO DIVULGE OUR FAITHFUL RETAINER'S WHEREABOUTS--
BUT, BATMAN! WE'VE GOT HIM DEAD TO RIGHTS!
--AND THAT WILL REQUIRE A TRICKY APPROACH!

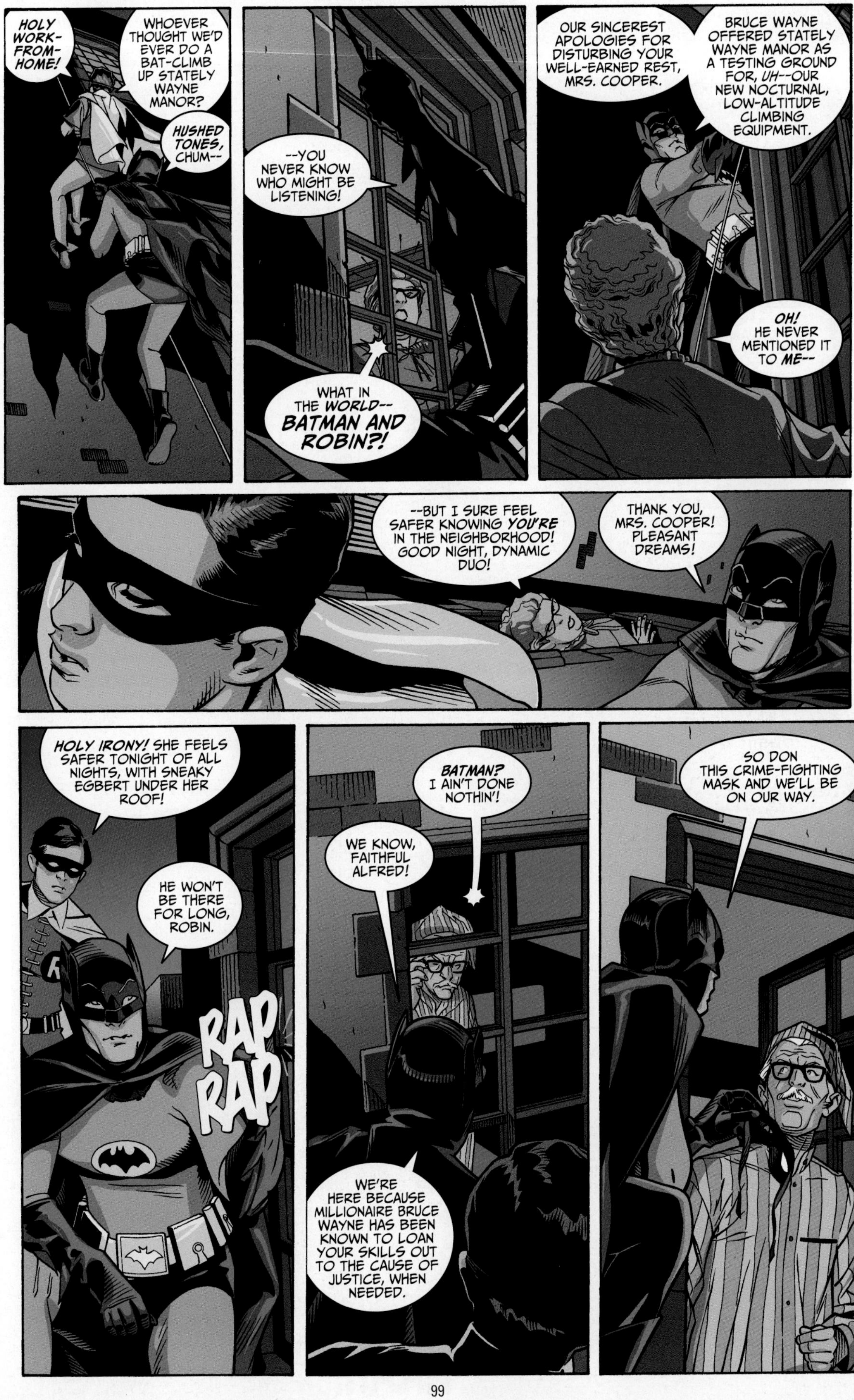
HOLY WORK-FROM-HOME!
WHOEVER THOUGHT WE'D EVER DO A BAT-CLIMB UP STATELY WAYNE MANOR?
HUSHED TONES, CHUM--
--YOU NEVER KNOW WHO MIGHT BE LISTENING!
WHAT IN THE WORLD-- BATMAN AND ROBIN?!
OUR SINCEREST APOLOGIES FOR DISTURBING YOUR WELL-EARNED REST, MRS. COOPER.
BRUCE WAYNE OFFERED STATELY WAYNE MANOR AS A TESTING GROUND FOR, UH--OUR NEW NOCTURNAL, LOW-ALTITUDE CLIMBING EQUIPMENT.
OH! HE NEVER MENTIONED IT TO ME--
--BUT I SURE FEEL SAFER KNOWING YOU'RE IN THE NEIGHBORHOOD! GOOD NIGHT, DYNAMIC DUO!
THANK YOU, MRS. COOPER! PLEASANT DREAMS!
HOLY IRONY! SHE FEELS SAFER TONIGHT OF ALL NIGHTS, WITH SNEAKY EGBERT UNDER HER ROOF!
HE WON'T BE THERE FOR LONG, ROBIN.
RAP RAP
BATMAN? I AIN'T DONE NOTHIN'!
WE KNOW, FAITHFUL ALFRED!
WE'RE HERE BECAUSE MILLIONAIRE BRUCE WAYNE HAS BEEN KNOWN TO LOAN YOUR SKILLS OUT TO THE CAUSE OF JUSTICE, WHEN NEEDED.
SO DON THIS CRIME-FIGHTING MASK AND WE'LL BE ON OUR WAY.

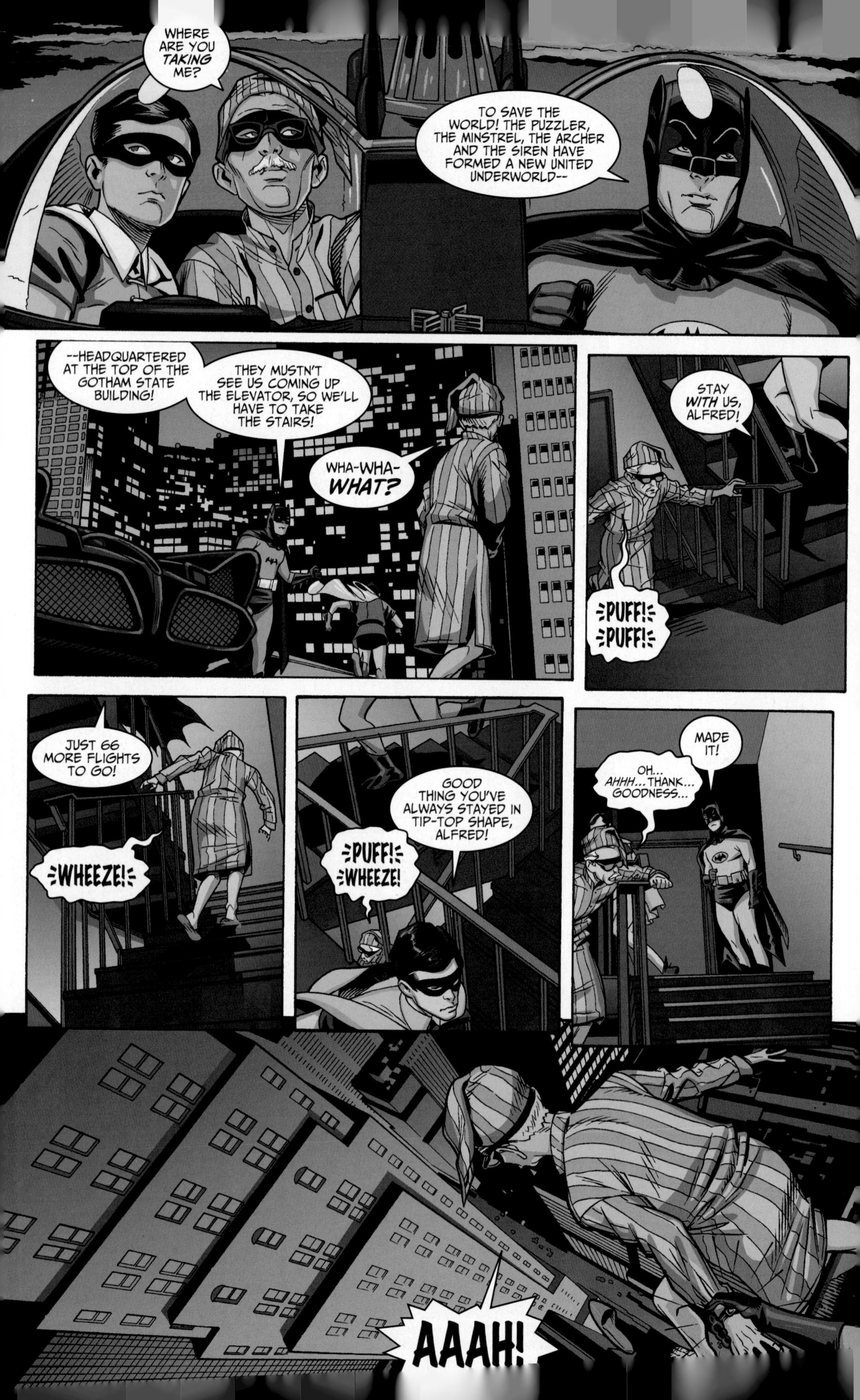
WHERE ARE YOU *TAKING* ME?
TO SAVE THE WORLD! THE PUZZLER, THE MINSTREL, THE ARCHER AND THE SIREN HAVE FORMED A NEW UNITED UNDERWORLD--
--HEADQUARTERED AT THE TOP OF THE GOTHAM STATE BUILDING!
THEY MUSTN'T SEE US COMING UP THE ELEVATOR, SO WE'LL HAVE TO TAKE THE STAIRS!
WHA-WHA-WHAT?
STAY *WITH* US, ALFRED!
PUFF! PUFF!
JUST 66 MORE FLIGHTS TO GO!
WHEEZE!
GOOD THING YOU'VE ALWAYS STAYED IN TIP-TOP SHAPE, ALFRED!
PUFF! WHEEZE!
MADE IT!
OH... *AHHH*... THANK... GOODNESS...
AAAH!

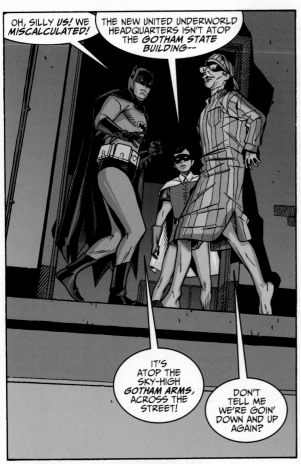

OH, SILLY US! WE MISCALCULATED! THE NEW UNITED UNDERWORLD HEADQUARTERS ISN'T ATOP THE GOTHAM STATE BUILDING--

IT'S ATOP THE SKY-HIGH GOTHAM ARMS, ACROSS THE STREET!

DON'T TELL ME WE'RE GOIN' DOWN AND UP AGAIN?

NOT AT ALL, ALFRED! WE CAN CROSS THE BAT-BRIDGE!

WHAT? NO!

WHOOSH

COME ACROSS, ALFRED!

I CAN'T DO IT! I AIN'T ATHLETIC LIKE YOU!

NONSENSE, ALFRED! YOU'VE ACCOMPLISHED THIS FEAT DOZENS OF TIMES!

I-- I CAN'T, I TELLS YA!

STOP PRETENDING, ALFRED!

I'M NOT ALFRED!

WE KNEW THAT, EGBERT!

TELL US WHERE ALFRED IS--

--AND WE'LL REEL YOU BACK IN!

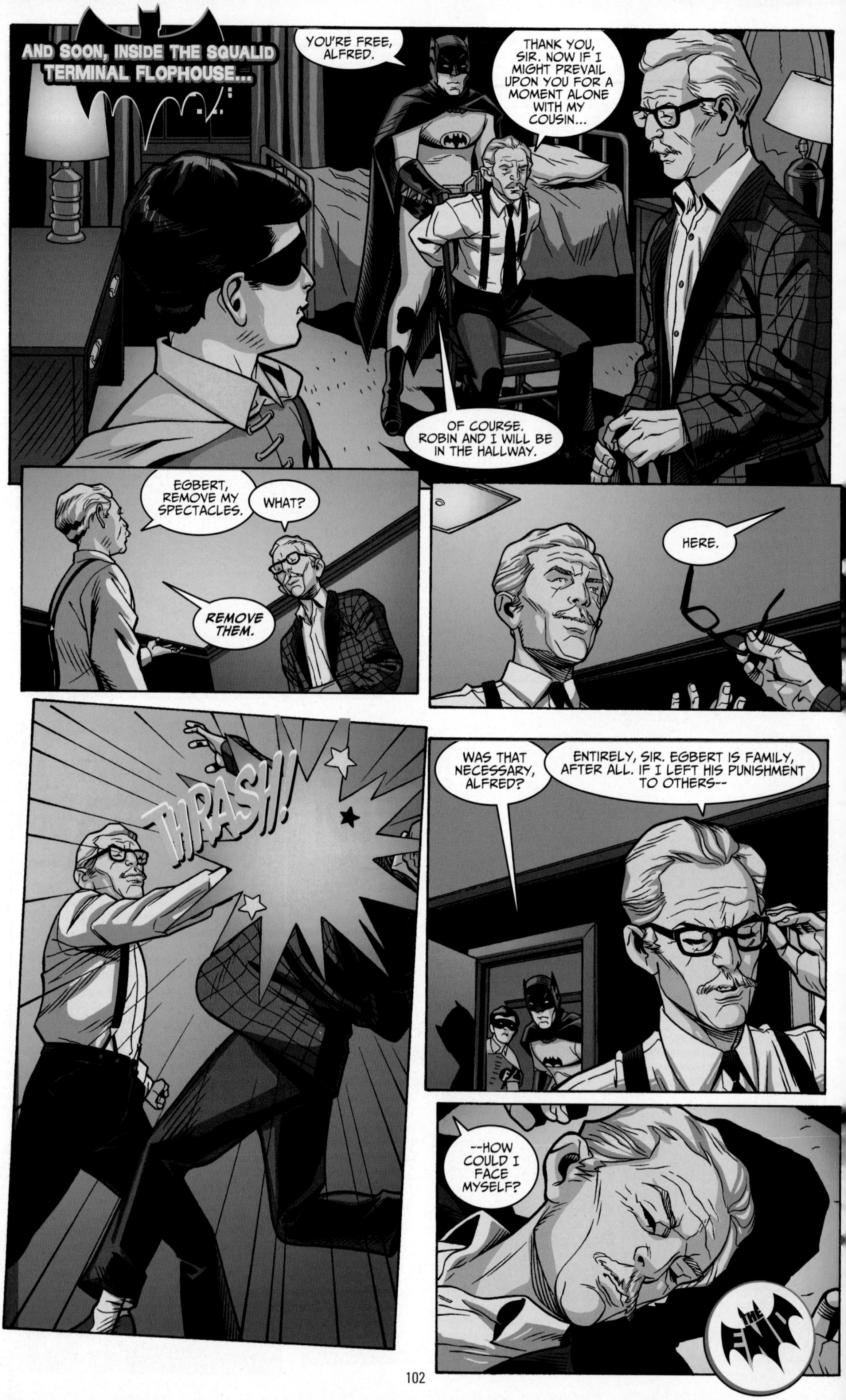
AND SOON, INSIDE THE SQUALID TERMINAL FLOPHOUSE...
YOU'RE FREE, ALFRED.
THANK YOU, SIR. NOW IF I MIGHT PREVAIL UPON YOU FOR A MOMENT ALONE WITH MY COUSIN...
OF COURSE. ROBIN AND I WILL BE IN THE HALLWAY.
EGBERT, REMOVE MY SPECTACLES.
WHAT?
REMOVE THEM.
HERE.
THRASH!
WAS THAT NECESSARY, ALFRED?
ENTIRELY, SIR. EGBERT IS FAMILY, AFTER ALL. IF I LEFT HIS PUNISHMENT TO OTHERS--
--HOW COULD I FACE MYSELF?
THE END

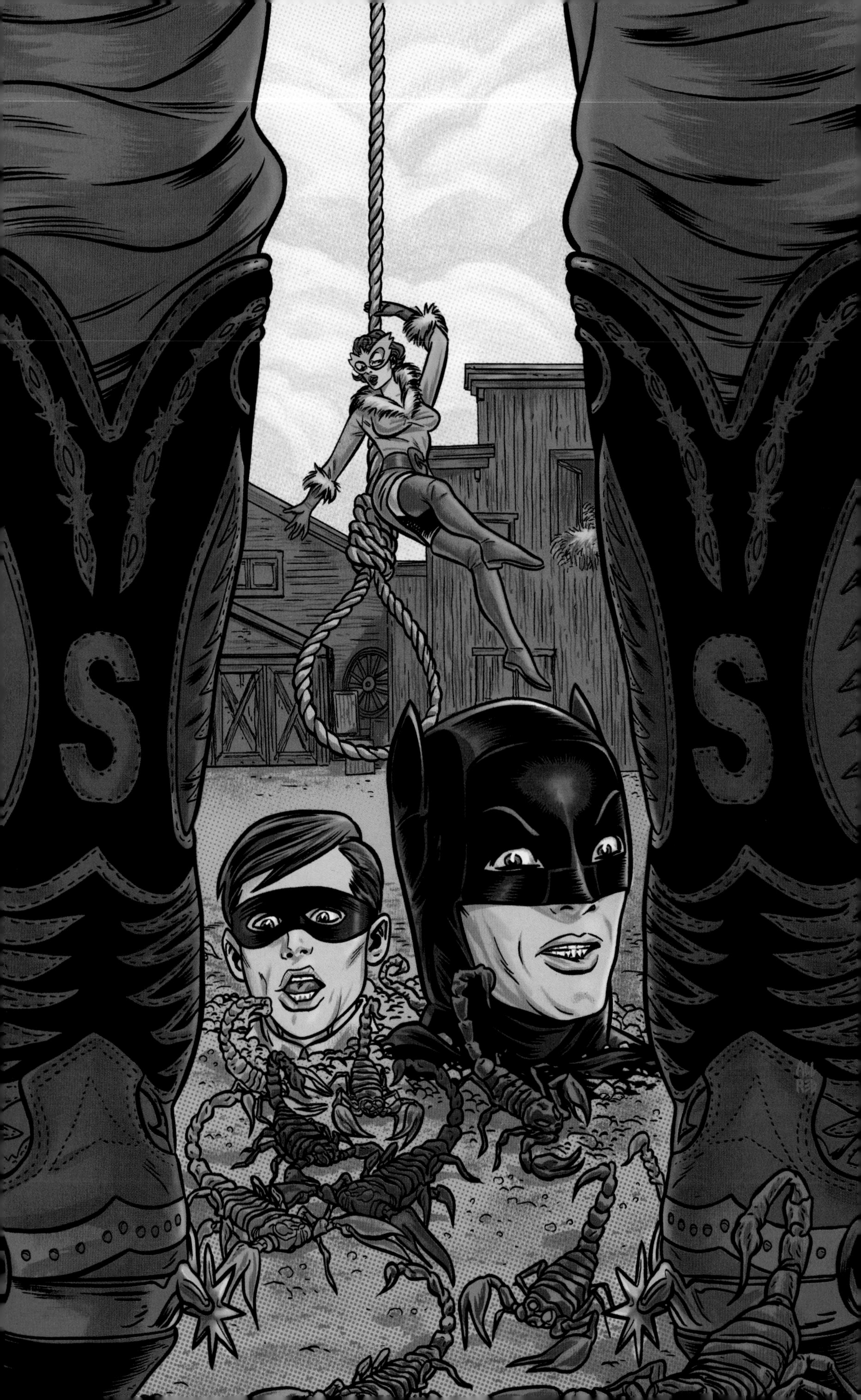

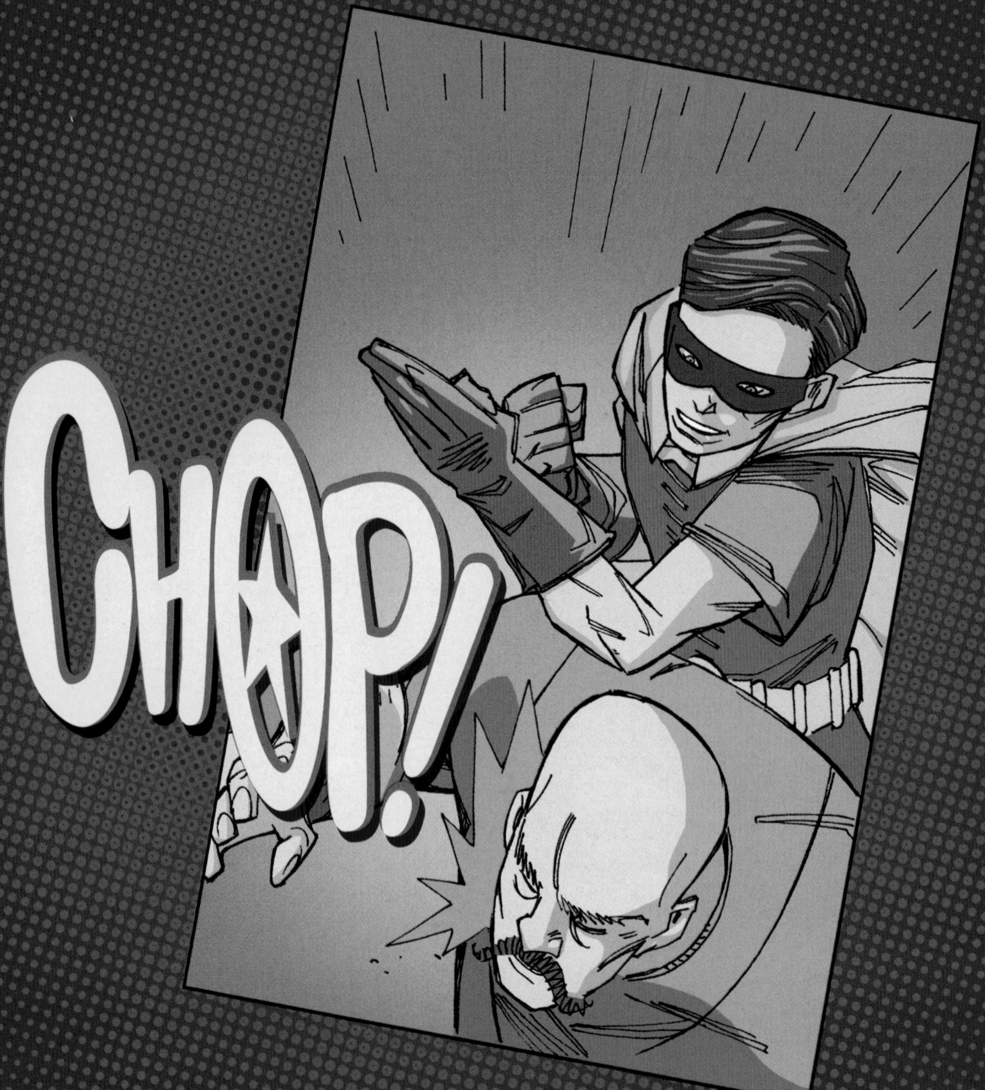
CHOP!

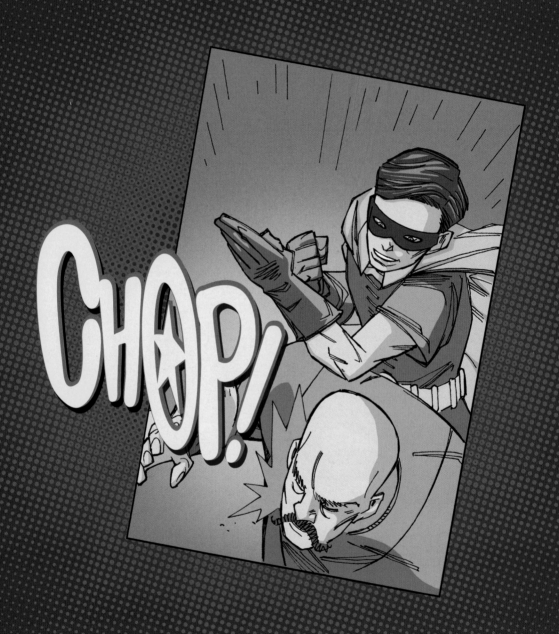

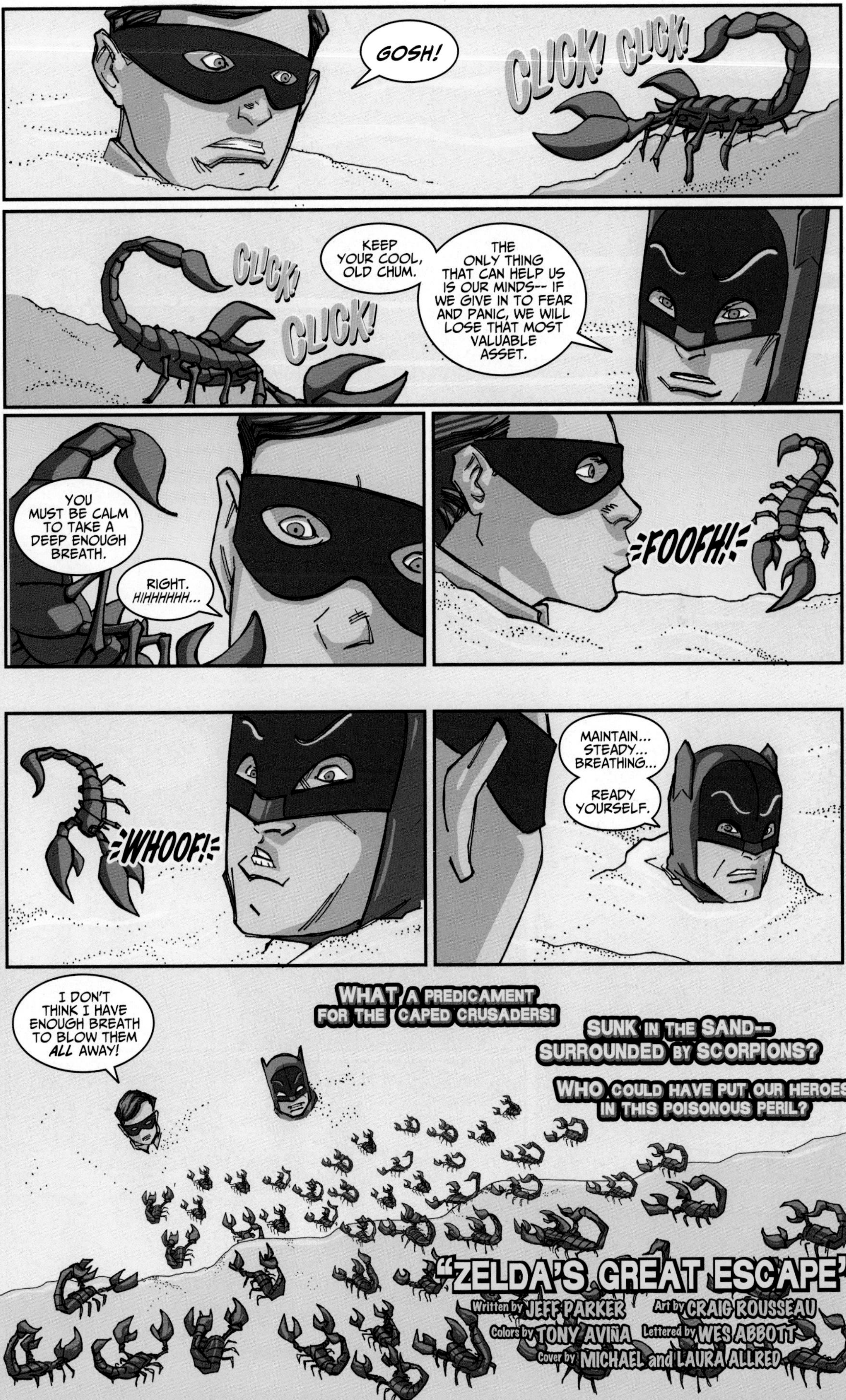
GOSH!
CLICK! CLICK!
CLICK!
CLICK!
KEEP YOUR COOL, OLD CHUM.
THE ONLY THING THAT CAN HELP US IS OUR MINDS-- IF WE GIVE IN TO FEAR AND PANIC, WE WILL LOSE THAT MOST VALUABLE ASSET.
YOU MUST BE CALM TO TAKE A DEEP ENOUGH BREATH.
RIGHT. HIHHHHHH...
FOOFH!
WHOOF!
MAINTAIN... STEADY... BREATHING...
READY YOURSELF.
I DON'T THINK I HAVE ENOUGH BREATH TO BLOW THEM ALL AWAY!
WHAT A PREDICAMENT FOR THE CAPED CRUSADERS!
SUNK IN THE SAND-- SURROUNDED BY SCORPIONS?
WHO COULD HAVE PUT OUR HEROES IN THIS POISONOUS PERIL?
"ZELDA'S GREAT ESCAPE"
Written by JEFF PARKER Art by CRAIG ROUSSEAU
Colors by TONY AVIÑA Lettered by WES ABBOTT
Cover by MICHAEL and LAURA ALLRED

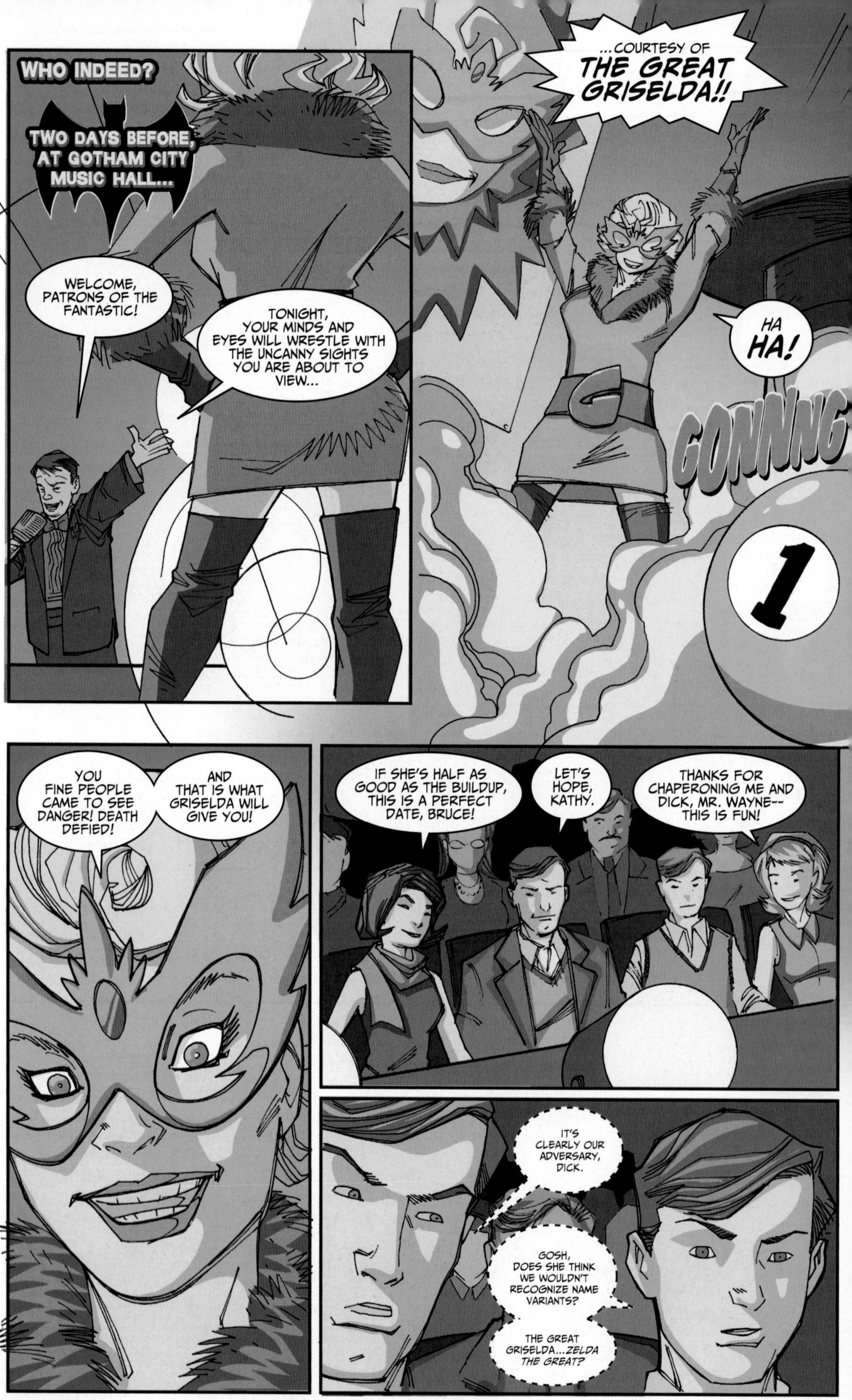
WHO INDEED?
TWO DAYS BEFORE, AT GOTHAM CITY MUSIC HALL...
WELCOME, PATRONS OF THE FANTASTIC!
TONIGHT, YOUR MINDS AND EYES WILL WRESTLE WITH THE UNCANNY SIGHTS YOU ARE ABOUT TO VIEW...
...COURTESY OF THE GREAT GRISELDA!!
HA HA!
GONNNG
1
YOU FINE PEOPLE CAME TO SEE DANGER! DEATH DEFIED!
AND THAT IS WHAT GRISELDA WILL GIVE YOU!
IF SHE'S HALF AS GOOD AS THE BUILDUP, THIS IS A PERFECT DATE, BRUCE!
LET'S HOPE, KATHY.
THANKS FOR CHAPERONING ME AND DICK, MR. WAYNE-- THIS IS FUN!
IT'S CLEARLY OUR ADVERSARY, DICK.
GOSH, DOES SHE THINK WE WOULDN'T RECOGNIZE NAME VARIANTS?
THE GREAT GRISELDA...ZELDA THE GREAT?

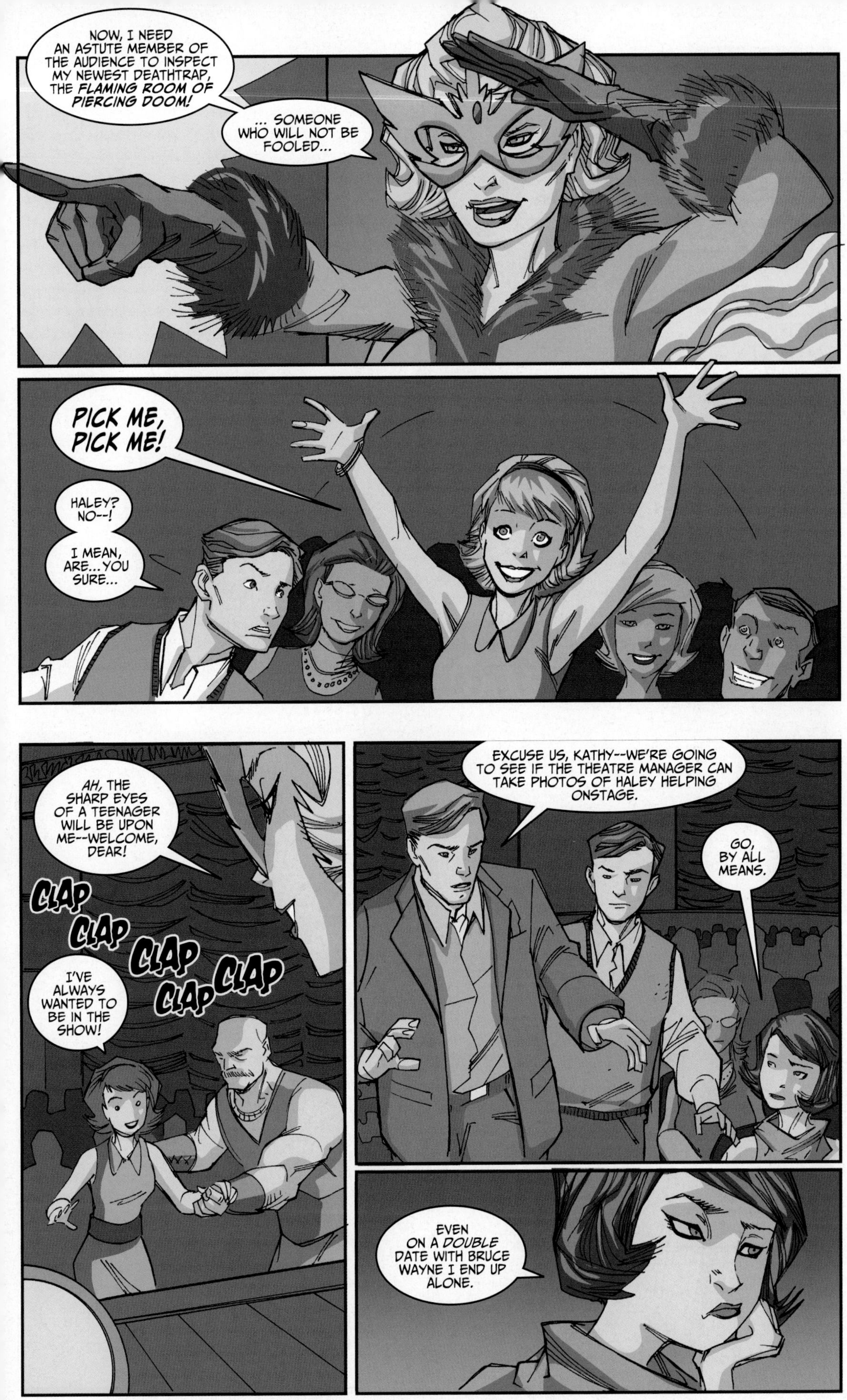
NOW, I NEED AN ASTUTE MEMBER OF THE AUDIENCE TO INSPECT MY NEWEST DEATHTRAP, THE FLAMING ROOM OF PIERCING DOOM!
... SOMEONE WHO WILL NOT BE FOOLED...
PICK ME, PICK ME!
HALEY? NO--!
I MEAN, ARE...YOU SURE...
AH, THE SHARP EYES OF A TEENAGER WILL BE UPON ME--WELCOME, DEAR!
CLAP CLAP CLAP CLAP CLAP
I'VE ALWAYS WANTED TO BE IN THE SHOW!
EXCUSE US, KATHY--WE'RE GOING TO SEE IF THE THEATRE MANAGER CAN TAKE PHOTOS OF HALEY HELPING ONSTAGE.
GO, BY ALL MEANS.
EVEN ON A DOUBLE DATE WITH BRUCE WAYNE I END UP ALONE.

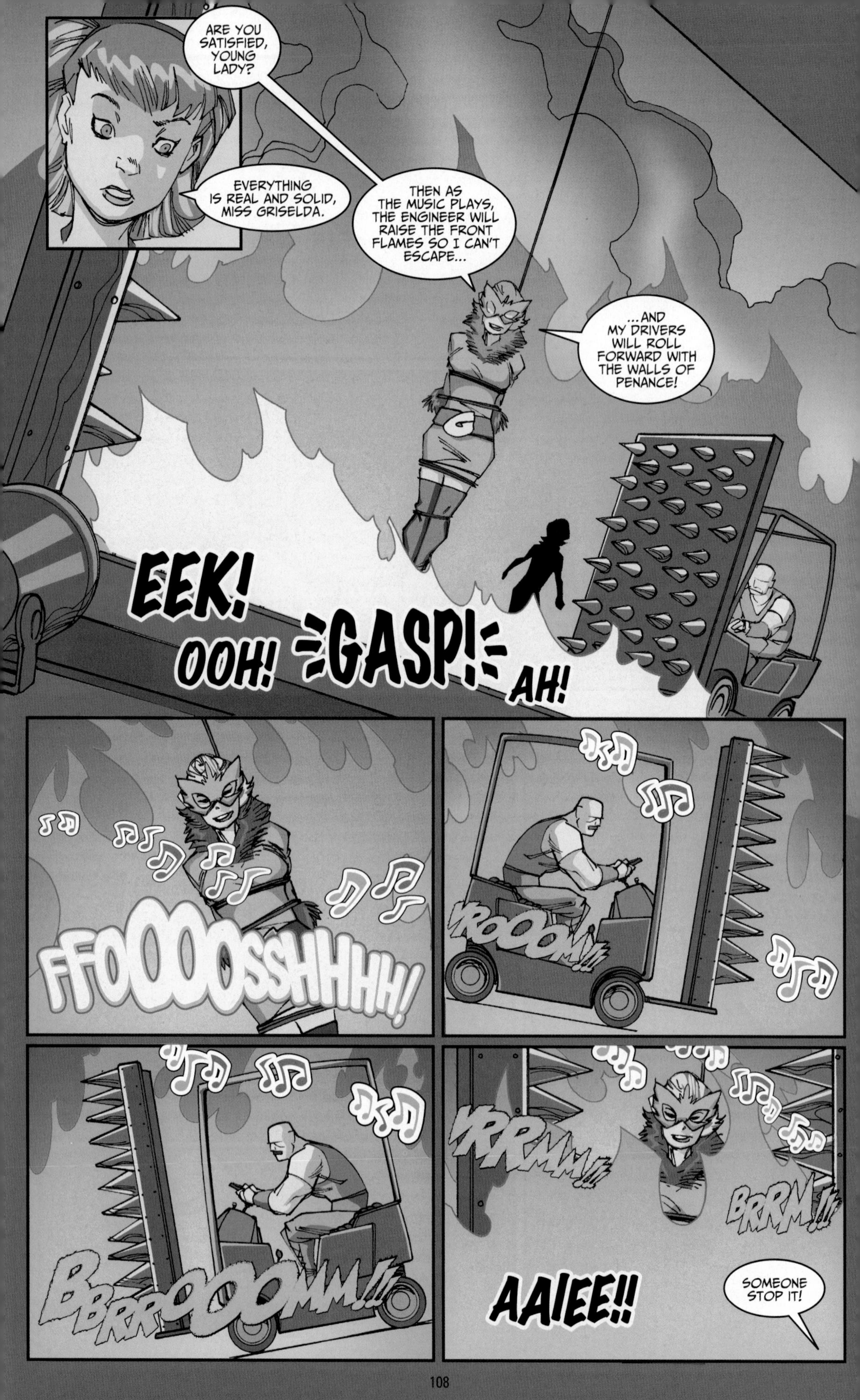
ARE YOU SATISFIED, YOUNG LADY?
EVERYTHING IS REAL AND SOLID, MISS GRISELDA.
THEN AS THE MUSIC PLAYS, THE ENGINEER WILL RAISE THE FRONT FLAMES SO I CAN'T ESCAPE...
...AND MY DRIVERS WILL ROLL FORWARD WITH THE WALLS OF PENANCE!
EEK!
OOH!
GASP!
AH!
FFOOOOSSHHHH!
VROOOM!!
BBRRROOOMM!!
VRRMM!!
BRRM!!
AAIEE!!
SOMEONE STOP IT!

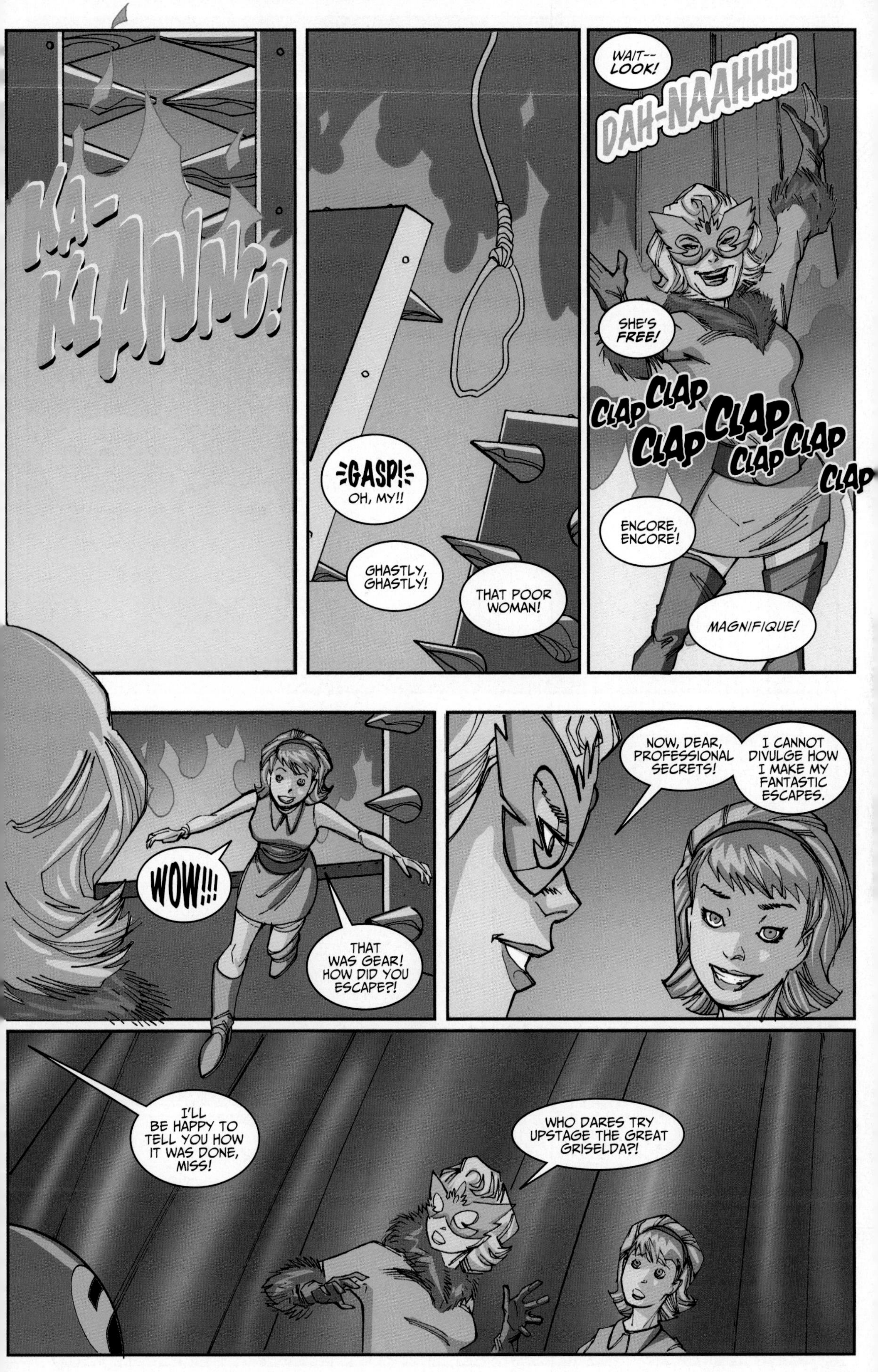
KA-KLANNG!
GASP! OH, MY!!
GHASTLY, GHASTLY!
THAT POOR WOMAN!
WAIT-- LOOK!
DAH-NAAHH!!!
SHE'S FREE!
CLAP CLAP CLAP CLAP CLAP CLAP CLAP
ENCORE, ENCORE!
MAGNIFIQUE!
WOW!!!
THAT WAS GEAR! HOW DID YOU ESCAPE?!
NOW, DEAR, PROFESSIONAL SECRETS!
I CANNOT DIVULGE HOW I MAKE MY FANTASTIC ESCAPES.
I'LL BE HAPPY TO TELL YOU HOW IT WAS DONE, MISS!
WHO DARES TRY UPSTAGE THE GREAT GRISELDA?!

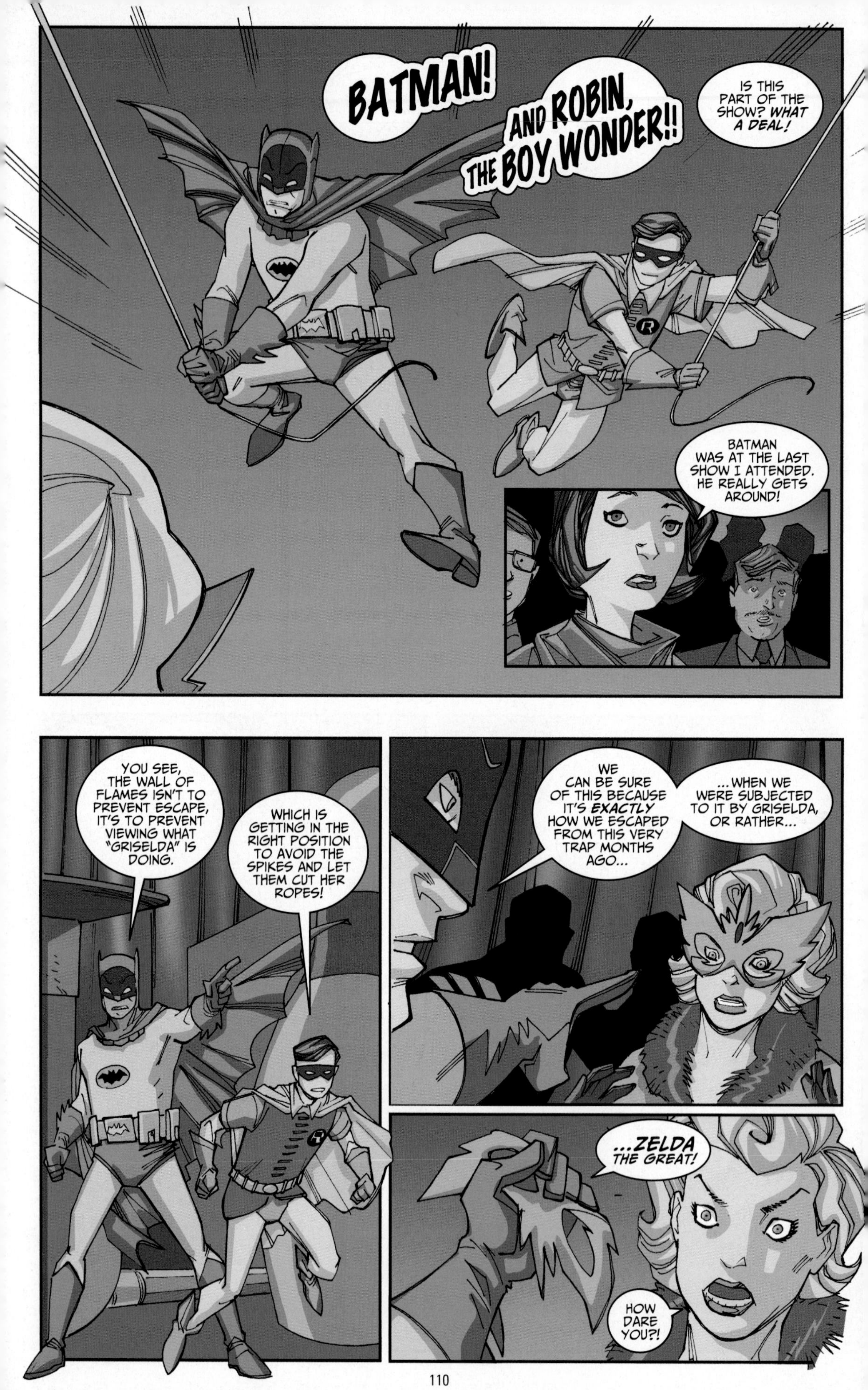
BATMAN!
AND ROBIN, THE BOY WONDER!!
IS THIS PART OF THE SHOW? WHAT A DEAL!
BATMAN WAS AT THE LAST SHOW I ATTENDED. HE REALLY GETS AROUND!
YOU SEE, THE WALL OF FLAMES ISN'T TO PREVENT ESCAPE, IT'S TO PREVENT VIEWING WHAT "GRISELDA" IS DOING.
WHICH IS GETTING IN THE RIGHT POSITION TO AVOID THE SPIKES AND LET THEM CUT HER ROPES!
WE CAN BE SURE OF THIS BECAUSE IT'S EXACTLY HOW WE ESCAPED FROM THIS VERY TRAP MONTHS AGO...
...WHEN WE WERE SUBJECTED TO IT BY GRISELDA, OR RATHER...
...ZELDA THE GREAT!
HOW DARE YOU?!

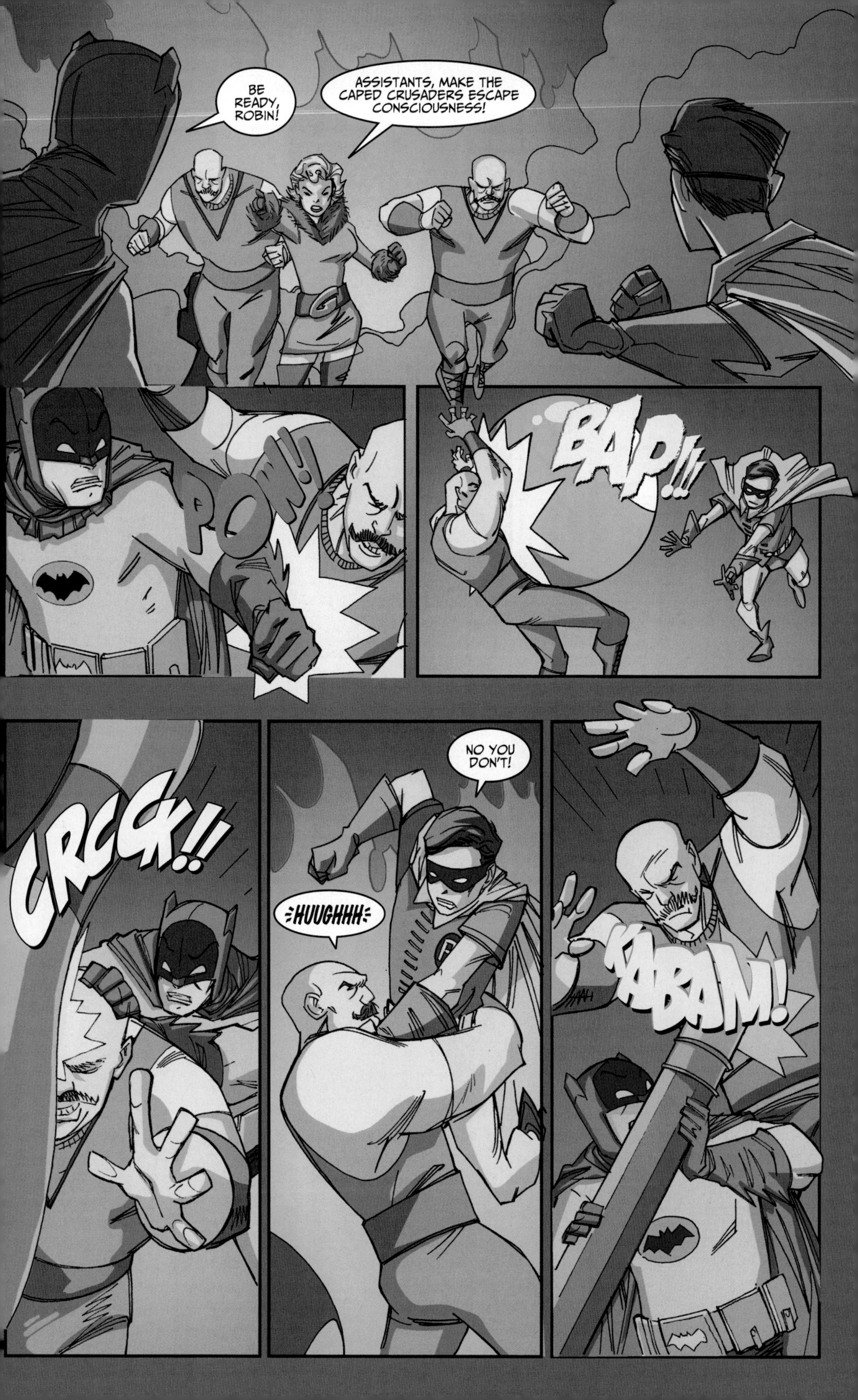
BE READY, ROBIN!
ASSISTANTS, MAKE THE CAPED CRUSADERS ESCAPE CONSCIOUSNESS!
POW!
BAP!!!
CRCCK!!
NO YOU DON'T!
HUUGHHH
KABAM!

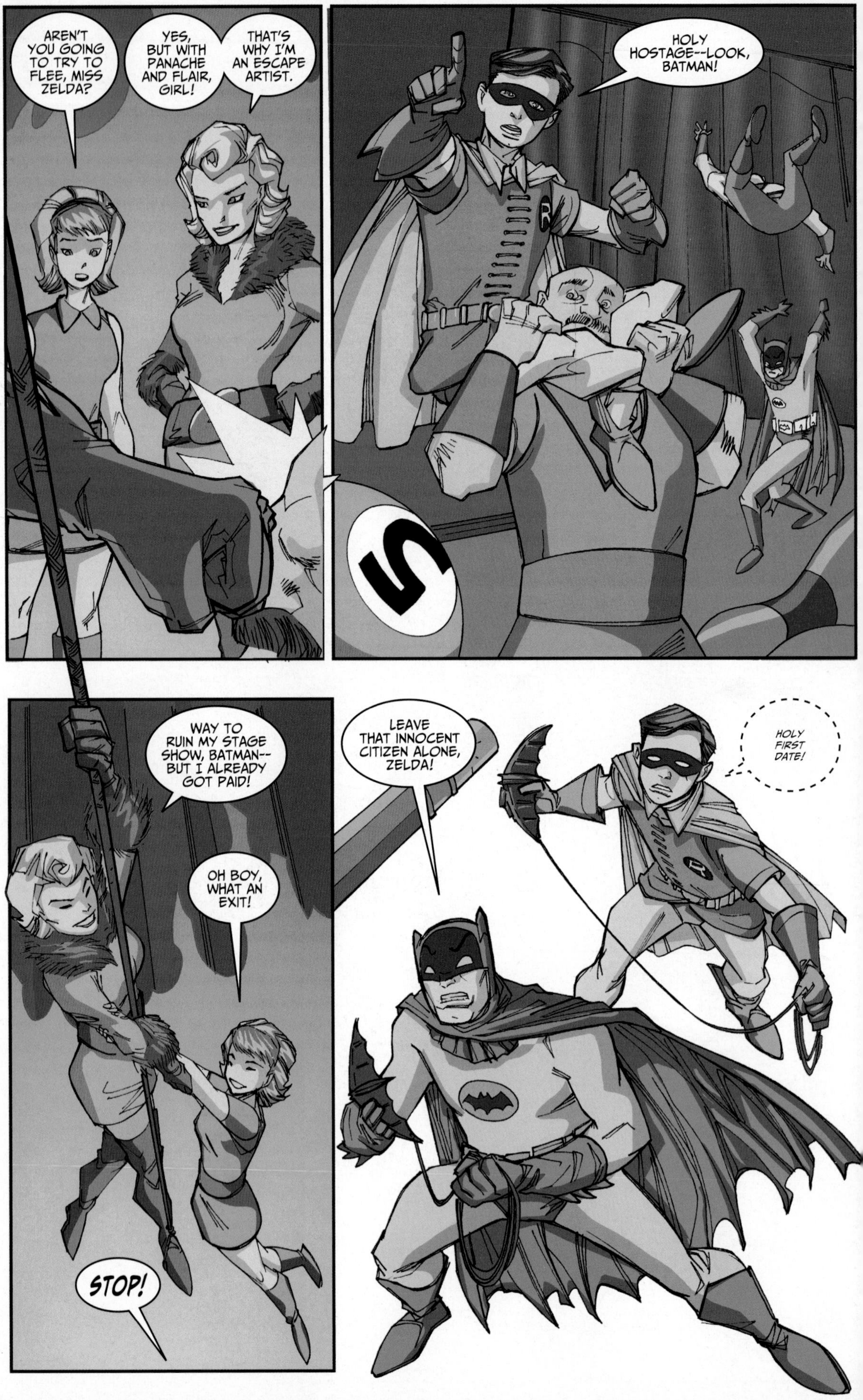
AREN'T YOU GOING TO TRY TO FLEE, MISS ZELDA?
YES, BUT WITH PANACHE AND FLAIR, GIRL!
THAT'S WHY I'M AN ESCAPE ARTIST.
HOLY HOSTAGE--LOOK, BATMAN!
WAY TO RUIN MY STAGE SHOW, BATMAN--BUT I ALREADY GOT PAID!
OH BOY, WHAT AN EXIT!
STOP!
LEAVE THAT INNOCENT CITIZEN ALONE, ZELDA!
HOLY FIRST DATE!

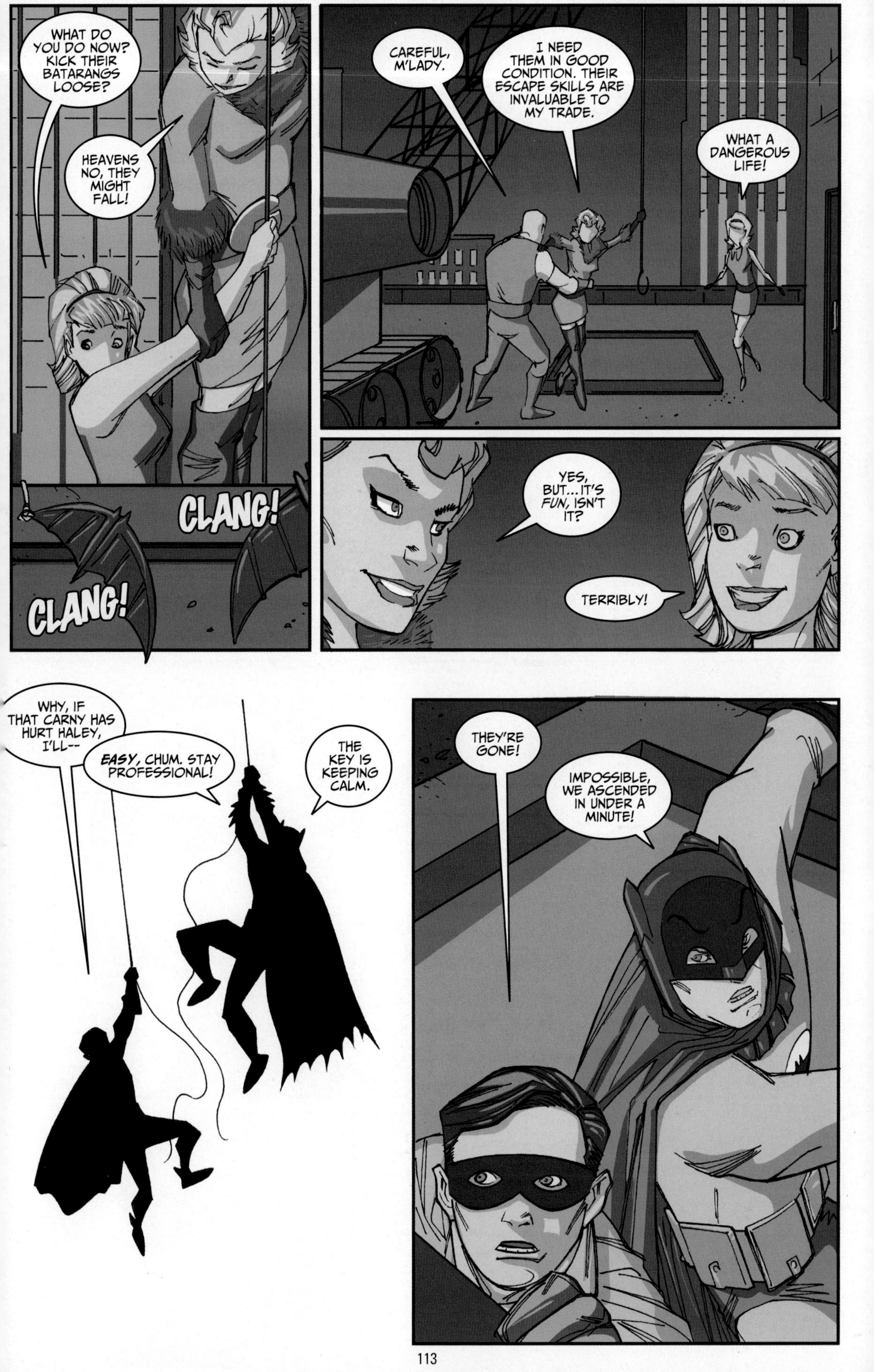
WHAT DO YOU DO NOW? KICK THEIR BATARANGS LOOSE?
HEAVENS NO, THEY MIGHT FALL!
CLANG!
CLANG!
CAREFUL, M'LADY.
I NEED THEM IN GOOD CONDITION. THEIR ESCAPE SKILLS ARE INVALUABLE TO MY TRADE.
WHAT A DANGEROUS LIFE!
YES, BUT...IT'S *FUN*, ISN'T IT?
TERRIBLY!
WHY, IF THAT CARNY HAS HURT HALEY, I'LL--
EASY, CHUM. STAY PROFESSIONAL!
THE KEY IS KEEPING CALM.
THEY'RE GONE!
IMPOSSIBLE, WE ASCENDED IN UNDER A MINUTE!

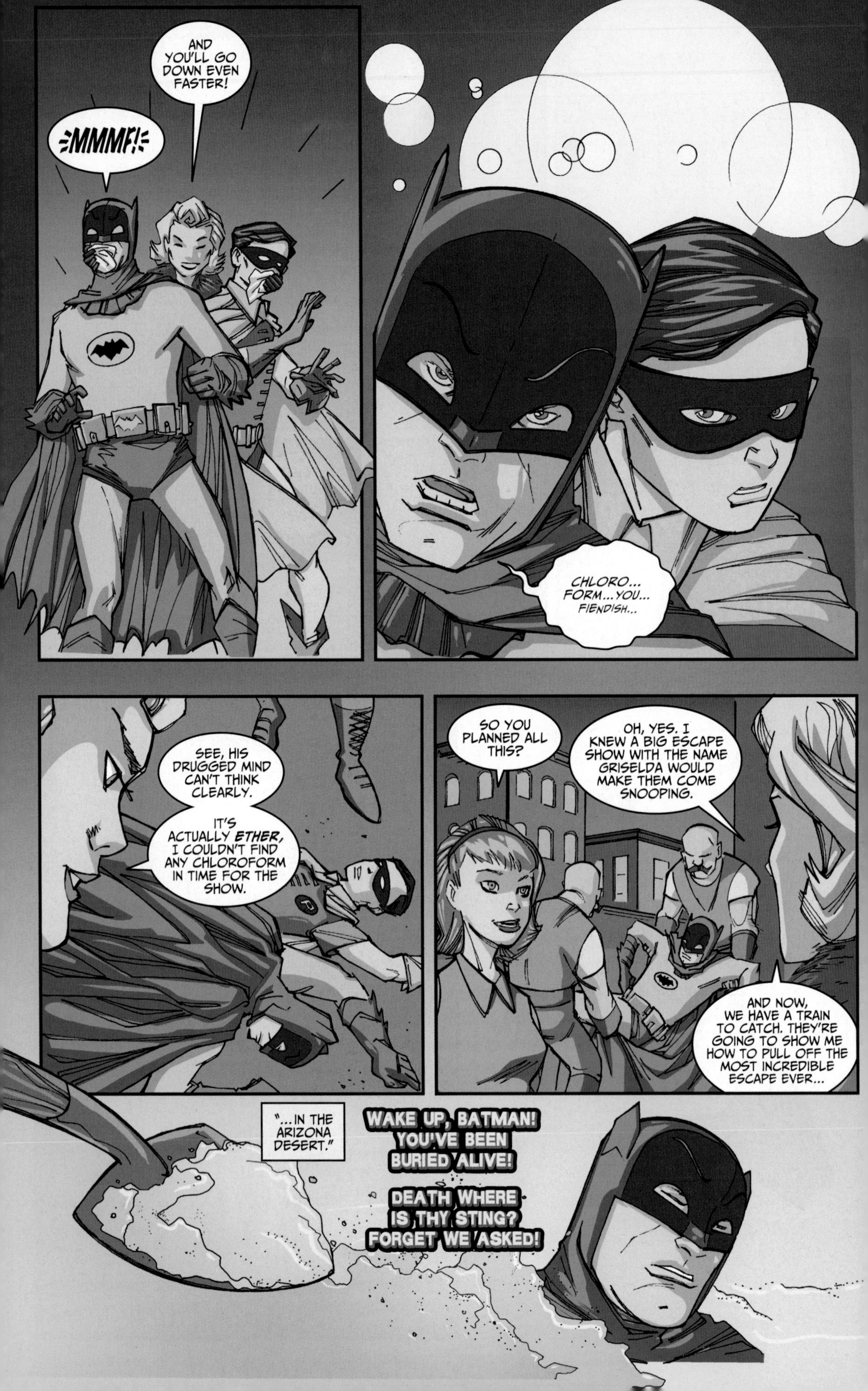
AND YOU'LL GO DOWN EVEN FASTER!
MMMF!
CHLORO... FORM... YOU... FIENDISH...
SEE, HIS DRUGGED MIND CAN'T THINK CLEARLY.
IT'S ACTUALLY ETHER, I COULDN'T FIND ANY CHLOROFORM IN TIME FOR THE SHOW.
SO YOU PLANNED ALL THIS?
OH, YES. I KNEW A BIG ESCAPE SHOW WITH THE NAME GRISELDA WOULD MAKE THEM COME SNOOPING.
AND NOW, WE HAVE A TRAIN TO CATCH. THEY'RE GOING TO SHOW ME HOW TO PULL OFF THE MOST INCREDIBLE ESCAPE EVER...
"...IN THE ARIZONA DESERT."
WAKE UP, BATMAN! YOU'VE BEEN BURIED ALIVE!
DEATH WHERE IS THY STING? FORGET WE ASKED!

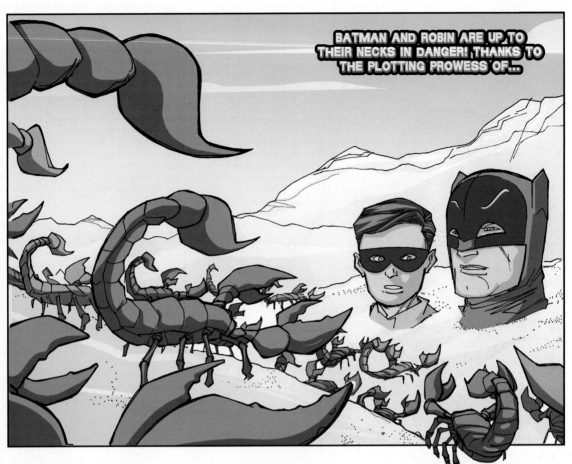

BATMAN AND ROBIN ARE UP TO THEIR NECKS IN DANGER! THANKS TO THE PLOTTING PROWESS OF...

...ZELDA THE GREAT!

SO EXCITING, MISS ZELDA! HOW DO YOU THINK THEY'RE GOING TO ESCAPE?

WELL, HALEY, NORMALLY THEY WOULD PROBABLY FISH AROUND FOR SOMETHING IN THOSE INCREDIBLE UTILITY BELTS.

BUT THEY CAN'T MOVE THEIR ARMS! I HAVE NO IDEA WHAT THEY'LL DO.

OH... WHAT IF-- WHAT IF THEY CAN'T ESCAPE?

THEN I'LL HAVE TO DO SOMETHING I REALLY DON'T ENJOY.

ABANDON THIS ACT FOR AN ALL-NEW DEATH TRAP.

COME ON, SCORPION WRANGLERS, GET ALL OF THEM IN. IT HAS TO BE VISUALLY IMPRESSIVE!

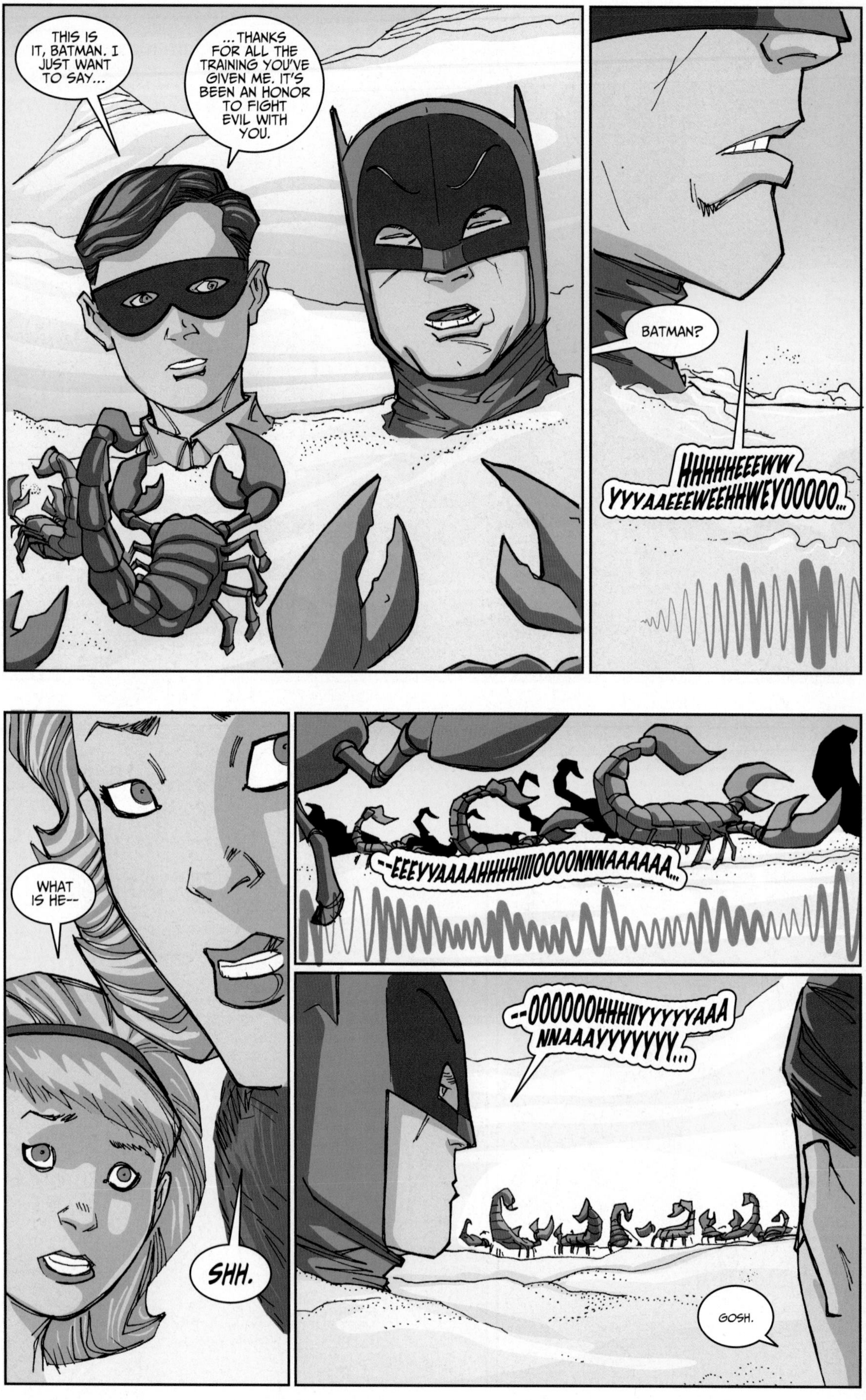
THIS IS IT, BATMAN. I JUST WANT TO SAY...
...THANKS FOR ALL THE TRAINING YOU'VE GIVEN ME. IT'S BEEN AN HONOR TO FIGHT EVIL WITH YOU.
BATMAN?
HHHHHEEEWW YYYAAEEEWEEHHWEYOOOOO...
WHAT IS HE--
SHH.
--EEEYYAAAAHHHHIIIIOOOONNNAAAAAA...
--OOOOOOHHHIIYYYYYAAA NNAAAYYYYYYY...
GOSH.

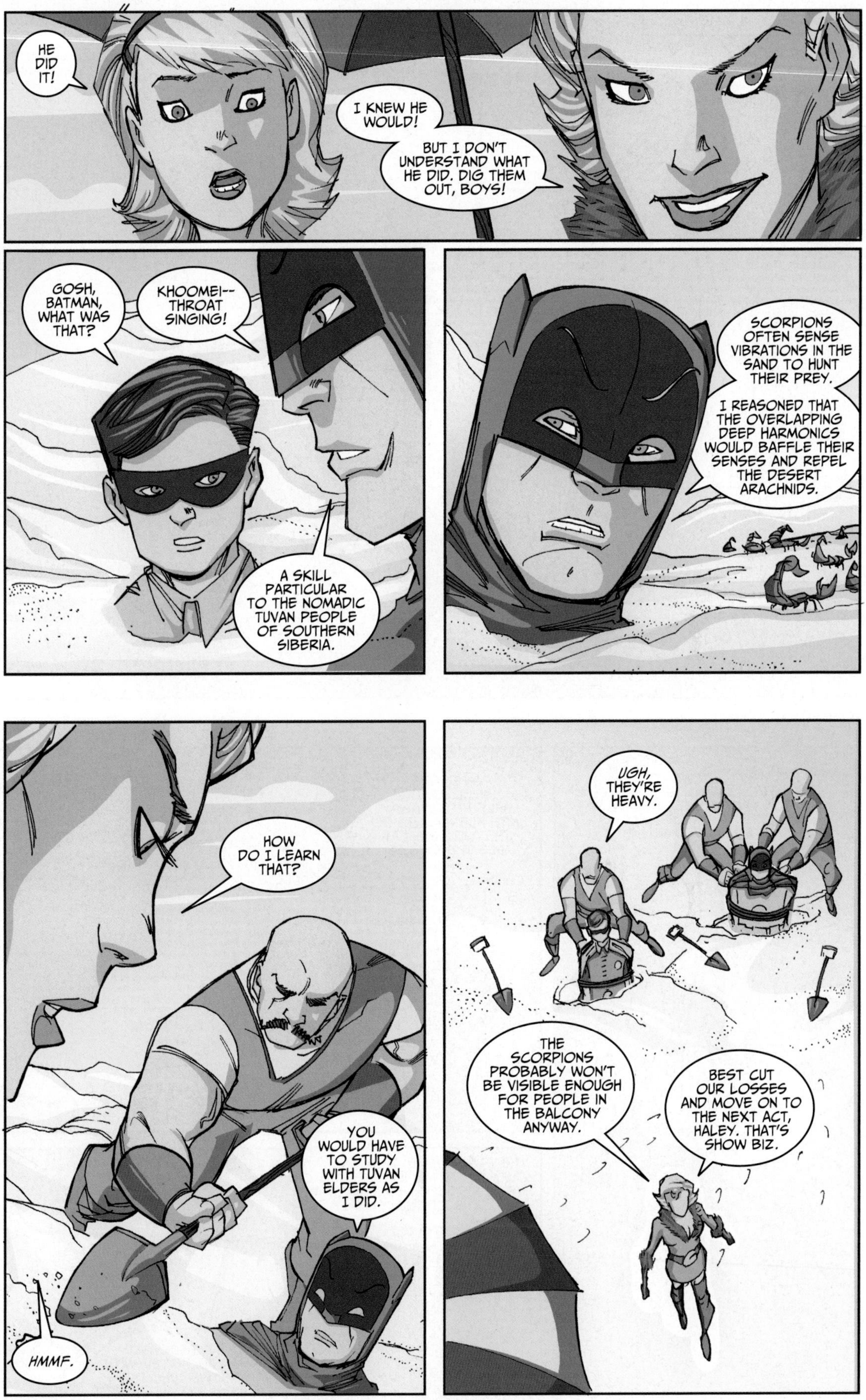
HE DID IT!
I KNEW HE WOULD!
BUT I DON'T UNDERSTAND WHAT HE DID. DIG THEM OUT, BOYS!
GOSH, BATMAN, WHAT WAS THAT?
KHOOMEI-- THROAT SINGING!
A SKILL PARTICULAR TO THE NOMADIC TUVAN PEOPLE OF SOUTHERN SIBERIA.
SCORPIONS OFTEN SENSE VIBRATIONS IN THE SAND TO HUNT THEIR PREY.
I REASONED THAT THE OVERLAPPING DEEP HARMONICS WOULD BAFFLE THEIR SENSES AND REPEL THE DESERT ARACHNIDS.
HOW DO I LEARN THAT?
YOU WOULD HAVE TO STUDY WITH TUVAN ELDERS AS I DID.
HMMF.
UGH, THEY'RE HEAVY.
THE SCORPIONS PROBABLY WON'T BE VISIBLE ENOUGH FOR PEOPLE IN THE BALCONY ANYWAY.
BEST CUT OUR LOSSES AND MOVE ON TO THE NEXT ACT, HALEY. THAT'S SHOW BIZ.

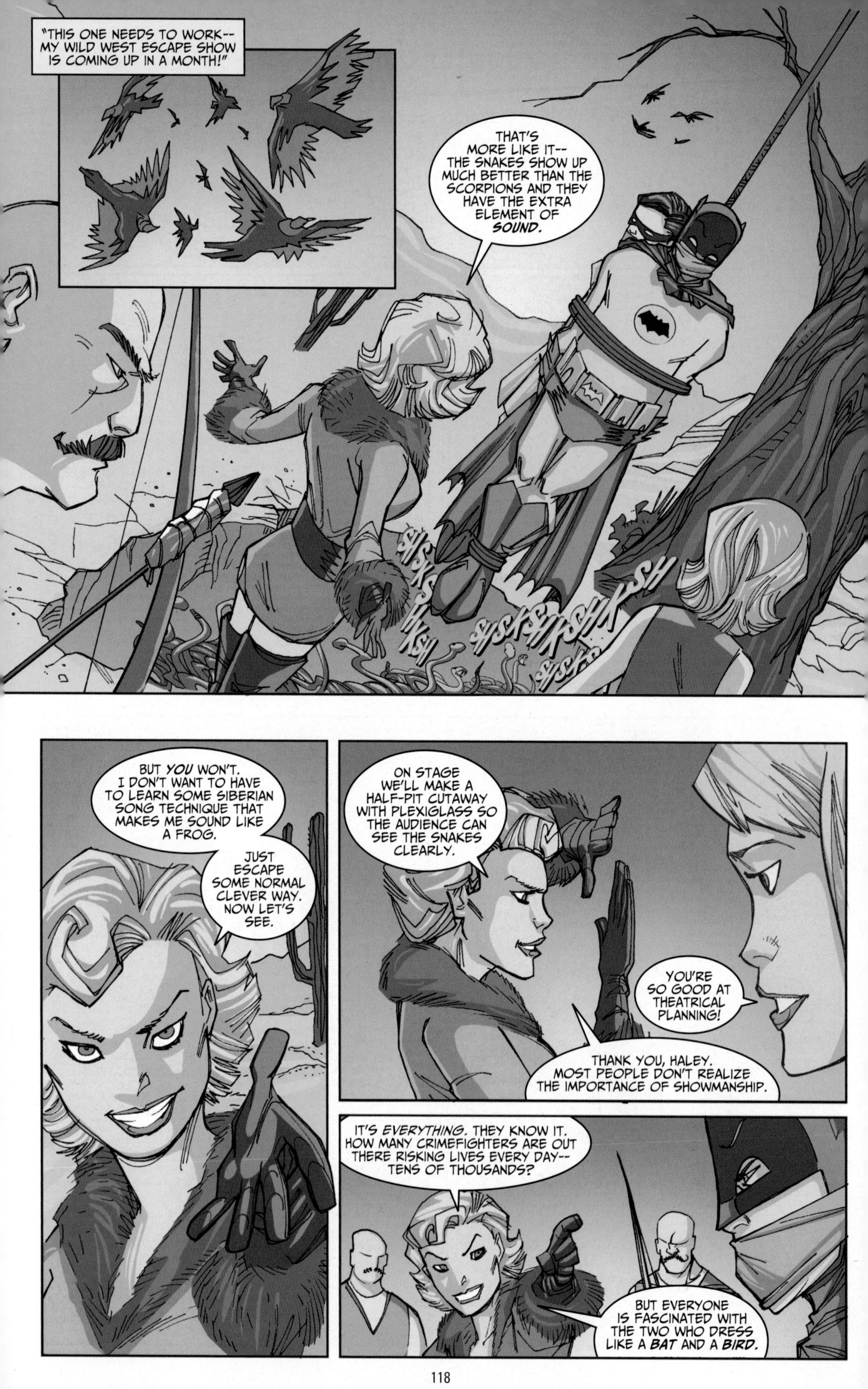
"THIS ONE NEEDS TO WORK-- MY WILD WEST ESCAPE SHOW IS COMING UP IN A MONTH!"
THAT'S MORE LIKE IT-- THE SNAKES SHOW UP MUCH BETTER THAN THE SCORPIONS AND THEY HAVE THE EXTRA ELEMENT OF *SOUND*.
BUT *YOU* WON'T. I DON'T WANT TO HAVE TO LEARN SOME SIBERIAN SONG TECHNIQUE THAT MAKES ME SOUND LIKE A FROG.
JUST ESCAPE SOME NORMAL CLEVER WAY. NOW LET'S SEE.
ON STAGE WE'LL MAKE A HALF-PIT CUTAWAY WITH PLEXIGLASS SO THE AUDIENCE CAN SEE THE SNAKES CLEARLY.
YOU'RE SO GOOD AT THEATRICAL PLANNING!
THANK YOU, HALEY. MOST PEOPLE DON'T REALIZE THE IMPORTANCE OF SHOWMANSHIP.
IT'S *EVERYTHING*. THEY KNOW IT. HOW MANY CRIMEFIGHTERS ARE OUT THERE RISKING LIVES EVERY DAY-- TENS OF THOUSANDS?
BUT EVERYONE IS FASCINATED WITH THE TWO WHO DRESS LIKE A *BAT* AND A *BIRD*.

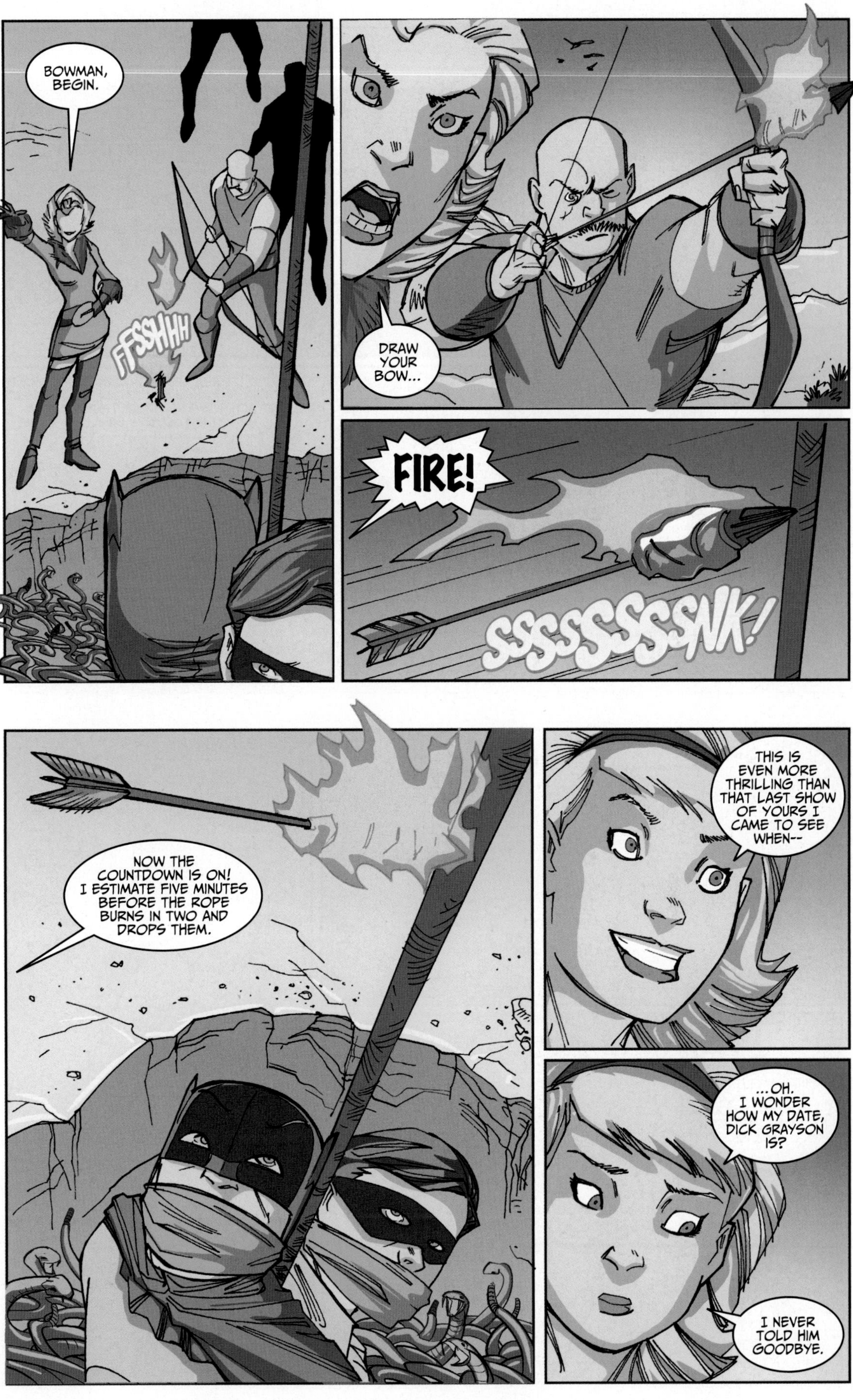

BOWMAN, BEGIN.
FFSSHHH
DRAW YOUR BOW...
FIRE!
SSSSSSSSNK!
NOW THE COUNTDOWN IS ON! I ESTIMATE FIVE MINUTES BEFORE THE ROPE BURNS IN TWO AND DROPS THEM.
THIS IS EVEN MORE THRILLING THAN THAT LAST SHOW OF YOURS I CAME TO SEE WHEN--
...OH. I WONDER HOW MY DATE, DICK GRAYSON IS?
I NEVER TOLD HIM GOODBYE.

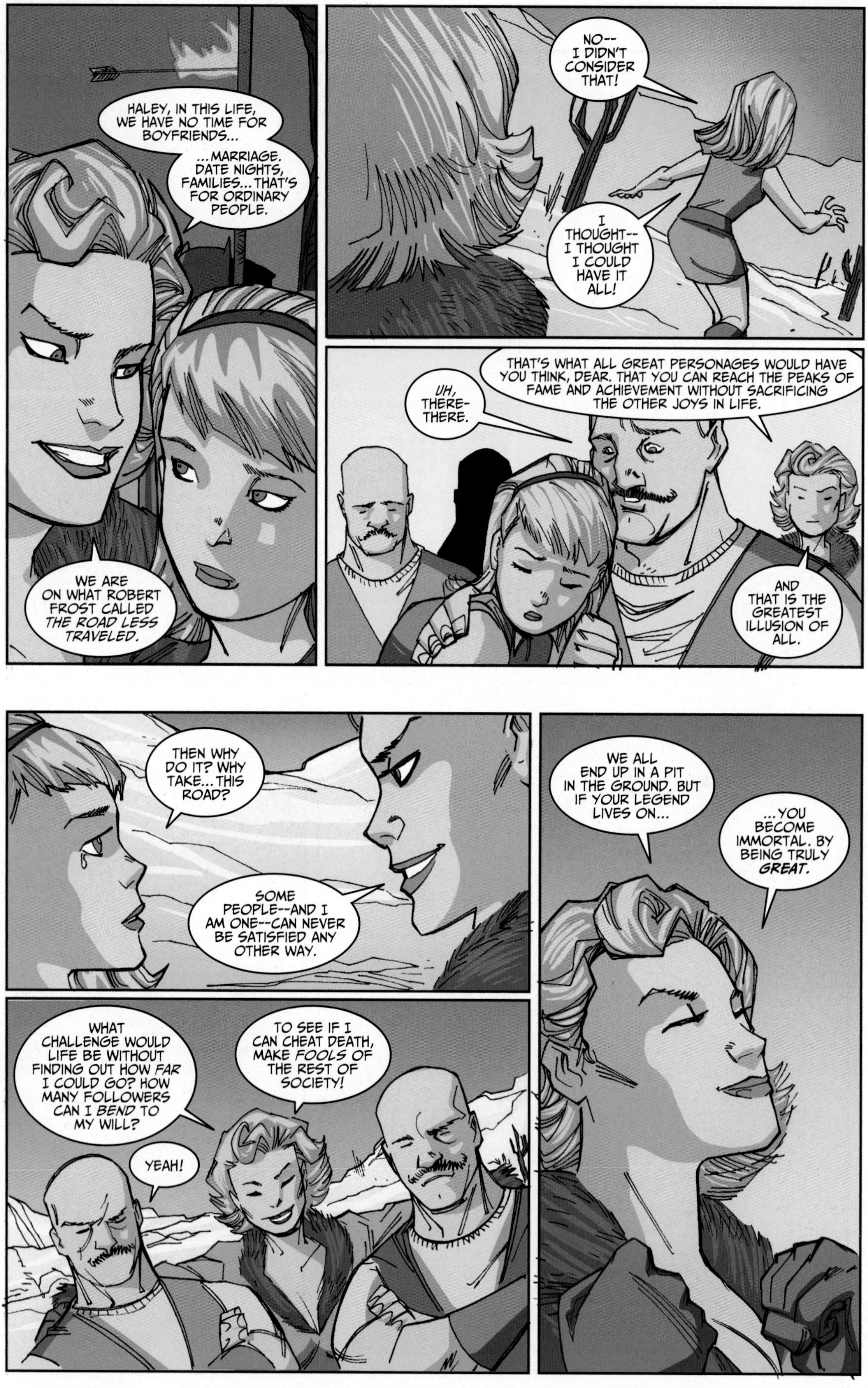
HALEY, IN THIS LIFE, WE HAVE NO TIME FOR BOYFRIENDS...
...MARRIAGE. DATE NIGHTS, FAMILIES...THAT'S FOR ORDINARY PEOPLE.
WE ARE ON WHAT ROBERT FROST CALLED *THE ROAD LESS TRAVELED.*
NO-- I DIDN'T CONSIDER THAT!
I THOUGHT-- I THOUGHT I COULD HAVE IT ALL!
UH, THERE-THERE.
THAT'S WHAT ALL GREAT PERSONAGES WOULD HAVE YOU THINK, DEAR. THAT YOU CAN REACH THE PEAKS OF FAME AND ACHIEVEMENT WITHOUT SACRIFICING THE OTHER JOYS IN LIFE.
AND THAT IS THE GREATEST ILLUSION OF ALL.
THEN WHY DO IT? WHY TAKE...THIS ROAD?
SOME PEOPLE--AND I AM ONE--CAN NEVER BE SATISFIED ANY OTHER WAY.
WHAT CHALLENGE WOULD LIFE BE WITHOUT FINDING OUT HOW *FAR* I COULD *GO?* HOW MANY FOLLOWERS CAN I *BEND* TO MY WILL?
TO SEE IF I CAN CHEAT DEATH, MAKE *FOOLS* OF THE REST OF SOCIETY!
YEAH!
WE ALL END UP IN A PIT IN THE GROUND. BUT IF YOUR LEGEND LIVES ON...
...YOU BECOME IMMORTAL. BY BEING TRULY *GREAT.*

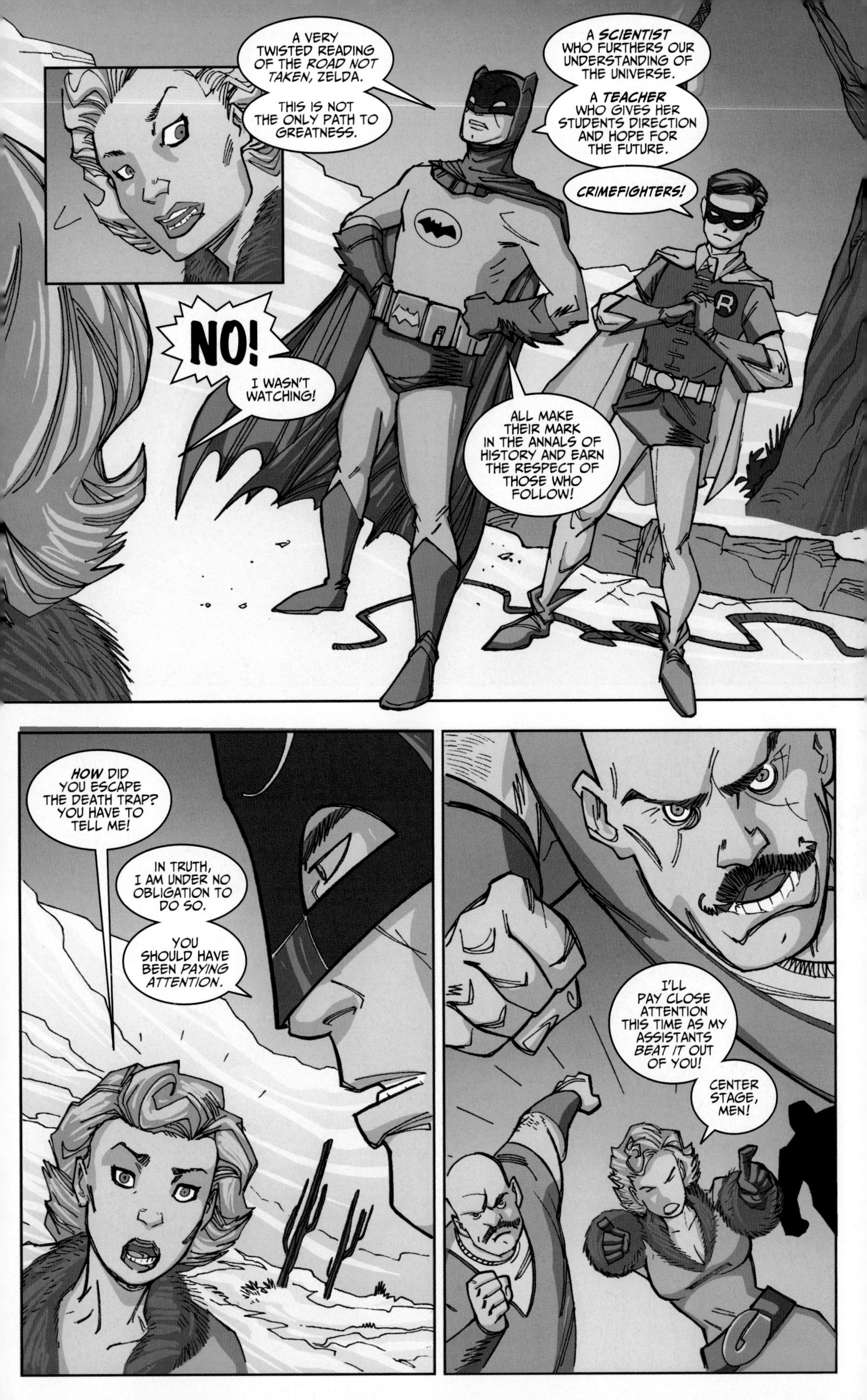
A VERY TWISTED READING OF THE *ROAD NOT TAKEN*, ZELDA.
THIS IS NOT THE ONLY PATH TO GREATNESS.
A *SCIENTIST* WHO FURTHERS OUR UNDERSTANDING OF THE UNIVERSE.
A *TEACHER* WHO GIVES HER STUDENTS DIRECTION AND HOPE FOR THE FUTURE.
CRIMEFIGHTERS!
NO!
I WASN'T WATCHING!
ALL MAKE THEIR MARK IN THE ANNALS OF HISTORY AND EARN THE RESPECT OF THOSE WHO FOLLOW!
HOW DID YOU ESCAPE THE DEATH TRAP? YOU HAVE TO TELL ME!
IN TRUTH, I AM UNDER NO OBLIGATION TO DO SO.
YOU SHOULD HAVE BEEN *PAYING ATTENTION*.
I'LL PAY CLOSE ATTENTION THIS TIME AS MY ASSISTANTS *BEAT IT* OUT OF YOU!
CENTER STAGE, MEN!

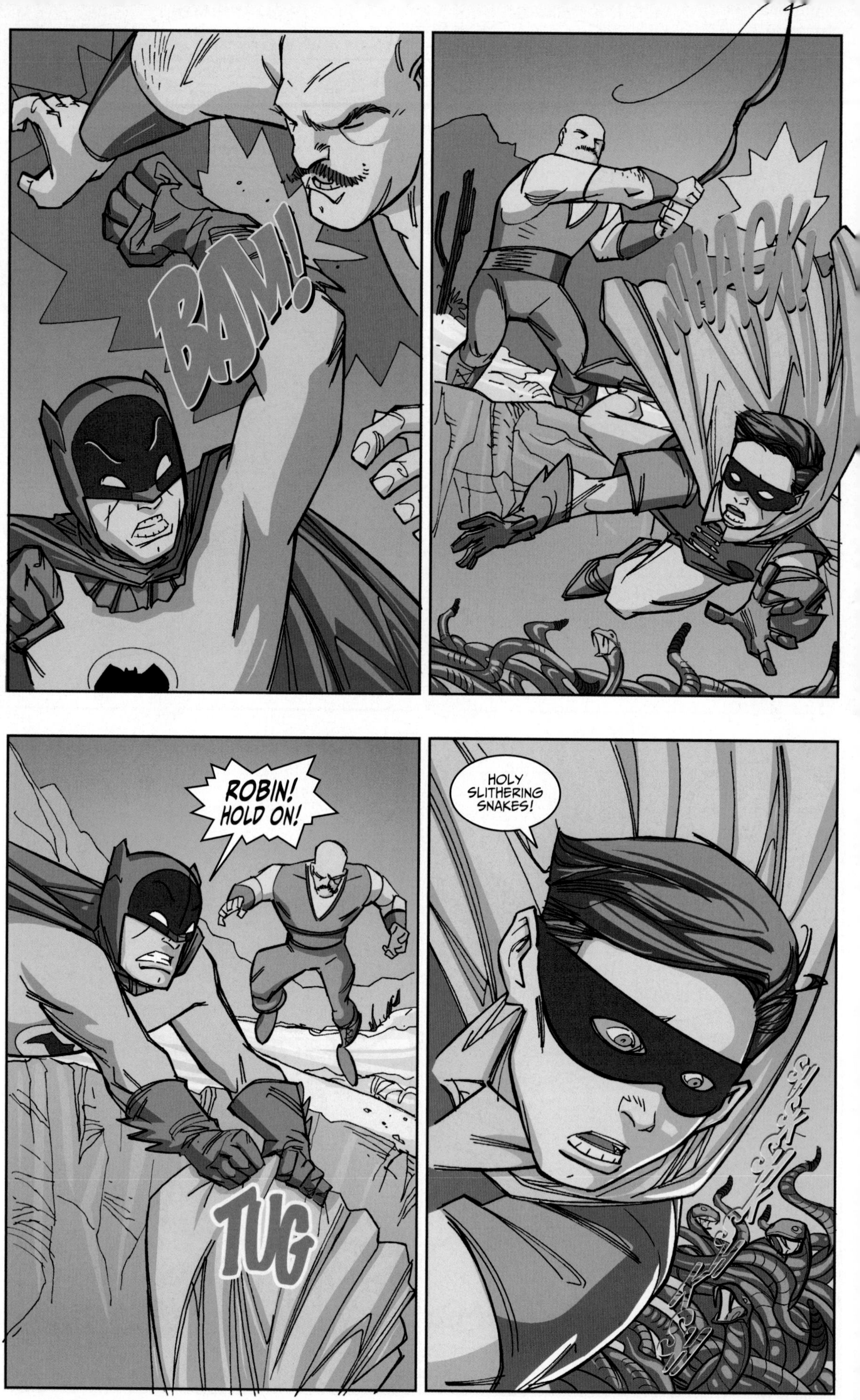
BAM!
WHACK!
ROBIN! HOLD ON!
TUG
HOLY SLITHERING SNAKES!

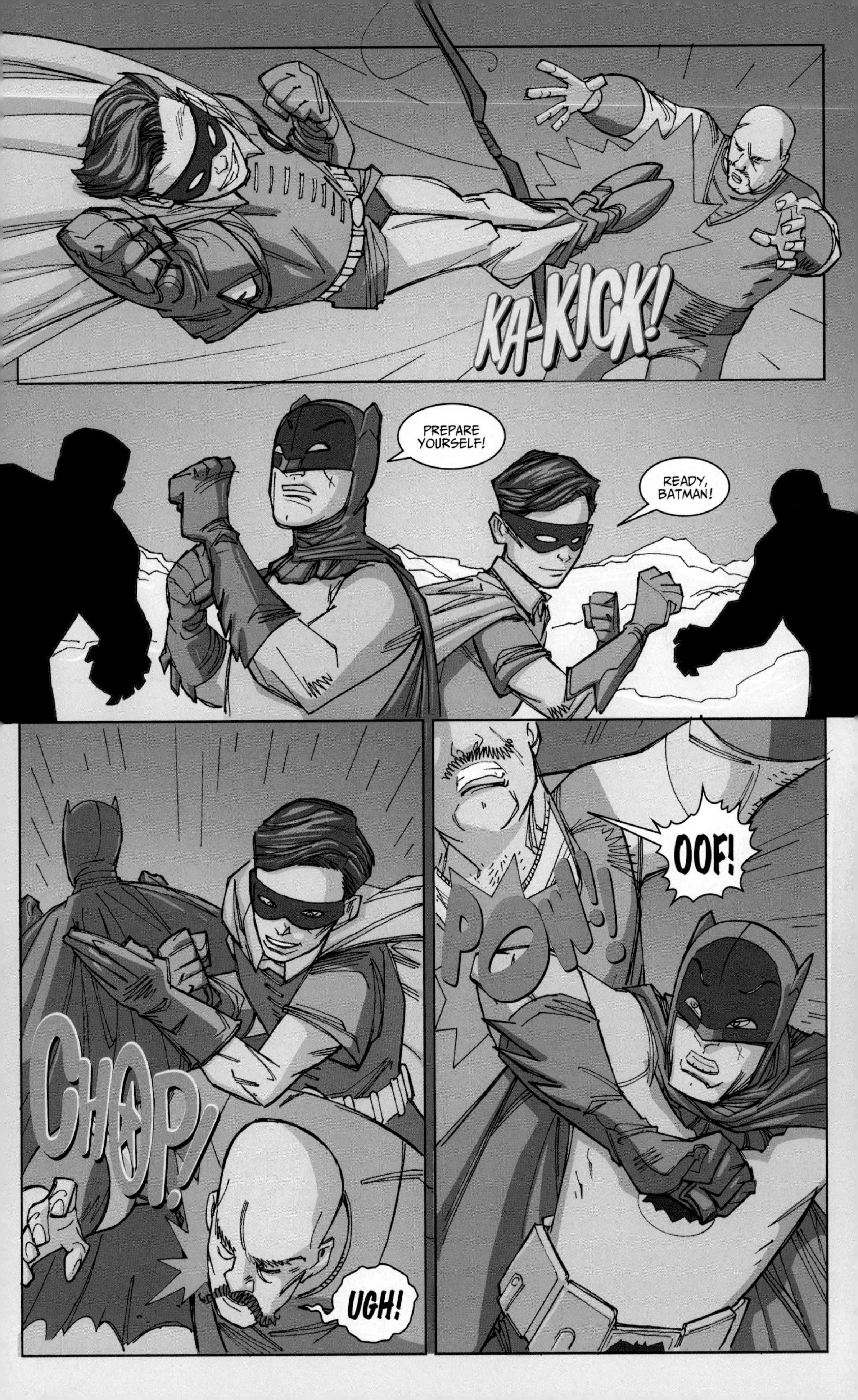
KA-KICK!
PREPARE YOURSELF!
READY, BATMAN!
CHOP!
UGH!
POW!!
OOF!

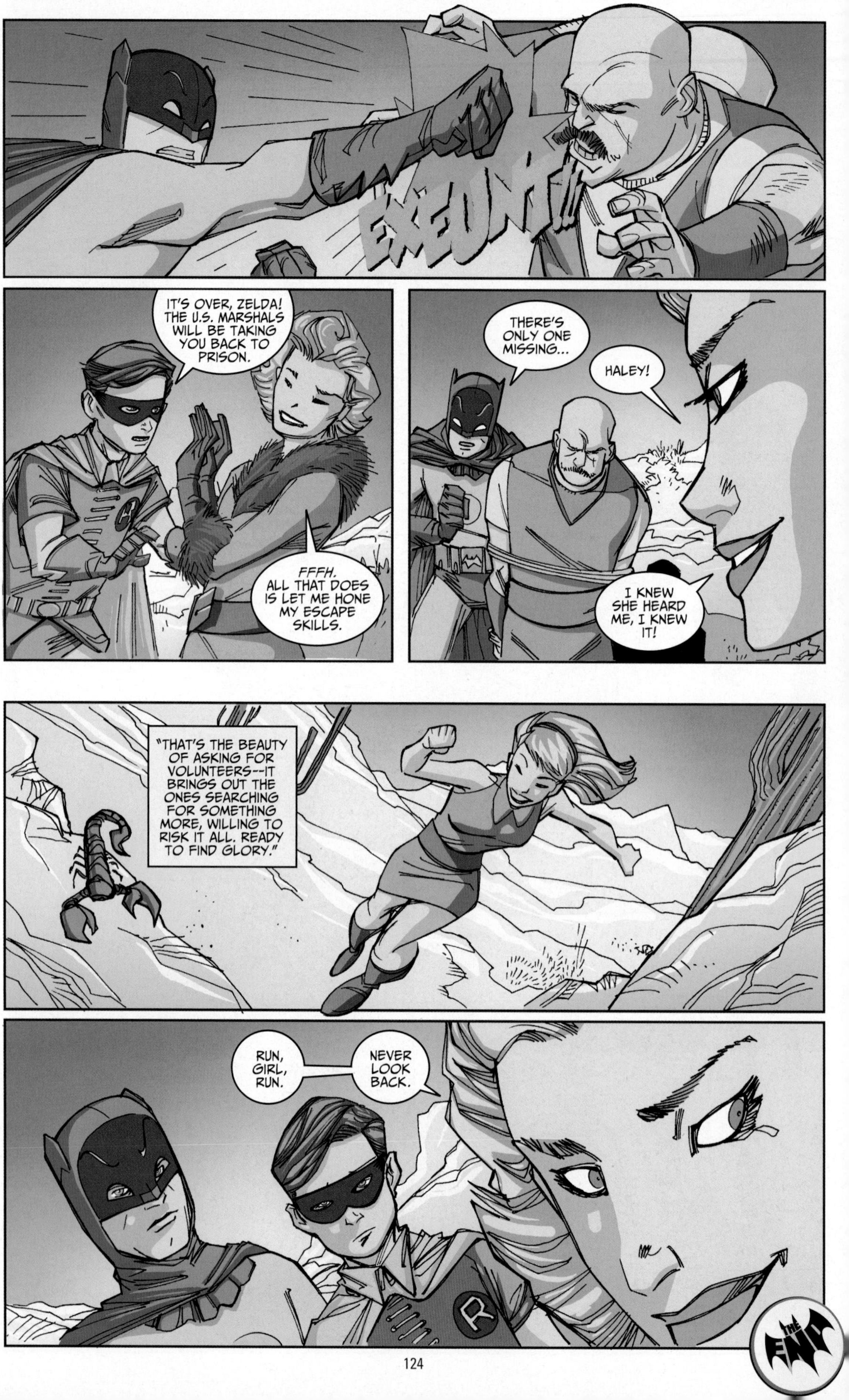
EXEUNT!!
IT'S OVER, ZELDA! THE U.S. MARSHALS WILL BE TAKING YOU BACK TO PRISON.
FFFH. ALL THAT DOES IS LET ME HONE MY ESCAPE SKILLS.
THERE'S ONLY ONE MISSING...
HALEY!
I KNEW SHE HEARD ME, I KNEW IT!
"THAT'S THE BEAUTY OF ASKING FOR VOLUNTEERS--IT BRINGS OUT THE ONES SEARCHING FOR SOMETHING MORE, WILLING TO RISK IT ALL. READY TO FIND GLORY."
RUN, GIRL, RUN.
NEVER LOOK BACK.
R
THE END

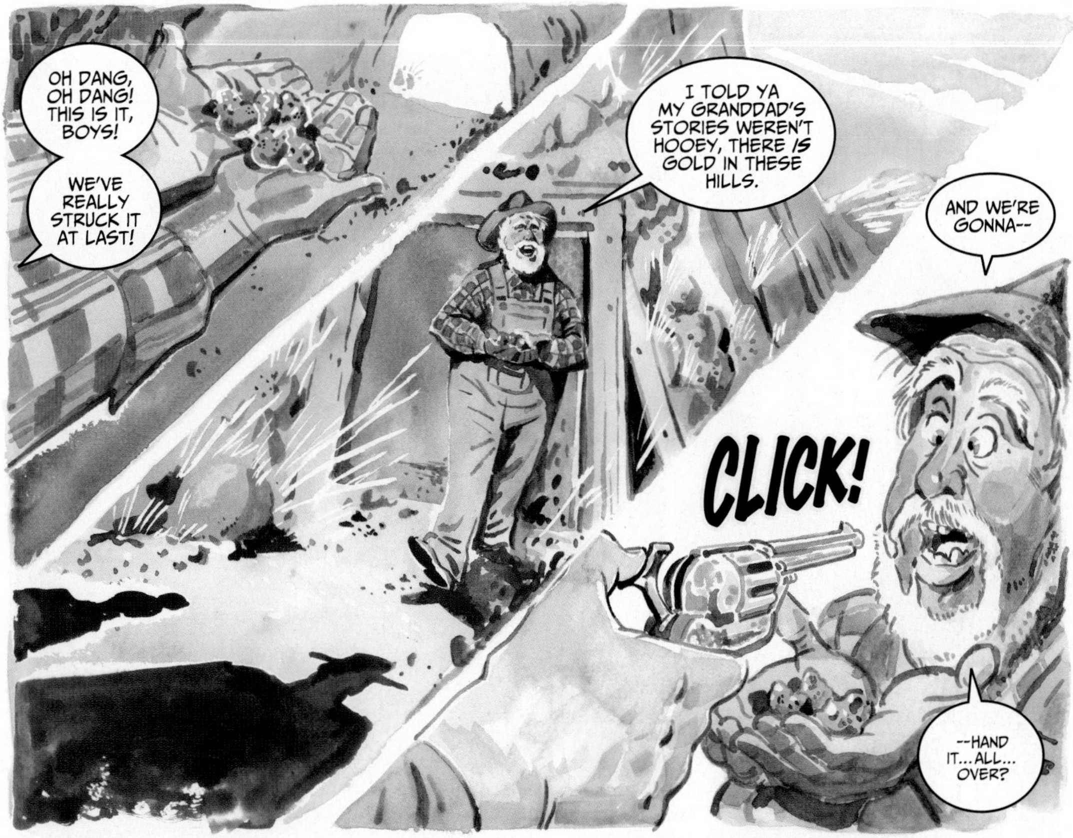
OH DANG, OH DANG! THIS IS IT, BOYS!
WE'VE REALLY STRUCK IT AT LAST!
I TOLD YA MY GRANDDAD'S STORIES WEREN'T HOOEY, THERE *IS* GOLD IN THESE HILLS.
AND WE'RE GONNA--
CLICK!
--HAND IT... ALL... OVER?

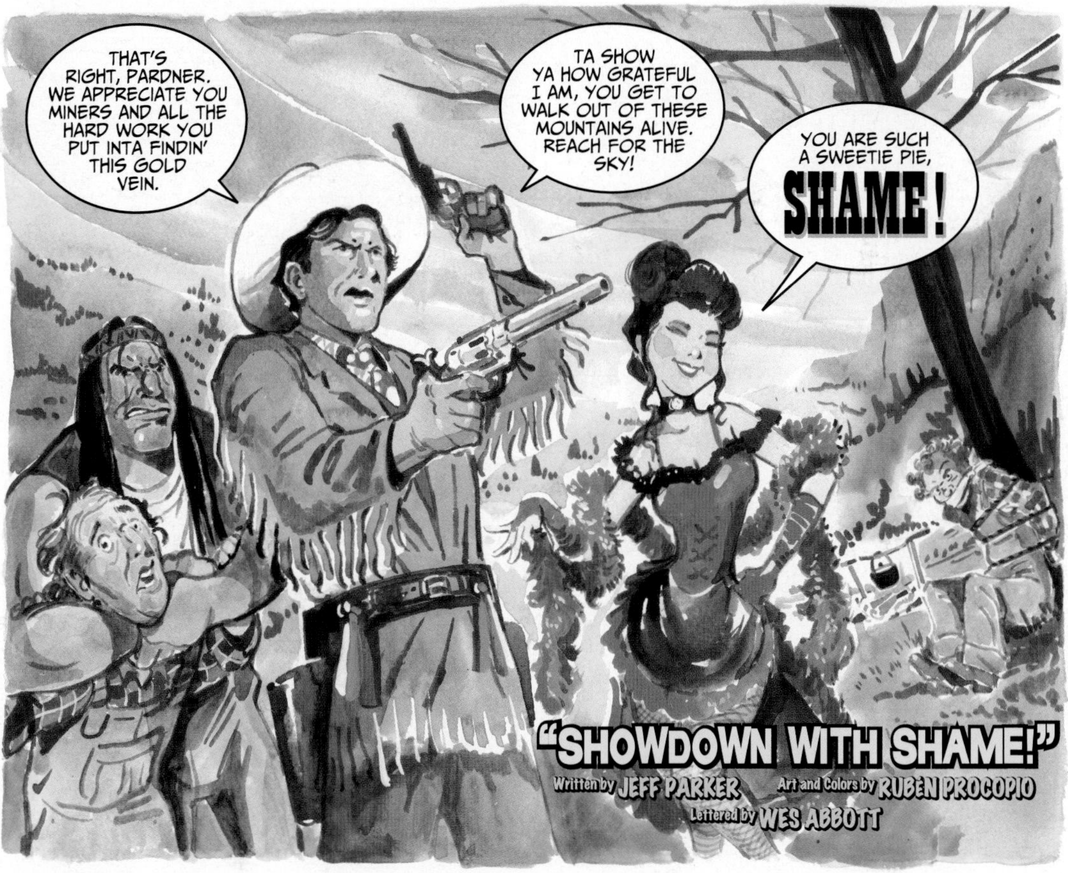
THAT'S RIGHT, PARDNER. WE APPRECIATE YOU MINERS AND ALL THE HARD WORK YOU PUT INTA FINDIN' THIS GOLD VEIN.
TA SHOW YA HOW GRATEFUL I AM, YOU GET TO WALK OUT OF THESE MOUNTAINS ALIVE. REACH FOR THE SKY!
YOU ARE SUCH A SWEETIE PIE, SHAME!
"SHOWDOWN WITH SHAME!"
Written by JEFF PARKER Art and Colors by RUBEN PROCOPIO
Lettered by WES ABBOTT

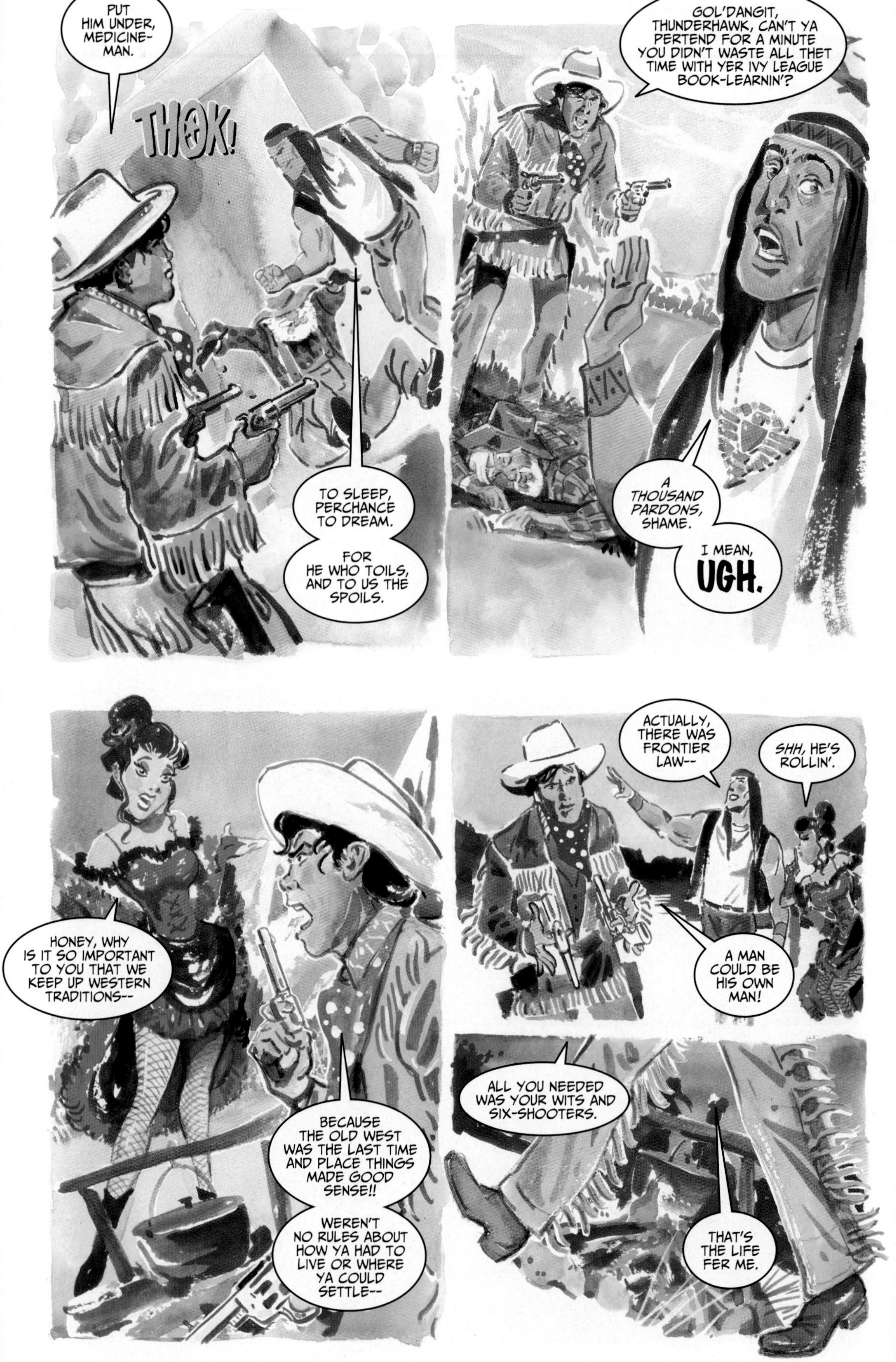
PUT HIM UNDER, MEDICINE-MAN.
THOK!
TO SLEEP, PERCHANCE TO DREAM.
FOR HE WHO TOILS, AND TO US THE SPOILS.
GOL'DANGIT, THUNDERHAWK, CAN'T YA PERTEND FOR A MINUTE YOU DIDN'T WASTE ALL THET TIME WITH YER IVY LEAGUE BOOK-LEARNIN'?
A THOUSAND PARDONS, SHAME.
I MEAN, UGH.
HONEY, WHY IS IT SO IMPORTANT TO YOU THAT WE KEEP UP WESTERN TRADITIONS--
BECAUSE THE OLD WEST WAS THE LAST TIME AND PLACE THINGS MADE GOOD SENSE!!
WEREN'T NO RULES ABOUT HOW YA HAD TO LIVE OR WHERE YA COULD SETTLE--
ACTUALLY, THERE WAS FRONTIER LAW--
SHH, HE'S ROLLIN'.
A MAN COULD BE HIS OWN MAN!
ALL YOU NEEDED WAS YOUR WITS AND SIX-SHOOTERS.
THAT'S THE LIFE FER ME.

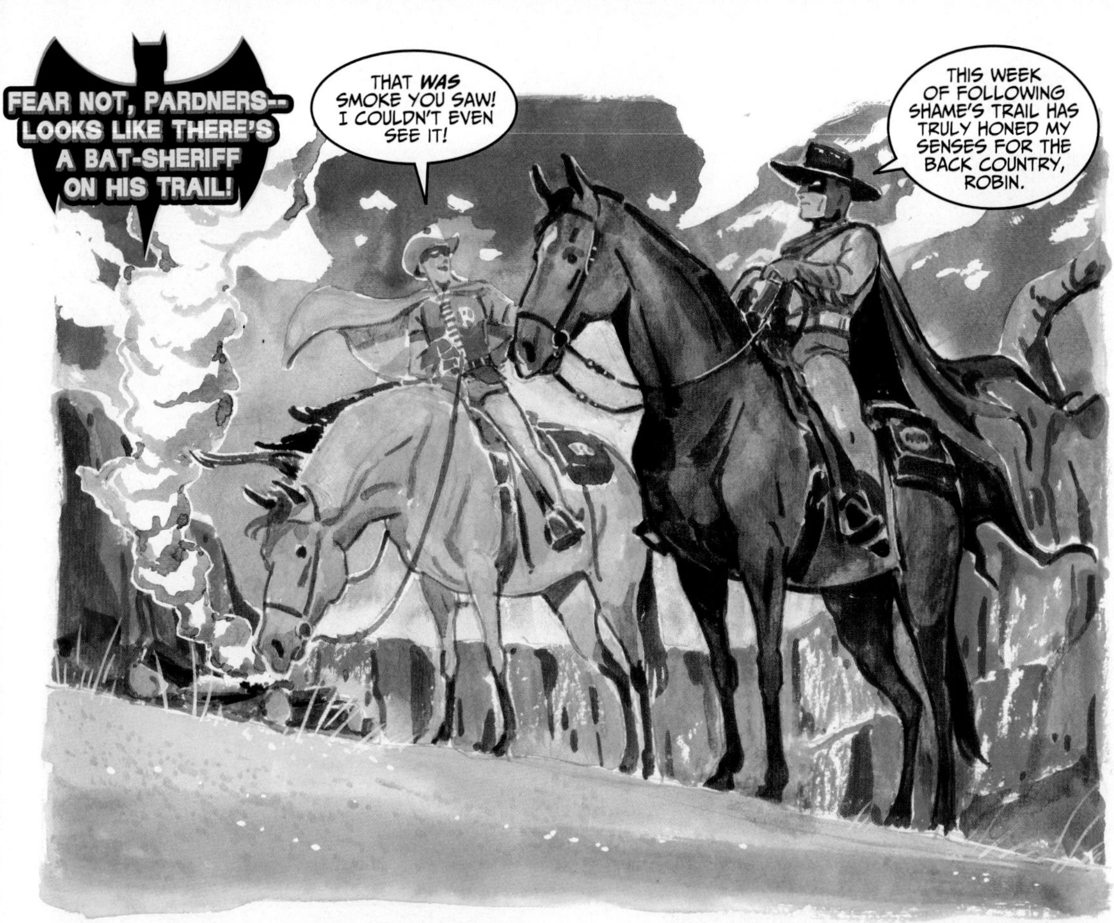
FEAR NOT, PARDNERS-- LOOKS LIKE THERE'S A BAT-SHERIFF ON HIS TRAIL!
THAT WAS SMOKE YOU SAW! I COULDN'T EVEN SEE IT!
THIS WEEK OF FOLLOWING SHAME'S TRAIL HAS TRULY HONED MY SENSES FOR THE BACK COUNTRY, ROBIN.

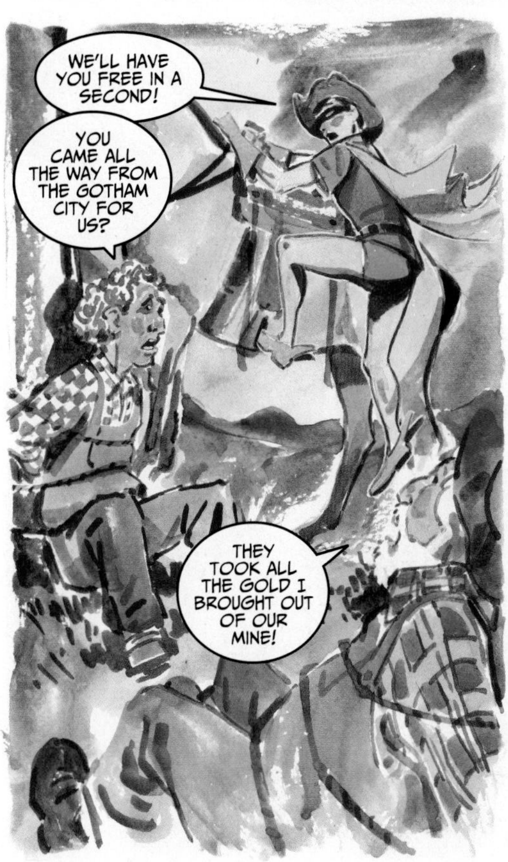
WE'LL HAVE YOU FREE IN A SECOND!
YOU CAME ALL THE WAY FROM THE GOTHAM CITY FOR US?
THEY TOOK ALL THE GOLD I BROUGHT OUT OF OUR MINE!

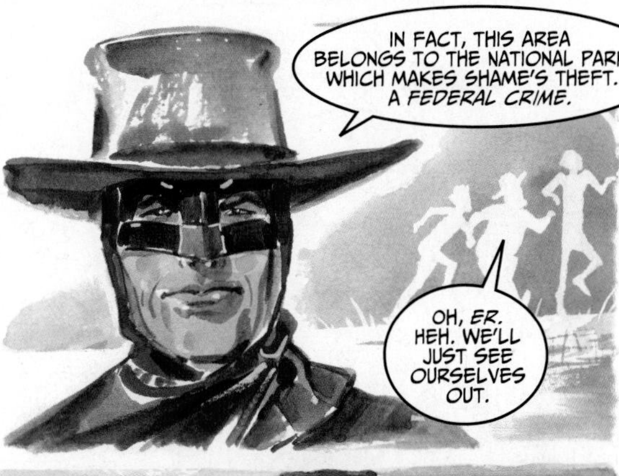
IN FACT, THIS AREA BELONGS TO THE NATIONAL PARKS. WHICH MAKES SHAME'S THEFT... A FEDERAL CRIME.
OH, ER. HEH. WE'LL JUST SEE OURSELVES OUT.

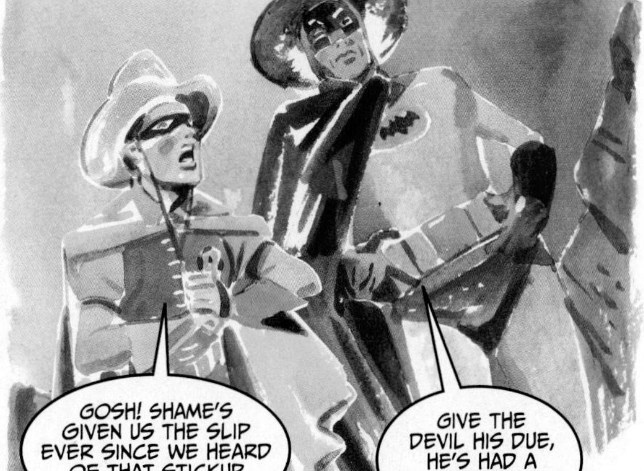
GOSH! SHAME'S GIVEN US THE SLIP EVER SINCE WE HEARD OF THAT STICKUP IN ARIZONA.
GIVE THE DEVIL HIS DUE, HE'S HAD A LEGENDARY RUN THIS TIME.

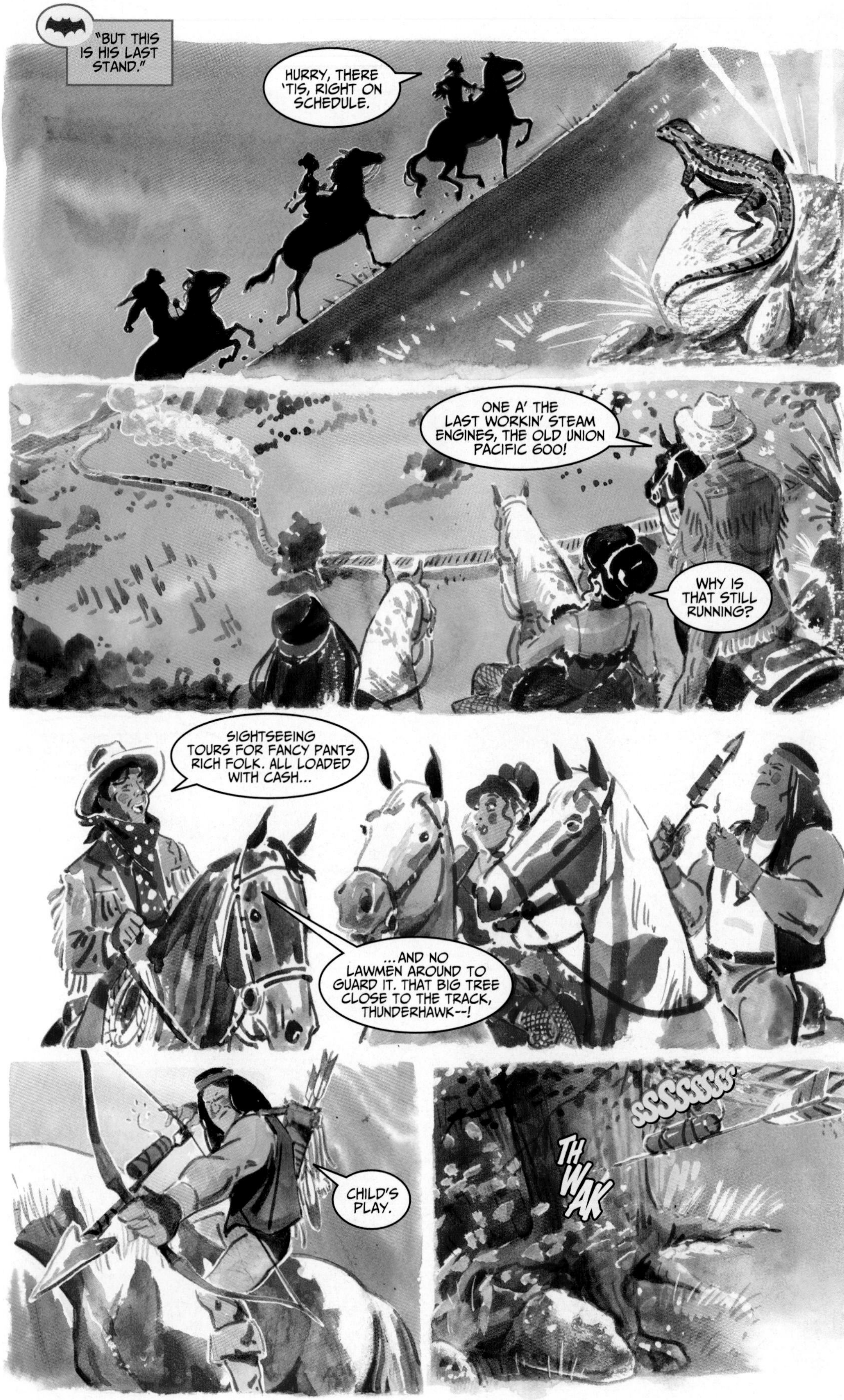

"BUT THIS IS HIS LAST STAND."
HURRY, THERE 'TIS, RIGHT ON SCHEDULE.
ONE A' THE LAST WORKIN' STEAM ENGINES, THE OLD UNION PACIFIC 600!
WHY IS THAT STILL RUNNING?
SIGHTSEEING TOURS FOR FANCY PANTS RICH FOLK. ALL LOADED WITH CASH...
...AND NO LAWMEN AROUND TO GUARD IT. THAT BIG TREE CLOSE TO THE TRACK, THUNDERHAWK--!
CHILD'S PLAY.
SSSSSSSS
THWAK

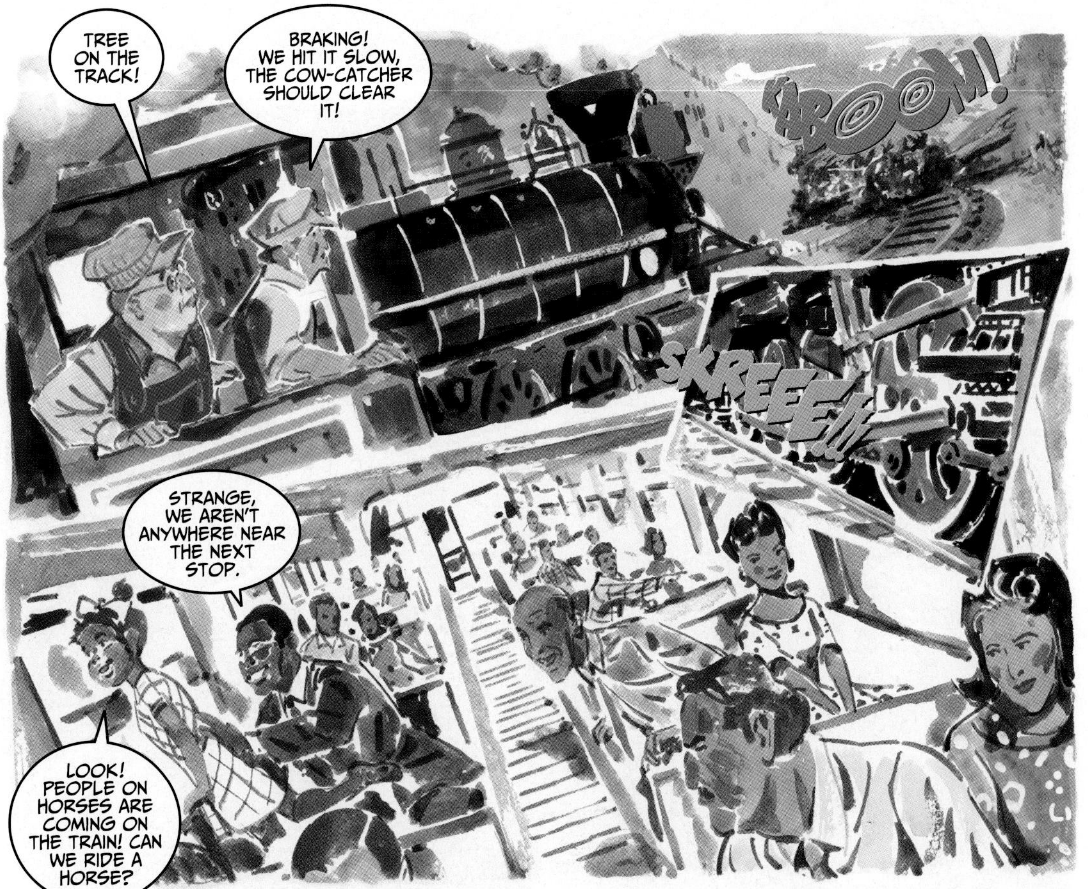
TREE ON THE TRACK!
BRAKING! WE HIT IT SLOW, THE COW-CATCHER SHOULD CLEAR IT!
KABOOM!
SKREEEE!!!
STRANGE, WE AREN'T ANYWHERE NEAR THE NEXT STOP.
LOOK! PEOPLE ON HORSES ARE COMING ON THE TRAIN! CAN WE RIDE A HORSE?

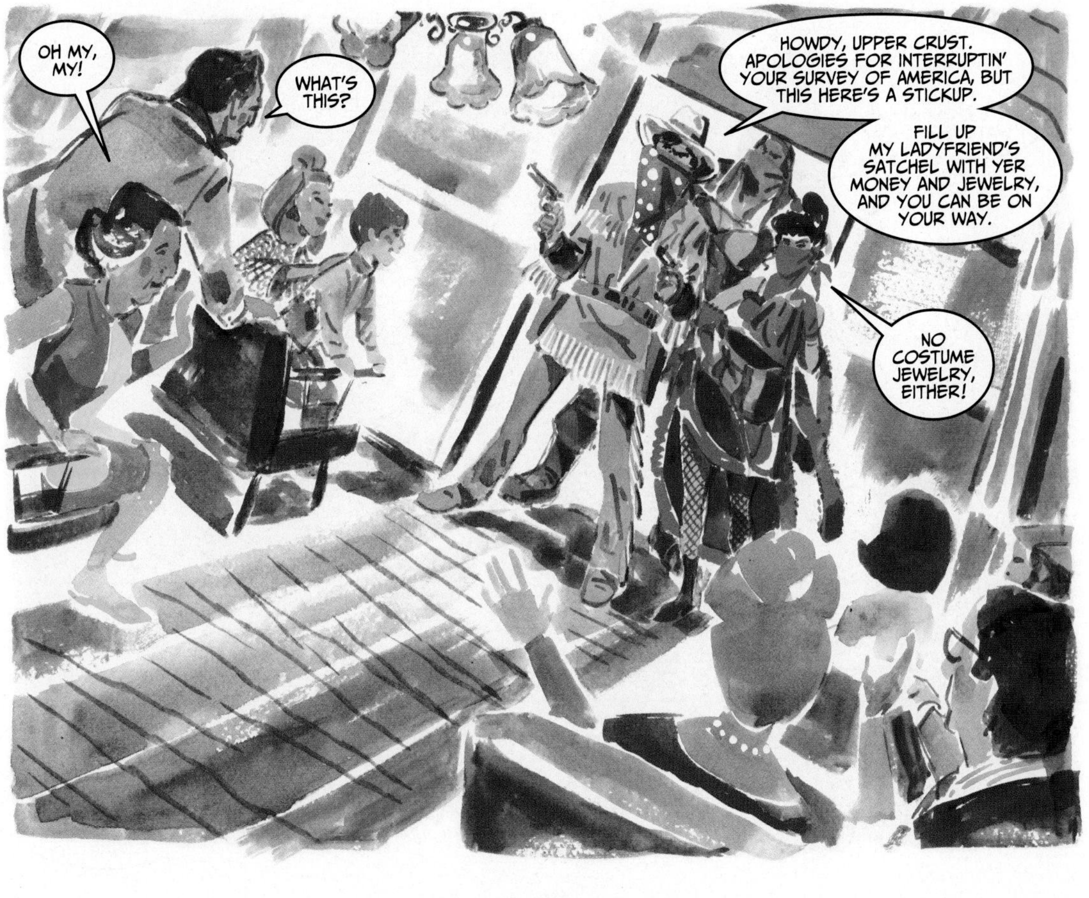
OH MY, MY!
WHAT'S THIS?
HOWDY, UPPER CRUST. APOLOGIES FOR INTERRUPTIN' YOUR SURVEY OF AMERICA, BUT THIS HERE'S A STICKUP.
FILL UP MY LADYFRIEND'S SATCHEL WITH YER MONEY AND JEWELRY, AND YOU CAN BE ON YOUR WAY.
NO COSTUME JEWELRY, EITHER!

FAN-TASTIC! THE TOUR REALLY WENT ALL OUT FOR THIS!
SEE, HONEY, THIS IS JUST LIKE A TRAIN ROBBERY THEY WOULD HAVE BACK IN THE OLD WEST!
NEAT!
YEAH, IT'S EXACTLY LIKE IT...
BLAM!
...'CAUSE IT IS!
AAAHH!
THAT'S RIGHT...AND DON'T FORGET YOUR EXPENSIVE WATCHES.
KEEP IT COMIN', THIS WON'T BREAK YA.
AND YEARS FROM NOW YOU CAN STILL BE TELLIN' ANYONE WHO'LL LISTEN ABOUT THE ONE BIT A' EXCITEMENT YOU HAD IN YER LIFE.

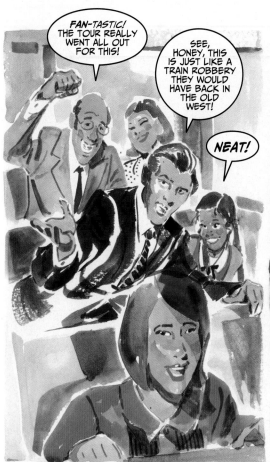

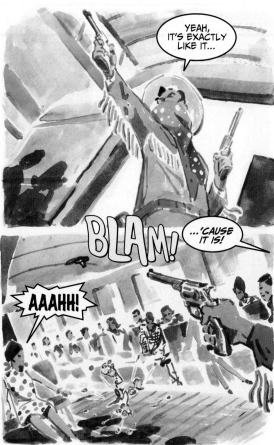

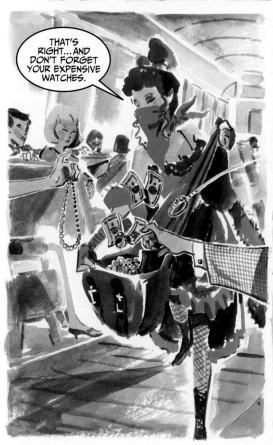

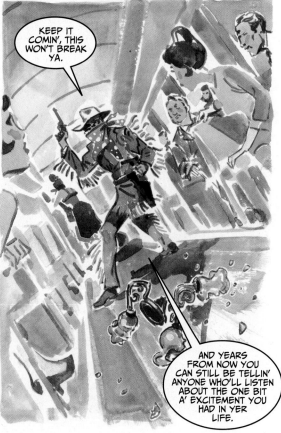

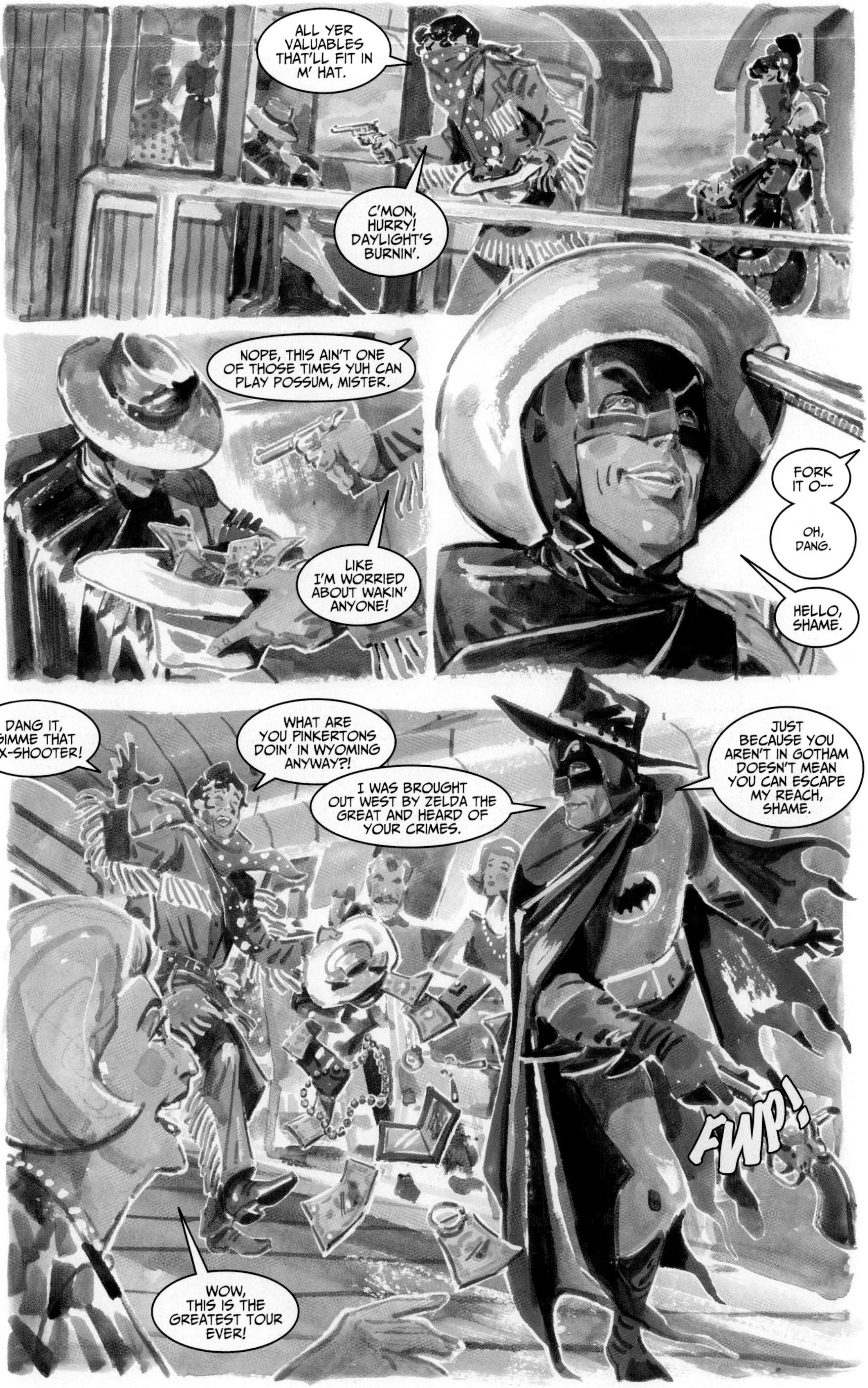
ALL YER VALUABLES THAT'LL FIT IN M' HAT.
C'MON, HURRY! DAYLIGHT'S BURNIN'.
NOPE, THIS AIN'T ONE OF THOSE TIMES YUH CAN PLAY POSSUM, MISTER.
LIKE I'M WORRIED ABOUT WAKIN' ANYONE!
FORK IT O--
OH, DANG.
HELLO, SHAME.
DANG IT, GIMME THAT SIX-SHOOTER!
WHAT ARE YOU PINKERTONS DOIN' IN WYOMING ANYWAY?!
I WAS BROUGHT OUT WEST BY ZELDA THE GREAT AND HEARD OF YOUR CRIMES.
JUST BECAUSE YOU AREN'T IN GOTHAM DOESN'T MEAN YOU CAN ESCAPE MY REACH, SHAME.
FWP!
WOW, THIS IS THE GREATEST TOUR EVER!

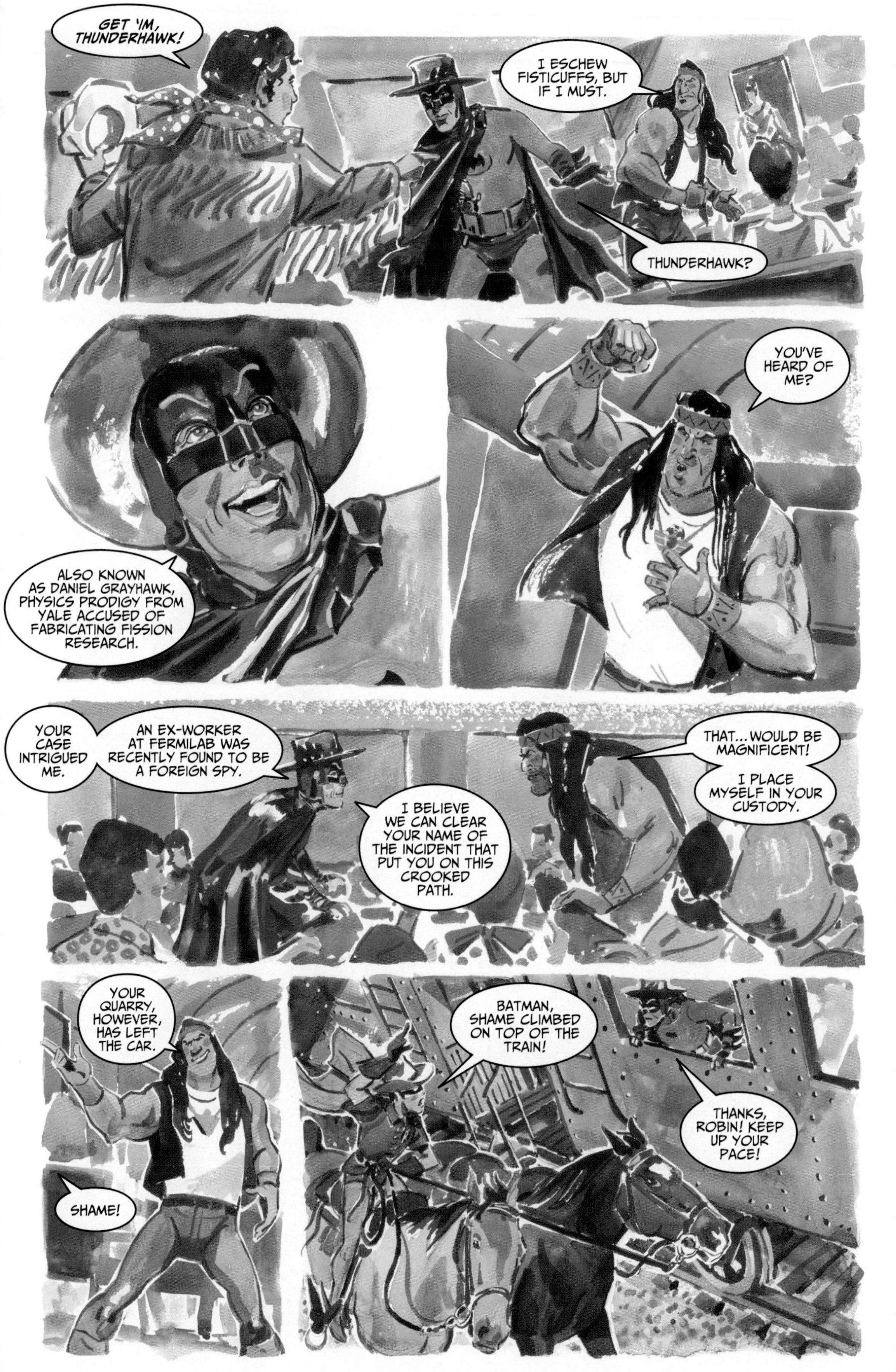
GET 'IM, THUNDERHAWK!
I ESCHEW FISTICUFFS, BUT IF I MUST.
THUNDERHAWK?
YOU'VE HEARD OF ME?
ALSO KNOWN AS DANIEL GRAYHAWK, PHYSICS PRODIGY FROM YALE ACCUSED OF FABRICATING FISSION RESEARCH.
YOUR CASE INTRIGUED ME.
AN EX-WORKER AT FERMILAB WAS RECENTLY FOUND TO BE A FOREIGN SPY.
I BELIEVE WE CAN CLEAR YOUR NAME OF THE INCIDENT THAT PUT YOU ON THIS CROOKED PATH.
THAT...WOULD BE MAGNIFICENT!
I PLACE MYSELF IN YOUR CUSTODY.
YOUR QUARRY, HOWEVER, HAS LEFT THE CAR.
SHAME!
BATMAN, SHAME CLIMBED ON TOP OF THE TRAIN!
THANKS, ROBIN! KEEP UP YOUR PACE!

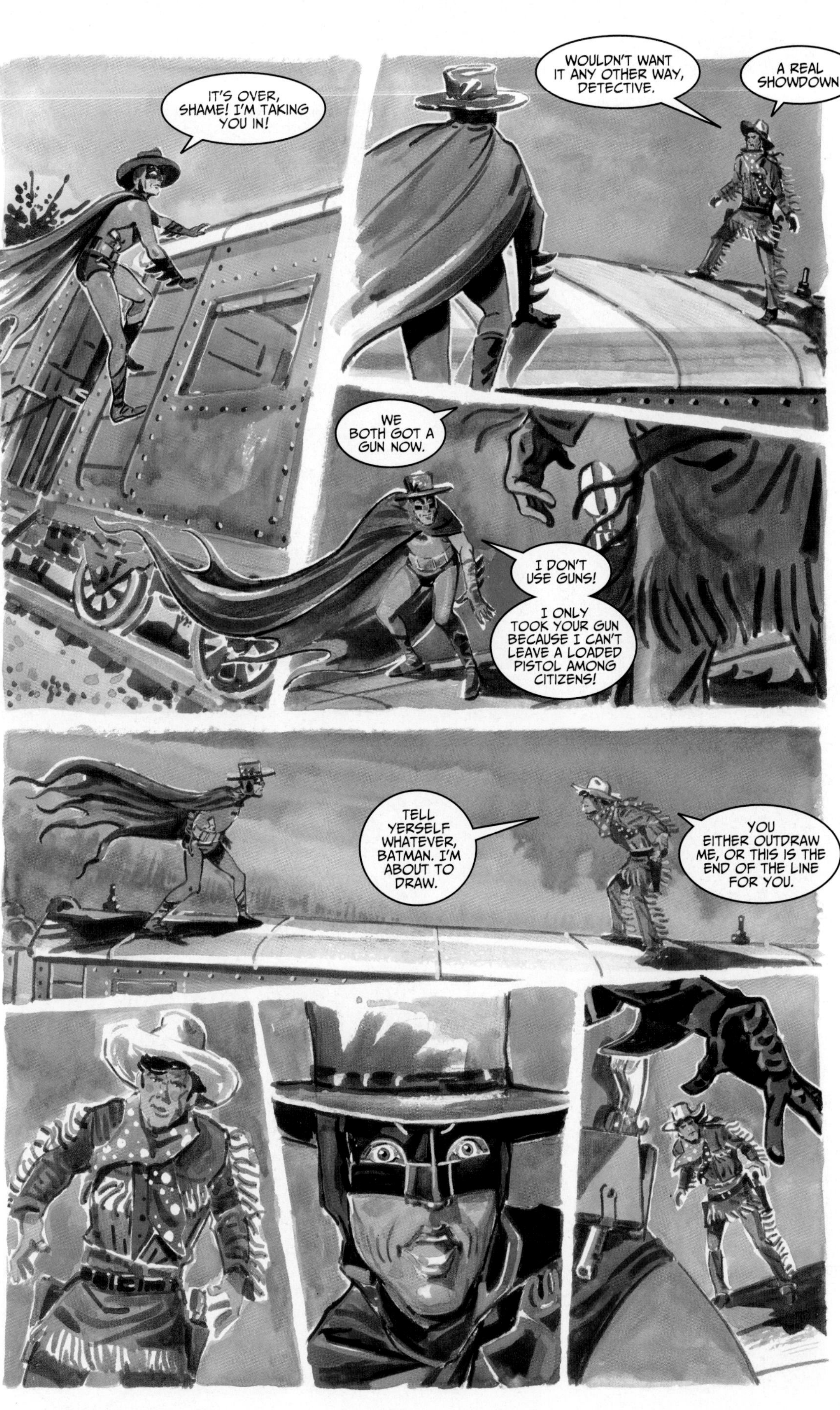
IT'S OVER, SHAME! I'M TAKING YOU IN!
WOULDN'T WANT IT ANY OTHER WAY, DETECTIVE.
A REAL SHOWDOWN.
WE BOTH GOT A GUN NOW.
I DON'T USE GUNS!
I ONLY TOOK YOUR GUN BECAUSE I CAN'T LEAVE A LOADED PISTOL AMONG CITIZENS!
TELL YERSELF WHATEVER, BATMAN. I'M ABOUT TO DRAW.
YOU EITHER OUTDRAW ME, OR THIS IS THE END OF THE LINE FOR YOU.

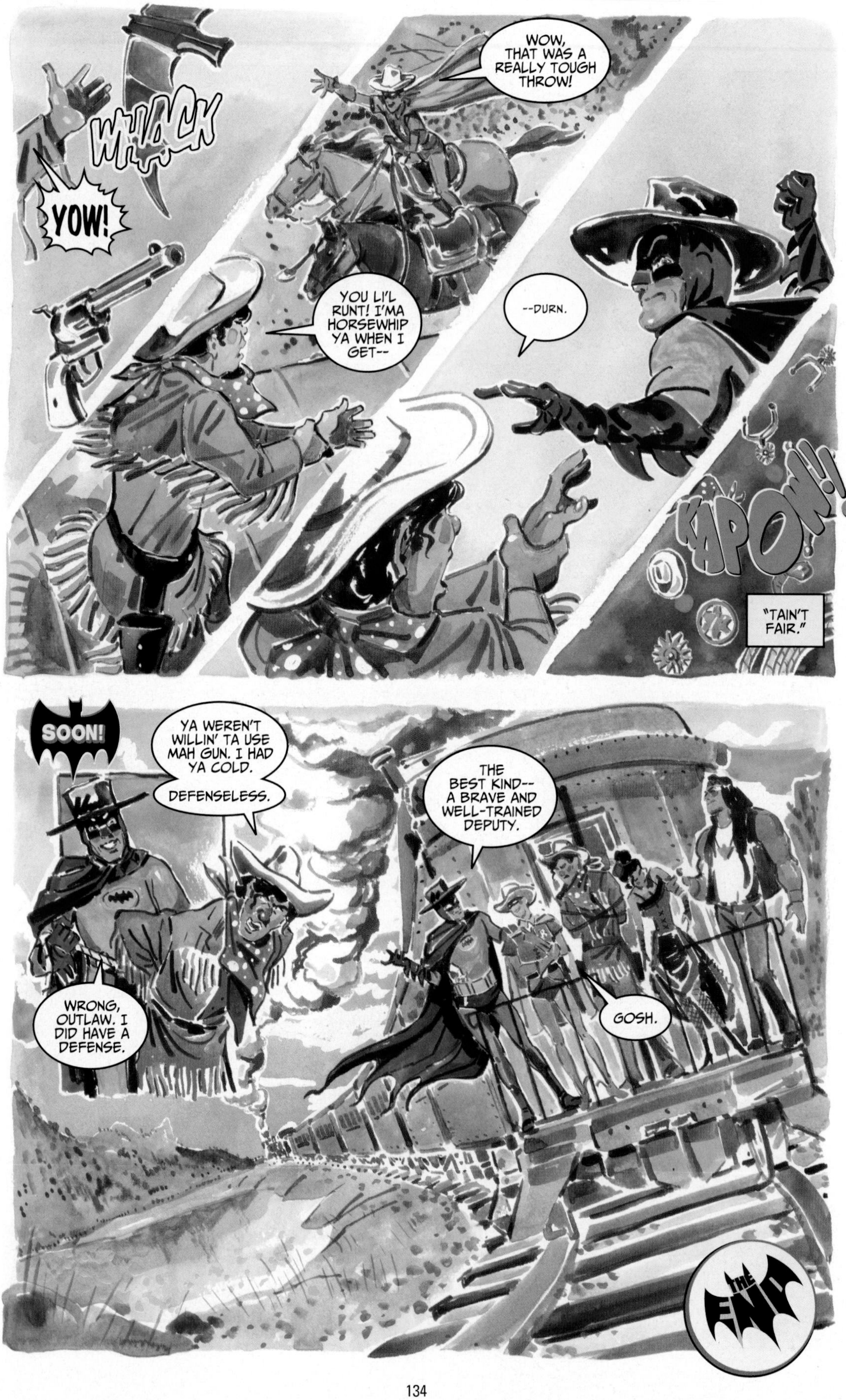
WHACK
YOW!
WOW, THAT WAS A REALLY TOUGH THROW!
YOU LI'L RUNT! I'MA HORSEWHIP YA WHEN I GET--
--DURN.
KAPOW!!
"TAIN'T FAIR."
SOON!
YA WEREN'T WILLIN' TA USE MAH GUN. I HAD YA COLD.
DEFENSELESS.
WRONG, OUTLAW. I DID HAVE A DEFENSE.
THE BEST KIND-- A BRAVE AND WELL-TRAINED DEPUTY.
GOSH.
THE END

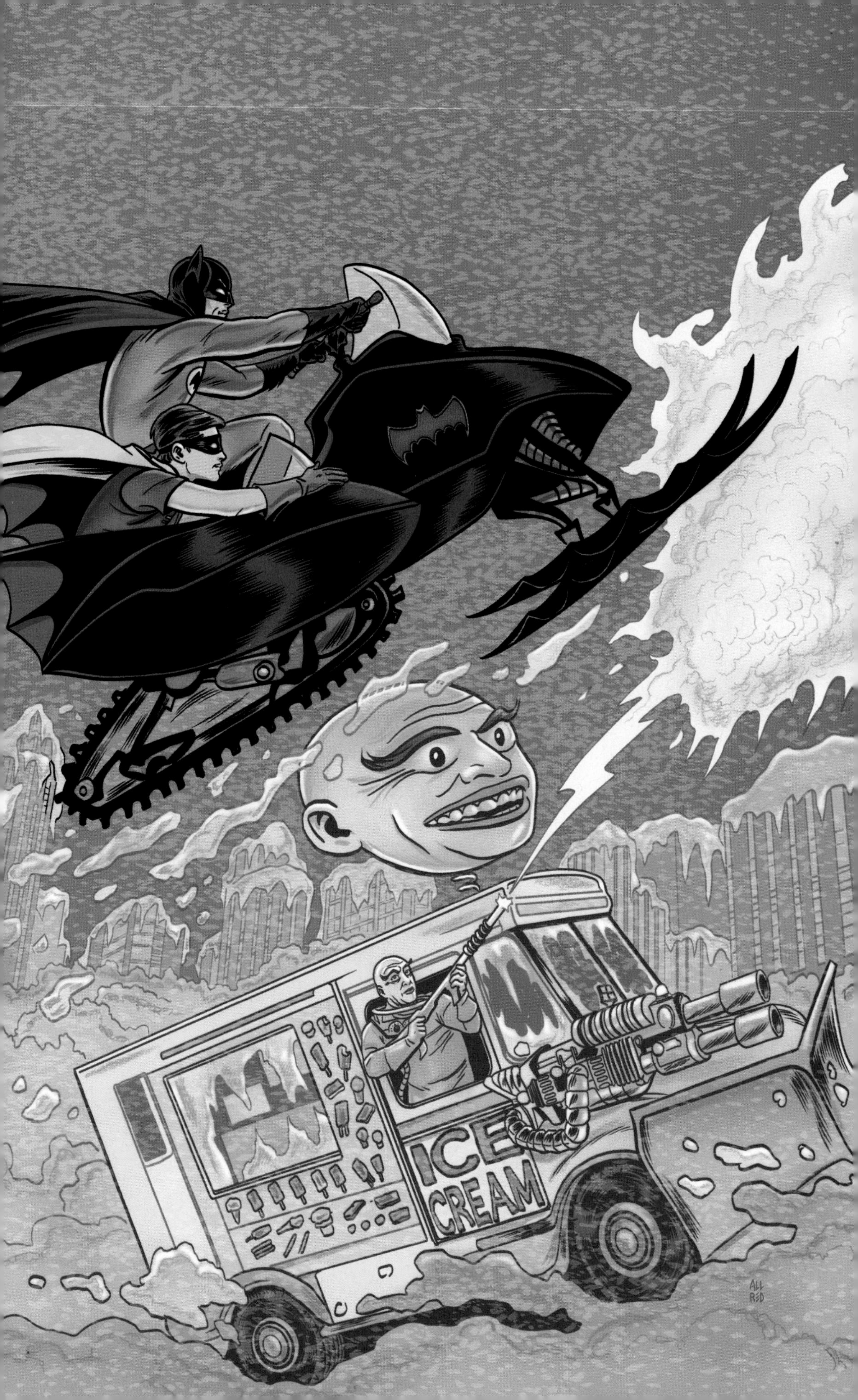

ICE
CREAM
ALL
RED

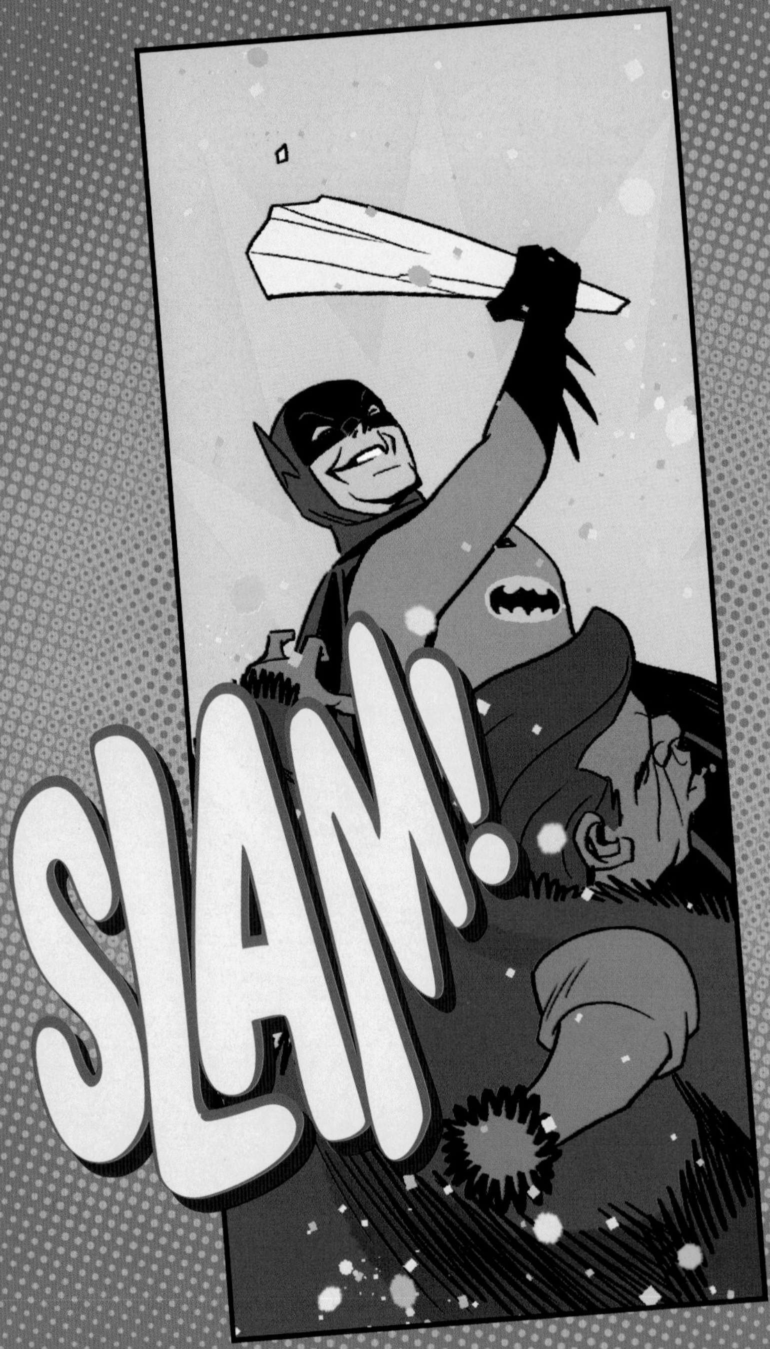
SLAM!

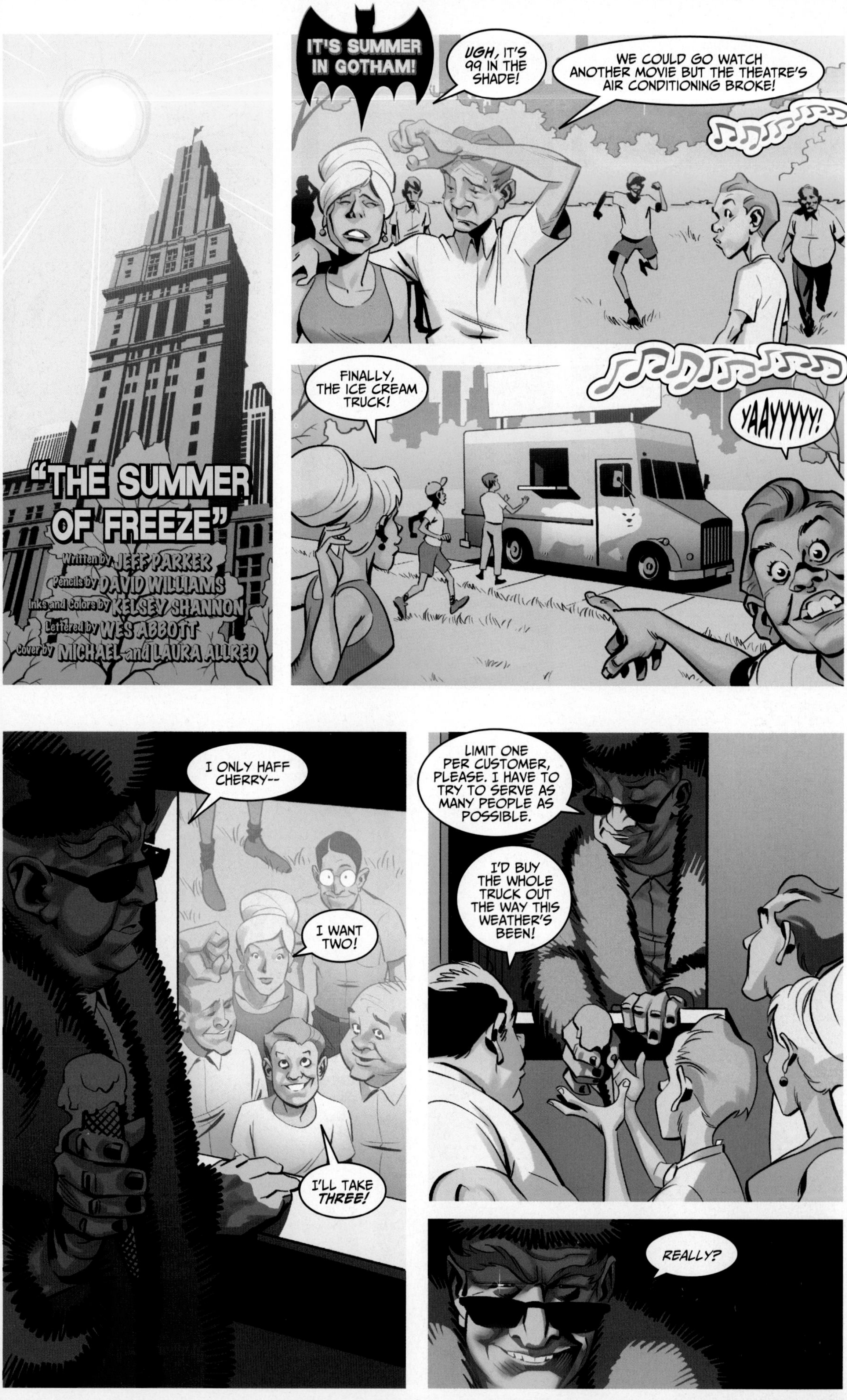
"THE SUMMER OF FREEZE"
Written by JEFF PARKER
Pencils by DAVID WILLIAMS
Inks and Colors by KELSEY SHANNON
Lettered by WES ABBOTT
Cover by MICHAEL and LAURA ALLRED
IT'S SUMMER IN GOTHAM!
UGH, IT'S 99 IN THE SHADE!
WE COULD GO WATCH ANOTHER MOVIE BUT THE THEATRE'S AIR CONDITIONING BROKE!
FINALLY, THE ICE CREAM TRUCK!
YAAYYYYY!
I ONLY HAFF CHERRY--
I WANT TWO!
I'LL TAKE THREE!
LIMIT ONE PER CUSTOMER, PLEASE. I HAVE TO TRY TO SERVE AS MANY PEOPLE AS POSSIBLE.
I'D BUY THE WHOLE TRUCK OUT THE WAY THIS WEATHER'S BEEN!
REALLY?

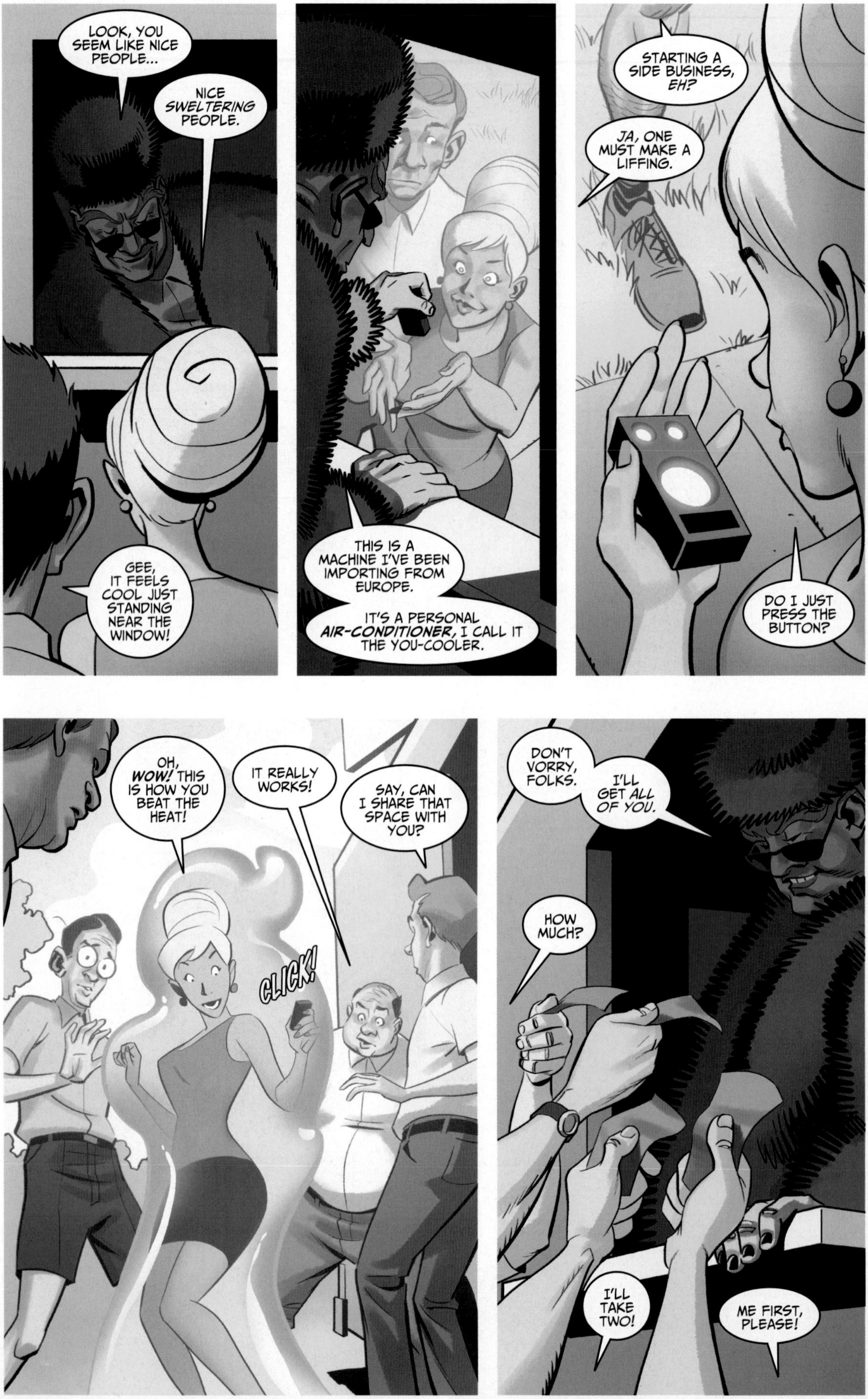
LOOK, YOU SEEM LIKE NICE PEOPLE...
NICE SWELTERING PEOPLE.
GEE, IT FEELS COOL JUST STANDING NEAR THE WINDOW!
THIS IS A MACHINE I'VE BEEN IMPORTING FROM EUROPE.
IT'S A PERSONAL AIR-CONDITIONER, I CALL IT THE YOU-COOLER.
STARTING A SIDE BUSINESS, EH?
JA, ONE MUST MAKE A LIFFING.
DO I JUST PRESS THE BUTTON?
OH, WOW! THIS IS HOW YOU BEAT THE HEAT!
IT REALLY WORKS!
SAY, CAN I SHARE THAT SPACE WITH YOU?
CLICK!
DON'T VORRY, FOLKS.
I'LL GET ALL OF YOU.
HOW MUCH?
I'LL TAKE TWO!
ME FIRST, PLEASE!

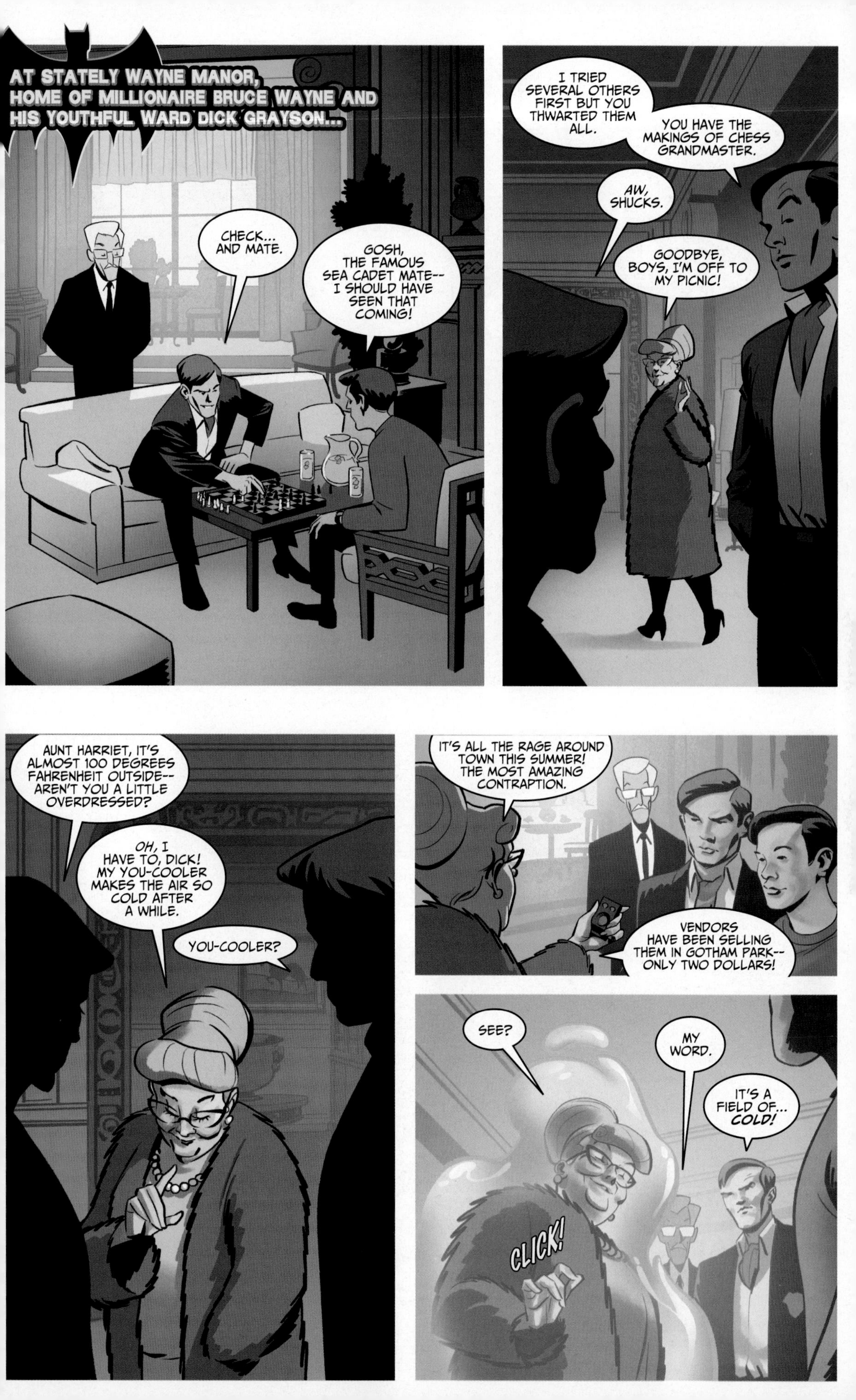
AT STATELY WAYNE MANOR, HOME OF MILLIONAIRE BRUCE WAYNE AND HIS YOUTHFUL WARD DICK GRAYSON...
CHECK... AND MATE.
GOSH, THE FAMOUS SEA CADET MATE-- I SHOULD HAVE SEEN THAT COMING!
I TRIED SEVERAL OTHERS FIRST BUT YOU THWARTED THEM ALL.
YOU HAVE THE MAKINGS OF CHESS GRANDMASTER.
AW, SHUCKS.
GOODBYE, BOYS, I'M OFF TO MY PICNIC!
AUNT HARRIET, IT'S ALMOST 100 DEGREES FAHRENHEIT OUTSIDE-- AREN'T YOU A LITTLE OVERDRESSED?
OH, I HAVE TO, DICK! MY YOU-COOLER MAKES THE AIR SO COLD AFTER A WHILE.
YOU-COOLER?
IT'S ALL THE RAGE AROUND TOWN THIS SUMMER! THE MOST AMAZING CONTRAPTION.
VENDORS HAVE BEEN SELLING THEM IN GOTHAM PARK-- ONLY TWO DOLLARS!
SEE?
MY WORD.
IT'S A FIELD OF... COLD!
CLICK!

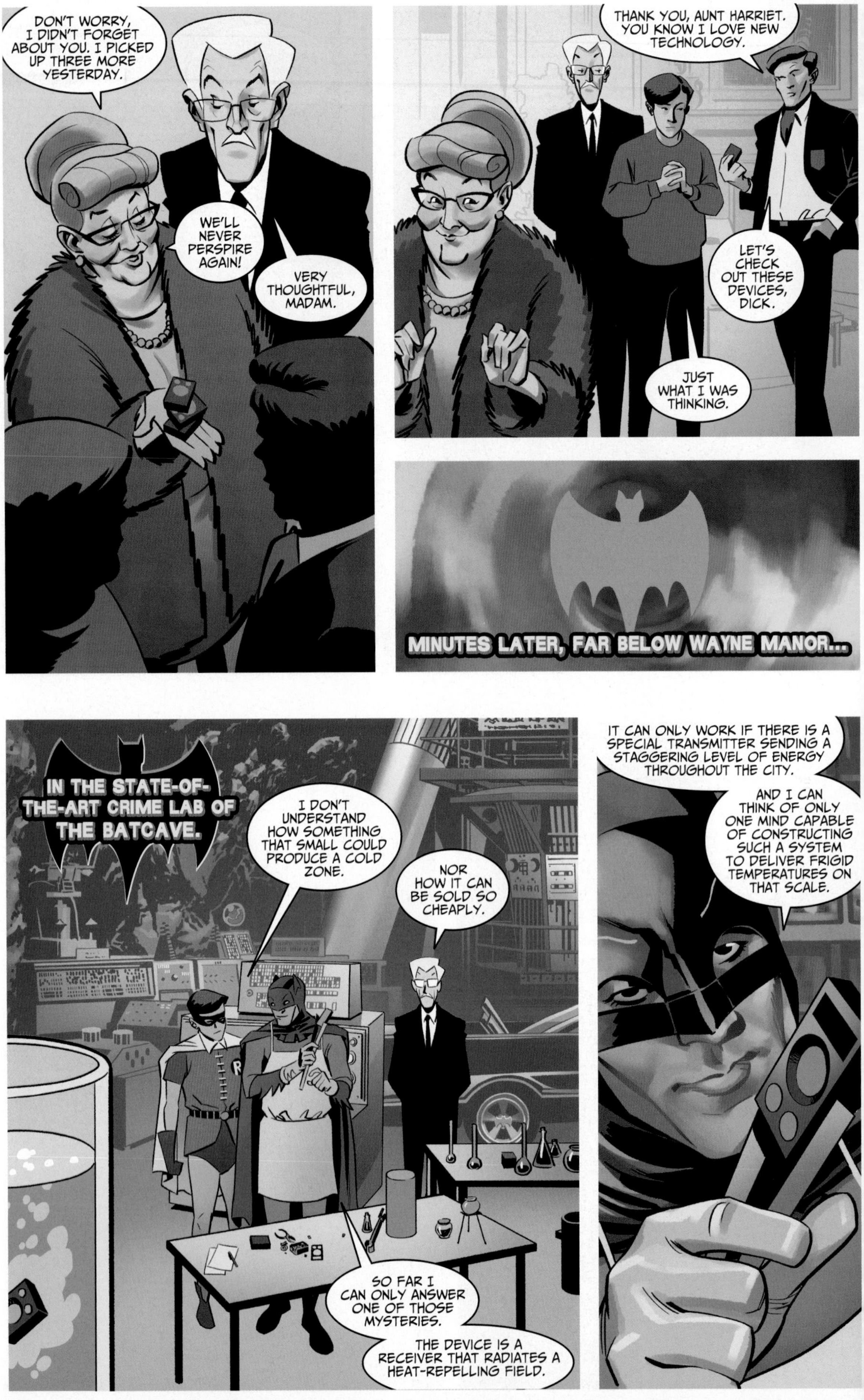
DON'T WORRY, I DIDN'T FORGET ABOUT YOU. I PICKED UP THREE MORE YESTERDAY.
WE'LL NEVER PERSPIRE AGAIN!
VERY THOUGHTFUL, MADAM.
THANK YOU, AUNT HARRIET. YOU KNOW I LOVE NEW TECHNOLOGY.
LET'S CHECK OUT THESE DEVICES, DICK.
JUST WHAT I WAS THINKING.
MINUTES LATER, FAR BELOW WAYNE MANOR...
IN THE STATE-OF-THE-ART CRIME LAB OF THE BATCAVE.
I DON'T UNDERSTAND HOW SOMETHING THAT SMALL COULD PRODUCE A COLD ZONE.
NOR HOW IT CAN BE SOLD SO CHEAPLY.
SO FAR I CAN ONLY ANSWER ONE OF THOSE MYSTERIES.
THE DEVICE IS A RECEIVER THAT RADIATES A HEAT-REPELLING FIELD.
IT CAN ONLY WORK IF THERE IS A SPECIAL TRANSMITTER SENDING A STAGGERING LEVEL OF ENERGY THROUGHOUT THE CITY.
AND I CAN THINK OF ONLY ONE MIND CAPABLE OF CONSTRUCTING SUCH A SYSTEM TO DELIVER FRIGID TEMPERATURES ON THAT SCALE.

MISTER FREEZE!

THE COMMISSAR OF COLD.

INDEED.

HE MUST HAVE SOME INSANE SCHEME FOR HIS TWISTED NOTION OF REVENGE AGAINST YOU!

I DON'T KNOW THAT IT'S ALL THAT TWISTED, ROBIN.

HE WAS A PIONEER IN CRYO-SCIENCE BUT RESENTFUL THAT HIS WORK RAN SHORT OF FUNDING. DESPERATION DROVE HIM TO STEAL THE EQUIPMENT HE NEEDED.

IT'S BATMAN!

STOP HIM AT ALL COSTS! FOR MY WORK!

CLINK!

PSSSSSS

AAHHH!!!

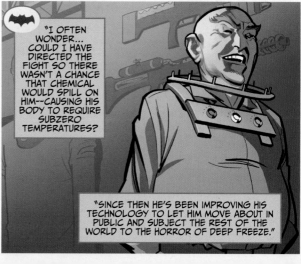

"I OFTEN WONDER... COULD I HAVE DIRECTED THE FIGHT SO THERE WASN'T A CHANCE THAT CHEMICAL WOULD SPILL ON HIM--CAUSING HIS BODY TO REQUIRE SUBZERO TEMPERATURES?

"SINCE THEN HE'S BEEN IMPROVING HIS TECHNOLOGY TO LET HIM MOVE ABOUT IN PUBLIC AND SUBJECT THE REST OF THE WORLD TO THE HORROR OF DEEP FREEZE."

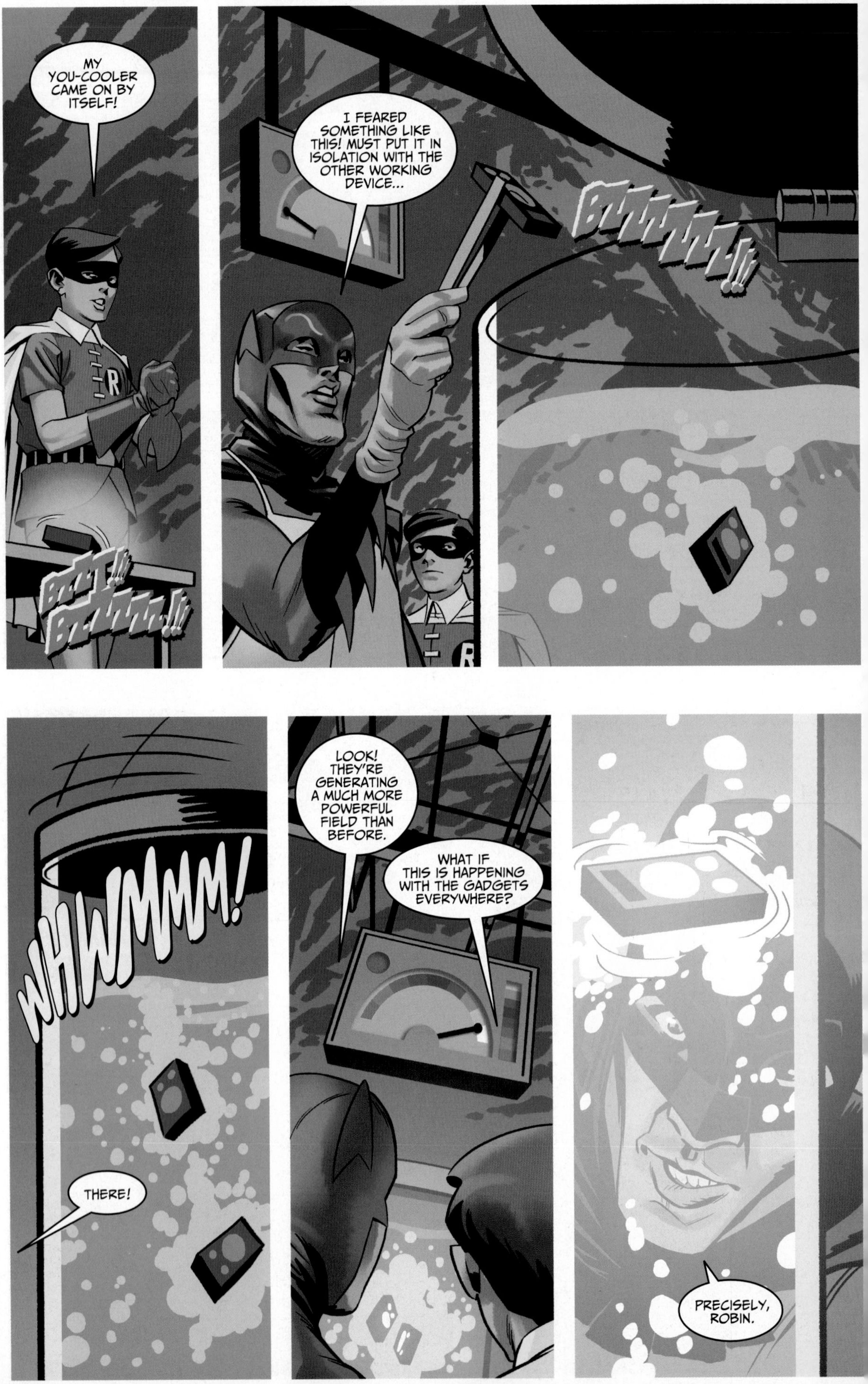
MY YOU-COOLER CAME ON BY ITSELF!
BZZT!! BZZZZZ!!
I FEARED SOMETHING LIKE THIS! MUST PUT IT IN ISOLATION WITH THE OTHER WORKING DEVICE...
BZZZZZZ!!
WHWMMM!
THERE!
LOOK! THEY'RE GENERATING A MUCH MORE POWERFUL FIELD THAN BEFORE.
WHAT IF THIS IS HAPPENING WITH THE GADGETS EVERYWHERE?
PRECISELY, ROBIN.

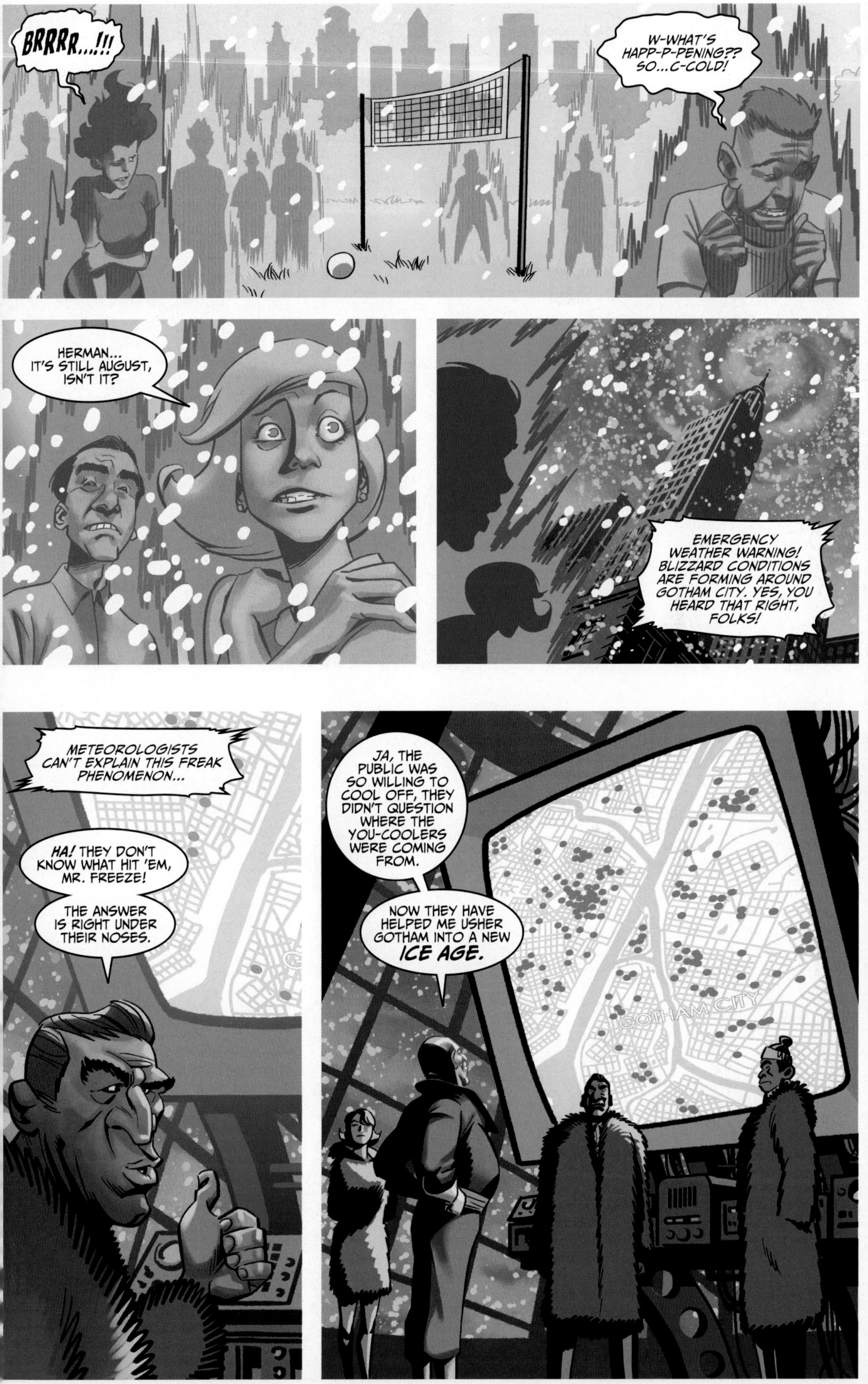
BRRRR...!!!
W-WHAT'S HAPP-P-PENING?? SO...C-COLD!
HERMAN... IT'S STILL AUGUST, ISN'T IT?
EMERGENCY WEATHER WARNING! BLIZZARD CONDITIONS ARE FORMING AROUND GOTHAM CITY. YES, YOU HEARD THAT RIGHT, FOLKS!
METEOROLOGISTS CAN'T EXPLAIN THIS FREAK PHENOMENON...
HA! THEY DON'T KNOW WHAT HIT 'EM, MR. FREEZE!
THE ANSWER IS RIGHT UNDER THEIR NOSES.
JA, THE PUBLIC WAS SO WILLING TO COOL OFF, THEY DIDN'T QUESTION WHERE THE YOU-COOLERS WERE COMING FROM.
NOW THEY HAVE HELPED ME USHER GOTHAM INTO A NEW ICE AGE.
GOTHAM CITY

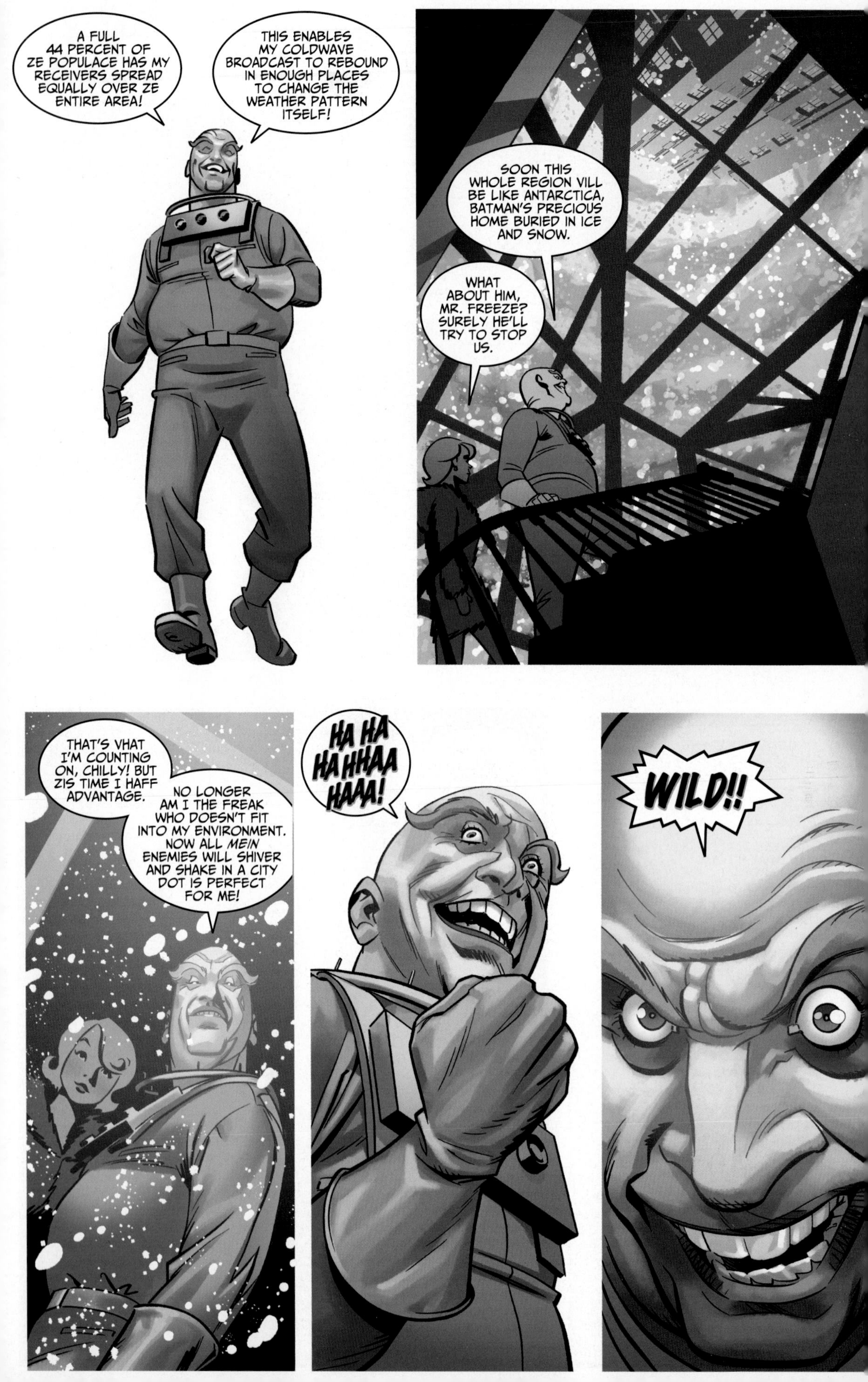
A FULL 44 PERCENT OF ZE POPULACE HAS MY RECEIVERS SPREAD EQUALLY OVER ZE ENTIRE AREA!
THIS ENABLES MY COLDWAVE BROADCAST TO REBOUND IN ENOUGH PLACES TO CHANGE THE WEATHER PATTERN ITSELF!
SOON THIS WHOLE REGION VILL BE LIKE ANTARCTICA, BATMAN'S PRECIOUS HOME BURIED IN ICE AND SNOW.
WHAT ABOUT HIM, MR. FREEZE? SURELY HE'LL TRY TO STOP US.
THAT'S VHAT I'M COUNTING ON, CHILLY! BUT ZIS TIME I HAFF ADVANTAGE.
NO LONGER AM I THE FREAK WHO DOESN'T FIT INTO MY ENVIRONMENT. NOW ALL *MEIN* ENEMIES WILL SHIVER AND SHAKE IN A CITY DOT IS PERFECT FOR ME!
HA HA HA HHAA HAAA!
WILD!!

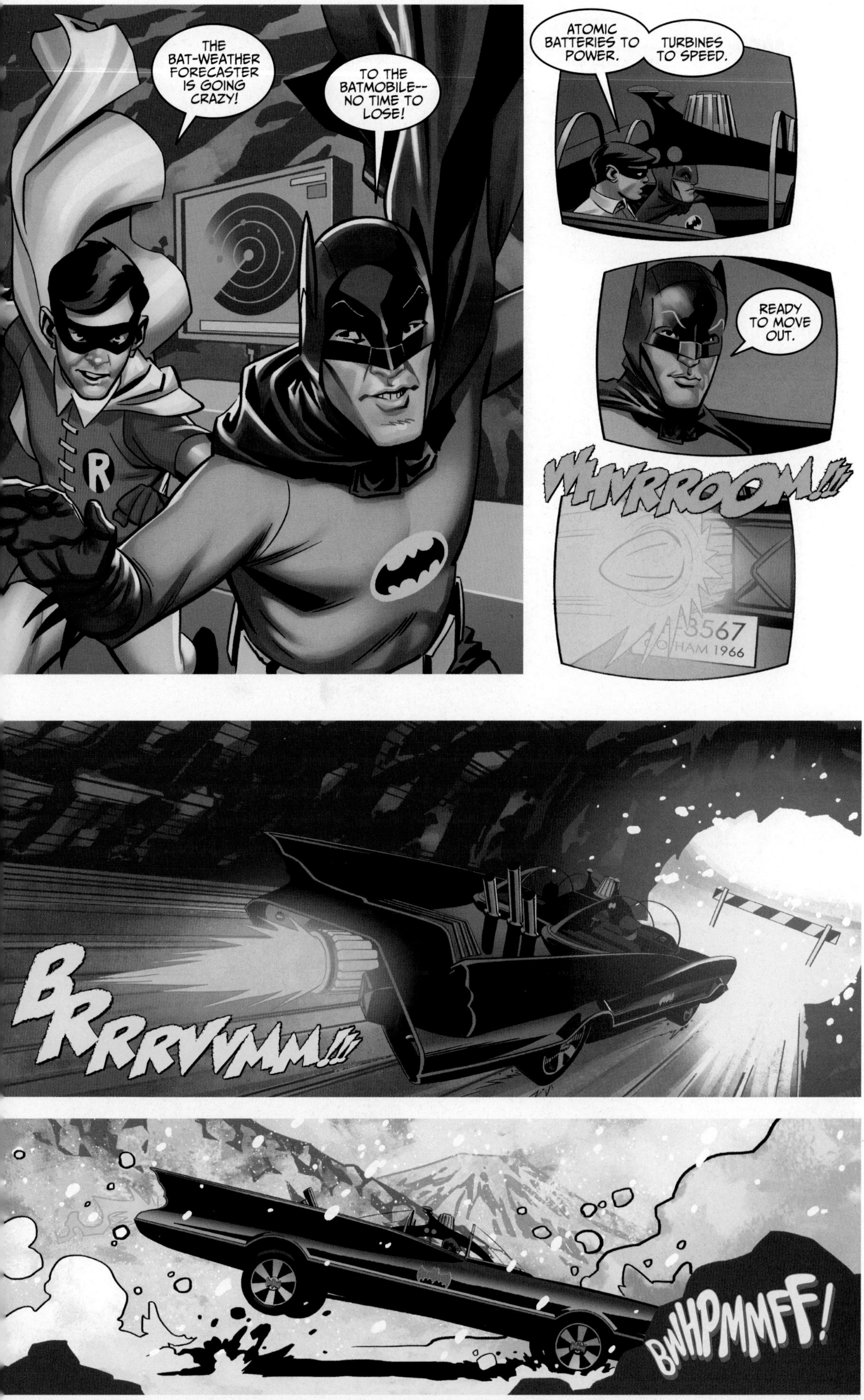
THE BAT-WEATHER FORECASTER IS GOING CRAZY!
TO THE BATMOBILE-- NO TIME TO LOSE!
ATOMIC BATTERIES TO POWER.
TURBINES TO SPEED.
READY TO MOVE OUT.
WHVRROOM!!!
3567
GOTHAM 1966
BRRRVVMM!!!
BWHPMMFF!

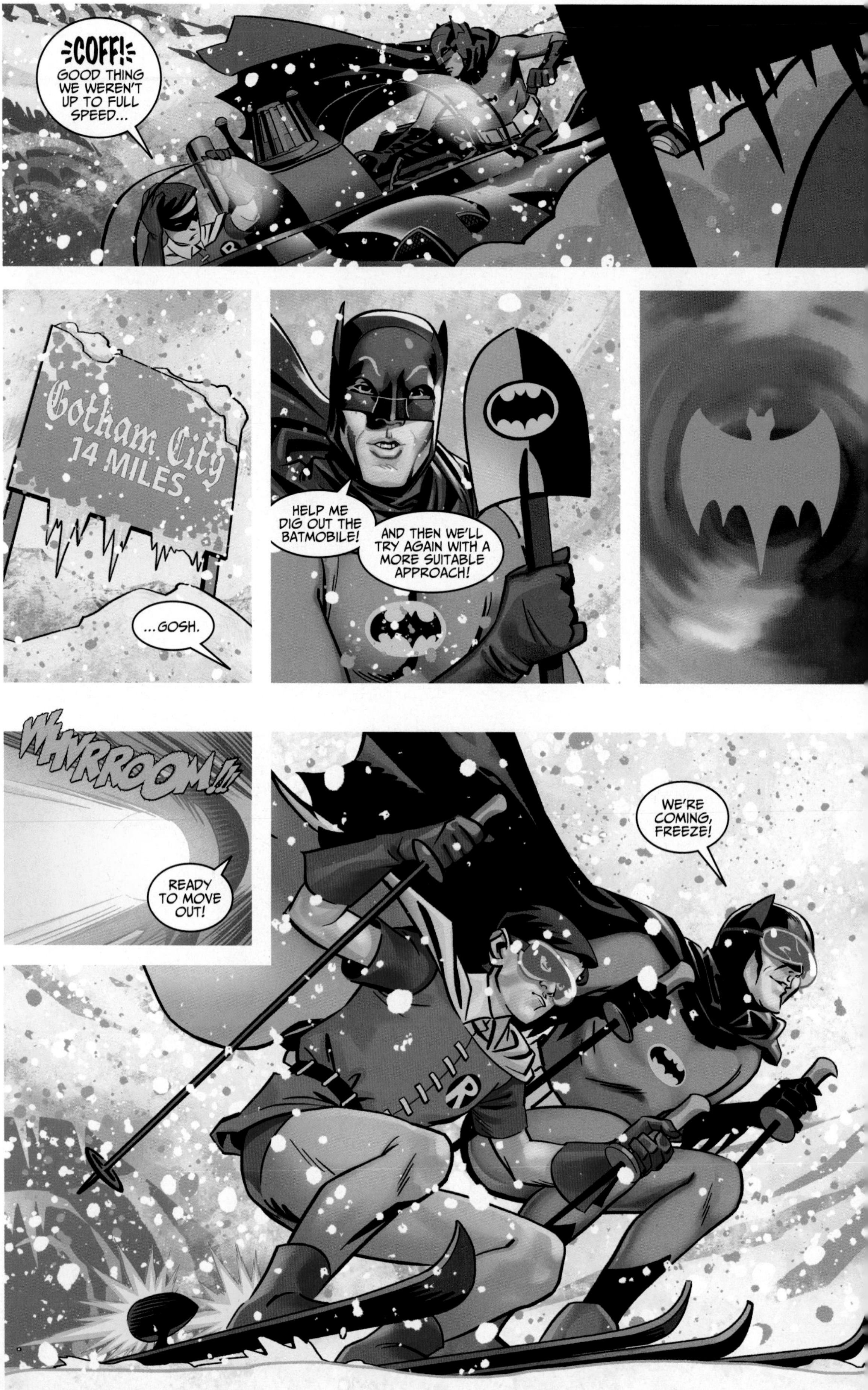
COFF!
GOOD THING WE WEREN'T UP TO FULL SPEED...
Gotham City
14 MILES
...GOSH.
HELP ME DIG OUT THE BATMOBILE!
AND THEN WE'LL TRY AGAIN WITH A MORE SUITABLE APPROACH!
VVHVRROOM!!!
READY TO MOVE OUT!
WE'RE COMING, FREEZE!

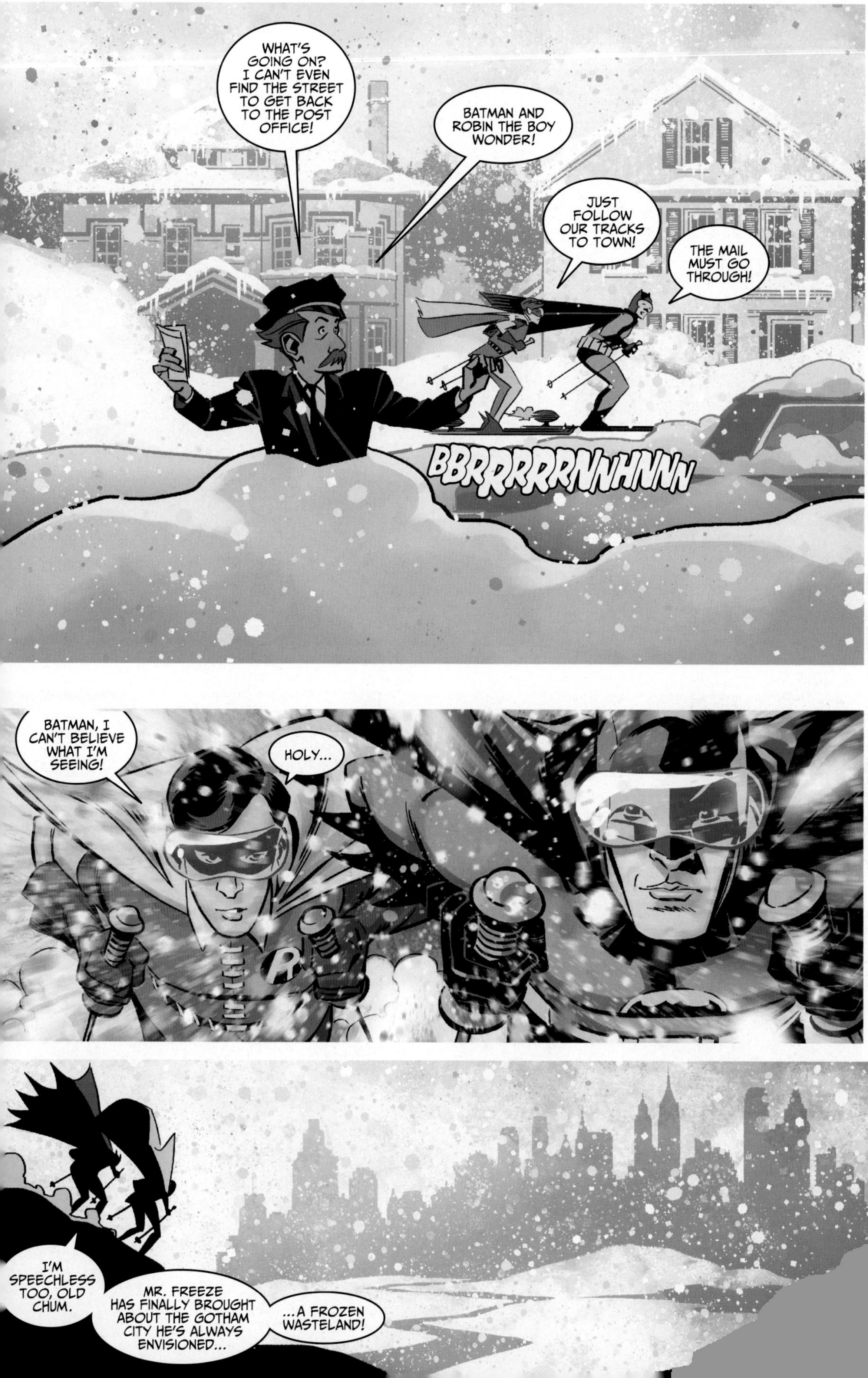
WHAT'S GOING ON? I CAN'T EVEN FIND THE STREET TO GET BACK TO THE POST OFFICE!
BATMAN AND ROBIN THE BOY WONDER!
JUST FOLLOW OUR TRACKS TO TOWN!
THE MAIL MUST GO THROUGH!
BBRRRRRNNHNNN
BATMAN, I CAN'T BELIEVE WHAT I'M SEEING!
HOLY...
I'M SPEECHLESS TOO, OLD CHUM.
MR. FREEZE HAS FINALLY BROUGHT ABOUT THE GOTHAM CITY HE'S ALWAYS ENVISIONED...
...A FROZEN WASTELAND!

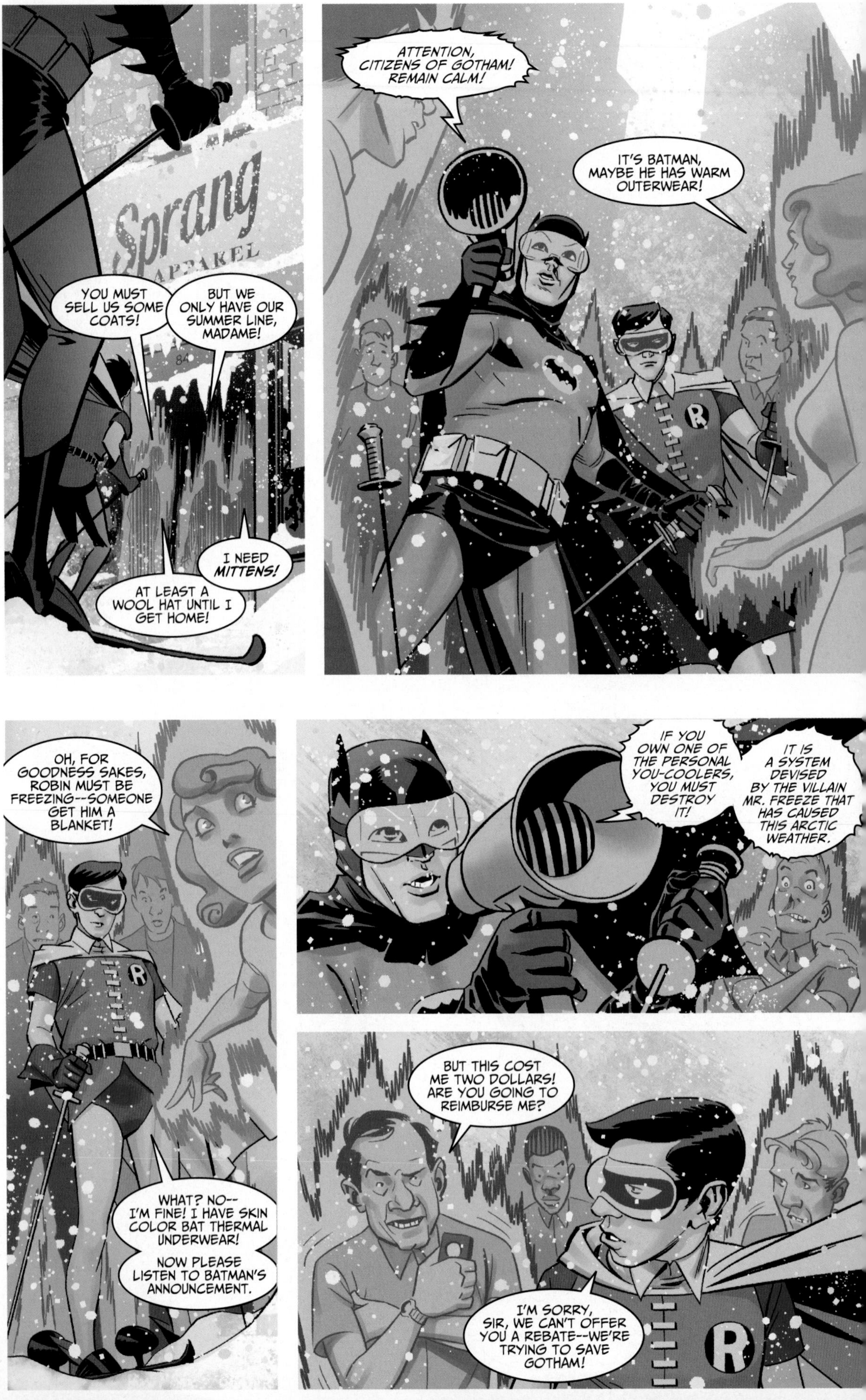
Sprang
APPAREL
YOU MUST SELL US SOME COATS!
BUT WE ONLY HAVE OUR SUMMER LINE, MADAME!
I NEED MITTENS!
AT LEAST A WOOL HAT UNTIL I GET HOME!
ATTENTION, CITIZENS OF GOTHAM! REMAIN CALM!
IT'S BATMAN, MAYBE HE HAS WARM OUTERWEAR!
OH, FOR GOODNESS SAKES, ROBIN MUST BE FREEZING--SOMEONE GET HIM A BLANKET!
WHAT? NO-- I'M FINE! I HAVE SKIN COLOR BAT THERMAL UNDERWEAR!
NOW PLEASE LISTEN TO BATMAN'S ANNOUNCEMENT.
IF YOU OWN ONE OF THE PERSONAL YOU-COOLERS, YOU MUST DESTROY IT!
IT IS A SYSTEM DEVISED BY THE VILLAIN MR. FREEZE THAT HAS CAUSED THIS ARCTIC WEATHER.
BUT THIS COST ME TWO DOLLARS! ARE YOU GOING TO REIMBURSE ME?
I'M SORRY, SIR, WE CAN'T OFFER YOU A REBATE--WE'RE TRYING TO SAVE GOTHAM!

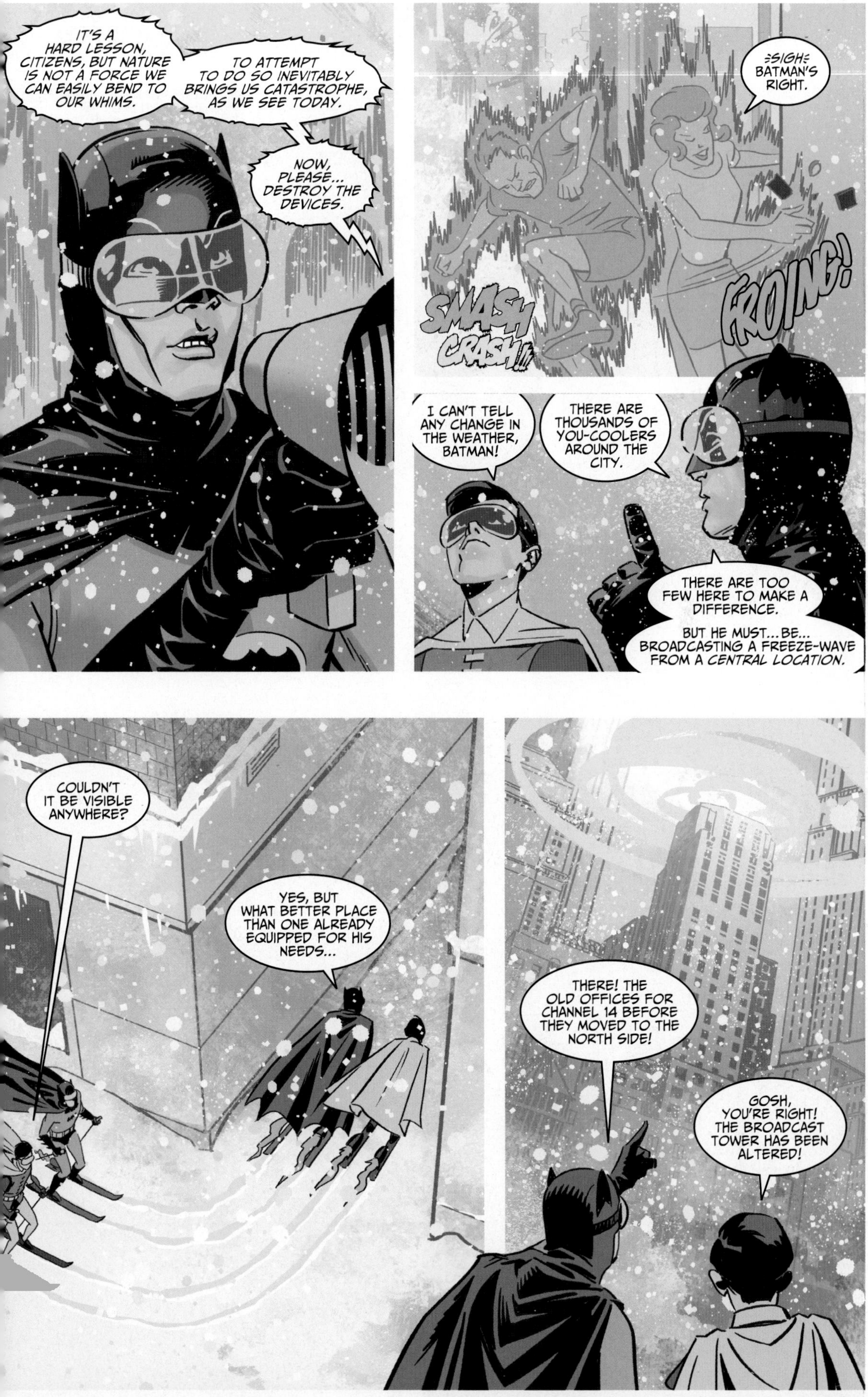
IT'S A HARD LESSON, CITIZENS, BUT NATURE IS NOT A FORCE WE CAN EASILY BEND TO OUR WHIMS.
TO ATTEMPT TO DO SO INEVITABLY BRINGS US CATASTROPHE, AS WE SEE TODAY.
NOW, PLEASE... DESTROY THE DEVICES.
SMASH CRASH!!
FROING!
=SIGH= BATMAN'S RIGHT.
I CAN'T TELL ANY CHANGE IN THE WEATHER, BATMAN!
THERE ARE THOUSANDS OF YOU-COOLERS AROUND THE CITY.
THERE ARE TOO FEW HERE TO MAKE A DIFFERENCE.
BUT HE MUST...BE... BROADCASTING A FREEZE-WAVE FROM A CENTRAL LOCATION.
COULDN'T IT BE VISIBLE ANYWHERE?
YES, BUT WHAT BETTER PLACE THAN ONE ALREADY EQUIPPED FOR HIS NEEDS...
THERE! THE OLD OFFICES FOR CHANNEL 14 BEFORE THEY MOVED TO THE NORTH SIDE!
GOSH, YOU'RE RIGHT! THE BROADCAST TOWER HAS BEEN ALTERED!

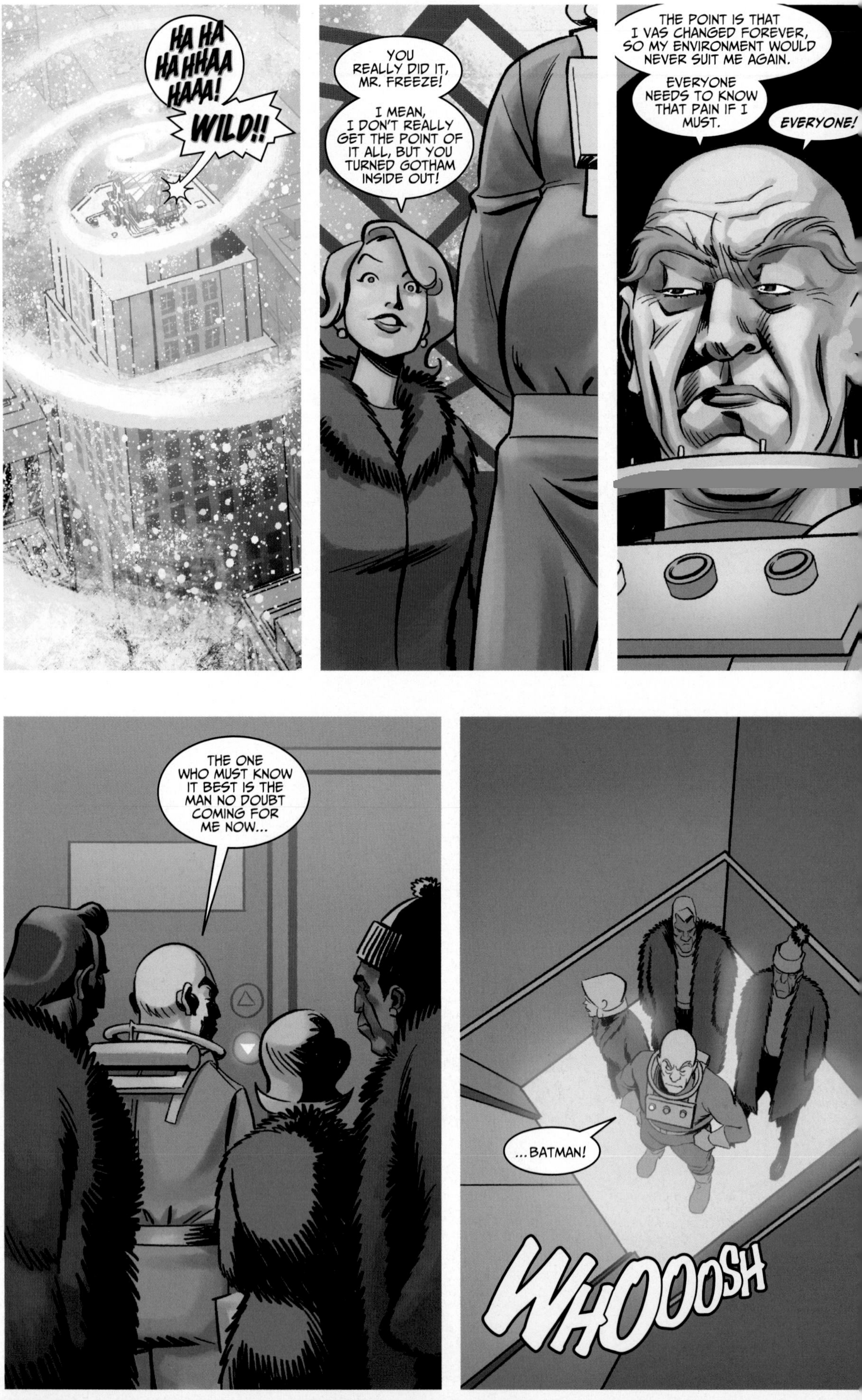
HA HA HA HHAA HAAA!
WILD!!
YOU REALLY DID IT, MR. FREEZE!
I MEAN, I DON'T REALLY GET THE POINT OF IT ALL, BUT YOU TURNED GOTHAM INSIDE OUT!
THE POINT IS THAT I VAS CHANGED FOREVER, SO MY ENVIRONMENT WOULD NEVER SUIT ME AGAIN.
EVERYONE NEEDS TO KNOW THAT PAIN IF I MUST.
EVERYONE!
THE ONE WHO MUST KNOW IT BEST IS THE MAN NO DOUBT COMING FOR ME NOW...
...BATMAN!
WHOOOSH

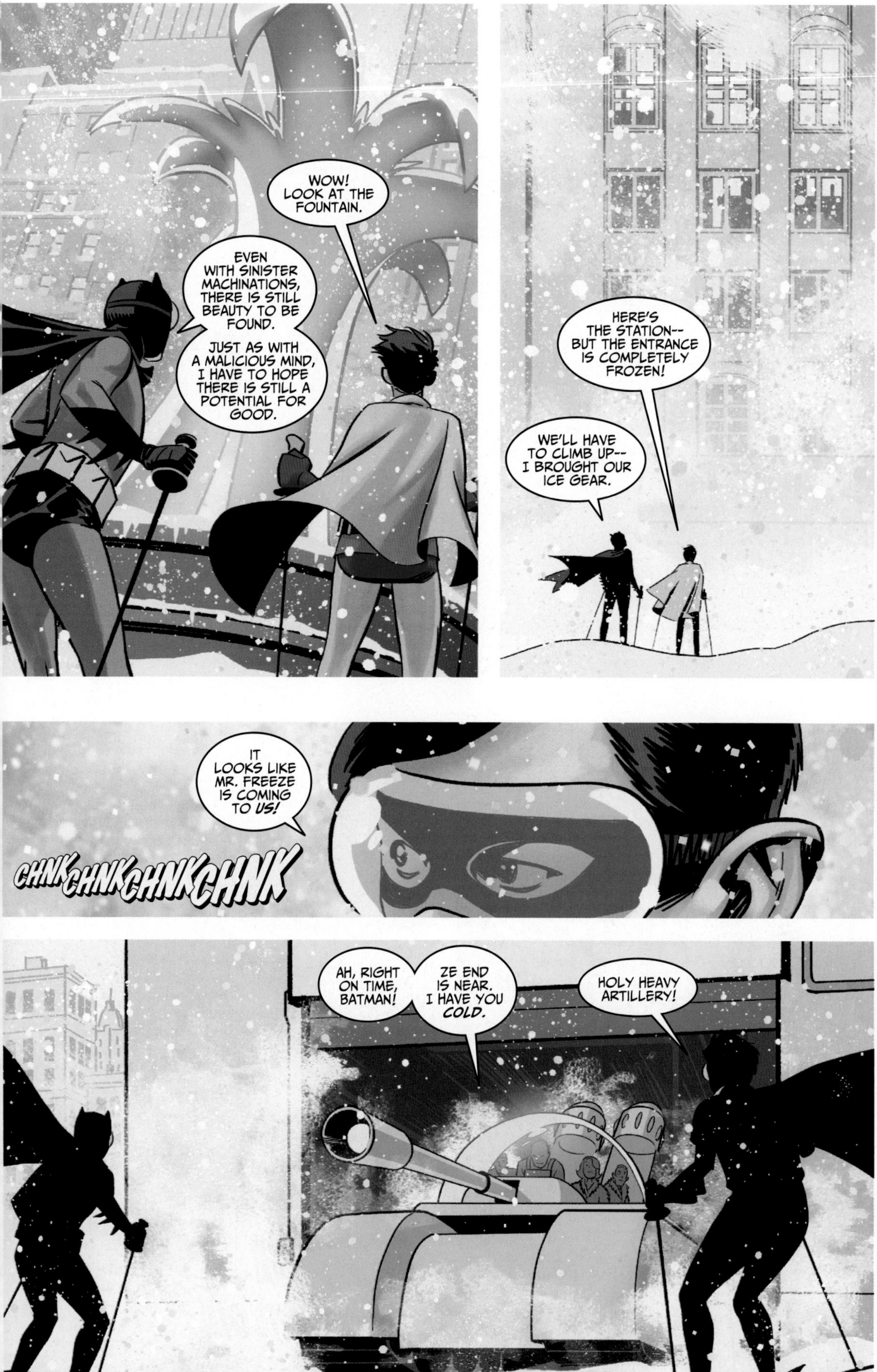
WOW! LOOK AT THE FOUNTAIN.
EVEN WITH SINISTER MACHINATIONS, THERE IS STILL BEAUTY TO BE FOUND.
JUST AS WITH A MALICIOUS MIND, I HAVE TO HOPE THERE IS STILL A POTENTIAL FOR GOOD.
HERE'S THE STATION-- BUT THE ENTRANCE IS COMPLETELY FROZEN!
WE'LL HAVE TO CLIMB UP-- I BROUGHT OUR ICE GEAR.
IT LOOKS LIKE MR. FREEZE IS COMING TO US!
CHNKCHNKCHNKCHNK
AH, RIGHT ON TIME, BATMAN!
ZE END IS NEAR. I HAVE YOU COLD.
HOLY HEAVY ARTILLERY!

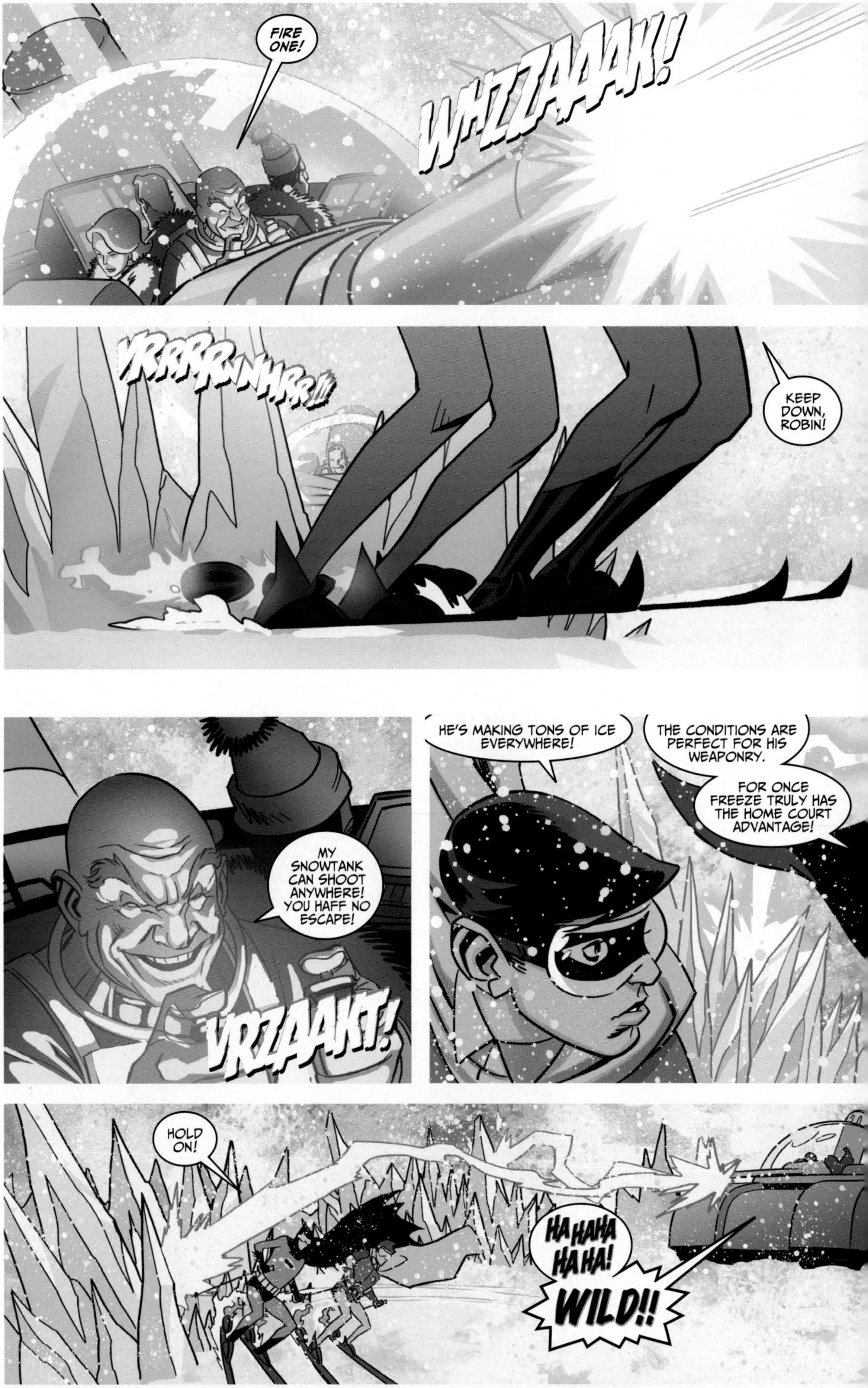
FIRE ONE!
WHZZAAAK!
VRRRRRNHRR!!!
KEEP DOWN, ROBIN!
MY SNOWTANK CAN SHOOT ANYWHERE! YOU HAFF NO ESCAPE!
VRZAAKT!
HE'S MAKING TONS OF ICE EVERYWHERE!
THE CONDITIONS ARE PERFECT FOR HIS WEAPONRY.
FOR ONCE FREEZE TRULY HAS THE HOME COURT ADVANTAGE!
HOLD ON!
HA HAHA HA HA!
WILD!!

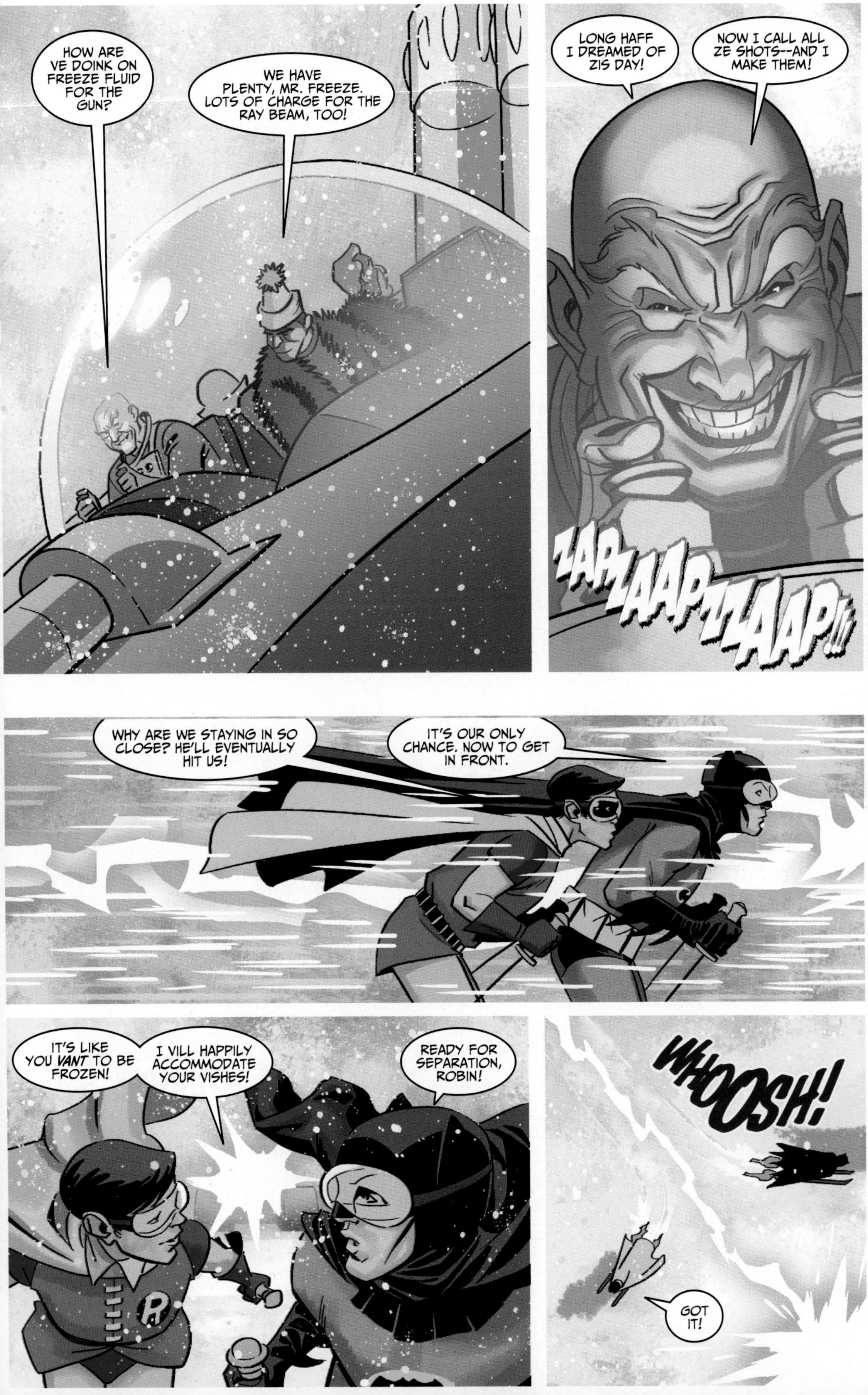
HOW ARE VE DOINK ON FREEZE FLUID FOR THE GUN?
WE HAVE PLENTY, MR. FREEZE. LOTS OF CHARGE FOR THE RAY BEAM, TOO!
LONG HAFF I DREAMED OF ZIS DAY!
NOW I CALL ALL ZE SHOTS--AND I MAKE THEM!
ZAP ZAAP ZZAAP!!!
WHY ARE WE STAYING IN SO CLOSE? HE'LL EVENTUALLY HIT US!
IT'S OUR ONLY CHANCE. NOW TO GET IN FRONT.
IT'S LIKE YOU *VANT* TO BE FROZEN!
I VILL HAPPILY ACCOMMODATE YOUR VISHES!
READY FOR SEPARATION, ROBIN!
WHOOSH!
GOT IT!

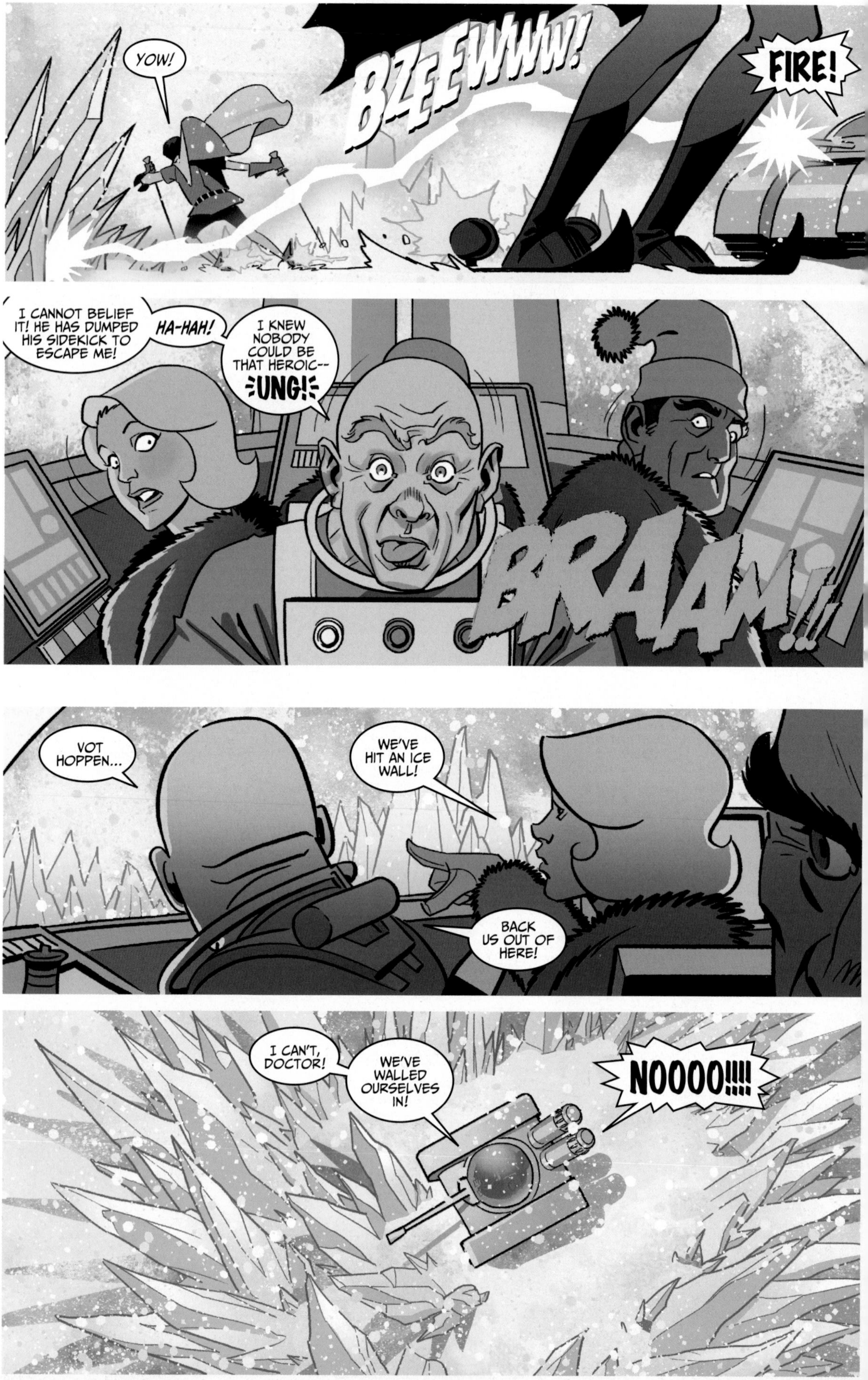
YOW!
BZEEWWW!
FIRE!
I CANNOT BELIEF IT! HE HAS DUMPED HIS SIDEKICK TO ESCAPE ME!
HA-HAH!
I KNEW NOBODY COULD BE THAT HEROIC--
UNG!
BRAAM!!
VOT HOPPEN...
WE'VE HIT AN ICE WALL!
BACK US OUT OF HERE!
I CAN'T, DOCTOR!
WE'VE WALLED OURSELVES IN!
NOOOO!!!!

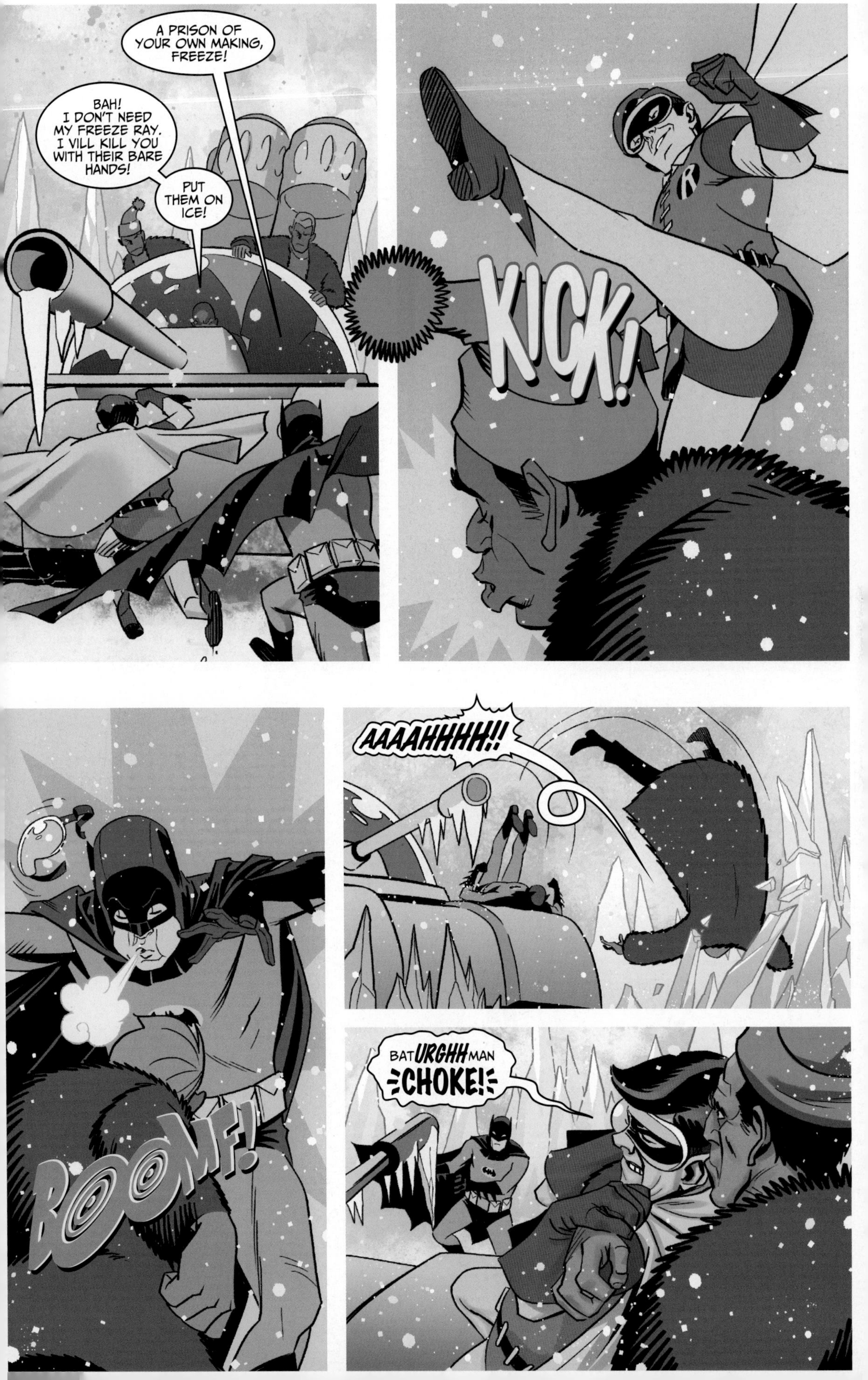
A PRISON OF YOUR OWN MAKING, FREEZE!
BAH! I DON'T NEED MY FREEZE RAY. I VILL KILL YOU WITH THEIR BARE HANDS!
PUT THEM ON ICE!
KICK!
BOOMF!
AAAAHHHH!!
BAT URGHH MAN
CHOKE!

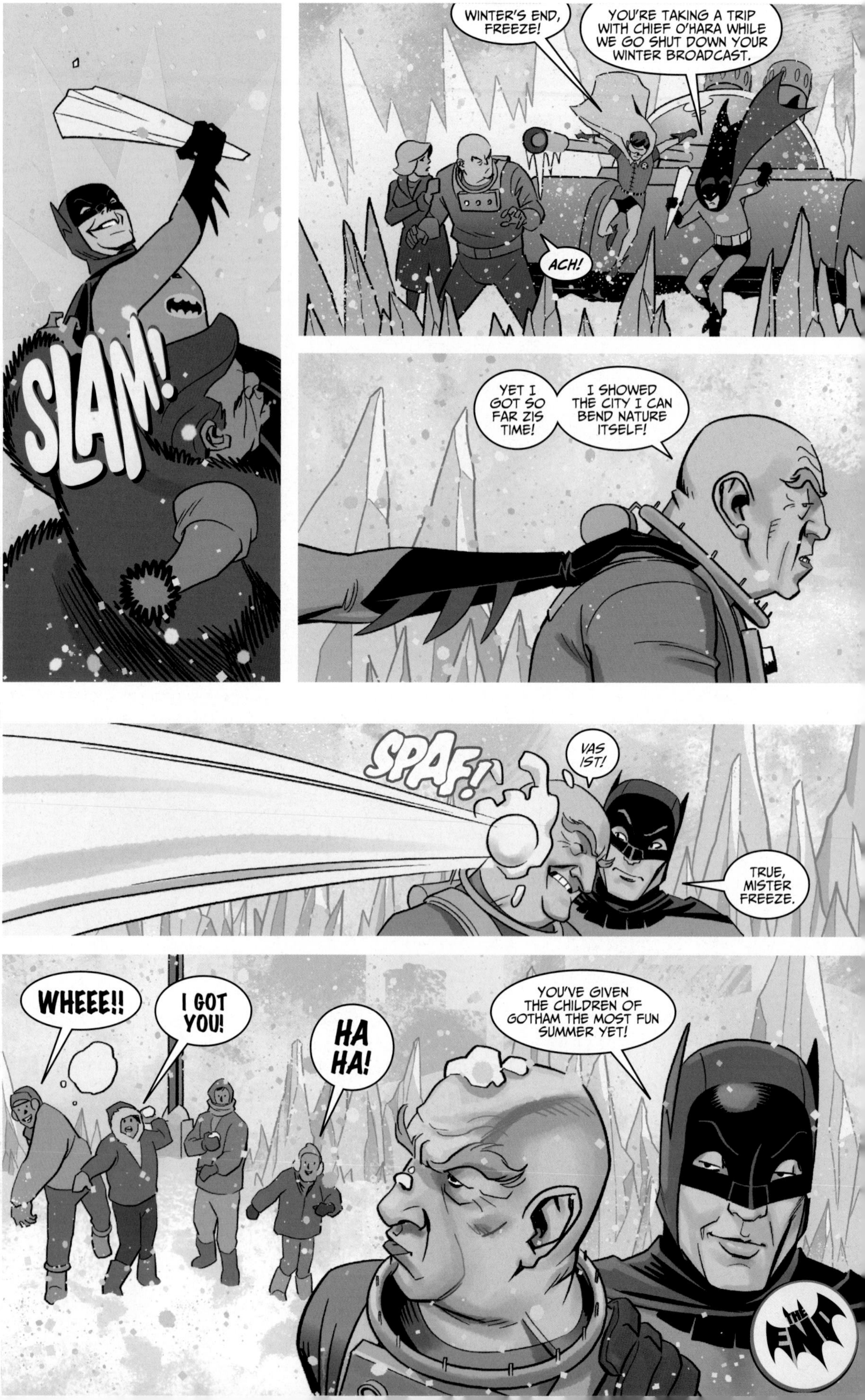
SLAM!
WINTER'S END, FREEZE!
YOU'RE TAKING A TRIP WITH CHIEF O'HARA WHILE WE GO SHUT DOWN YOUR WINTER BROADCAST.
ACH!
YET I GOT SO FAR ZIS TIME!
I SHOWED THE CITY I CAN BEND NATURE ITSELF!
SPAF!
VAS IST!
TRUE, MISTER FREEZE.
WHEEE!!
I GOT YOU!
HA HA!
YOU'VE GIVEN THE CHILDREN OF GOTHAM THE MOST FUN SUMMER YET!
THE END

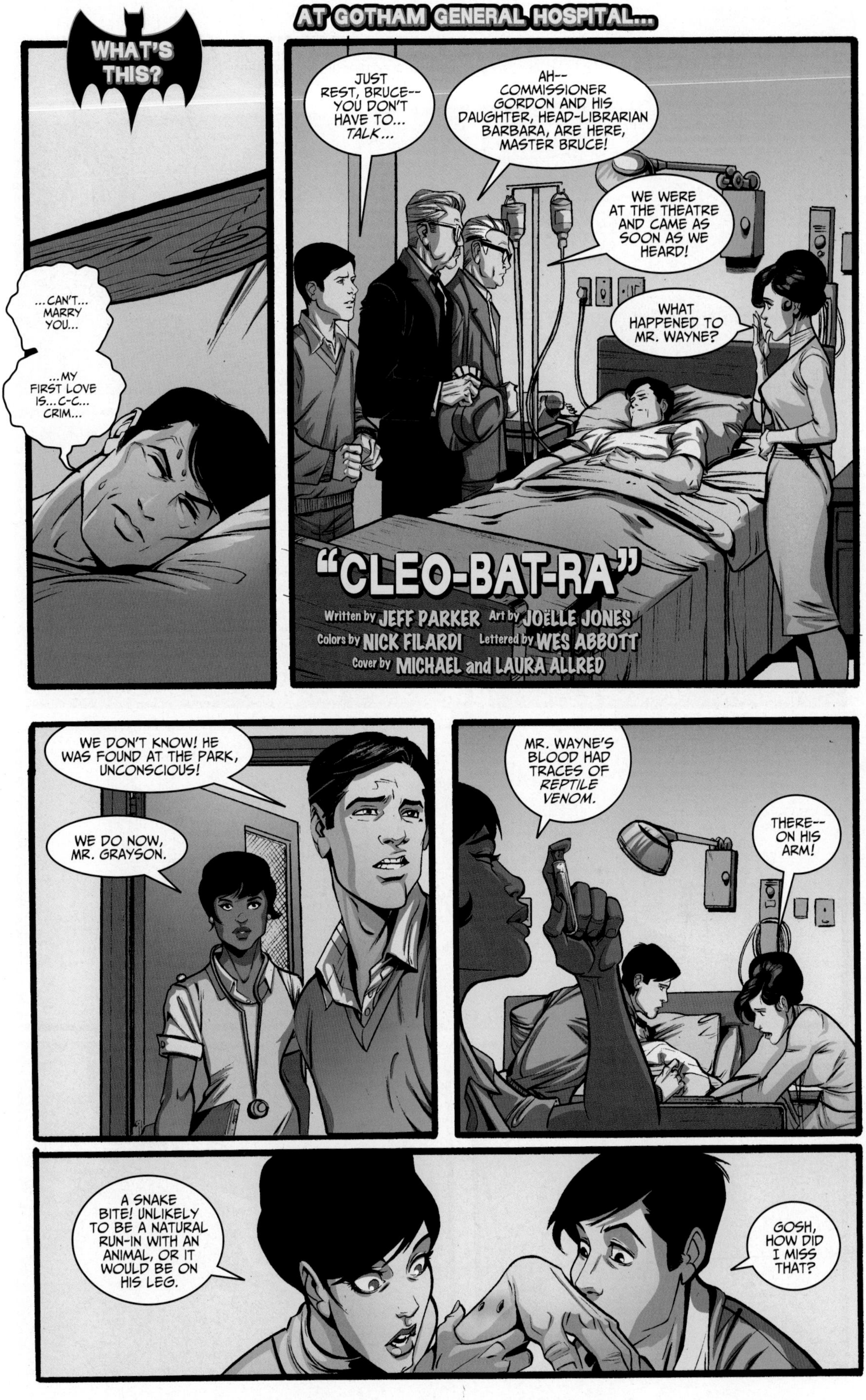
AT GOTHAM GENERAL HOSPITAL...
WHAT'S THIS?
...CAN'T... MARRY YOU...
...MY FIRST LOVE IS...C-C... CRIM...
JUST REST, BRUCE-- YOU DON'T HAVE TO... TALK...
AH-- COMMISSIONER GORDON AND HIS DAUGHTER, HEAD-LIBRARIAN BARBARA, ARE HERE, MASTER BRUCE!
WE WERE AT THE THEATRE AND CAME AS SOON AS WE HEARD!
WHAT HAPPENED TO MR. WAYNE?
"CLEO-BAT-RA"
Written by JEFF PARKER Art by JOËLLE JONES
Colors by NICK FILARDI Lettered by WES ABBOTT
Cover by MICHAEL and LAURA ALLRED
WE DON'T KNOW! HE WAS FOUND AT THE PARK, UNCONSCIOUS!
WE DO NOW, MR. GRAYSON.
MR. WAYNE'S BLOOD HAD TRACES OF REPTILE VENOM.
THERE-- ON HIS ARM!
A SNAKE BITE! UNLIKELY TO BE A NATURAL RUN-IN WITH AN ANIMAL, OR IT WOULD BE ON HIS LEG.
GOSH, HOW DID I MISS THAT?

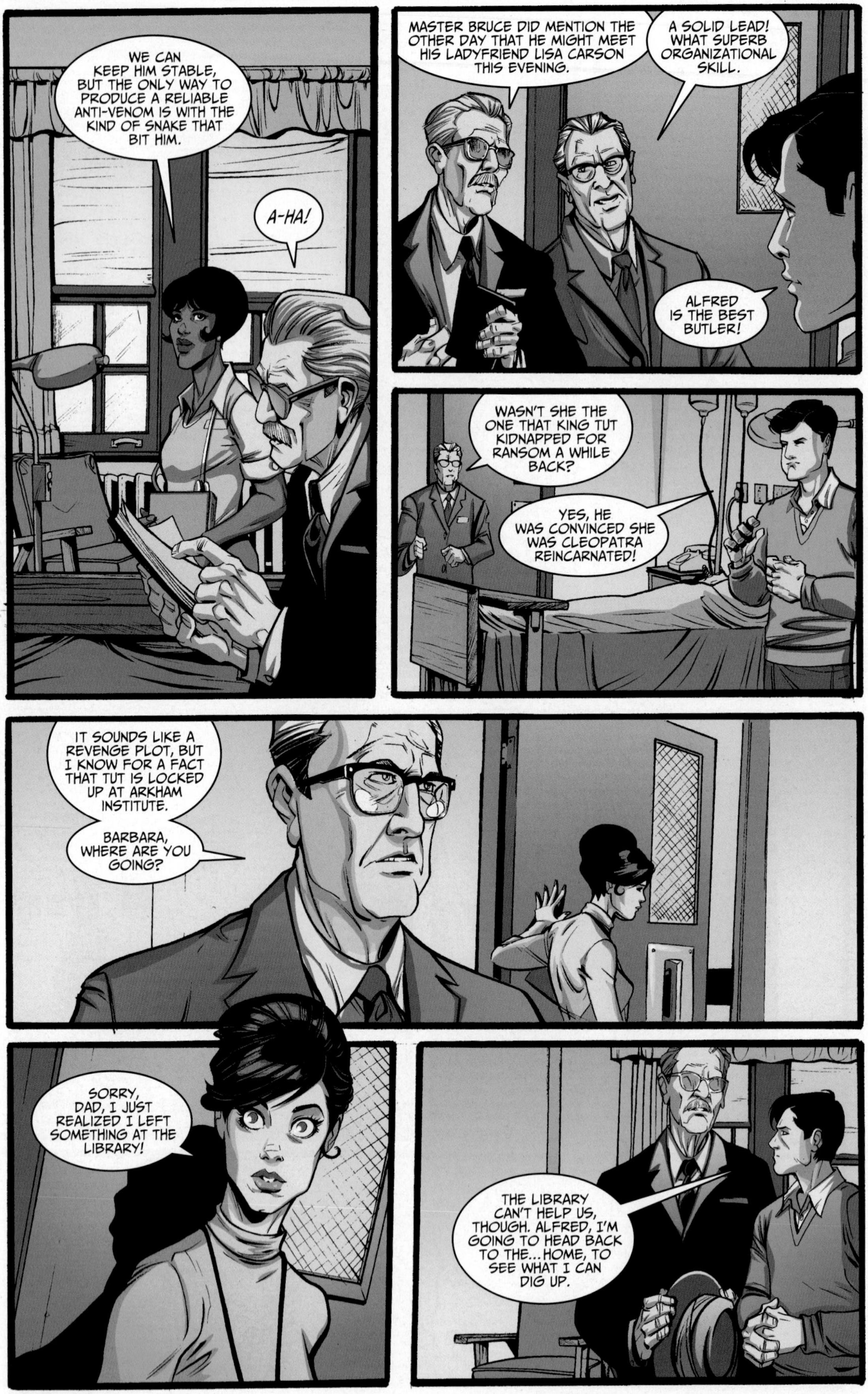
WE CAN KEEP HIM STABLE, BUT THE ONLY WAY TO PRODUCE A RELIABLE ANTI-VENOM IS WITH THE KIND OF SNAKE THAT BIT HIM.
A-HA!
MASTER BRUCE DID MENTION THE OTHER DAY THAT HE MIGHT MEET HIS LADYFRIEND LISA CARSON THIS EVENING.
A SOLID LEAD! WHAT SUPERB ORGANIZATIONAL SKILL.
ALFRED IS THE BEST BUTLER!
WASN'T SHE THE ONE THAT KING TUT KIDNAPPED FOR RANSOM A WHILE BACK?
YES, HE WAS CONVINCED SHE WAS CLEOPATRA REINCARNATED!
IT SOUNDS LIKE A REVENGE PLOT, BUT I KNOW FOR A FACT THAT TUT IS LOCKED UP AT ARKHAM INSTITUTE.
BARBARA, WHERE ARE YOU GOING?
SORRY, DAD, I JUST REALIZED I LEFT SOMETHING AT THE LIBRARY!
THE LIBRARY CAN'T HELP US, THOUGH. ALFRED, I'M GOING TO HEAD BACK TO THE...HOME, TO SEE WHAT I CAN DIG UP.

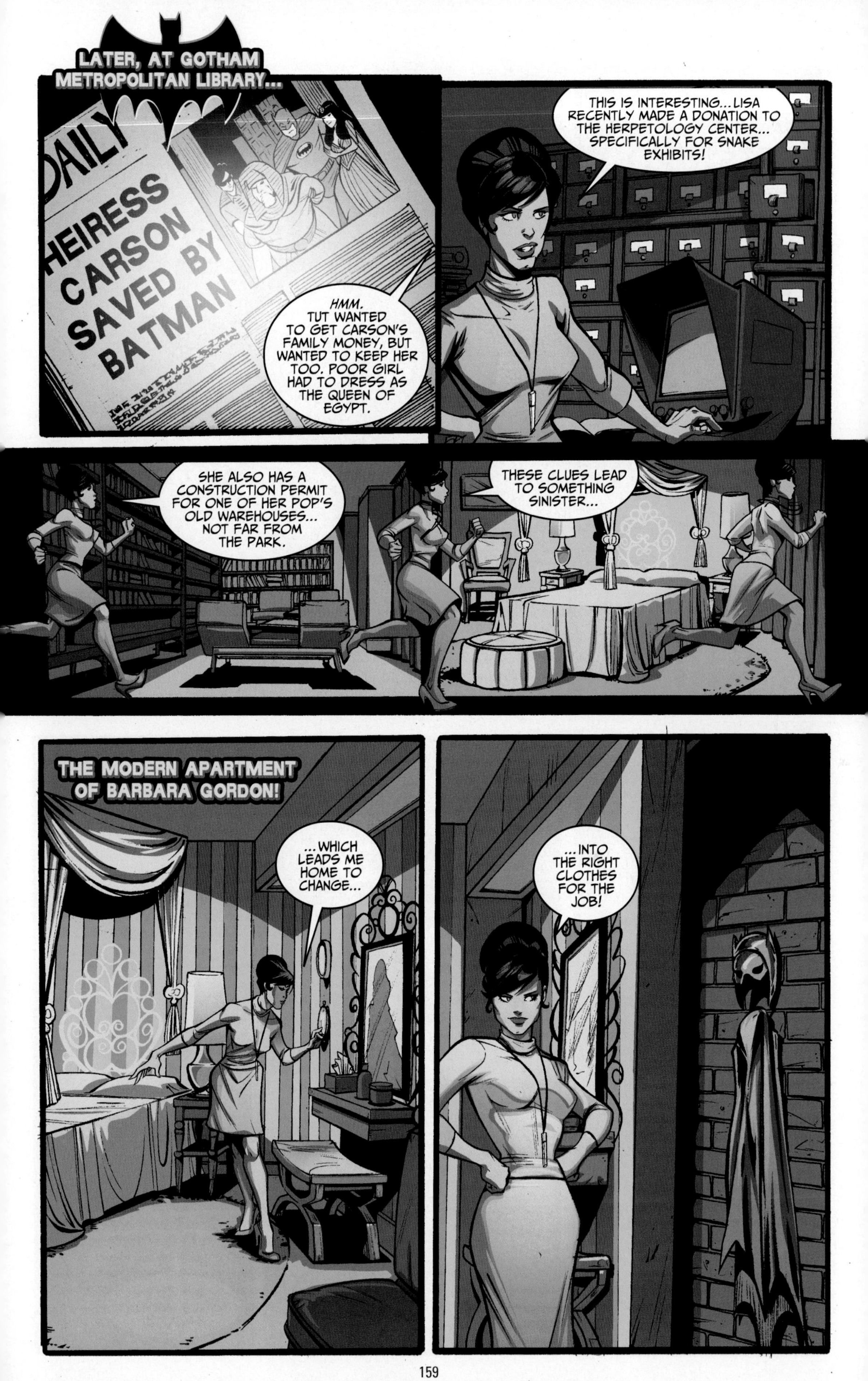

LATER, AT GOTHAM METROPOLITAN LIBRARY...
DAILY
HEIRESS CARSON SAVED BY BATMAN
HMM. TUT WANTED TO GET CARSON'S FAMILY MONEY, BUT WANTED TO KEEP HER TOO. POOR GIRL HAD TO DRESS AS THE QUEEN OF EGYPT.
THIS IS INTERESTING...LISA RECENTLY MADE A DONATION TO THE HERPETOLOGY CENTER... SPECIFICALLY FOR SNAKE EXHIBITS!
SHE ALSO HAS A CONSTRUCTION PERMIT FOR ONE OF HER POP'S OLD WAREHOUSES... NOT FAR FROM THE PARK.
THESE CLUES LEAD TO SOMETHING SINISTER...
THE MODERN APARTMENT OF BARBARA GORDON!
...WHICH LEADS ME HOME TO CHANGE...
...INTO THE RIGHT CLOTHES FOR THE JOB!

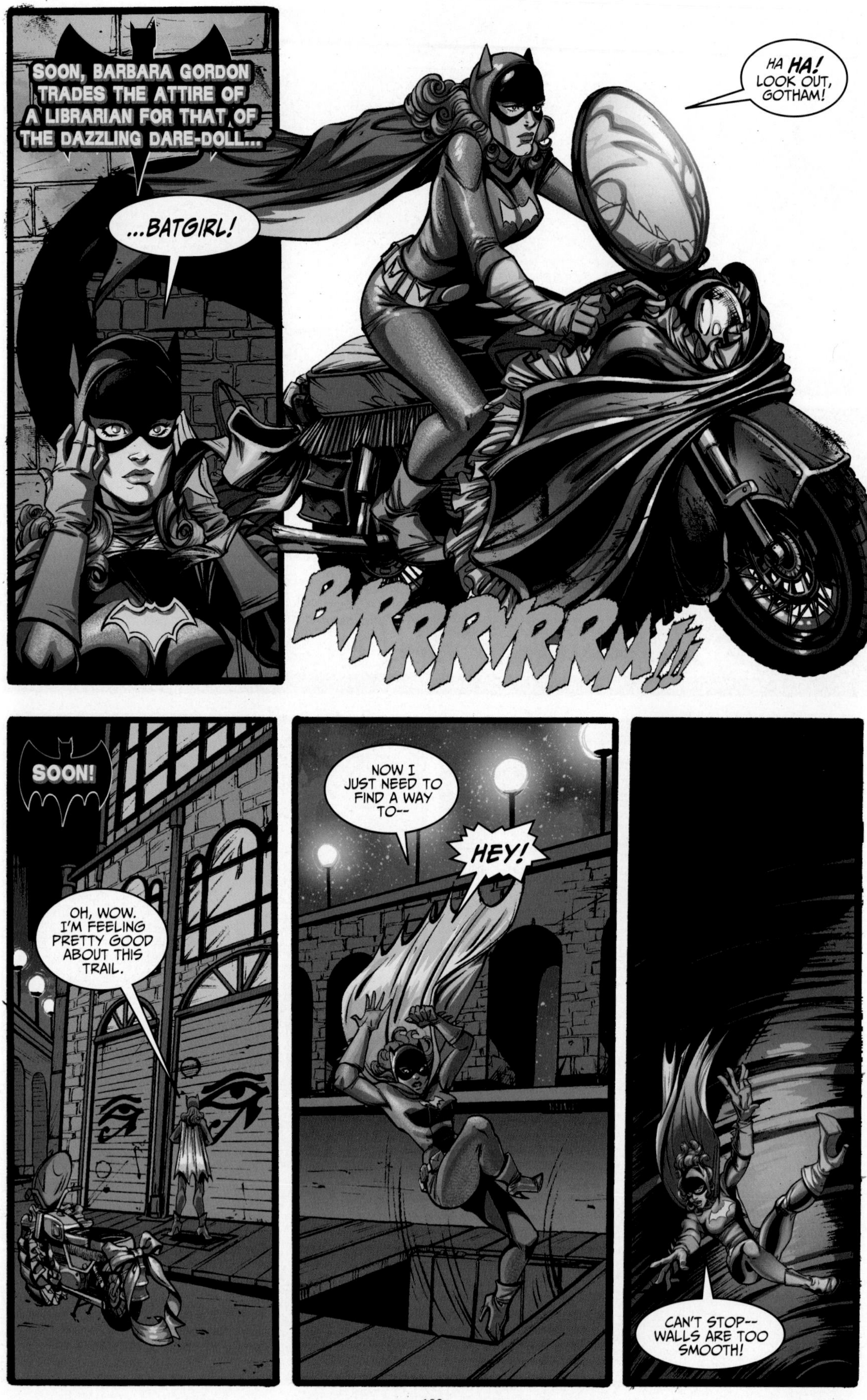
SOON, BARBARA GORDON TRADES THE ATTIRE OF A LIBRARIAN FOR THAT OF THE DAZZLING DARE-DOLL...
...BATGIRL!
HA HA! LOOK OUT, GOTHAM!
BVRRRVRRM!!
SOON!
OH, WOW. I'M FEELING PRETTY GOOD ABOUT THIS TRAIL.
NOW I JUST NEED TO FIND A WAY TO--
HEY!
CAN'T STOP-- WALLS ARE TOO SMOOTH!

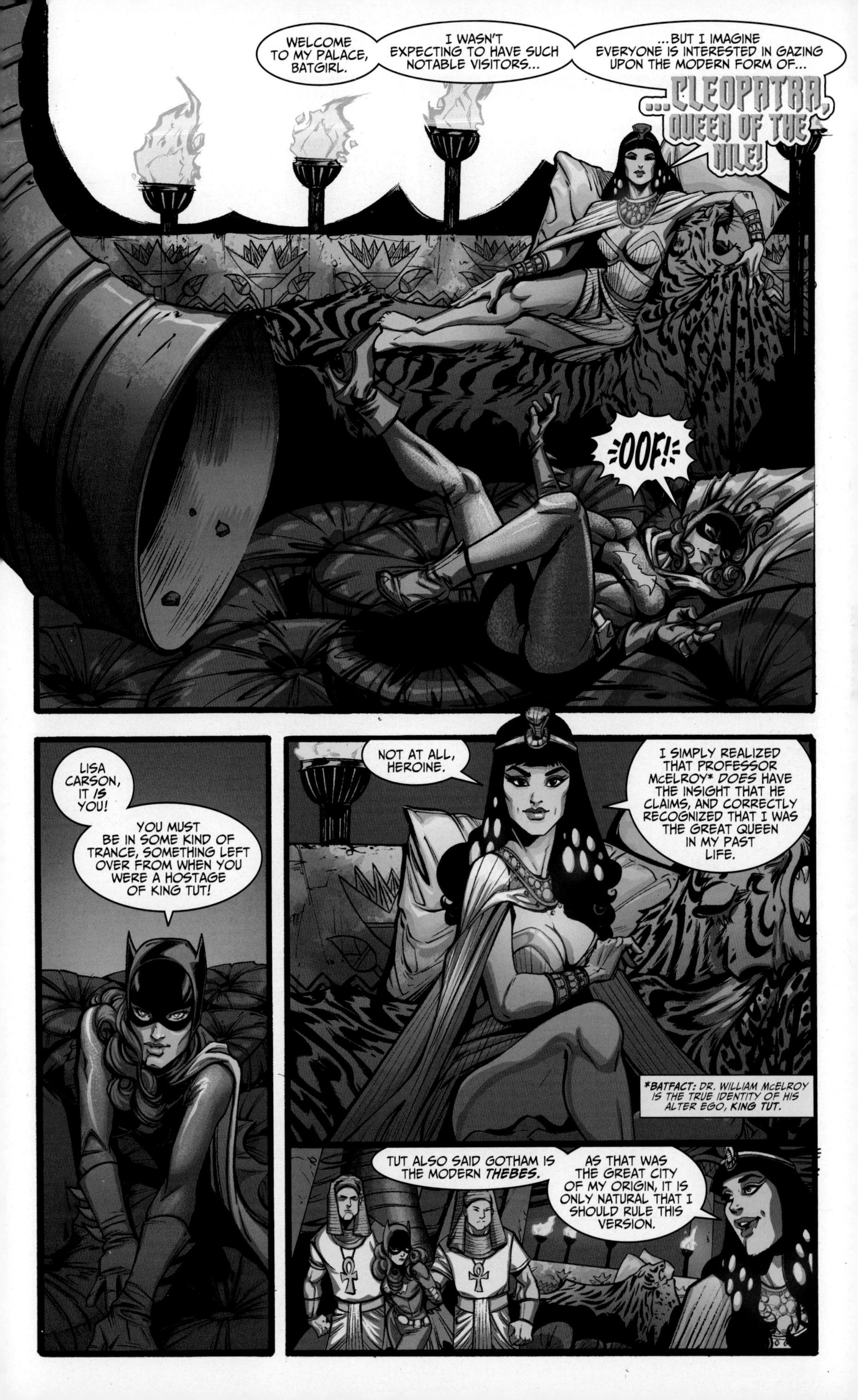
WELCOME TO MY PALACE, BATGIRL.
I WASN'T EXPECTING TO HAVE SUCH NOTABLE VISITORS...
...BUT I IMAGINE EVERYONE IS INTERESTED IN GAZING UPON THE MODERN FORM OF...
...CLEOPATRA, QUEEN OF THE NILE!
OOF!
LISA CARSON, IT IS YOU!
YOU MUST BE IN SOME KIND OF TRANCE, SOMETHING LEFT OVER FROM WHEN YOU WERE A HOSTAGE OF KING TUT!
NOT AT ALL, HEROINE.
I SIMPLY REALIZED THAT PROFESSOR McELROY* DOES HAVE THE INSIGHT THAT HE CLAIMS, AND CORRECTLY RECOGNIZED THAT I WAS THE GREAT QUEEN IN MY PAST LIFE.
*BATFACT: DR. WILLIAM McELROY IS THE TRUE IDENTITY OF HIS ALTER EGO, KING TUT.
TUT ALSO SAID GOTHAM IS THE MODERN THEBES.
AS THAT WAS THE GREAT CITY OF MY ORIGIN, IT IS ONLY NATURAL THAT I SHOULD RULE THIS VERSION.

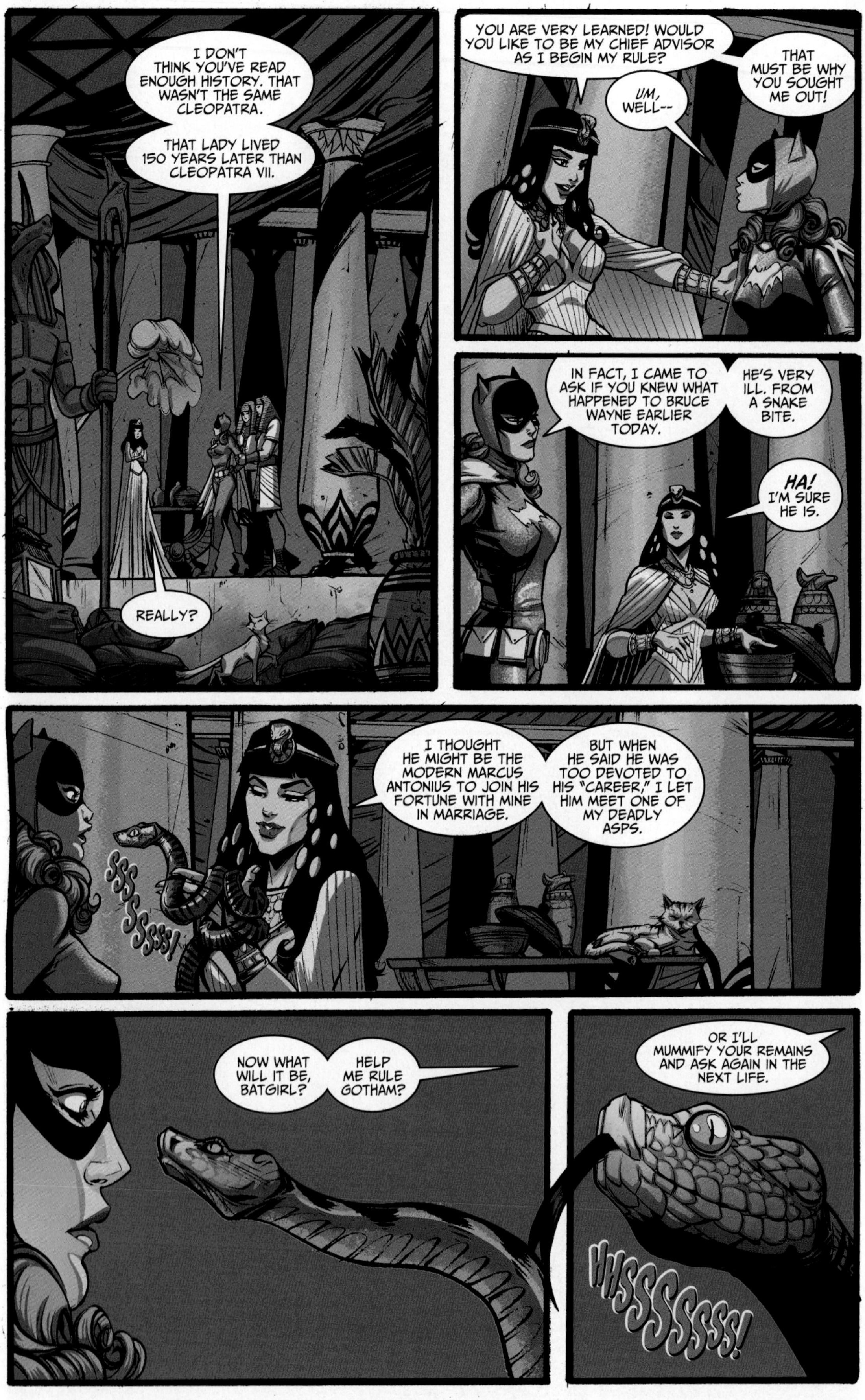
I DON'T THINK YOU'VE READ ENOUGH HISTORY. THAT WASN'T THE SAME CLEOPATRA.
THAT LADY LIVED 150 YEARS LATER THAN CLEOPATRA VII.
REALLY?
YOU ARE VERY LEARNED! WOULD YOU LIKE TO BE MY CHIEF ADVISOR AS I BEGIN MY RULE?
UM, WELL--
THAT MUST BE WHY YOU SOUGHT ME OUT!
IN FACT, I CAME TO ASK IF YOU KNEW WHAT HAPPENED TO BRUCE WAYNE EARLIER TODAY.
HE'S VERY ILL. FROM A SNAKE BITE.
HA! I'M SURE HE IS.
I THOUGHT HE MIGHT BE THE MODERN MARCUS ANTONIUS TO JOIN HIS FORTUNE WITH MINE IN MARRIAGE.
BUT WHEN HE SAID HE WAS TOO DEVOTED TO HIS "CAREER," I LET HIM MEET ONE OF MY DEADLY ASPS.
SSSSSSSS!
NOW WHAT WILL IT BE, BATGIRL?
HELP ME RULE GOTHAM?
OR I'LL MUMMIFY YOUR REMAINS AND ASK AGAIN IN THE NEXT LIFE.
HHSSSSSSSS!

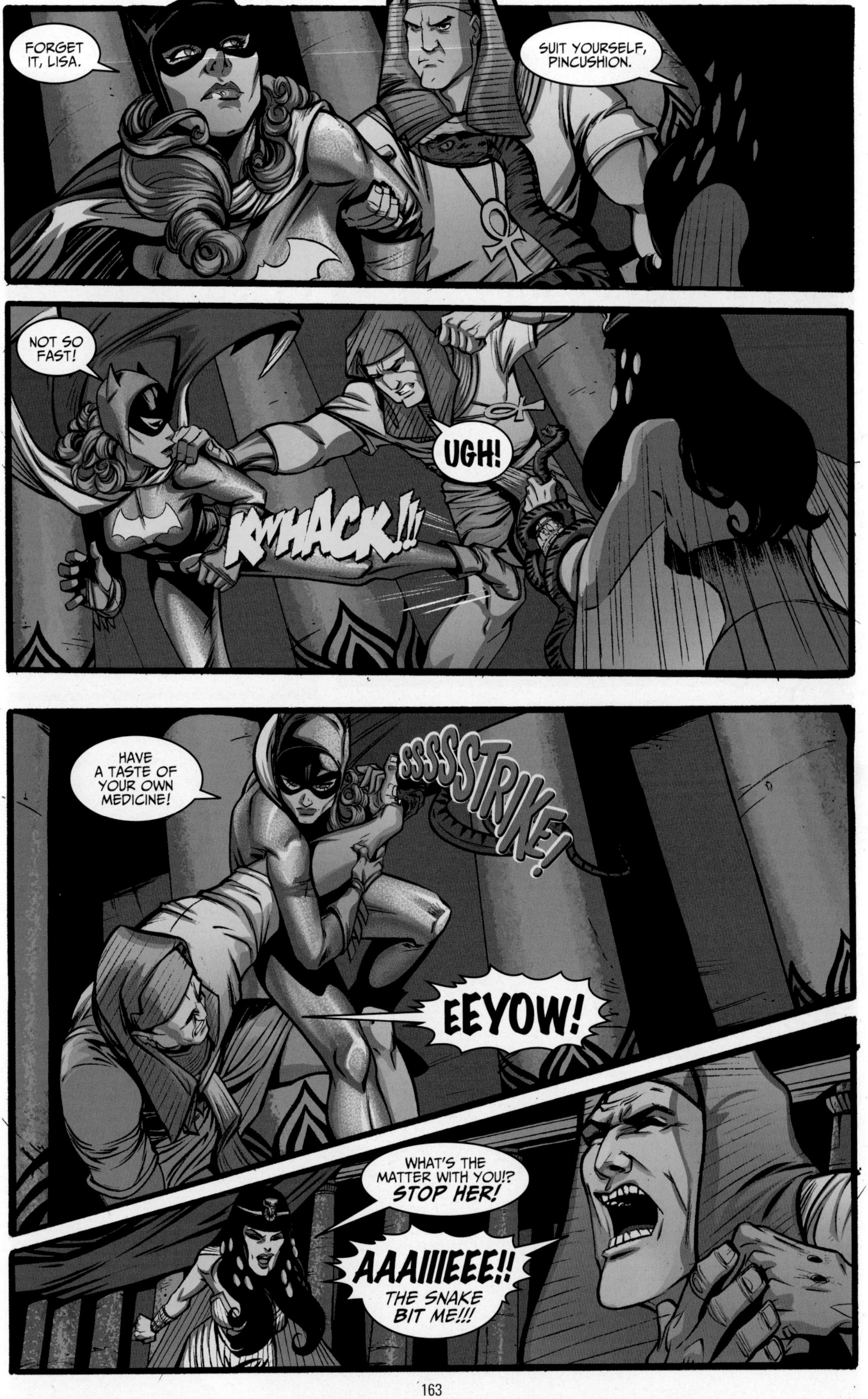
FORGET IT, LISA.
SUIT YOURSELF, PINCUSHION.
NOT SO FAST!
UGH!
KWHACK!!
HAVE A TASTE OF YOUR OWN MEDICINE!
SSSSSTRIKE!
EEYOW!
WHAT'S THE MATTER WITH YOU!? STOP HER!
AAAIIIEEE!! THE SNAKE BIT ME!!!

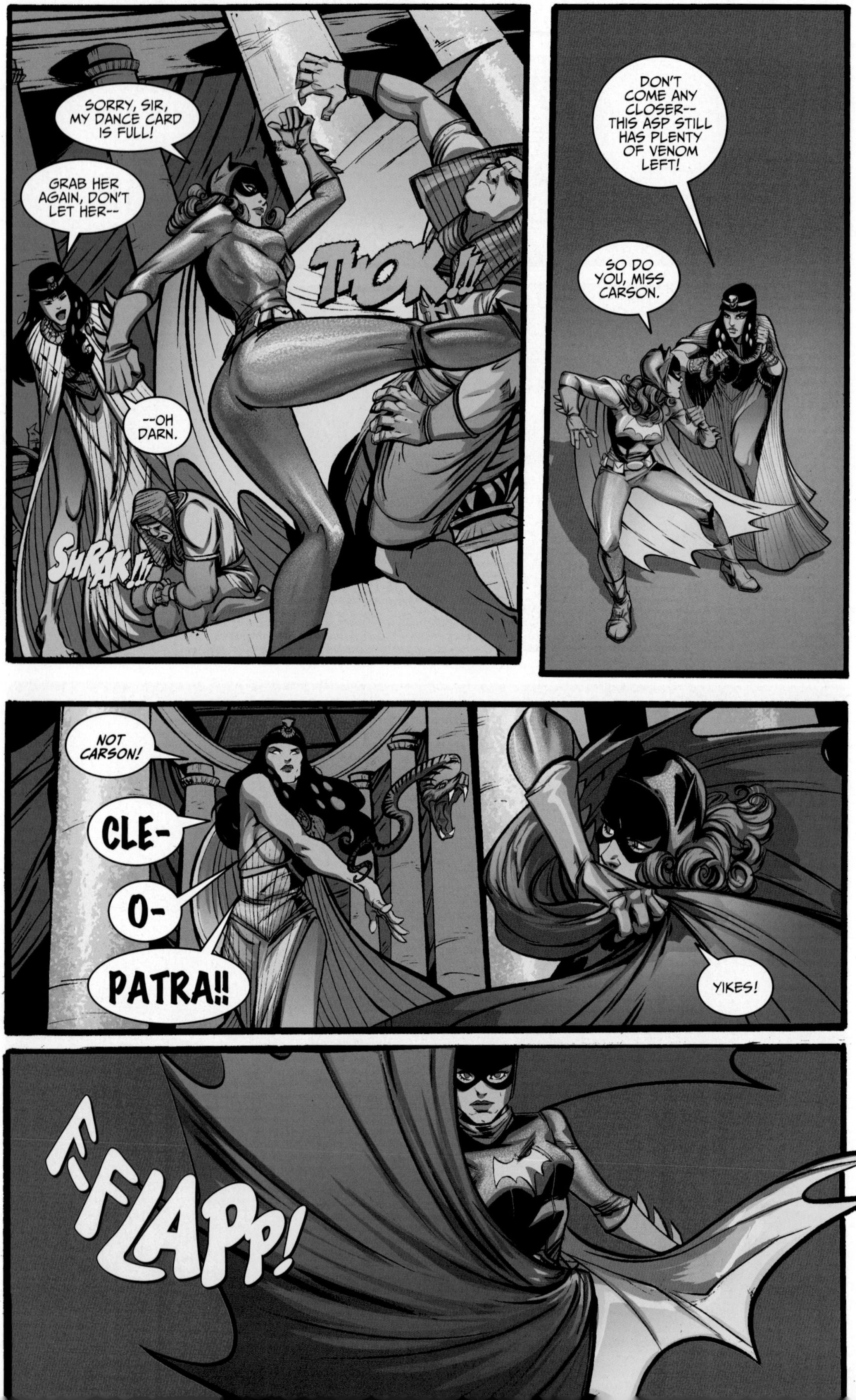
SORRY, SIR, MY DANCE CARD IS FULL!
GRAB HER AGAIN, DON'T LET HER--
THOK!!
--OH DARN.
SHRAK!!
DON'T COME ANY CLOSER-- THIS ASP STILL HAS PLENTY OF VENOM LEFT!
SO DO YOU, MISS CARSON.
NOT CARSON!
CLE-
O-
PATRA!!
YIKES!
F-FLAPP!

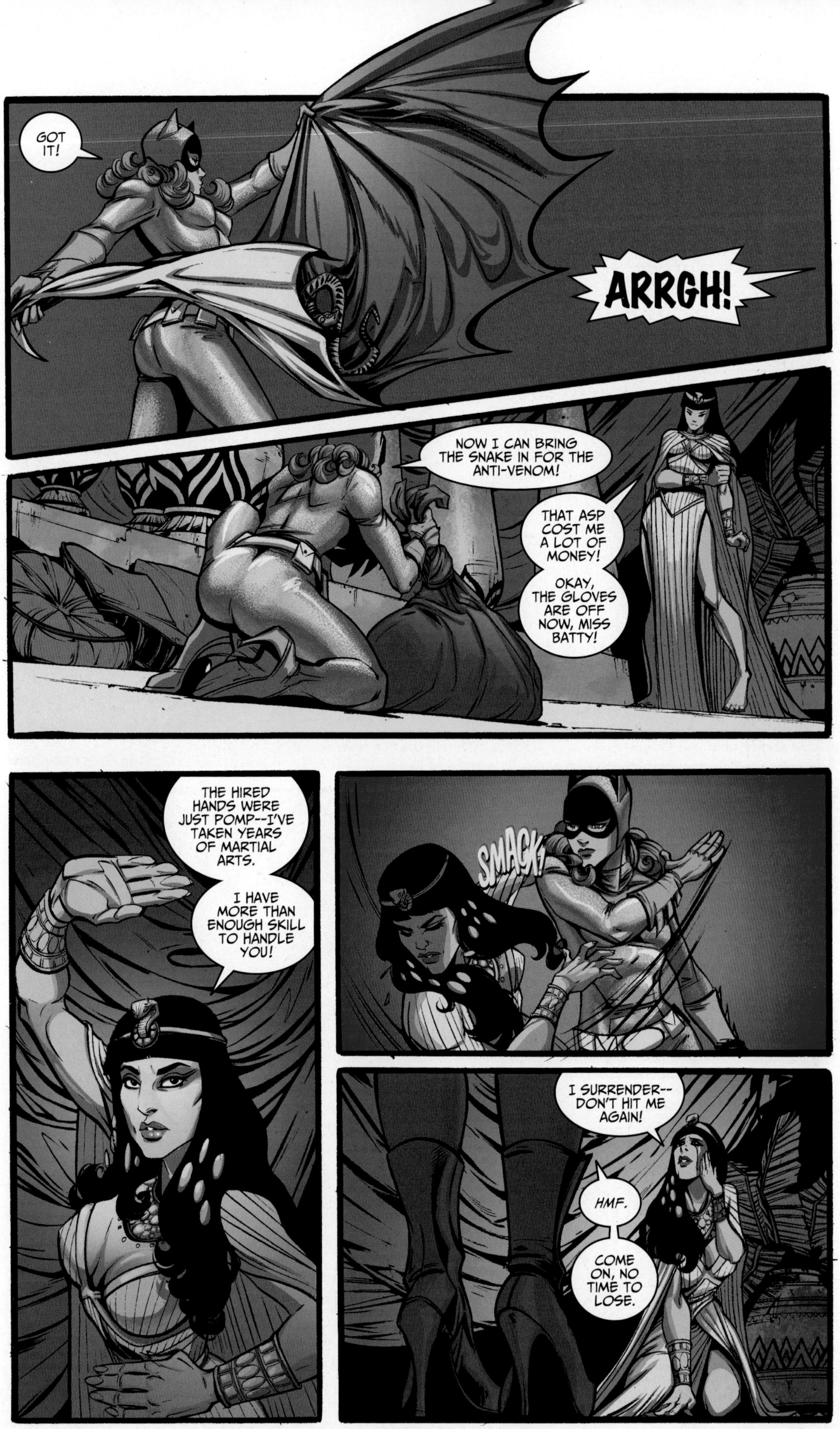

GOT IT!
ARRGH!
NOW I CAN BRING THE SNAKE IN FOR THE ANTI-VENOM!
THAT ASP COST ME A LOT OF MONEY!
OKAY, THE GLOVES ARE OFF NOW, MISS BATTY!
THE HIRED HANDS WERE JUST POMP--I'VE TAKEN YEARS OF MARTIAL ARTS.
I HAVE MORE THAN ENOUGH SKILL TO HANDLE YOU!
SMACK!
I SURRENDER--DON'T HIT ME AGAIN!
HMF.
COME ON, NO TIME TO LOSE.

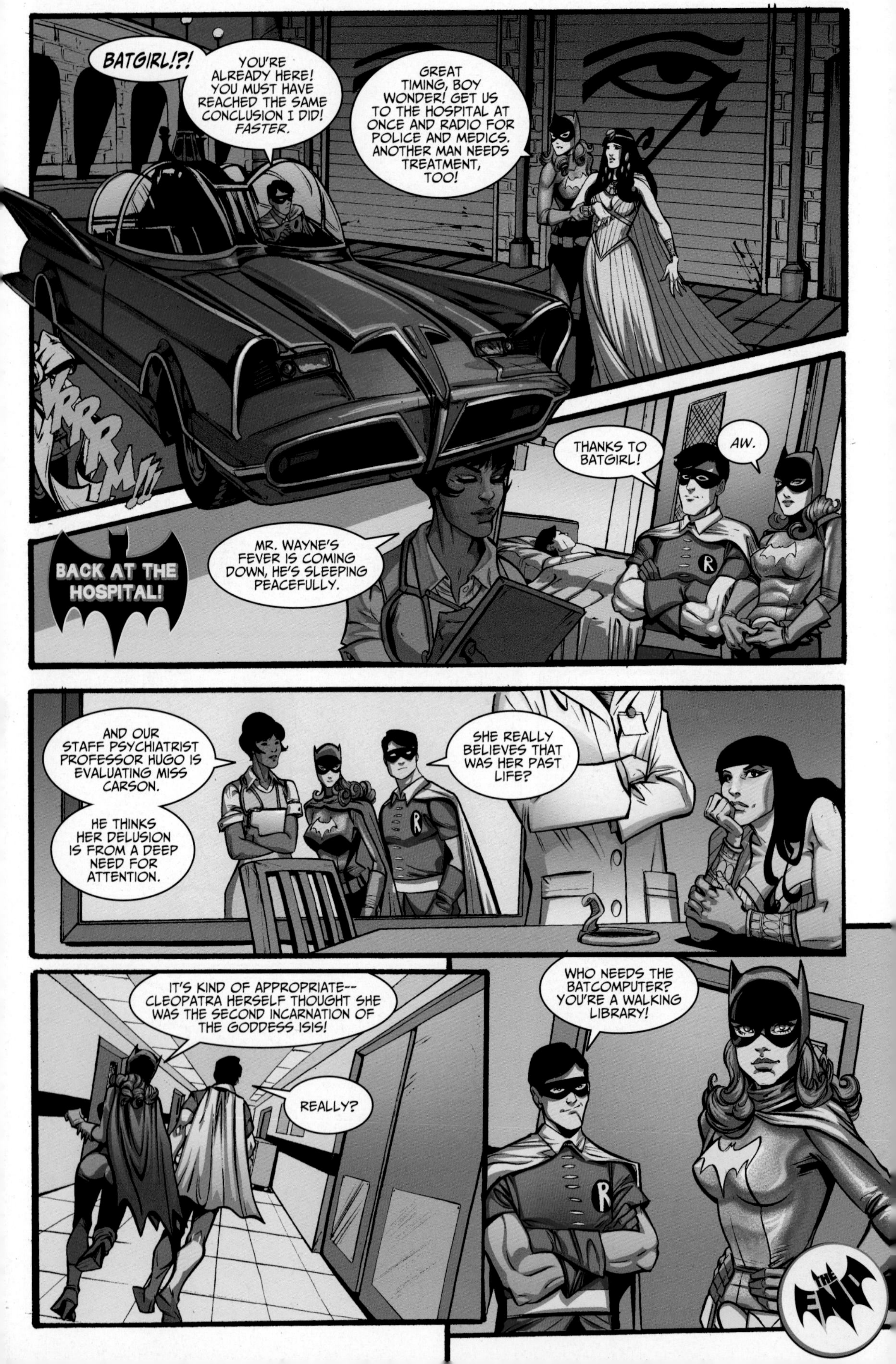
BATGIRL!?!
YOU'RE ALREADY HERE! YOU MUST HAVE REACHED THE SAME CONCLUSION I DID! FASTER.
GREAT TIMING, BOY WONDER! GET US TO THE HOSPITAL AT ONCE AND RADIO FOR POLICE AND MEDICS. ANOTHER MAN NEEDS TREATMENT, TOO!
VRRRRM!!
BACK AT THE HOSPITAL!
MR. WAYNE'S FEVER IS COMING DOWN, HE'S SLEEPING PEACEFULLY.
THANKS TO BATGIRL!
AW.
AND OUR STAFF PSYCHIATRIST PROFESSOR HUGO IS EVALUATING MISS CARSON.
HE THINKS HER DELUSION IS FROM A DEEP NEED FOR ATTENTION.
SHE REALLY BELIEVES THAT WAS HER PAST LIFE?
IT'S KIND OF APPROPRIATE-- CLEOPATRA HERSELF THOUGHT SHE WAS THE SECOND INCARNATION OF THE GODDESS ISIS!
REALLY?
WHO NEEDS THE BATCOMPUTER? YOU'RE A WALKING LIBRARY!
THE END

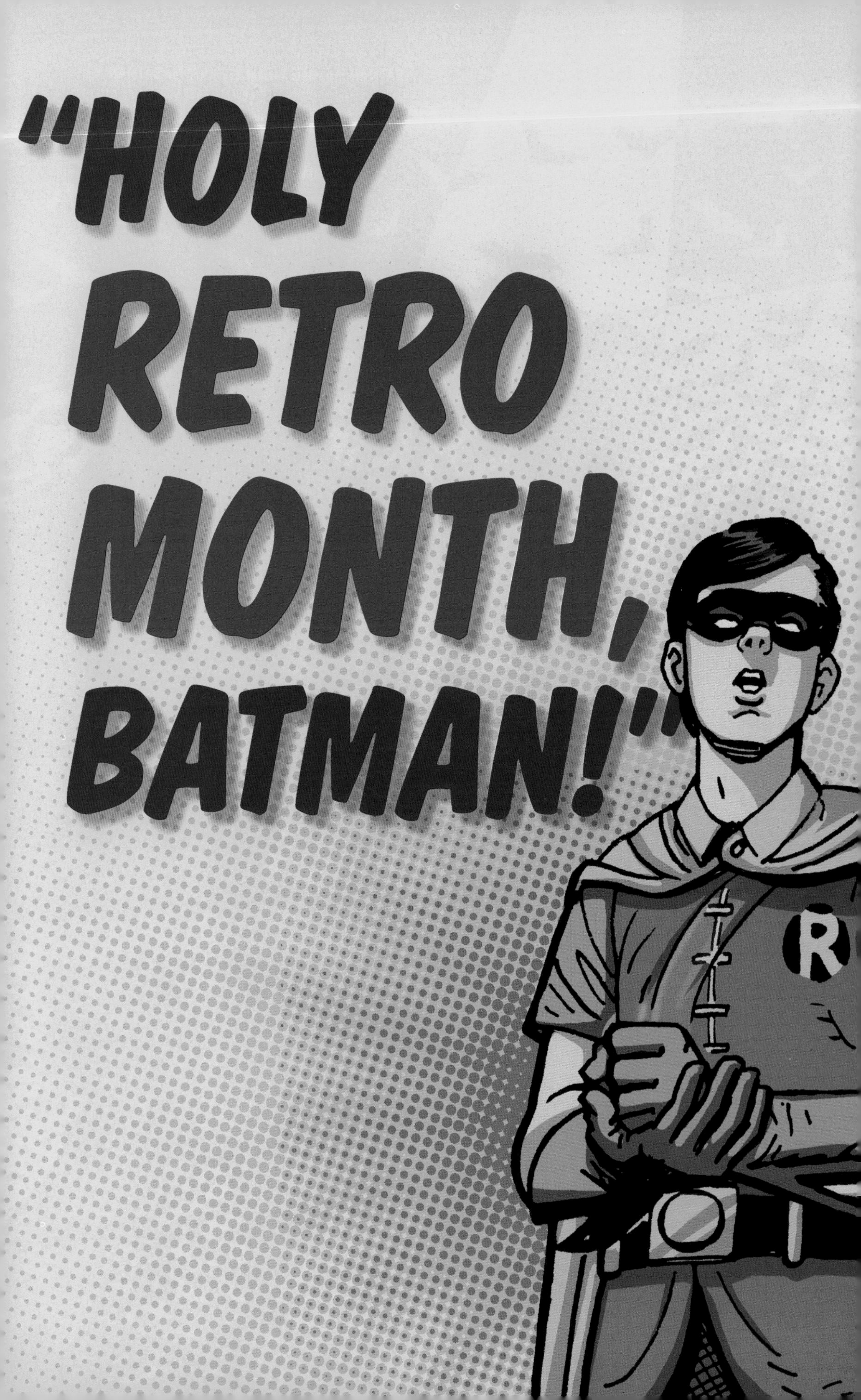
"HOLY RETRO MONTH, BATMAN!"
R

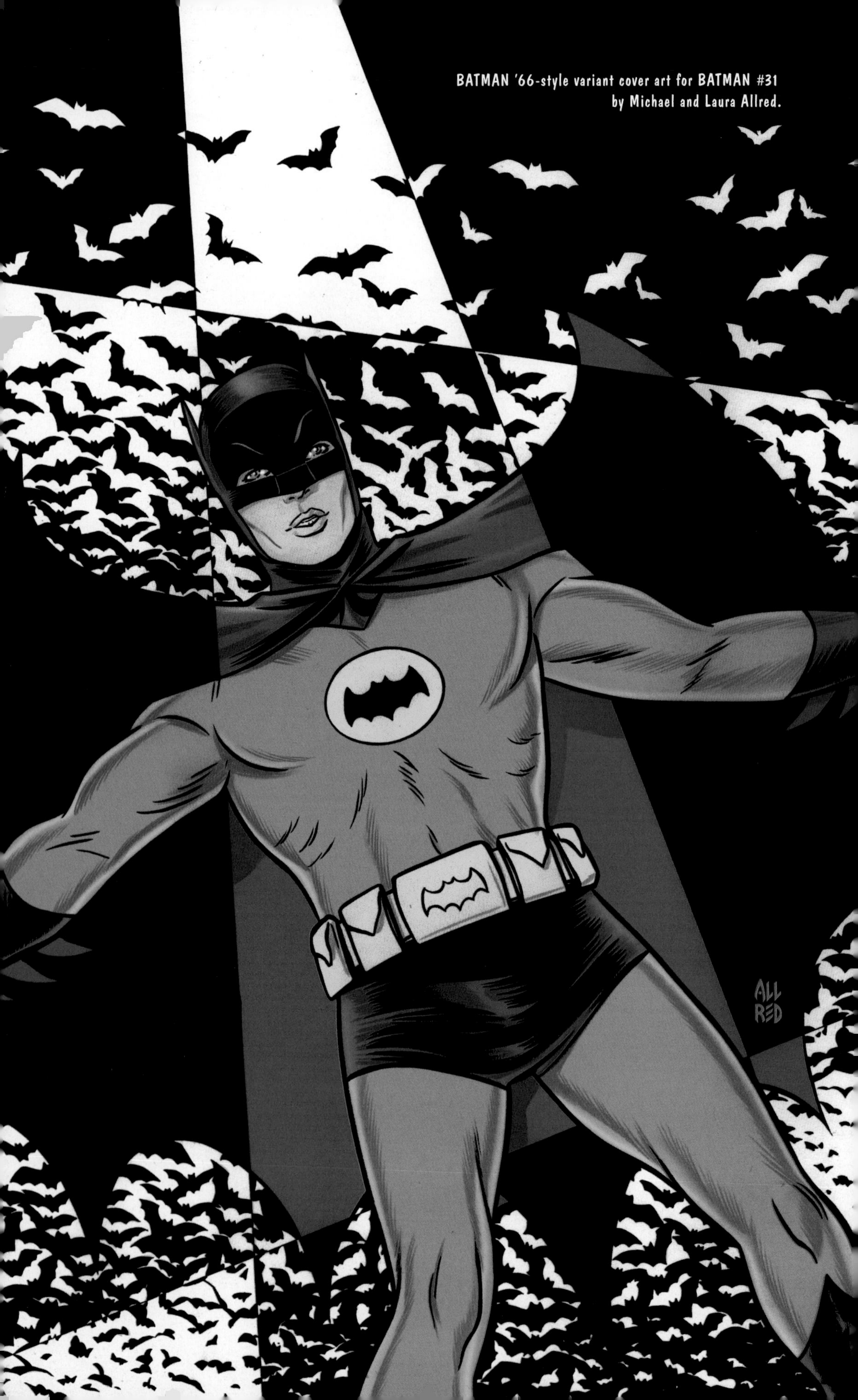
ALL
RED

BATMAN '66-style variant cover art for BATMAN #31
by Michael and Laura Allred.

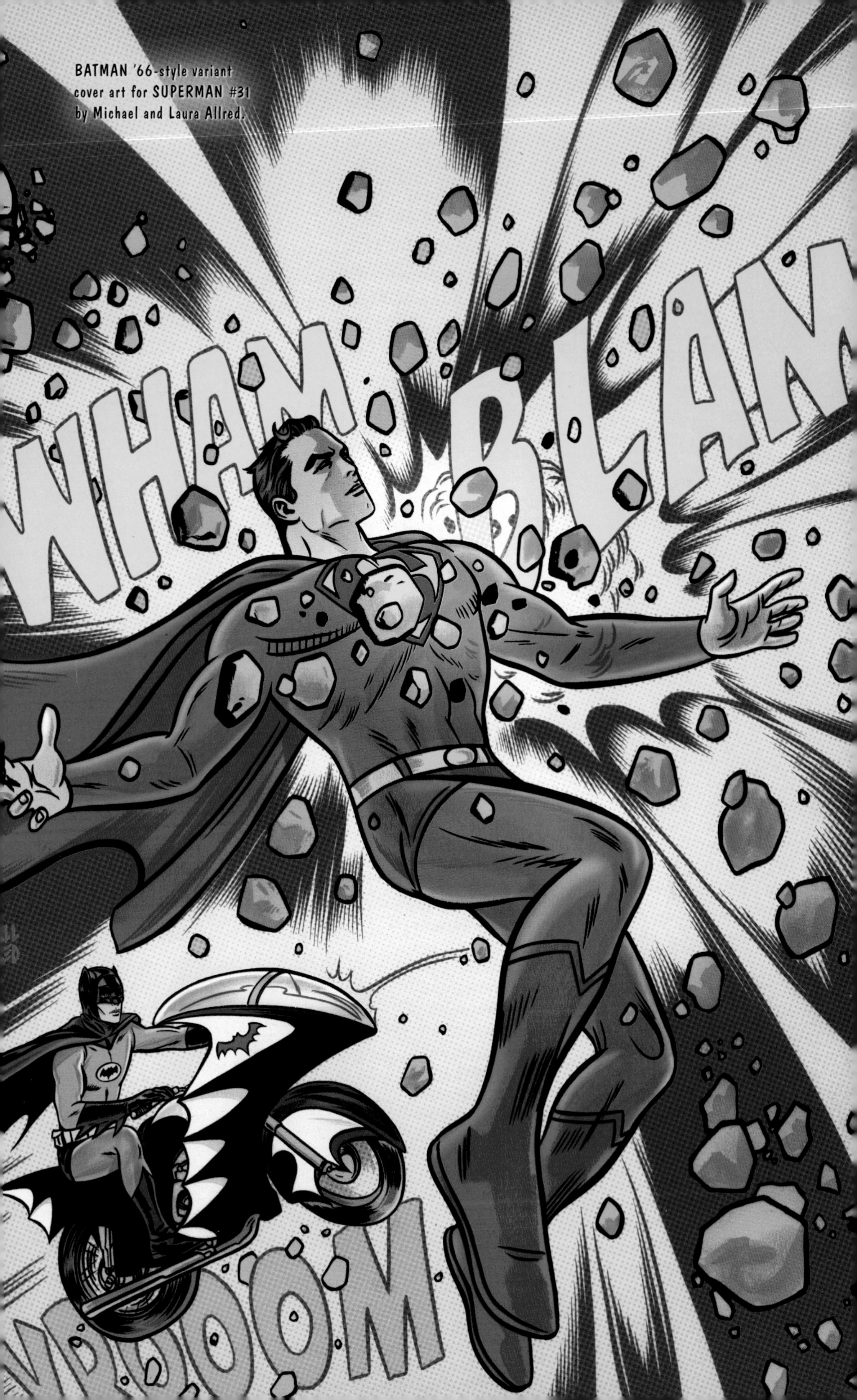
WHAM
BLAM

BATMAN '66-style variant cover art for SUPERMAN #31 by Michael and Laura Allred.

BATMAN '66-style variant cover art for BATWOMAN #31
by Michael and Laura Allred.

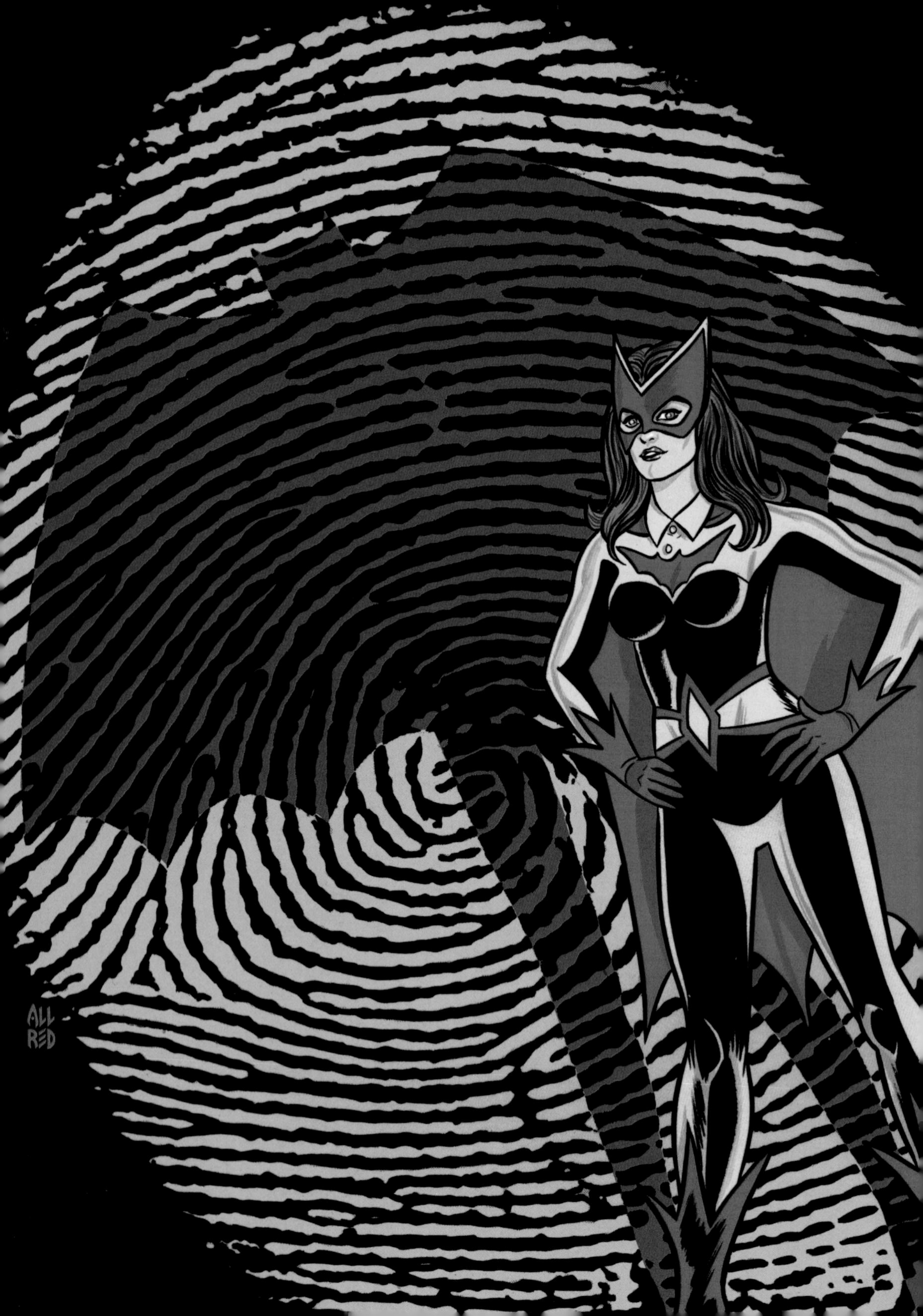
ALL
RED

BATMAN '66-style variant cover art for EARTH 2 #23
by Michael and Laura Allred.

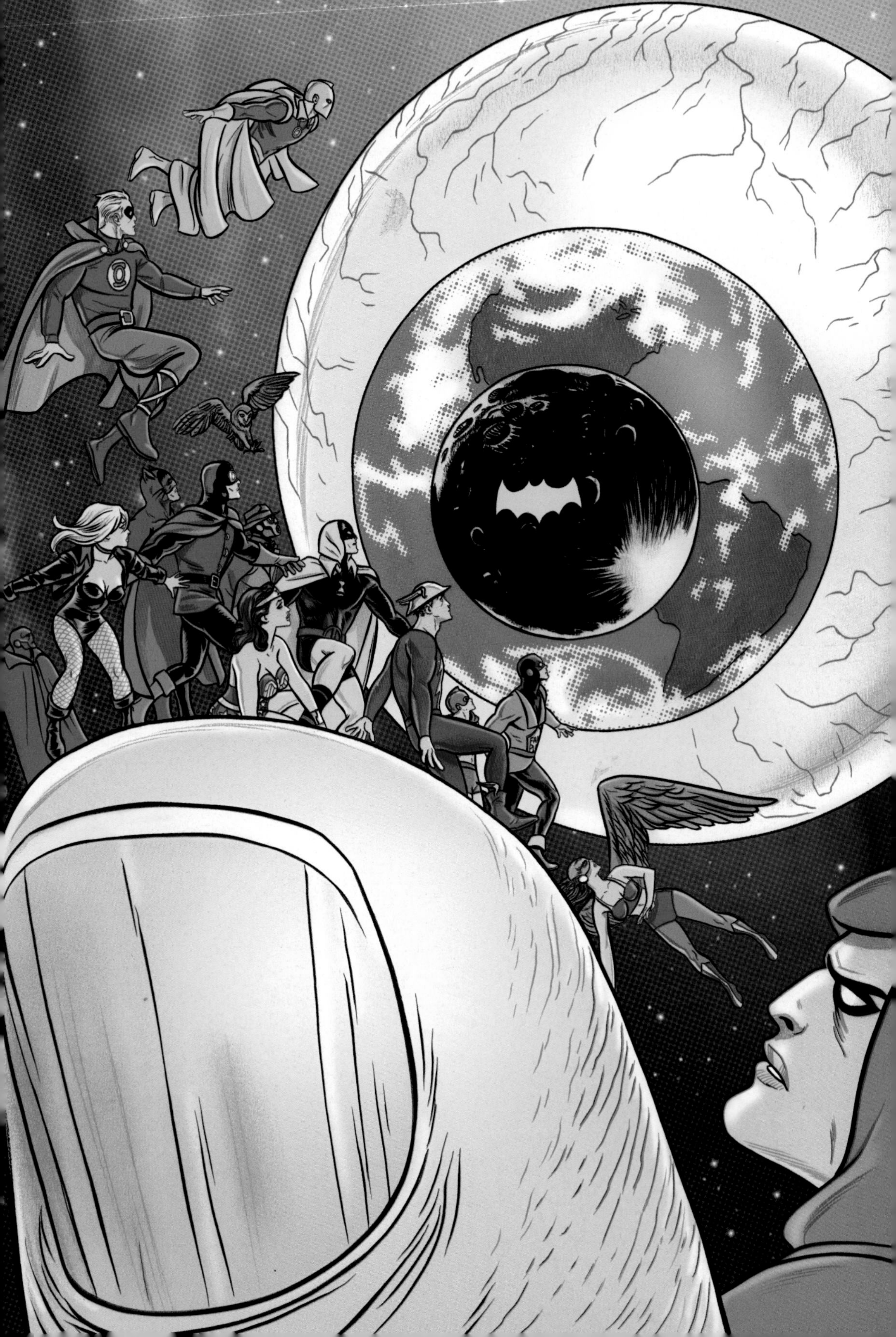

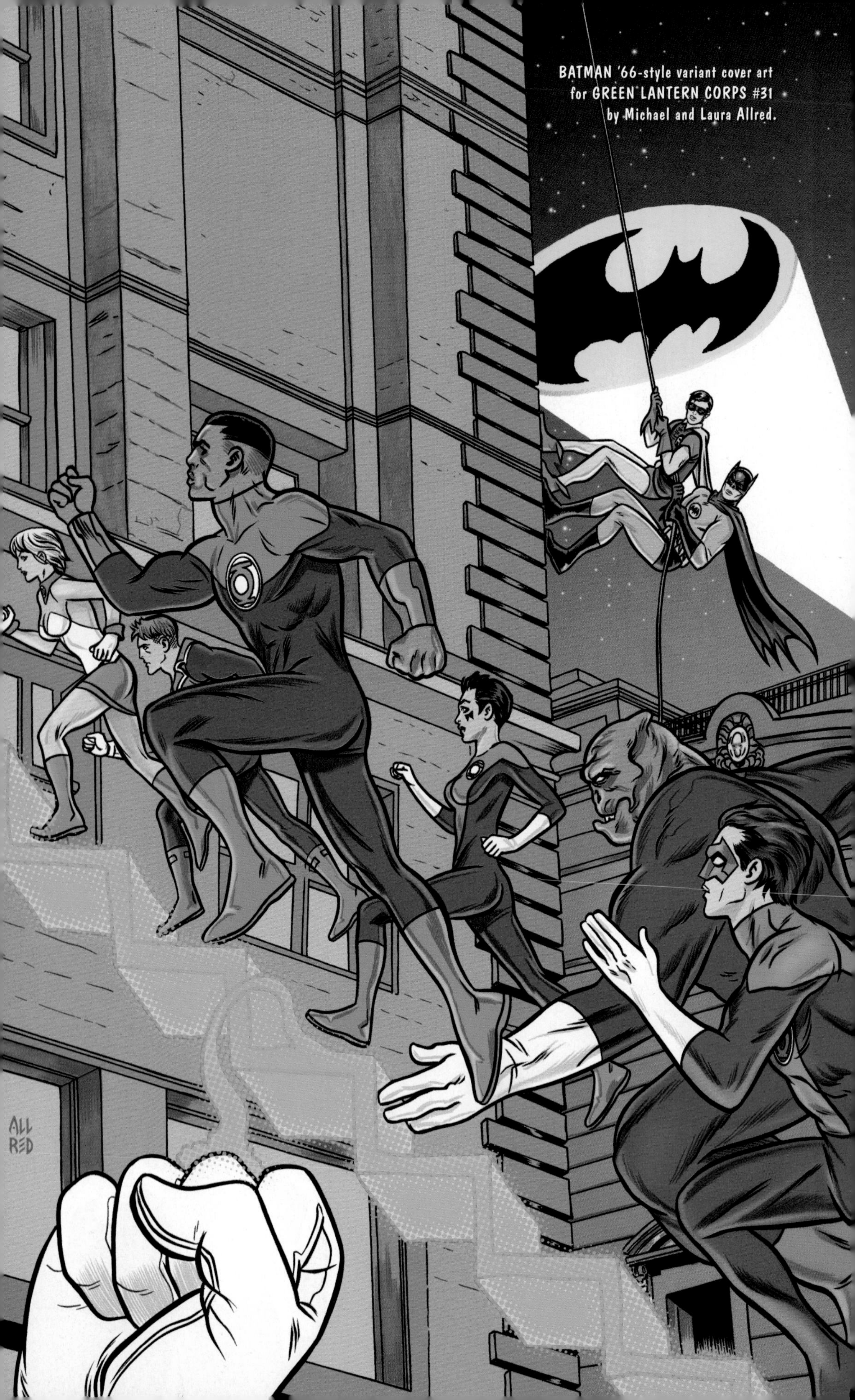
ALL
RED

BATMAN '66-style variant cover art
for GREEN LANTERN CORPS #31
by Michael and Laura Allred.

BATMAN '66-style variant cover art for BATGIRL #31
by Michael and Laura Allred.

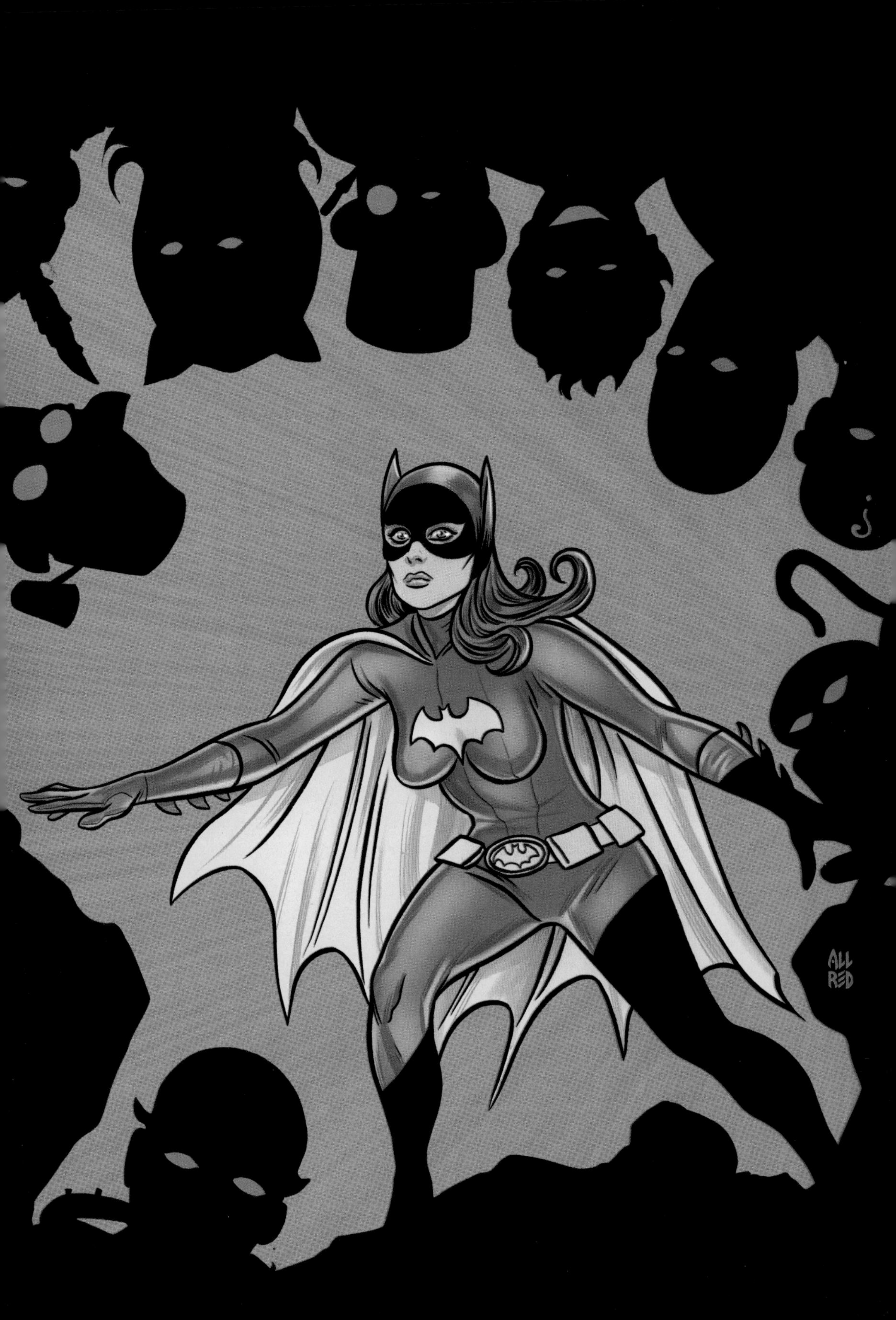

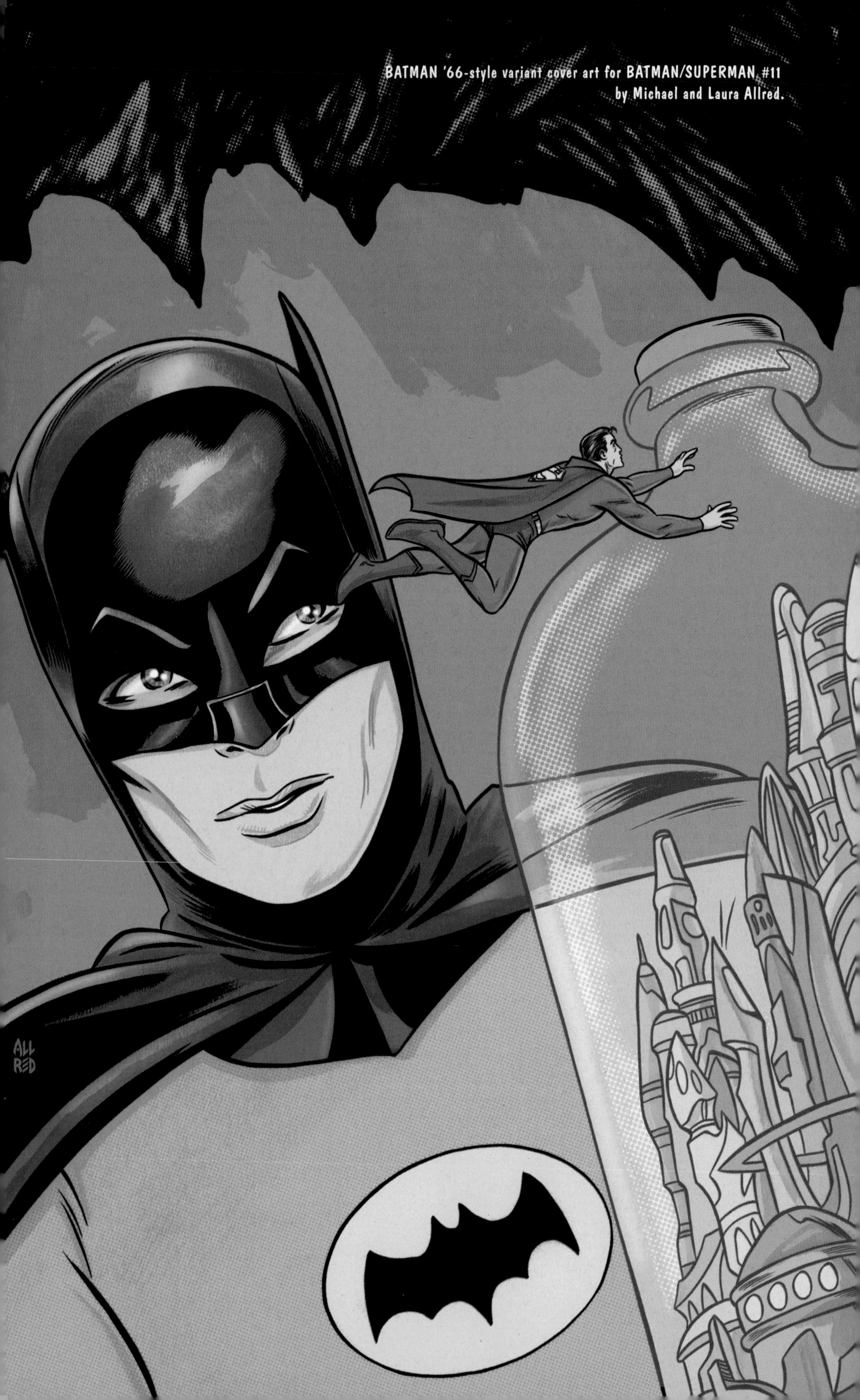
ALL
RED

BATMAN '66-style variant cover art for BATMAN/SUPERMAN #11
by Michael and Laura Allred.

BATMAN '66-style variant cover art for WONDER WOMAN #31
by Michael and Laura Allred.

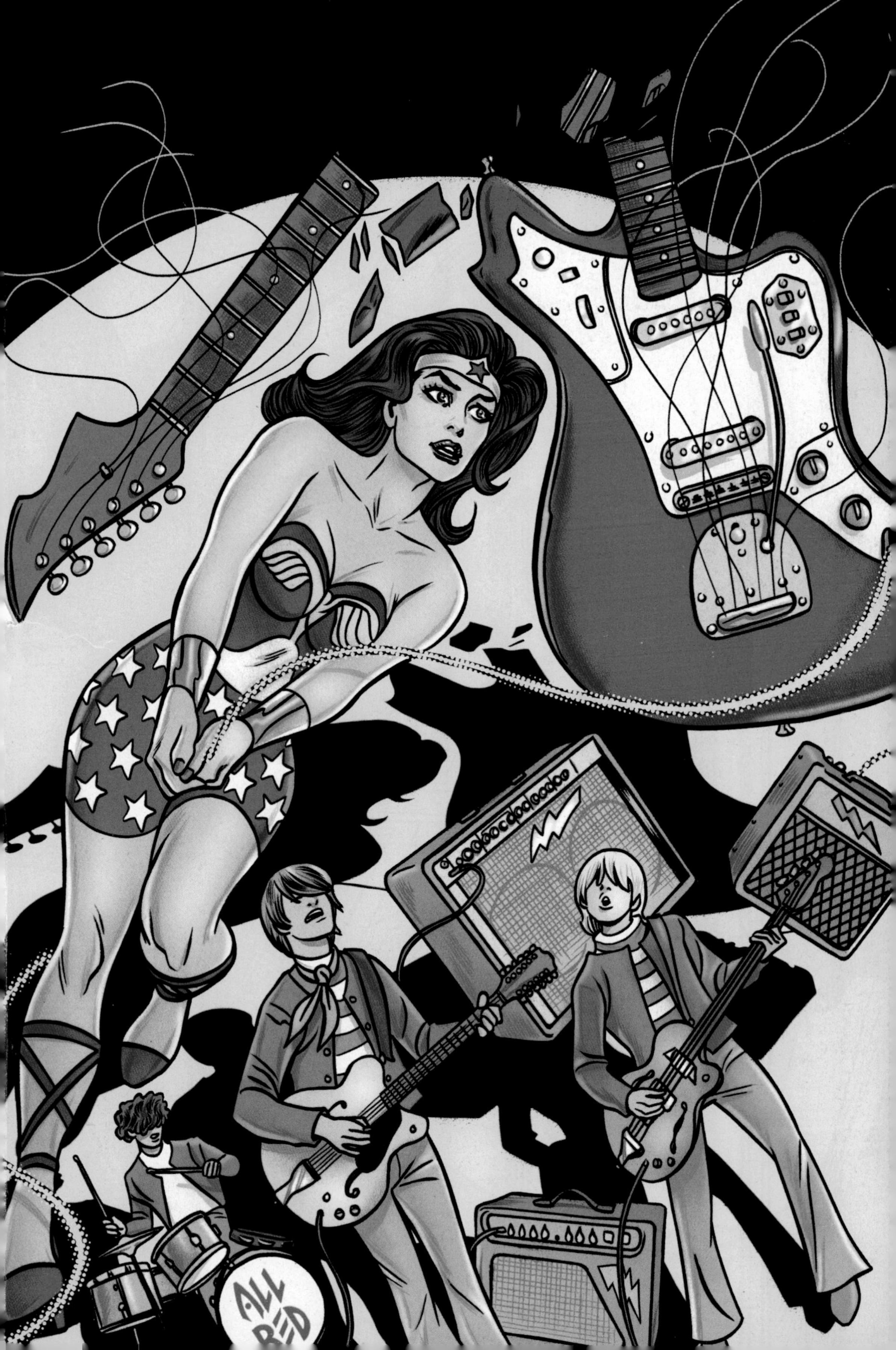
ALL

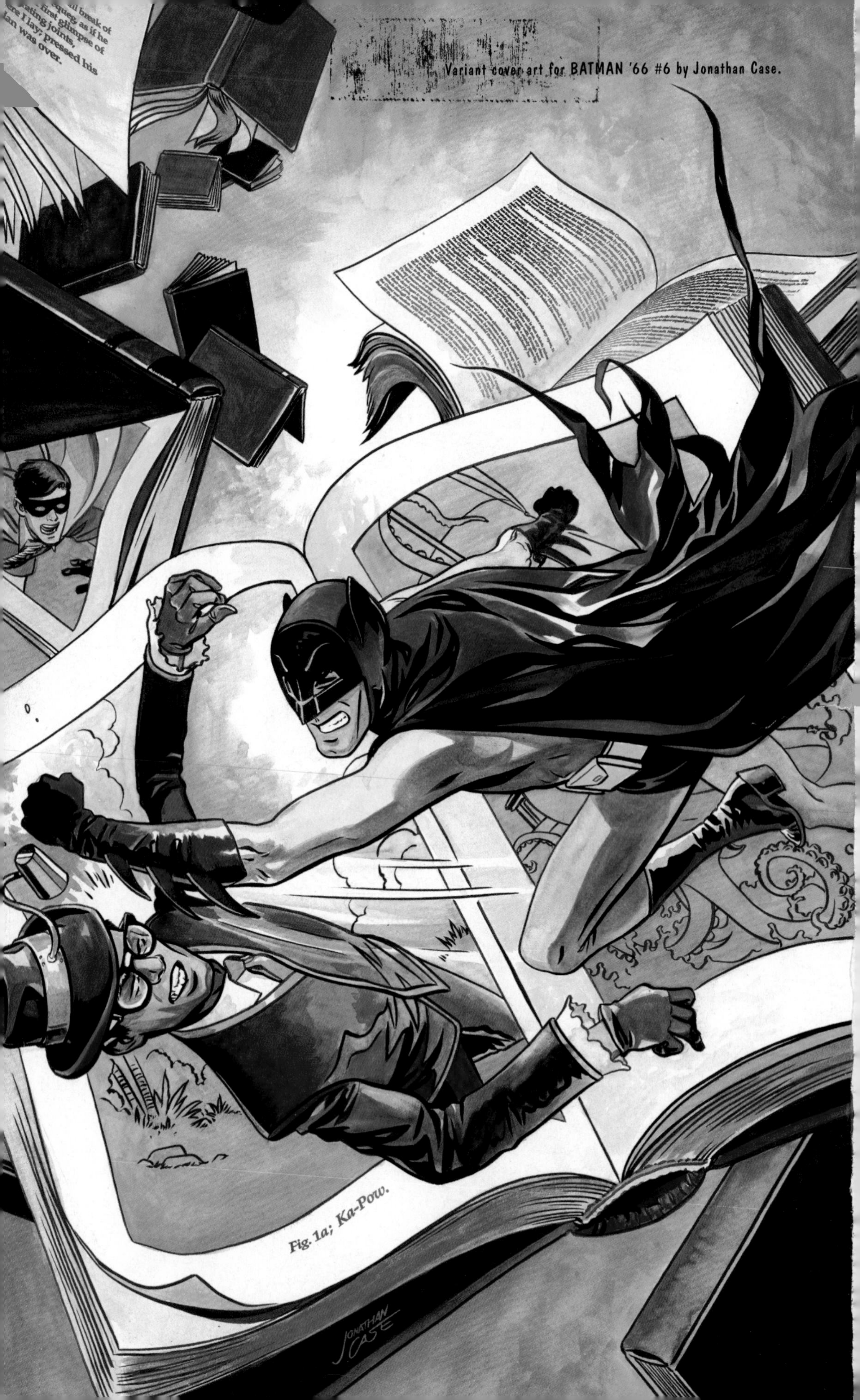
Fig. 1a; Ka-Pow.
JONATHAN CASE

Variant cover art for BATMAN '66 #6 by Jonathan Case.